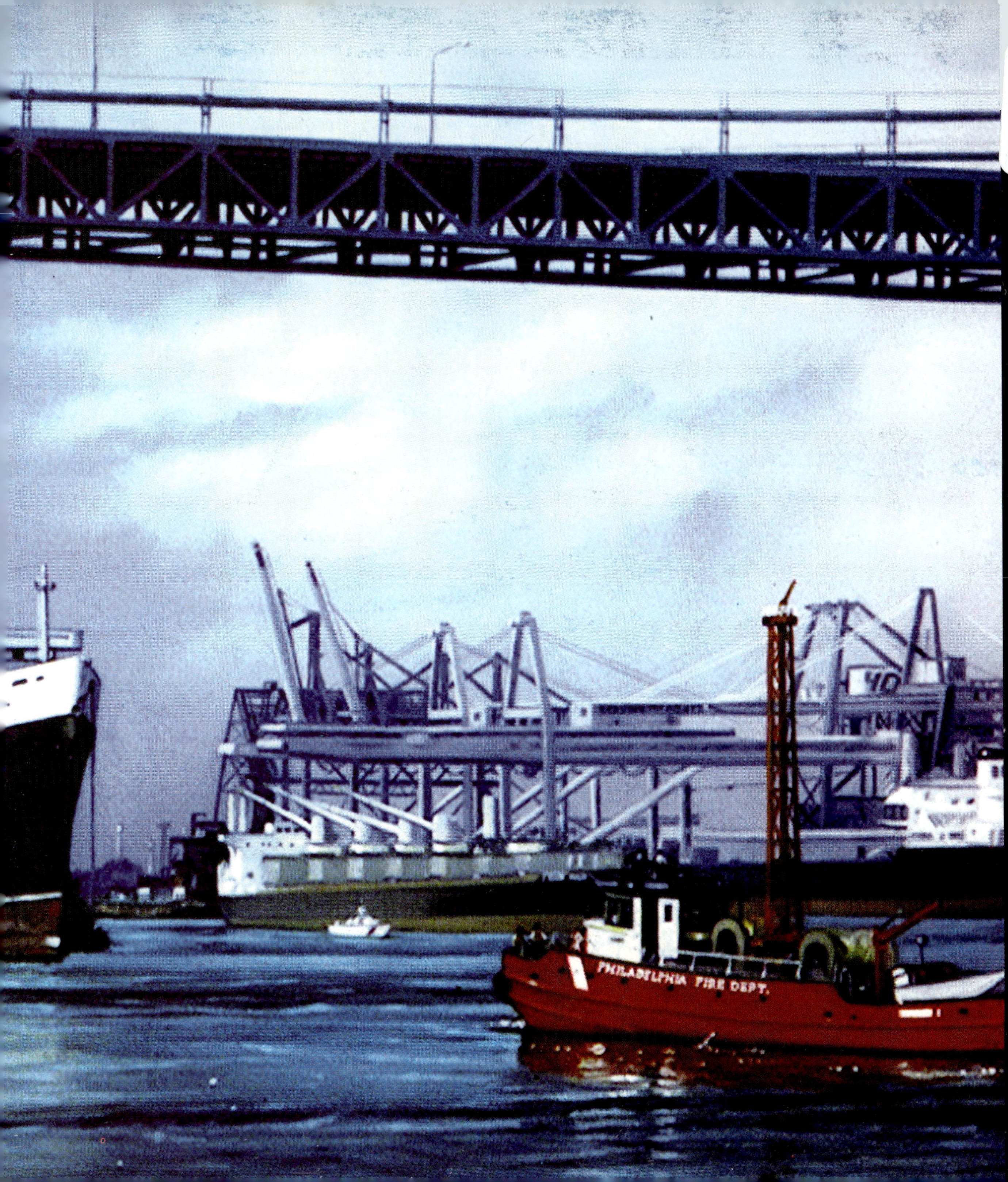
PHILADELPHIA FIRE DEPT.

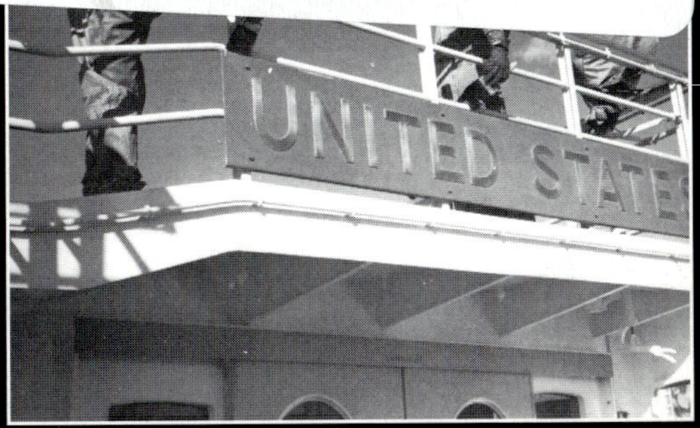
UNITED STATE

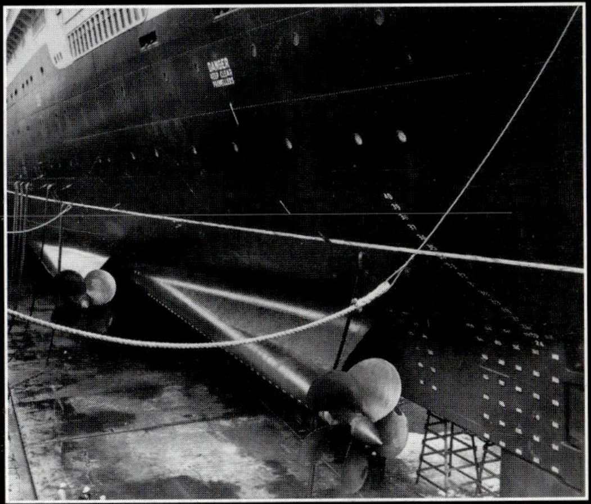

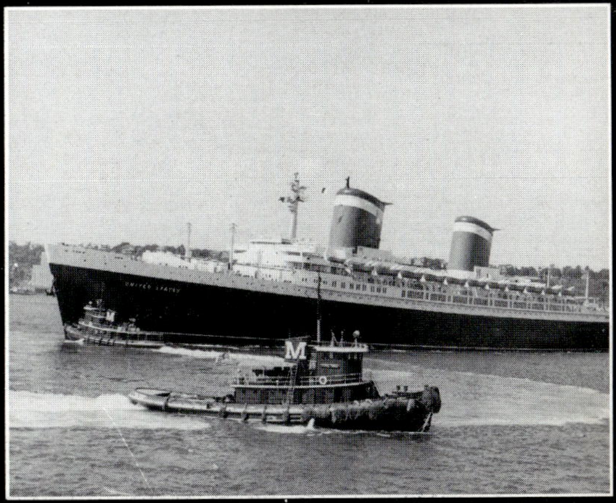

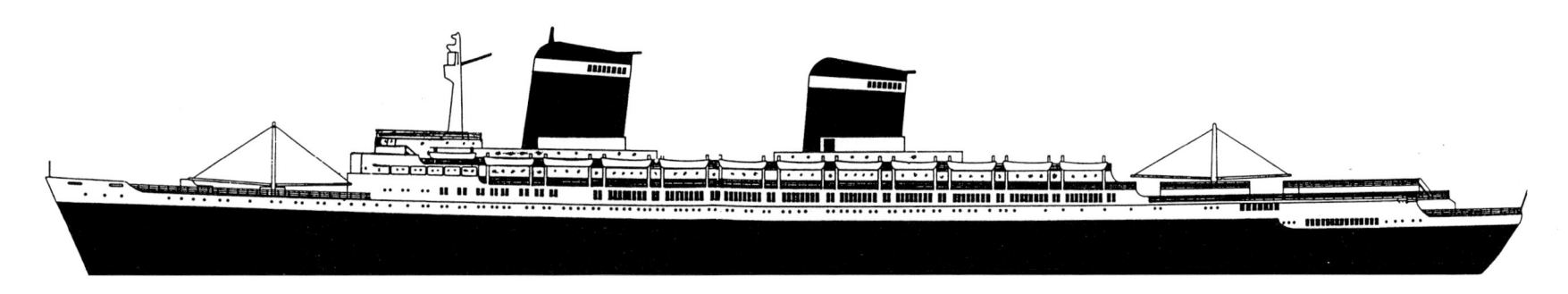

S.S. United States

Acknowledgments

The SS United States Foundation would like to acknowledge the following institutions and individuals who helped to guide this book to publication: The Mariner's Museum, Newport News Virginia, Frank O. Braynard, Susan Gibbs, Mark Thompson, Laer Pearce & Associates, *The New York Times*, The RMS Queen Mary, Cynthia Gayton, The American Merchant Marine Academy, National Endowment For The Arts, Mike Alexander, Mike Alfano, Hugh Lydiard, Bruce A. Lehman, Commodore Leroy Alexanderson, the SSUSF Advisory Board and the members and supporters of the SS United States Foundation throughout the world.

The SS United States Foundation Board of Directors:

Robert Hudson Westover, Chairman
Paul Robinson, Vice Chairman
Susan Gibbs, Director
Daniel McSweeney, Director
Tom Fulton, Director

This book is dedicated to the memories of William Francis Gibbs and Lawrence Robert Westover.

Turner
Publishers

Turner Publishing Company
Publishers of America's History
P.O. Box 3101
Paducah, Kentucky 42002-3101

Co-published by
Mark A. Thompson, Associate Publisher

For book publishing write to:
M.T. Publishing Company, Inc.
P.O. Box 6802
Evansville, Indiana 47719-6802

Pre-Press work by M.T. Publishing Company, Inc.
Graphic Designer: Elizabeth A. Dennis
Cover Design: Paul Robinson

For information about purchasing the CD-Rom: "The S.S. *United States* – A History in Advertising 1951-1968" contact: www.archivesofadvertising.com

Original artwork reproduced on endsheets with permission of Robert C. Semler.

Copyright © 2002
SS United States Foundation

This book or any part thereof may not be reproduced without the written consent of SS United States Foundation and the Publishers.

The materials were compiled and produced using available information; Turner Publishing Company, M.T. Publishing Company, Inc., and SS United States Foundation regret they cannot assume liability for errors or omissions.

Library of Congress
Control Number: 2002110102
ISBN: 1-56311-824-6

Printed in the United States of America

Limited Edition of 750 copies of which this book is number 385

Contents

Foreword by Susan Gibbs — 4

Introduction by Robert Hudson Westover — 6

"The Big Ship" by Frank Braynard — 10

Adrift: 1982 through 1996 by Robert Hudson Westover — 145

Save the *United States* — The Story of the S.S. United States Foundation by Robert Hudson Westover — 148

Passenger and Crew Stories — 153

Supplemental History by Bill DiBenedetto — 163

Index — 172

Foreword

My grandfather, William Francis Gibbs (who we always called W.F.), died when I was five years old. When I was seven, the *S.S. United States* stopped running. It was a blessing that my grandfather went first; that even in his final days, he could imagine the "big ship" charging across the sea, engines humming. Growing up, my exposure to the ship was rather limited. On special occasions, like Thanksgiving and Christmas, we would dine on fancy white china plates with gold trim and eagle insignias from the ship's first class dining room. Various images of the ship were framed on our walls, including an enormous Christmas card showing the *S.S. United States* passing majestically through New York Harbor. There was also a small oil painting showing my grandfather's silhouette, a shadowy, solitary figure on a pier facing the ship as she left port. But in all of my years, I had never been on the ship itself.

Last summer, the SSUnited States Foundation convened its 2001 Annual Meeting at the Philadelphia Seaport Museum, only a short drive from Pier 82 on the Delaware River where the *S.S. United States* is docked. We were told that the ship's owner might allow our group on board. Anticipating this prospect, I set out to read as much about the ship as possible. I searched through boxes stacked in the attic marked "Gibbs Memorabilia" and came across folders of faded newspaper clips chronicling the ship's sea trials, old Gibbs & Cox newsletters, letters from my grandfather to his sister Bertha describing the ship's construction, and the travel diaries of my grandmother, Vera Cravath Gibbs, from the early transatlantic crossings. In poring though these attic treasures, I began to understand my grandparents' love for the ship and the values she embodied. I started to feel the power of "the big U," and how she has instilled such passion in those close to her.

Heading down the highway toward the ship last summer, I entertained my family by reading excerpts of my grandmother's diaries aloud. The mounting excitement during the ship's 1952 sea trials was palpable:

"On the ship were scenes of great activity. A great many men were scrubbing floors, or polishing this and that. Most of the furniture was in already. The movie theater I thought a gem: soft gray, with fluted walls, the chairs were most comfortable.

"One room had black walls with brilliant diamond stars of illuminated glass. I thought they were magnified snowflakes, but no, they were heavenly bodies. The ballroom was a triumph. Between the bar and the dance floor were glass screens, pure crystal, engraved with the most exquisite designs.

"Already, the cooks were stirring up savory soups. They expected 500 passengers on the trial – Tables were set in the dining salon. There were unusually attractive vases of mixed flowers on every table, really a most charming variety – the caterer had fabricated a model of the ship, about three feet long, in sugar, which was conspicuously placed and lighted in the dining salon.

"...Darkness fell, and then all the lights came on the big ship. Suddenly she seemed like a fairy palace. At that moment she didn't seem real. She suggested a shiny presence that had suddenly just happened. For a few moments one forgot all the headaches it had taken to build her, all the "man hours" that had been expended to create her. We just looked at her as a child gazes at a Christmas tree, full of wonder."

We made it to the SS United States Foundation's annual meeting, and then we soon received the word. We would be allowed on board. The meeting dispersed, and we caravaned to Pier 82. Because of safety concerns, not all of us could go on. Children were forbidden. Hence, my husband and nine-year old daughter were left to stare at the huge rusting vessel from the dock as I struggled to climb into the darkened interior via a rope and a plank. As a small group of us began to make our way through the ship's cavernous corridors, a reporter from the *Philadelphia Inquirer* asked me what it felt like to be on the ship for the first time. I found such a simple question surprisingly difficult to answer. As we shined our flashlights through the dining room, completely empty except for stark metal stumps marking where tables once were, it was so hard to imagine the ship in its prime, lit up and bustling with waiters, flowers and musicians. I murmured something to the reporter about how the ship described by my grandparents was so alive, so full of energy. This ship was a shadow of that, so dark and near death.

As my feet crunched on the deck's rusting paint, I was so relieved that it was me, not my grandfather, who was on this journey on this day. What a relief that when my grandfather died, the ship was still running strong. But as I stood on the deck and looked down at my daughter crying on the pier because she wanted so badly to come on board, I thought to myself, there is still time. We still have a chance to save this ship. Let us make the most of the time we are given.

The ship's great claim to fame lay in her dash across the Atlantic in 1952, trouncing the speed record held by Britain's *Queen Mary*. My grandmother's diaries describe the all-night celebrations as the ship reached Bishops Light, the orchestras playing until the wee hours, the snake dances of giddy, inebriated passengers stomping and twirling up and down the decks as dawn broke. This triumphant voyage was the high-water mark of my grandfather's life. His conception of "a great and premier ship for the Atlantic" was first sketched in 1914. My grandfather's persistence – some might use the word obsession – was legendary. After the *S.S. United States'* maiden voyage, my grandmother mused in her diary:

"The trip of trips was now drawing to a close. When I look back on the weeks, months, and years that W. F. spent on the *S.S. United States*, I wonder how his enthusiasm remained undiminished. The series of disappointments that he had to face, the political battles he had to face, all those went on for so long. Those aggravations kept repeating themselves with slight variations, over and over again. What I always wondered was why the wellspring of W.F.'s enthusiasm didn't dry up. I am reminded of what Edmund Burke wrote: "The nerve that never relaxes, the thought that never wanders, the purpose that never wavers, these are the masters of victory."

After the ship's record-breaking run, my grandfather, a formal man with very few sentimental tendencies, wrote a thank-you note to my grandmother. She had carefully affixed the typed note into one of her prized albums. I suspect she treasured this expression of appreciation:

"I thought you did your part in adding to the gay spirit of this trip and it was a great pleasure to be with you on such a momentous occasion. I am afraid that I could not be as entertaining as I would have liked, but it seemed to me that whenever I got settled down, something came up which made it necessary to put one's mind to the main business at hand.

Many thanks for your long continued patience and enthusiasm about this ship. I have many times thought that you must get tired of being about with a person who seemed to have but one thing in mind. However, you can agree, it was quite a big thing."

The *S.S. United States* was a "big thing" to my grandfather not just because of its physical size. For him, the ship expressed the biggest and the best of the American spirit. Upon receiving an award from Philadelphia's Franklin Institute in 1953, he reflected:

"The people who (contributed to building the *S.S. United States*) understood what they were doing. They knew that they were trying for the greatest ship in the world and they knew that they were doing it as trustees for the citizens of the United States. They were made aware of that by continuous preaching, and I have the feeling that the reason that this was possible in the United States, with all of its checks and balances, all the difficulties of discussion of all kinds by those opposed to ships and those for ships, all of the arguments that would be made as to the type of design, and all the rest of it, I feel that this result coming out of it indicates the strength of a free society and individual initiative. It is a tribute to the American system."

In rereading this speech, I found myself hoping that the American system so appreciated by my grandfather would work to the ship's advantage during its most desperate hour. Would the efforts of the *SS United States* Foundation and others prevail in reversing the ship's fortunes? Would the ship's place in history be preserved and commemorated? Could the U.S. government, which commissioned the ship in the first place, play a role in her preservation? Could all of us who have known and loved this ship join together to ensure her salvation?

After my tour of the ship, I began walking back to our van parked at Pier 82 with my husband, daughter, the Chairman of the SS United States Foundation Robert Westover, and a few others. As we gazed at the ship from the asphalt, a sadness hung over the group. My daughter was still in tears at being forbidden entry. Robert tried to console her, insisting that when the ship is saved and restored, she could invite all of her friends on board, that it would be quite a party.

Those of us whose imaginations have been captured by this magnificent ship have different reasons for working to save her. My connection goes deep, and anchors me between past and future generations. Shortly after our visit to the ship, my daughter completed a school assignment on a "family heirloom." She chose to write about our set of china plates from the *S.S. United States*.

"We keep our plates from the *S.S. United States* in a nice cupboard where they are safe. I've seen the ship in a Pennsylvania harbor. I felt very special to be there and I felt very proud that my great grandfather made this wonderful ship. When I'm alone sometimes I think that the plates symbolize all the memories of the past. I feel very special that I have this great grandfather that helped our country."

As our van pulled away from the pier, I thought, I hope Robert is right. I hope that my children and my grandchildren will have more than a set of plates to mark the *S.S. United States* and her role in our nation's history. I hope there will be a big old party, with snake dances up and down the decks and music playing strong. I hope the ship once again instills happiness among those who get to know her. She certainly gave happiness to my family, and to my grandfather most of all. There is one page of my grandmother's diary, describing the ship's triumphant return from one of her early sea trials, that I especially treasure:

"We all got out and began to wander down the Yard in the direction of the sea. The *Champlain* was in, one of our fastest aircraft carriers. There was a big cargo vessel in, too. The Yard was quite crowded. Again, twilight produced magic. After a while she (the *S.S. United States*) was righted. We watched her as she approached. It seemed as if she came perilously near the shore at one time.

"This, of course, makes no sense whatsoever, but it conveys some of the varying emotions we went through. One little boy, not more than six years old, was overheard to say, "I saw her the other day. I think she is the most beautiful thing I have ever seen!" She crept past the various docks. I had a glimpse of her as I stood between the *Champlain* and the freighter. Then, she reached her own dock. The three tugs, of course, were nestling around her. The big ship and the tugs engaged in quite a conversation: First, would be the deep voice of the big ship; then the tugs would answer, first by a medium squeak, then a high one. This went on for some time while she was turning into the dock. It took quite a while, of course.

"The first person we saw come off, I think, was Admiral Lee, then W.F.'s secretaries, Mr. Kelly and Mr. Connelly, and then, after a while, W.F. and Frederick Gibbs. Everyone coming off looked more than cheerful.

"When W.F. came off he had to wait for someone, so he perched himself on a post right by the side of the ship, and there he sat with his knees up to his chin, just looking at his ship – He was inside the lines, so we could not speak to him. Therefore, he was left in peace, just looking at the big and beautiful thing he created.

"I think that will be one of my happiest memories."

Please help us restore the dignity and magnificence this great ship once held for not only my family, but for so many Americans. Join our campaign, become a member of the SS United States Foundation, write your senators and congressmen, start a local chapter. Combining our talents, we can restore and revitalize the *S.S. United States* for generations to come.

Susan L. Gibbs
Washington, D.C.
October 3, 2001

Introduction

"Every ship has a soul" – Franklin Roosevelt

Throughout millennia, man has attempted to conquer the seas. Alexander the Great built one of the first great naval fleets to help administer his multinational empire as well as overwhelm his enemies. For thousands of year ships were essentially – in Western Culture – vessels designed to navigate the Mediterranean and Black Sea. It wasn't until Columbus set out to circumnavigate the globe, that ships, as the world would come to know them, were built. The earliest trans-Atlantic vessels were crude by modern standards, but very efficient. They consisted of three to four decks and had enough provisions to sustain them for months at a time. Their navigation devices were rudimentary, but accurate, relying on the age-old system of using the stars to find one's position and destination.

For several centuries, tall mast schooners were the preferred form of sea travel. Many advancements in sea travel were added to the great wooden vessels, but nothing compared to the advancements that would attend the competition for sea travel between the old and the new world in the late 19th Century. Then White Star launched *Teutonic* one of the first "great ships" to dispense with sails altogether. However, tradition dies hard, and the ships that would follow – for nearly a century – would have mock sailing-type masts. It was not until the great *United States* was launched that all pretense to the masted sailing ships would be entirely done away with – the national flagship would have no forward mast. A 50ft high all aluminum radar lookout "mast" was placed above the wheel house – giving the graceful *United States* such a modern and sleek look that all other ships that followed would (like so many other features) try to emulate it.

By the time *Teutonic* was launched it was apparent that British steamships would forever change our concept of sea travel. The stakes were so high for which company could build the fastest and biggest ships, that a competition, known as the race for the fabled Blue Riband was inaugurated in 1860. The first vessel to hold the coveted title as "world's fastest" was the *Great Western*. Although the *Great Western* had taken the speed record 30 years earlier, it was given the title as "first" because it was the first to achieve recognition as the ship to beat. The race was originally designed for the ship which would deliver the British Empire's mail the fastest but soon became the hallmark for passengers as well.

Once immigrants in large numbers began to cross into the Americas, "largest" also became important. Ships then began to be built in a scale that is still impressive by today's standards. The *Great Eastern* for example, was nearly 700 feet long and was capable of carrying over two thousand passengers! Although the vessel was never profitable, she eventually found work laying cable across the Atlantic.

One of the first great ships that not only was successful, but the largest and fastest in the world, was the *Mauritania*. The vessel could cross the Atlantic at speeds of over 17 knots and was also a floating palace. The race to build the fastest and greatest had by now become an all out arms race between the European powers. France hurried to out strip the English but Germany did it. With the launch of Germany's *Bremen*, the English lost the Blue Riband for the first time in nearly a quarter of a century.

Because the competition for the fastest ships was so tight and so financially exhaustive, several shipping lines didn't even try. These lines would push for luxury instead of engineering. White Star is the most famous of the lines that opted for form over function and paid the greatest price of all in human lives. White Star's master plan was to build three super luxury ships, the *Olympic*, the *Titanic* and the *Gigantic*. Two of the three sisters would meet horrific fates, while the *Olympic* would have a successful career and sail until her scrapping twenty years later.

The tragedy of the *Titanic* still haunts the world. It is a story, not only of heroisms and arrogance but also of just plain bad engineering. The vessels launched in Ireland by White Star, as mentioned above, were never supposed to be great engineering wonders.

It is for this reason that White Star's publicist pushed the luxury aspect of the vessels. A brilliant publicity move, that brought the three sisters the international attention they badly needed to fill their cabins. However, as is still the problem in many corporate structures of today, hype leads the day, and engineers were forced to comply with the glamorous images their managers were promoting.

It was for this reason – aesthetics – that the extra lifeboats were removed from the doomed *Titanic*. They, the extra boats, made the vessel seem clunky and less sleek. Still, White Star needed to tie-in some engineering hoopla, as the public had become accustomed to hearing about the great advancements these shipping lines were seemingly creating with every new vessel. So, the *Titanic* became "unsinkable." Unsinkable? Even engineering of that time knew that was laughable. Not only was the *Titanic* not unsinkable, it was an engineering hodgepodge. With bulkheads that could be flooded after five decks, there was no possible way this ship could be considered unsinkable. It was a design – the bulkheads – that had been used in another ships that had sunk in the past. So why the hype? Puffery. Advertising and Public Realtions gone amok. No one in the press cared to hear some nobody engineer cry fowl. So the spin went out and the passengers bought tickets and some lifeboats – deemed unnecessary—were removed. The tragedy that followed would never be forgotten.

It is with the sinking of *Titanic* that the story of the *SS United States* begins, because it was the very tragedy of the *Titanic* that inspired the young son of a prominent Philadelphia family to dream one day of building, not only an enormous 1000 ft vessel, but to make it safe. William Francis Gibbs was 17 years old when he stood at Penns Landing on Philadelphia's Delaware River waterfront and envisioned his super ship that would one day change the way ships were built ever since.

William Francis Gibbs reluctantly followed his family's request and went to an ivy league university to get his Law degree. He went reluctantly, because he already knew what he wanted to do and that was to build ships. It was at the age of 8 that Gibbs got a first hand look at a great transatlantic vessel. It was the launching of the *St. Louis* in Philadelphia. The boy was so impressed by the massive vessel that he resolutely made up his mind to build ships.

19 years later, he started the firm Gibbs and Cox with his brother Frederic and began his first major ship design project. After World War I, Gibbs and Cox got the largest refit contract of a merchant ship in American history. The ship, a war prize from Germany was renamed the *Leviathan* and would be brought under American ownership by United States Lines. The *Leviathan*, originally called the *Valterland*, was an enormous ship of over 50,000 tons. She was nearly 900 ft in length and was a 120 ft at the beam.

The *Leviathan* project gave Gibbs the most perfect training ground for a ship builder. He was involved with every aspect of rebuilding the vessel from keel to the top of her funnels. And she was grand. The *Leviathan* with an Olympic size swimming pool and décor to rival any European palace quickly became the favorite way to cross by Americans of distinction including Rudolph Valentino and Gloria Swanson.

But for all the marvelous rework Gibbs put into the adopted United States Lines flagship, she would remain exactly that, a reworked "foreign" liner. Gibbs would work from that day forward to get his super ship built. It would take him nearly the rest of his life before his ship of dreams would become a reality.

Many ships would follow—over five thousand to be exact—giving Gibbs the distinction of being the most prolific naval architect of the 20th Century, or any century for that matter. Over the years, Gibbs would examine in detail the greatest ships ever built. He was frequently to be found in the engine rooms of the *Maratania*, the *Normandy* and the *Queen Mary*.

Gibbs cared little for the frills and opulence associated with the above-mentioned vessels. He was more impressed with speed and efficiency. It was during the competition between the *Normandy* and the *Queen Mary* for the Blue Riband that Gibbs learned the enormous investment required to have a vessel of 1000 ft in length to also hold the speed record. For every knot above 21 on a ship, the same amount of money in engineering costs had to go into the ship.

Needless to say, this type of investment could only take place with government involvement. Something the Europeans had been doing for nearly 100 years, but something the United States government took very little interest in. From the launching of the *Queen Mary* and *Normandy* in the mid 1930s, Gibbs would have to wait nearly another twenty years to see his dream break all world records and take her place in history as one of the greatest engineering feats of all time.

As destiny would have it, Gibbs having to wait so long to build his super ship, proved to be fortuitous. Since the crossing of the *Teutonic* to New York in mid-1800s, the warm opulence of wood paneled suites were the required décor of all transatlantic crossers. In fact, more rare wood was used in the building of the *Queen Mary* then all of Buckingham Palace!

However, with this traditional country manner atmosphere came also the risk of fire. It was rare, a raging fire on board a luxury ship, but when it happened the effects were disastrous. Two of the greatest ships ever built, the *Normandy* and *Queen Elizabeth* were both completely destroyed because of fire. And it happened to a ship Gibbs had designed.

The burning of Gibbs' *Morro Castle* is still to date, one of the most horrific sea disasters of all time. The 531 ft *Morro Castle* had set out to sea on September 8, 1934. Not long after a fire erupted in her hull. It spread with such intensity and heat that many bodies were burned beyond recognition. 133 persons died that horrible day. To add to the horror, tides pushed the smoldering vessel onto the shores of a resort. There she lay a terrifying smoldering tomb, causing hundreds to come day after day to morbidly gaze on the dead ship. A catastrophe like that of the *Morro Castle* might have destroyed a lesser man's confidence, and eventually his reputation and career, but Gibbs pressed on to create safer and safer vessels. His *SS United States* is still considered the safest vessel ever put to sea.

Gibbs' next great project was to out shine everything that had come before. His new ship would set the standard for American ship builders. The *SS America* was the United States first large transatlantic vessel. Although she only weighed in at 34,000 tons and was just under 725ft, her hull design and propulsion systems were streamlined and some of the most efficient technologies put to sea. The *America* was christened by Eleanor Roosevelt in 1939 and would almost immediately be repainted in battleship gray to be used as a troop transport during WWII. Renamed the *West Point*, the *America* carried hundreds of thousands of men to conflict in the South Pacific. This one vessel alone helped reduce the length of the war by many months.

In fact, her war career was so successful, that the brass at the Pentagon decided to let Gibbs begin the designs of a ship that would not only out maneuver, out run, but also serve as a merchant luxury liner that could be converted into a troop transport for more than 14,000 men. The first blue prints were drawn up in 1948. Not long after, the skeptic's voices rang in. It was too expensive. No ship of a 1000 ft in length could be as maneuverable as Gibbs was promising and it certainly would never achieve speeds any greater than the *Queen Mary* (then the fastest ship in the world). But as always, Gibbs pressed on and was give dry dock 488 in Newport News shipyard to build the nation's first super ship and what would become the prototype of America's modern super Navy.

In his quest to secure approval for the building of his super ship, Gibbs relied on the political diplomacy of the president of United States Lines, the affable General Franklin. Franklin worked along side Gibbs to ensure the great ship became a reality. Franklin shared in Gibbs' vision and knew that the Philadelphian was the only naval architect who could carry off such a feat of engineering prowess. In later years, Gibbs would with appreciation acknowledge that had Franklin not been at the helm of United States Lines, the *SS United States* would have never been built.

Tom Brokaw's book *The Greatest Generation* has brought awareness to the legacy of those who fought to save the world from the influence of intolerance and despotism. It was an American generation of men and women who unified on all levels of society. At the beginning of the 1950s the stratification between the haves and the have naughts was the smallest it had ever been in American history. The wage difference between the average factory worker and the executives was only 40 percent. This was in part due to the collective consciousness of the war mentality.

No one wanted to consider themselves that much better than the average Joe, who not just five years before the building began on the *United States* may have saved a young officer's life, who now was the executive of the firm "Joe" was working in and rely upon for help. It was in this atmosphere of comradery that the *United States* was conceived. One only has to look at photographs of the *Queen Mary* and *Queen Elizabeth* speeding across the Atlantic with 15,000 troops on board, pressed nearly shoulder to shoulder in some cases, that the concept of oneness – of all for one and one for all – dominated the Greatest Generation.

These men had saved the world, together, and now they were about to lay the blue prints of a new greatest civilization, one that would have no rival in the history of the world. This spirit of righteous victory was galvanized across all sectors of society. There was nothing Americans could not do if we put our minds to it. Because this was before the heady years of space exploration and enormous advances in air travel, the oceans and who ruled them was on the minds of all those who sought to keep the United States in control of a world that could quickly unravel if not closely monitored.

The Pentagon was faced with a daunting challenge. The country had to create a great Navy. America's battleships were as powerful as any on the seas, but it would take more than military prowess to keep watch over the new world order. We had to prove that not only did we have a Navy as great as any, we had to prove to the world that our Navy and our American built ships were so far beyond any other nation's that the dominance of the seas would not even be a question – even to Great Britain.

Up to this point we had yet, in this country, to build any ship of great size and speed. The *Queen Mary* at 1018ft in length had held the speed record for nearly 20 years. She and her sister ship the *Queen Elizabeth* were credited to having shortened the length of the European conflict in WWII by as much as a year. The enormous vessels carrying between them 30,000 men on a single crossing were faster and stealthier than any vessel in our entire Navy. The English had had centuries to perfect the art of shipbuilding. Now we Americans were going to take them on and build the greatest symbol of victory a nation could.

During the heavy trade years of the turn of the century and until the building of the *United States*, Western nations sought to build not only profitable transatlantic ocean liners but nothing short of symbols of their nations. Because these ships were the largest moving objects ever built, whichever nation had the queen of seas as their flagship was the nation that ruled the seas.

It was time for the United States to take the helm, as it were. In the highest security since the building of the atomic bomb, the first blueprints of the new super ship were laid out by General Franklin and William Francis Gibbs on a table before Pentagon brass. The questions were many. How much money was it going to cost? Would it be civilian or military?

Eventually, a duel purpose vessel was decided upon, one that would serve as a merchant super liner ferrying passengers from New York to Europe, but could also be used in time of war as a troop transport.

William Francis Gibbs was the only one considered up to the task. If he failed, he would be relegated to just another naval architect, if he succeeded his super ship would become not only a symbol of the nation and victory, but the very prototype of our nation's modern super Navy. No one who heard Gibbs speak of what this ship would do when completed could have actually believed him. Not only was this man promising the most powerful ship ever built, but an engineering feat of such magnitude that it would shatter all preconceived notions speed, maneuverability, safety and technologies that would have to be invented as they went along. In other words, this native from Philadelphia was promising one of the greatest engineering feats of all time.

Newport News shipyard in Virginia would be the site for the laying of hull number 488. Heavy security would be in place at all times. No one could enter or leave the dry dock unless they passed through a tight security contingent. 3000 of the best ship builders from all over the nation were summoned to Newport News. None turned down the opportunity to take part in building the new super ship. From the placement of the first shipment of high tinseled steal, even the vendors for Newport News knew something incredible was being built in dry dock number 12. However, before hull 488 began to take shape, problems in design arose.

Many naval engineers disagreed adamantly with Gibbs, a strange man they said among themselves. A man who wore black everyday and lurked around the construction of this ship like some specter out of a Shakespearian play. Who was he after all? He had never even been formally schooled in naval engineering. And when they heard of what he planned to do, well, many laughed, but none deserted. Gibbs' plan must have seemed laughable to many. This man was going to build not only the fastest ship in the world, but also a ship that would be 1000 ft in length and carry upwards of 15,000 during times of crisis. To accomplish the speeds he wanted, Gibbs super ship would have to weigh less than 55,000 tons. The *Queen Mary*, a ship of nearly the same dimensions, weighed in at over 80,000 tons. There was no possible way that using existing ship building technology that this ship would weigh in at anything less than 75,000 tons. It was simply impossible.

Gibbs didn't think so. He proposed using aluminum to bring down the weight of his vessel. A lot of aluminum. When the order came in to Alcoa headquarters, no one could believe it. The Newport News shipyard, which had hardly ever ordered any significant amounts of aluminum before had just placed the largest single order in history. Over 5000 tons. And it was for just one ship!

Now Gibbs was really over doing it. He had lost his mind. Not only was this lightweight material going to be used extensively throughout the superstructure of the super ship, but also the entire superstructure would be made of aluminum! The engineers were in a tailspin of frustration. Even if the super structure could be built, the electrolyses, caused by the friction of aluminum meeting metal would eat through the structure and bring it crashing down in a matter of a few years.

Gibbs didn't think so. In fact, in other ships he had used the same combination, with insulation between the metals that worked like a charm. The construction proceeded with Gibbs' aluminum superstructure plan approved.

One of the reasons Gibbs was given the go ahead for many of his radical engineering ideas was because he had had a 40-year track record of highly successful naval ships that greatly pleased the brass in the Pentagon. However, because the brass had agreed to pay the lion's share of the new ship's construction costs, they would have a hand in many details. This would ultimately effect most importantly the over all length of the ship. Gibbs had wanted his super ship to be in excess of 1000ft. But the Navy needed a troop transport that could get through the Panama Canal. This meant that Gibbs' ship could be no wider than 90 feet at the beam and 950 feet in length. This would give the vessel several feet of clearance when entering the locks in the canal.

Gibbs was livid. What kind of super ship was only 950 ft in length? Through his persuasive abilities, he learned as a law student, Gibbs managed to convince the Navy that his ship could be fitted out to the limits of no other ship that had ever crossed the Panama Canal. In the end, Gibbs was approved to design a ship 990 ft in length (just under his 1000ft minimum) and 101 feet at the beam. In other words, Gibbs ship when launched would be the third largest ship in the world and largest ever built to traverse the Panama Canal – with only 6 inches to spare!

But, the in-depth history of this ship and its construction is better left to be told by our nation's foremost maritime historian, Frank Braynard. His seminal work on the *SS United States* entitled *The Big Ship* has been reprinted here in this the 50th anniversary commemorative book on the history of the national flagship.

Robert Hudson Westover

The ship at port with anchor up and tie-offs to dock. (Photo by Andrew Malmsea courtesy of Sven Olefeldt)

Author's Note

There is every indication at this printing that the superliner *United States* still lives! She may well sail again, proud flagship of the American Merchant Marine. Her story is not ended.

And what a story it has been. "The Big Ship," as she was lovingly known at Gibbs & Cox, on whose drawingboards she was designed, is an achievement that should rank with the Pyramids or, the great cathedrals of the Middle Ages. She is a marvel of ingenuity and her construction is a monument to American naval architecture and marine engineering. She was one of the most popular and most successful of all Atlantic liners in her 17 years on the high seas. She was and remains the greatest passenger ship ever built for operation under the American flag.

This work is intended to be plain and simply "a book about the Big Ship." That was what the late Frederic H. Gibbs asked me to write in my last interview with him. It does not pretend in any sense to be a technical or even a definitive treatment of this truly amazing saga. It does hope to document the extraordinary achievement of the Gibbs brothers, William Francis and Frederic H., for the *United States* was a lifelong assignment for both of them. Their careers had other highlights, of course, but from their earliest days their joint dream was the construction of "the Big Ship." Most of the credit has always gone to William Francis Gibbs, for he was the older and the more vocal of the two brothers, but their successes were joint successes.

This book is dedicated to Frederic H. Gibbs, whose last wish in life was to make it possible for the creation of this work as one further small way of honoring his distinguished brother. A special word of thanks is due to the many friends in the distinguished firm of Gibbs & Cox, listed alphabetically: Charles J. Altenburg, Walter C. Bachman, Thomas Buermann, H.L. Culpepper, Rebekah T. Dallas, Matthew Forrest, Walter Malmstrom, Henry Meyer, V. Moynihan, Frank Patz, B.O. Smith, and Norman Zippler.

Many friends in U.S. Lines also helped, particularly Kenneth Gautier, Nicholas Bachko and Cliff Morgan. And there were others in the Maritime Administration who assisted, notably Capt. Thomas A. King, J.C. Fernanders, John E. Murray, and Walter E. Oates. John R. Kane, formerly with the Newport News Shipbuilding Corp., was most helpful, as were Phyllis Stephenson and James M. Griffith. Of course The Mariners' Museum was a prime source of inspiration and assistance, from Director William D. Wilkinson down, including my patient editor Robert H. Burgess, and others such as Ardie L. Kelly, John O. Sands and Steve Laise. A most cordial word of thanks to interior decorator and designer Anne Urquhart is called for also.

Additional help came from the following: Capt. Harry Allendorfer, Mrs. John W. Anderson, Mrs. William Bak, Alexander Crosby Brown, Lawrence J. Bates, Dennie B. Beattie, Jeff Blinn, Richard Berry; and also from M. Jean Caune, Robert Doyle, Clarence P. Gehrig, William J. Green, Allan E. Jordan, Bruce E. Kahler, Hans Marx, B.J. Nixon, J.R.P. O'Neill, Walter B. Perkins, David E. Perkins, Michael Shindler, Patrick J. Stephens, and John P. Walsh.

As this introduction was written Richard Hadley and his United States Cruises company had just moved the *United States* into drydock and found her hull in A1 condition. More power to their efforts to get her back into the cruising field.

A final and very special word of thanks to Gibbs & Cox, without whose encouragement and assistance this work would not have seen the light of day. In one of my last meetings with Frederic Gibbs, I sat spellbound as he told me stories of the earliest days of his and his brother's interest in ocean liners and of the origins of the *United States,* way back in World War I. And then he sat back in his large chair and paused, smiling. "I want a book on the big ship," he said. "Would you like to do it?" I answered: "Would I!"

Frank O. Braynard
June 10, 1980

1

The Beginnings

The story of the superliner *United States* is a remarkable epoch. She was a superb wonder ship in many ways; the supreme achievement of American maritime genius. She was a success beyond the most sanguine expectations of her designer and builders.

The opening in 1952 of her brief 17-year career on the route for which she was built was like a brilliant comet's arrival. She burst on the scene in a blaze of glory acidly described in Britain's *Punch* magazine: "After the loud and fantastic claims made in advance for the liner *United States* it comes as something of a disappointment to find them all true." In her recapturing of the Atlantic speed supremacy, her great popularity as a trans-Atlantic liner, and her remarkable record of trouble free operation, many saw a rebirth of America's maritime glory.

Behind the saga of the *United States* looms the gaunt figure of one man, a man whose talents and drive put him on the highest plateau among the most gifted of men. William Francis Gibbs, supported throughout his lifetime by his younger brother Frederic Herbert Gibbs, was that man. If ever there was a true perfectionist it was William Francis. And where else in all history has a perfectionist come so close to achieving perfection – not only with the *United States,* high point in his career, but all along the way in many other maritime milestones that stand to his credit. The mystical chain linking the man and the ship is profound and all embracing. Although thousands contributed to the creating of this wonder vessel, and Mr. Gibbs emphasized this many times, she was, perhaps as only rarely before, a one-man ship. Some might say this was the case with Moses Rogers and his tiny *Savannah,* of 1819, the first steam-powered ship to cross any ocean. Others would nominate Isambard Kingdom Brunel and his huge failure, the first *Leviathan,* better known as the *Great Eastern.* But there can never be the slightest question in that the superliner *United States* was William Francis Gibbs – and *vice versa.* The *United States* was the embodiment in steel of the spirit that made Gibbs such a superman. Supership-superman and a super merger of the two. This book will be an effort to show how such an amazing union was conceived, matured, evolved, and conquered all, a success story seldom equalled in any field of enterprise. Fortunately Mr. Gibbs did not live to see his masterpiece laid up, a victim of the rush into air travel and the triumph of the jet age.

It is not as if William Francis Gibbs was a superman, God-like man. He had very human qualities and salted into the story they add a strong strain of humor to the saga of the *United States.* His passion to outdo competitors, particularly British competitors, was one such characteristic. Another was his determination to have his own way. Also his almost paranoic demand for secrecy over whatever he was doing. And his delightful foibles: how he dressed his ancient felt hat on the one hand and his elegant, red-lined opera cape on the other; how he spoke those who had offices near his often heard him slugging his contemporaries with the strongest kind of language. Swearing was one of his weapons, and he used it liberally to slice up anyone who dared oppose him. How he got his way – skullduggery – was not alien to his makeup, as unwary opponents often discovered. More times than not they never knew what had hit them, he was so deft at deception and fancy stepping. And he managed to combine a temperament that was both self-effacing, on almost a Uriah Heep scale, with an eagerness for recognition and audience appreciation. Near the end, when he was hospitalized, one of his many dedicated aides found that what he wanted most in his hospital room was to hear tape recordings of his public addresses – interrupted continually by loud laughter. He was a superb public speaker.

There are so few genuine geniuses that find fulfillment that a look into the early life of William Francis Gibbs and his brother Frederic offers an exciting porthole into the birth of this most creative team. Born on August 24, 1886, in Philadelphia, William Francis was the son of a successful financier, William Warren Gibbs, a man who was said to be a director of more companies than any other man in America. Wealth and family position gave William Francis and his brother, born a year later, many advantages, but they had in themselves much more. Being the older, William Francis was the one who stepped out in front and continued to do so for the rest of his life. The younger brother, however, was never far

William Francis Gibbs in front of his ship.

behind, and together they made a mutually supportive pair which would function almost as a single unit throughout their long careers.

At the age of three William Francis began drawing ship pictures. He would never stop. In a very real sense he drew the lines of what would eventually be the *United States* before America entered the first world war. When he first began drawing, the largest ocean liner of the day was still Brunel's masterpiece, the *Great Eastern,* although she had long since ended her active career. Way ahead of her time she had last served in a most ignominious way as a huge sign board in the River Thames. The largest active passenger ships in the world the year Gibbs began to put ship pictures on paper were the historic Inman Line twin flyers *City of New York* and City *of Paris,* clipper bowed beauties with three tall smokestacks. They had popularized the concept of twin-screws, thus ending forever the ship owners' ancient reliance on wind power as insurance against the breakdown of a single-propeller ship. Despite this they were fitted with square yards and a full set of sails. Thought by many to have been among the most beautiful liners ever built, these graceful twin liners were of just over 10,000 gross tons, huge monsters compared to the 300-ton pioneer steamship *Savannah,* or the 2,000-ton clipper ships of the mid-century period. It was an age of lightning progress for steamships, and they were, indeed, "the only way to cross."

The coming of twin propellers was in itself one of the major evolutionary developments in liner history. Once the shipowner was confident that his pride and joy could make her way into port even if one propeller shaft failed, the era of sail was at an end. While sails had still been needed, the steamship had, in effect, remained an auxiliary sailing ship in basic design. With a long, low hull and only one level of deck houses and possibly a raised bridge on struts, her tall smokestack would often be hidden behind billowing canvas and, from the distance, might even be obscured by rigging and masts, particularly from a head on or a following position. A tell-tale trail of smoke would be the only sure distinction that these 19th Century steam vessels had over sailing craft. They should be called steam-sail ships. But with twin screws all this would quickly be changed and the change would come in amazing leaps. It was just at the start of this epoch era of speeded-up evolution in naval architecture that young William Francis Gibbs sketched his first ocean liner. No wonder he was enthralled by each new ocean passenger ship he saw moving in and out of New York port from his childhood summer home in Spring Lake, New Jersey. No wonder his mind looked to new and larger and faster and finer passenger ships.

Five historic liners would play important roles in the early motivation of the Gibbs brothers. Each was an outstanding vessel, each a very special ship and the two Gibbs boys knew them well. Fate was playing the cards in an almost brazen fashion, or were the two young men already in command? Certainly it had to be fate that brought William Francis Gibbs to the launching on November 12, 1894, of the liner *St. Louis* at Cramp's Shipyard in Philadelphia. And what more fitting opening to the career of America's most famous naval architect since the era of Donald McKay. He had only just turned eight, but the event was to be indelibly stamped on his memory. To understand the very real significance of this launching a quick glance back is necessary.

The significance of the *St. Louis,* the first of the five great Atlantic liners that would so influence William Francis Gibbs in his most formative years, comes into focus here. Launched in 1894 she was the first major trans-Atlantic steam passenger liner built in America since the Civil War. There had been big ships like the *Erie* and the *Ontario,* but they had been of wooden construction and were out of date when they were launched and proved dismal failures in no time. And there were four little Philadelphia-based liners of the International Navigation Company built in 1870.

But between the *Adriatic,* last of the Collins Line queens, and 1895 there were no first-class American-built liners on the Atlantic. None! The very construction of the *St. Louis* and her sister, the *St. Paul,* was an odd arrangement, which did not bespeak for permanence or long-range success. The International Navigation Company had been acquired by J.P. Morgan and the company wanted to make a big splash in the "big pond." It was decided to buy the two largest and finest ships on the Atlantic, the Inman Line record-breakers *City of Paris* and *City of New York.* But they were under foreign flag and had been built abroad. To permit them to sail under the American flag a special act of Congress had to be passed. Morgan had to pledge that his company would build two even larger ships in an American yard and operate them under the American flag. And so it was in an atmosphere of heady nationalism and high hopes that the *St. Louis* was launched. This was the beginning of the American Line, which eventually would become the United States Lines. As can be seen, it was a highly artificial situation which really had little hope of making a permanent improvement in our maritime debacle. The company would survive only because America would fall victim to three major wars in the next half century providing continuing financial stimulants to deepsea shipping. But discouraging realities meant little when Mrs. Grover Cleveland christened the 11,000-ton *St. Louis* with young William Francis Gibbs and his brother Frederic among the thousands of cheering spectators. It seemed like a rebirth of the American Merchant Marine.

"This was my first view of a great ship and from that day forward I dedicated my life to ships," said William Francis of that colorful launching. "I have never regretted it," he added. It was a moment of inspiration that would give point and purpose to his career. And few lives have ever fulfilled such dedication with such success.

Between this mind-stamping experience at the launching of the *St. Louis* and his first trans-oceanic voyage in June 1901, young William Francis had shown a precocious ability to learn. His father filled their home with quality magazines and professional journals. The highly technical engineering publication, *Cassier's Magazine,* had found its way into the house and immediately became a favorite of the eight-year-old genius. Although his father had a prejudice against engineers, thinking they were inarticulate and lacking in business ability, the young Gibbs knew what he wanted and managed to get it: books about ships and machinery. With the assistance of a small technical dictionary he learned the meanings of the technical words that he found in *Cassier's* and in other magazines. As so often was the case with a prodigy, the formal education of William Francis Gibbs was very much secondary to his own self-directed learning process. His motivation was so high that he did not really need the routines that others were forced to pass through. He entered the Delancey School in 1894 and quickly absorbed what help he could get there. His attendance was somewhat irregular due to frequent colds. But there was nothing irregular about his continuing dedication to great passenger ships once the seed had been planted at the launching of the *St. Louis* in 1895.

The four other ships that helped confirm the lifelong passion for great liners in the mind of young William Francis were the White Star Line's *Oceanic* and *Celtic* and the twin Cunarders *Lusitania* and *Mauretania*. These four were all British ships. His impressions of them and the traditions of the two great companies that owned them helped create in his young mind a strong competitive thrust that at times would surface as a powerful anti-British attitude. In the case of the *United States* his great goal was to out-do the British *Queen Mary*. His contacts with those four British liners produced other life-long thought patterns that would contribute much to the final dream fulfillment in the *United States*.

The evolution of the Atlantic liner as such had taken one tremendous burst forward in 1858 with the amazing ship *Great Eastern.* She had huge paddle wheels, a propeller, a full set of sails on six tall masts and five smokestacks. She was 680 feet in length, between perpendiculars, or well over twice as long as any other ship in the world when she was new. Her bulk measured 18,915 gross tons, giving her a tonnage measurement five times greater than any existing liner. After she came on the scene the terms "longest" and "largest" were simply put on the shelf and not used for the next half a century. She remained the longest and the largest well after she was scrapped in 1891. It was not until 1899 that a ship was built that exceeded her in length. That ship was the *Oceanic,* and we can be sure that William Francis Gibbs knew all about her from the moment her keel laying was announced at the famous Belfast, Ireland, yard of Harland & Wolff. She had a length of 685 feet, between perpendiculars, just five feet more than the *Great Eastern*. Of course her beam of 68 feet was far less than that of Brunel's masterpiece, which was 82 feet wide without counting her paddle wheels. Counting her paddles and their guards her total beam was 120 feet, still to this writing never equalled by any passenger ship ever built. The *Oceanic's* gross tonnage was 17,274 tons, well under that of the first *Leviathan*.

The *Oceanic* was a superb vessel. With her twin screw propulsion, sails were no longer necessary even in the mind of the most die-hard conservative. And so her superstructure could rise above the main deck and did. She had three decks of superstructure, including two promenade decks on top of each other. The crowning achievement of her designers, and the feature which doubtless made young William Francis Gibbs' eyes pop almost out of his head, were her twin smokestacks. They were without doubt the tallest stacks ever put on any liner up to that time, and followed the tall-stack tradition begun in 1889 by their beautiful predecessors, the *Majestic* and *Teutonic*. Giant stacks were to be a key part of the Gibbs dream, and the two huge smokestacks on the *United States* can be traced to this pre-1900 liner, the *Oceanic*. Whereas other naval architects would try to play down the stack, some eliminating it altogether, the Gibbs design always called for large, massive smokestacks.

Despite the glamorous appearance of the *Oceanic*, she was a failure in one major respect, speed, and her failure meant a major change in the philosophy of her owners. And this failure meant another lifelong goal in the thought pattern of William Francis, a goal that would see him insist on speed as a main feature in the design of the *United States*. The *Oceanic* emerged just as the Germans were successfully challenging Britain for the trans-Atlantic Blue Riband for the first time. Four German four-stackers in a row wrenched the speed crown from England and the new *Oceanic* came out just as this era of German speed supremacy was at its high point. Although she was a 21-knot ship, certainly one of the world's fastest, she could not equal the speed of either of the glamorous German racers of the day, *Kaiser Wilhelm Der Grosse* or *Deutschland*. Everyone knew two more German four-stackers of even greater speed were being planned. And so the directors of White Star decided, as the old century died and the new Twentieth Century began, to abandon the race for the speed crown and concentrate on very large ships which could boast great comfort, elegance, and steadiness instead. Perhaps the ghastly vibration of the *Deutschland* helped convince them that ship design had reached the point of diminishing returns as far as speed went. Whatever their reasoning, they made a change in emphasis and the magnificent *Oceanic* was never duplicated. She was one of history's rare things, a single ship.

With William Francis Gibbs watching from across the Atlantic, the company ordered four new ships of a very different style. Each would be the largest in the world when she was introduced, and at last the gross tonnage of the *Great Eastern* would be surpassed. Each would be very large in passenger capacity. Whereas the *Oceanic* had made a crossing in 5 days, 16 hours and 34 minutes, the new quartet would be scheduled to do the run in a comfortable eight or nine days at a maximum speed of 17 knots. The first of these new ships was launched on April 4th, 1901, and christened *Celtic*. She would be the first vessel in all time to exceed 20,000 tons. Also built by Harland & Wolff at Belfast, she would be considerably beamier than the *Oceanic,* but shorter. Her outline was utterly different: four masts and two relatively short stacks, much more traditional but far less exciting. Watching her construction timetable, William Francis planned his first trip to coincide with her maiden voyage. With his brother Frederic, he decided he would cross the Atlantic on the *Oceanic,* still the longest liner in the world, and return on the *Celtic,* the largest. They sailed in June in the finest cabin that the White Star flagship could offer. Frederic remembered how steady she was because he was able to build a house of blocks on the deck of his cabin and it did not fall over during the whole voyage. He was 13 years old and William Francis was going on 15. The boys knew all about the *Oceanic* long before they stepped aboard. They ate in her main dining saloon which measured 64 x 80 feet and was surmounted by a glass dome 21 feet square. They walked up and down her 400-foot long promenade deck, and they had plenty of time to admire her two tall buff and black smokestacks, emblems of luxury and elegance.

The new *Celtic* brought the two tall young Philadelphians home. They sailed from Liverpool, then the White Star Line's home port. Although the ship's First Class public rooms were luxurious in a mid-Victorian way, she was quite a different kind of ship from the *Oceanic*. She could carry 2,352 in Third Class, 347 in Second, and 160 in First. She took nine days to make the crossing and left in the mind of William Francis a strong feeling that speed was most important in the ideal Atlantic liner. Frederic was seasick and did not enjoy the fancy menus but William Francis sampled everything, from the Sweetbreads a la Demidoff to the Turkey Poulet and Ham, St. James. The round trip was important because it showed the Gibbs brothers two very different examples of the finest of modern British passenger ship design – the First Class flagship and the more common-sense money earner.

Already the *St. Louis* and her sistership *St. Paul* were falling behind in the competitive picture from all standpoints. They had never been record breakers. In size they were now far behind the leading liners of other nations, although only six years had passed since they were put into service. Their appointments were comfortable but far from ornate. They were the best under the American flag, however, and William Francis Gibbs was disappointed. A most patriotic person, he had hoped that the *St. Louis* and the *St. Paul* would be just the beginning of a new fleet of American-flag ships on the Atlantic. The great J. P. Morgan combine, however, preferred to put its money into ships of the White Star Line, which it also owned and did not seem interested in more ships for their one and only American-flag company, the American Line. They did add two slightly-larger copies of the *St. Louis* to the Red Star Line, the *Finland* and the *Kroonland,* however no one was even talking about new American speed queens or an American-flag superliner. But Gibbs began to think about one.

William Francis finished high school, keeping a close eye on maritime developments as he did. He literally devoured each new book on marine propulsion and ship design and he made it a point not to miss anything that was printed on the subject. He subscribed to all the technical journals in the field and read every page with a voracious appetite for new things that were happening. The most exciting new development in marine propulsion was the turbine. The Cunard Line, whose fortunes had fallen much too low for the happiness of most Britains, was rescued by the government in London by a promise of important financial help. In return the company pledged to build two new ships, which would not only be the world's largest, but the world's fastest. They would employ the new turbine engine, which in the first few years of the Twentieth Century had amazed everyone in the marine field with its new power and speed potential. Cunard's two new liners would recapture the speed record from Germany, or so everyone hoped, and they would be named *Lusitania* and *Mauretania*. Young William Francis watched eagerly for each article about their conception, their keel laying, their launching, and their trials.

The *Lusitania* was delivered in mid-1907 and was a triumph of design and style. With a length between perpendiculars of 762 feet and a gross tonnage of 31,550 she was larger than any other ship afloat. Her outline was magnificent; she looked like a racer from the tip of her knife-like prow to her beautiful counter stern. She had four tall smokestacks, beautifully proportioned and heroic in appearance. Unlike the four German four-stackers, her funnels were equally spaced. The German ships had two pair of stacks. To everyone's surprise the new ship did not immediately break the trans-Atlantic speed record as her trials indicated she could do. On her second passage, however, she set a new mark with a speed of 23.99 knots and a time of 4 days, 22 hours and 53 minutes from Cobh to Sandy Hook. The two Gibbs brothers had decided to make the maiden voyage of the *Mauretania* late in the year, and they booked passage over on the *Lusitania,* so they could compare how the two sisters operated. They had been built in different yards and the rivalry between them was already keen.

Comparison of the Gibbs Design-1915 and the *Vaterland*

	Vaterland	Gibbs Design-1915
Length overall	950 feet	1,001 feet
Beam	100 feet, 1 inch	106 feet
Depth	64 feet	74 feet
Draft	35 1/2 feet	35 feet
Gross Tonnage	54,000 gross	55,000 gross
Passenger capacity First	700	1,000
Second	600	800
Third/Steerage	1,050/1,700	1,200
Total	4,050	3,000
Crew	1,200	1,000

William Francis was impressed by the superb new *Lusitania.* She was nearly twice the tonnage of the *Oceanic,* new barely eight years before. Built by the same Scottish yard that would later turn out both the *Queen Mary* and the *Queen Elizabeth,* she was a great leap forward in luxury and spaciousness, boasting such innovations as elevators, an elaborate gymnasium, and Turkish baths. The *Mauretania* was built in England at Wallsend-on-Tyne. Although constructed to virtually identical plans, her tonnage came to only 30,696 gross. Gross tonnage measurement, as will be seen later in the computation of the tonnage of the *United States*, is a most variable kind of yardstick. But speed is a different kind of thing. The *Lusitania* had made 25.4 knots on her trials. Some months later the *Mauretania* broke this record with an amazing 26.04 knots. Everyone eagerly awaited her first crossing. She sailed on November 16,1907, with the Gibbs brothers aboard. William Francis was 21 and a very lanky six feet, 2 inches and a half in height. Frederic, at 19, matched him in height. They were in their element. One of the notables aboard was Andrew Lang, famed designer of the *Mauretania's* engines. There can be little doubt that William Francis would have had an introduction to meet him during the crossing. Although he was shy and generally retiring, when it came to an opportunity like this he would not have failed to take the fullest advantage of it. Bemuse of the winter season the *Mauretania* did not beat the record on this crossing but soon she showed herself to be the faster of the pair and took both eastbound and westbound speed records. The close-up contact with these outstanding new Cunard liners convinced William Francis Gibbs more than ever that speed was essential to the Atlantic liner. He would be so convinced of this that four decades later it would be one of the prime considerations in his design of the superliner *United States,* despite the fact that developments in air travel were making the whole question of speed for liners academic.

William Francis Gibbs had started his undergraduate work at Harvard in 1906. With an individualism that would become characteristic, he refused to follow the formal curriculum. He took those courses which interested him, everything he could find that touched upon naval architecture and marine engineering. As can be seen, he interrupted his studies in the fall of 1907 when he went abroad on the *Lusitania* and came home on the *Mauretania.* This was much more important, and rightly so, than any courses at Harvard. He continued to devour every book and technical study on his favorite subjects and worked like a fury to master the field. One of his favorite exercises was re-designing British battleships. He chose them to work with because he was able to find excellent printed data describing their construction and design. Working in secret behind a locked door in his Harvard dormitory to protect himself from ridicule from fellow students, he developed what would become a lifelong mania for secrecy. This phobia for secrecy would become one of the most difficult-to-live-with features of the construction and operation of the *United States* from the standpoint of the shipyard and the ship line involved. It produced a situation years after the completion of the ship when the president of the yard which built her was forced to ask the project manager in his own employ what the ship's top speed was. The employee, still under the influence of Mr. Gibbs, risked his position by refusing to divulge the information.

At Harvard Gibbs would cover the walls and floors of his college room with his own huge blueprints. Drawings of engines, boilers, propellers and the like were everywhere. Although there were no courses on naval architecture, Gibbs was training himself to master this complicated and highly technical field. He was equally intrigued with questions of steam pressure, heating surfaces, and the intricacies of a ship's power plant as with what a hull or a bow or a stern should look like. By 1910 he had learned all he could from courses on related subjects at Harvard. When he "graduated" he did so without receiving a degree, although years later the Harvard Chapter of Phi Beta Kappa made him an honorary member. Much against his own inclinations, but on the stern advice of his father, he then entered Columbia University Law School. His passion for ships and his utter disinterest in the law became more and more evident. That he managed to absorb enough of the legal jargon to more or less keep in step with his class is shown by an anecdote of those tiresome days. Once during one of those dull law classes he was completely absorbed in working out a complicated engineering problem, oblivious to all that was going on about him. Years later he recalled how, out of a haze, he heard his professor call out his name and ask him what he thought about the previous speaker's comments. All his classmates knew the professor had caught him off guard and listened with rapt attention. The thin young beanstalk rose to his feet with apparent poise and with due deliberation parrotted a phrase that the professor had himself used *ad nauseam:* "The former speaker's comments are interesting but immaterial and completely irrelevant." The reaction of his fellow students and even the professor was electric, responding with gales of laughter and hoots and howls and stamping of feet. He won his Bachelor of Law degree in 1913. He had also been taking graduate courses in economics and received at the same time his degree of Master of Arts. People were beginning to recognize that under his calm and almost retiring manner there was a dynamo of energy and ability that was extraordinary and would brook no interference from ordinary men.

For the next two years William Francis forced himself to work as a lawyer. He entered the New York law firm of William Osgood Morgan and disliked it intensely. Unfortunately, his father had undergone financial reverses and it was necessary for young William Francis not only to support himself but to help support his family. His memory of that period could bring back only one case, a law suit involving some plumbing matter. It was so protracted and so uninteresting that he quietly made up his mind to give up the law entirely and find some way to do what he knew he could do best – design ships. With no formal training in naval architecture this was a challenge, but he began it with keen enthusiasm and the fullest kind of help from his brother. Even during this period as a lawyer he had continued with his passionate hobby. Each weekend he would spend at the family home in Haverford, Pennsylvania, making new drawings, testing out new theories. His goal was clear. He would create a high-speed trans-Atlantic passenger liner of 1,000 feet in length. He had set this mark for himself as far back as 1908 or 1909. He pushed hard toward its accomplishment. Along the way he kept abreast of current events in both the liner and machinery fields. He had seen the *Mauretania* and the *Lusitania* deposed as the world's largest ships by the *Olympic* and her ill-fated sistership, the *Titanic*. Their tonnage was 46,000 gross. He knew that Germany was producing an even larger class of ship, starting with their 52,000-ton

Imperator and followed by the 54,000-ton *Vaterland*. He had watched the turbine engine take the place of the old reciprocating power plant and new that oil would soon replace coal as a source of power in ships. He knew of the first Diesel liner, the *Sealandia,* flying the Danish flag. He had heard of the so-called "electric drive," and thought it might produce the 20% additional speed that his ship would have to have over the *Mauretania*. Electricity was an important thing in his family and his father was president of the Electric Storage Battery Company. More than that, one of his classmates in college knew the Chief Engineer of the General Electric Company, a W.L.R. Emmet. Mr. Emmet was behind the "electric drive" concept. William Francis Gibbs was very sincere in his high goals and people began to take him seriously.

All through his law practice period he had been helped in deadly earnest by his brother Frederic. The latter provided the economic justification to the cause of the high-speed, 1,000-foot Atlantic liners that William Francis was determined to create. He dropped into the basket two striking new thoughts. One was to have the ships operate from Fort Pond Bay, a very deep pool of water between Montauk and Orient points at the eastern end of Long Island. This would save at least four hours on an Atlantic crossing. High speed railroad service would link the jumping off point with New York City. In this way the Long Island Railroad and its parent, the Pennsylvania Railroad, would become partners in the deal, leading to a second fresh bit of thinking. Pennsylvania Railroad ticket agents would not only sell rail tickets but would provide a network of ticket agencies for the trans-Atlantic steamship line. And as a natural corollary this great railroad would help finance the scheme. The Pennsylvania had long been interested in trans-Atlantic shipping, and in 1873 had founded the Keystone Line with four little liners of 3,400 gross tons each. This had been the beginning of the great International Mercantile Marine put together by J.P. Morgan.

In May, 1915, William Francis was far enough along in his original design work to take the fateful step. He abandoned all pretense of being a lawyer, gave up his only source of income and, with his brother's encouragement, began to devote full time to his 1,000-foot liner project. Despite his lack of formal training in the field of naval architecture and marine engineering, no man was better prepared for this staggering goal. Nevertheless, for the rest of his life, Mr. Gibbs would make a point of the fact that he had no degree in naval architecture and was really not a naval architect. One of the first things he did was to go to the General Electric headquarters in Schenectady to meet with Mr. Emmet. Frederic went with him, silently supportive and always there with an answer to a difficult question of business or practicality. They made a remarkable team. And this is the way it would continue for the rest of their lives. Both tall young men were well received by the General Electric executive. Obviously impressed with the ground work they had done, he agreed to have his company draw up the needed preliminary outlines of the electric driven machinery that the Gibbs 1,000-footers would need to have the power to break the trans-Atlantic speed record.

Unfortunately, none of the blueprints and drawings from this early period has survived except one conception of the ship as she might have looked had she been built at that moment. The design was that of a substantially stretchedout *Aquitania,* the ship built by Cunard to round out their three-ship express service. A plumb bow, very slightly raked and with a foredeck free of all small deck houses or well-deck, gave a fresh, new look to the design. The bridge rose much as in the *Olympic,* and without the upper pilot house added by the *Aquitania's* designers as an afterthought. Seventeen lifeboats ranged aft along the very long boat deck; none was nested on top of another, and Gibbs realized even then that this common practice was unsafe. A long, single promenade directly under the boat deck was open from its forward end to the stern. Below this there was a second promenade, glass enclosed for most of its length as in the *Olympic.* As her crowning feature the ship had four tall smokestacks, nicely raked. Instead of the evenly-spaced stacks as in the *Lusitania, Mauretania,* and all other subsequent British four-stackers, Gibbs returned with his design to the older way of doing it in pairs, like the four German speed queens, a trace of his anti-British sensitivity, perhaps. In his drawing he hinted at a single thick band near the top of each stack. It was shown with lighter shading on the otherwise black stack. A very obvious radio antenna stretched between the two tall pole masts forward and aft. Foretelling a most distinctive feature which Gibbs would use for the rest of his life, the four stacks were placed not equidistant from the twin masts, but forward, so as to give the impression of speed. Quite revolutionary, this stack and mast arrangement would be followed two decades later with the Gibbs-designed *America* and eventually in the *United States.* Below the two long promenade decks another superstructure deck rose from the main deck, painted white like the rest of the ship's upperworks. It showed no openings except the customary portholes.

Compared with the largest ship in service before the war, the Hamburg American liner *Vaterland,* the Gibbs four-stacker might be called slightly conservative, except for the funnel placing. The huge German liner had only three stacks, and one of these was a dummy, so the day of the four-stacker was numbered. Only two others were ever to be built, in fact. The *Vaterland* had a much higher bridge face and pilothouse, and Gibbs would have doubtless changed this feature of his design as was done with the *Aquitania* after she was completed. A platform at least four decks high was needed to permit reasonable visibility for the helmsman on ships of this size. In overall dimensions, however, the 1915 Gibbs 1,000-footer was not very much different from the *Vaterland.*

Perhaps more striking, however, is the similarity in overall exterior dimensions of the Gibbs 1915 design and the particulars of the *United States* built 30 years later.

The importance of the 30-knot speed was very real. Gibbs had not just picked it out of the air as a high goal to achieve. With such speed a pair of ships could operate a weekly service between Montauk and Southampton. Up until that point a weekly service required three 24-knot ships. This is why all the major ship lines built their premier ships in groups of three, such as the *Lusitania, Mauretania,* and *Aquitania* of Cunard Line, or the *Olympic, Titanic,* and *Gigantic,* of White Star, or the *Imperator, Vaterland,* and *Bismarck* of Hamburg American Line. But Gibbs would do it with just two ships. And the key to the very high speed he had to have was in his awareness of the electric drive, or so he thought. And all this puzzling out of things, this burning of the midnight oil to create a break-through ship design had been done not in the vast moulding loft at Belfast or on the design boards at Cramps on the Delaware but in the third floor bedroom of a private home near Philadelphia. After the successful meetings with General Electric's Emmet, many of the doubters, and there must have been plenty of them, would have had to change their tune and take the two lanky Gibbs boys seriously. But that was only the beginning. William Francis Gibbs always thought "big."

With Frederic plunging into new sets of cost studies and hard-headed financial prognostications on both the engineering and operating fronts, and with William Francis redrawing his blueprints and coming up with a much more modern design, the project moved into the year 1916. Their father's connections undoubtedly were most useful, but it was not only pull that enabled them to get an appointment to meet the Chief Constructor of the U.S. Navy in Washington, Admiral David W. Taylor. William Francis was learning not only how to be a naval architect but how to put his best foot forward. He was no longer a brash young man depending on guts and an engaging smile. He was in his twenty-ninth year and deadly serious. And he knew himself. He knew he was an extraordinary person. Admiral Taylor was impressed with the man, as well as what he had done; so impressed that he arranged a meeting with Josephus Daniels, Secretary of the Navy. The Secretary also liked what he saw and offered encouragement. What William Francis wanted the most was an opportunity to test his theories and his various hull designs in the Navy's towing tank later to be named in honor of Admiral Taylor. But before he could do this he realized that he needed the approval and backing of some top practical shipping man, and he aimed high. He would go to none other than Philip A.S. Franklin, head of the International Mercantile Marine (IMM). Mr. Franklin represented J.P. Morgan and controlled the largest fleet of passenger ships in the world.

Mr. Franklin was interested. He was interested enough to arrange a meeting with John Pierpont Morgan, Jr. It was a meeting that neither William Francis or his brother would ever forget. Frederic H. remembered it clearly 50 years later: "We were ushered into the great man's presence and welcomed in a gruff and business like way. My brother and I proceeded immediately to lay out our key designs and blueprints. As we did so my brother explained each special feature. Mr. Franklin watched attentively from the background. Mr. Morgan said absolutely nothing, but listened. There was tension in the air. I said very little, nodding or contributing a word or two as my brother outlined the commercial features of our plan." Then, suddenly, and without any explanation, the financier got up from behind his large desk and left the room. Mr. Franklin hurried out after him, leaving the two Gibbs brothers alone in the large paneled office. "That wait seemed like eternity," Frederic recalled. "It was about 20 minutes, but each minute was like an hour. We stood and looked at each other. I rolled up some of my biggest blueprints. My brother looked at his watch. Neither of us said a word. For the rest of my life I never have endured a wait like that one and then, suddenly, it was over. The door opened and Mr. Morgan strode back in and resumed his seat at the desk. My brother was about to speak, but Mr. Morgan held up his hand and said briskly: 'Very well, I will back you, how much money do you need to work up the final plans?'"

That was the end of the interview. And it was the beginning of the most famous naval architecture firm in twentieth century American history-Gibbs Bros., later Gibbs & Cox. An agreement was promptly drawn up and the two brothers were in business. They took office space in 11 Broadway, hired a small staff and began turning out new and more refined designs. On July 21, 1916, they were in Washington for their first model tests in the Navy tank. More tests were run in November and they confirmed the propulsion possibilities that had been anticipated in the Gibbs blueprints. The design called for a quadruple screw vessel with an 180,000 horsepower plant. The *Mauretania,* fastest ship in the world at that time, had 70,000 horsepower. The new Gibbs 1000-footers (two were planned, of course), would be large enough to be able to carry fuel for a cruising radius of 7,000 miles. They could sail to and from Europe without refueling, a major economic advantage with fuel cheaper in the United States than in Europe. While the model tests were going on they won further encouragement from the Pennsylvania Railroad. The Navy was most helpful. It looked as if nothing could stop them.

The July 21, 1916 model tested in the Taylor model tank has been preserved and hangs in The Mariners' Museum, Newport News, Virginia, at this writing. It shows a design considerably more modern than the original Gibbs four-stacker. That older artist's conception had been made public in 1915 but doubtless had been drawn several years before that. On the 1916 model the rake to the stem has been increased and, even more remarkable, the prow was flared out in a way that anticipated hull design for 30 years after that. The underwater portion of the hull forward was long and narrow. The placement of the four propellers differed only slightly from how they would be positioned on the *United States.* Most striking was the stern. The old counter stern, inherited from a century of sailing ship design, was gone and in its place was a modern-looking cruiser stern. The new design tested in 1916 was given the Gibbs Bros. designation – S-171.

The war in Europe had begun to strike close to home. With the sinking of the *Lusitania* in 1915 the strong pro-German sentiment in many parts of the country began to fade away and more and more it became apparent that America might enter the conflict on the side of Great Britain. The war gave Gibbs another cardinal principal for his 1,000-foot design, a principle that remained with him until it saw fulfillment in the *United States.* The new liners must not only be large and fast, but they must have military importance. The design was altered to permit a long, uncluttered after deck that could be used to house seaplanes. This innovative concept would be copied a decade later in a superliner designed by Theodore Ferris, and also by the North German Lloyd in their record-breaking twins *Bremen* and *Europa.* Gibbs was closely following, all developments involving merchant liners in the European war and knew about Cunard's old flyer *Campania,* which had been converted by the British Admiralty into a primitive but most useful aircraft carrier. Also noting how the British transformed other liners into armed auxiliary cruisers, he made provision in his design for gun emplacements forward and aft.

The Gibbs dream, however, became less and less real as war for America came to be more and more a certainty. In April, 1917, when the United States declared war on Germany, he was forced to put his grand plans on the shelf and support the war effort. He was made Assistant to the Chairman of the Shipping Control Committee of the General Staff of the Army. He watched with great interest the seizure and conversion of the world's largest liner at New York. Little did he realize that the *Leviathan,* ex *Vaterland,* would become his substitute for the 1,000-foot superliner at least for the next few years.

2
Two World Wars

The seeds for the *United States* were planted when William Francis Gibbs was a youth. They sprouted with his decision to give up the law and concentrate on marine design well before America's entry into the first world war. Gibb's war service was merely a brief interruption in his planning for "the big ship." His experience in the first world war taught him much that would benefit America in the second. He saw first-hand the consequences of a lack of standardization in ship design. And he learned the dangers of having many shipyards competing for workers, parts, and materials. After the war he went to Versailles as assistant to Edward N. Hurley, Chairman of the U.S. Shipping Board. On this assignment he met the top leaders of European shipping. But perhaps even more important, he sold himself and his concept for the S-171 to Mr. Hurley and the Shipping Board. J.P. Morgan was fading out of the shipping picture and the new patron for the 1,000-footers would be the United States Government itself. But William Francis remained with the International Mercantile Marine and on January 1, 1919, was appointed their Chief of Construction, with his brother Frederic Herbert as Assistant Chief.

The 1915 four-stacker artist's conception of the Gibbs express liner may be considered the first drawing of the *United States*. In 1919 a revised artist's conception was widely used in newspapers around America. *The New York Times* carried it over the entire eight columns of its rotogravure section under the following headline:

"DESIGN FOR THE TWO HUGE AMERICAN LINERS TO BE BUILT BY THE UNITED STATES SHIPPING BOARD FOR THE TRANS-ATLANTIC SERVICE"

A sub-caption was enthusiastic: "Each vessel to be 1,000 feet in Length, to Have Ten Decks, to be Oil Burning, and to Have a Speed of 30 Knots. The Construction of the Ships is to Begin at Once, and They are Expected to Cut the Ocean Passage to Four Days." There were many points of similarity with the *United States,* as she eventually appeared. The new ships were to be built under the supervision of the Navy Department and were to be built for conversion to naval auxiliaries. Gibbs went even farther; they could be converted to provide landing and launching space for seaplanes during wartime. The close ties with the Navy and the conversion potential would be two key ribs in the structuring of the liner *United States* thirty years later.

The artist's conception used by the *Times* was one of several that Gibbs prepared at this time. Two relatively short pole masts showed how Gibbs had moved ahead in his thinking since his 1915 design. The three stacks were twice as thick as the four tall funnels of the earlier conception. His various drawings show them all smoking, so none was a dummy. In the *Times* conception, the forward bridge structure appeared almost wedge-like in shape. Another drawing shows it as a rounded, three-deck high front end to the superstructure. In both designs this feature was far ahead of current ship design of that day. It would not be equalled on a real ship until the *Queen Elizabeth*. In all the 1919 designs, as in the four-stack conception of 1915, the stacks as a unit were placed forward of the midship point between the masts, giving the feeling of speed and thrust that would be a Gibbs trademark.

The hull design for S-171 was the subject of intensive testing in Washington throughout 1919, 1920, and 1921. William Francis Gibbs managed to break away from his work with IMM in New York to go to Washington to supervise the model tank work. His spirit of perfectionism came to be more and more evident to more and more people. Years later John Kane, assigned by the Newport News shipyard to be their staff contact man with Gibbs, would say that all during the construction of the *United States* he had the feeling that Gibbs was "looking over my shoulder continuously." Some penciled notes made by Gibbs on September 2, 1919, show that others would have had the same feeling then: "Arived model basin 8:10 and examined model 2264 carefully for about 40 minutes. At 8:50 it was placed in the water and it weighed 606 lbs., together with a 25 lb. bag of ballast and rope tackle. It should weigh to equal 59,835 tons, 1063 lbs. Mr. Krebs said the rope tackle weighed

17 lbs. so the ballast necessary will be (some figuring here) 474 lbs., which will equal (more figuring) 18 bags and 24 lbs. Mr. Krebs ordered only 18 bags and 4 lbs. put in, and I thought he was in error and called it to his attention. He went over his figures and found his error." Twenty-five runs of the model were made two days later with speeds varying from .95 knots to 5.16 knots. A speed of 4.26 knots was equal to 30 knots for the real ship.

Many different tests were made and more information about "the big ship" was established. Blueprints were issued with neat white lettering. They usually had the same heading, which included the phrase: "representing express passenger liner for the international Mercantile Marine designed by Wm. Francis Gibbs." The legend on many noted that the ships would be 995 feet in length with a beam of 107 feet. The model that was being used was 20 feet long and had a beam of 2.151 feet. One series of model experiments, for example, helped Gibbs realize the importance of long bilge keels to reduce ship's roll. Years later his conclusion that bilge keels were sufficient would lead him to reject the various stabilizers that were coming on the market in the late 1940s. The bilge keels on the S-171 would have been 248.8 feet long on the full-sized ship. They would have extended 99.5 feet forward of the midpoint and 149.3 feet aft. In the model tank experiments a report by the Navy noted that "without bilge keels it required 55 swings to reduce the angle of heel from 12 degrees to 2, while with the bilge keels on the model the same reduction was obtained with 14 swings." The tank work was expensive, but this did not deter perfectionist Gibbs, another characteristic that would drive shipyard people up the walls in later days. On March 12, 1920 as an illustration, Commander William McEntee of the model tank staff wrote to say that Gibbs' account was overrun to the amount of $101.84 with a few additional charges still to be added. He noted that as additional bilge keel experiments and self-propulsion tests were contemplated which would cost an estimated $450, he would need a check for $600 "so that the work may be continued with little delay." On March 16, William Francis sent the check requested, asking that he be advised "in advance the time when you will carry out the further tests." He wanted to be there.

While William Francis concentrated on technical experiments and tests, Frederic Herbert prepared new and more detailed studies of the advantages of linking the proposed 30-knot liners with the rail lines of France and the United States. A 12-page memorandum on the subject was dated September 30, 1919. It began by pointing out that the United States was spending $3,000,000,000 to build 13,000,000 tons of steel ships, of which "there are hardly more than a score of steamers which can be used as passenger carriers and those are too small to be seriously considered as competitors of the larger steamers sailing under foreign flags." Of the German liners seized when the United States entered the war, "only one, the *Leviathan,* ranks in the first class." The importance of express steamers to a nation's merchant marine was stressed and it was noted that the war had left the United States "with a tremendous preponderance of cargo steamers."

The report continued: "It was this situation which led the Shipping Board to consider the building of the first two 1,000-foot 30-knot express passenger and mail steamers in the world. This proposed advance in speed marks the greatest single step since the introduction of steam navigation. It is the opinion of those familiar with the shipping situation in the United States that the money invested in these two steamers will increase the total value of the Government investment in ships many times the outlay for the two liners." Much of the same reasoning would be used in the campaign to convince Congress that the building subsidies were justified for the *United States.*

The origins of the close ties that made the *United States* almost as much a Navy ship as a ship of the United States Lines could be seen in this 1919 report: "Such express liners would be of great advantage to the Navy in the time of war, since each one will be more than the equivalent of the highest type of scout cruiser. According to the suggestion of the Shipping Board, the Navy would handle the letting of contracts and pass upon the design of the steamers and supervise and inspect their construction for the Shipping Board." The Gibbs brothers were sure of their ground here as they would be three decades later. They had the closest of ties both with the Shipping Board and with the Navy and knew that, in the last analysis, it would be they who "supervised and inspected" any construction. But the report had still more ammunition:

"Used as transports, each of these steamers the experts of the Navy estimate, could carry over 12,000 men to France in less than four days, or the same number could be carried from New Orleans to the Panama Canal in two days." One thing the report did not point out was that the ships would be too wide to pass through the Panama Canal. This problem would fester in the minds of the Gibbs brothers, and when the *United States* was designed she would be just narrow enough to permit such passage. The memo noted that Congress had passed a law which President Wilson had approved that doubled the former ocean mail payment rate for steamers which could maintain a speed of 30 knots. "The Post Office Department is anxious to take advantage of this provision of the law and get the unquestioned advantage of the quicker ocean transportation for the mails."

Frederic Gibbs explained the importance of reducing time spent in port and having the maximum number of round trips per year, and then he added: "From this it follows that it is most advantageous to select ports which will (a) decrease the distance steamed; (b) allow the steamer to reach the pier and dock and undock with the least possible reduction of speed caused by shallow water, narrow channels, tidal conditions, or harbor congestion, and (c) give easy and convenient rail connections to the interior." All these goals could be accomplished, his report said, by using Fort Pond Bay at the eastern entrance to Long Island Sound, and Brest, France. The steaming distance between Brest and Fort Pond Bay "is reduced by about 100 miles over the New York, Plymouth, Cherbourg, Southampton route." Both Brest and Fort Pond Bay could be reached by wide and deep channels "which can be traversed by large steamers without reduction of speed."

New York harbor in those days was one of the most congested ports in the world, with over 500 tugs, countless railroad car floats, and many ferry lines, not to mention river, coastal, and deep sea shipping. The vast empty reaches of Fort Pond Bay, between Montauk and Orient points, would seem like a pilot's heaven. Frederic Gibbs painted a glowing word picture of how good it would be for his 30-knot express steamers: "The steamers could come at practically full speed up to their pier and enter without the necessity of turning as in the case at New York. When leaving it would only be necessary to reverse once and then go ahead at full speed without any assistance from tugs. In the operation of docking and undocking there would be no interference from the tide at any stage or time, day or night. The danger of collision now present and growing worse at New York would be removed."

All this detailed advance thinking illustrated how superb a team Frederic and William Francis Gibbs were developing into. It would be such thinking that would be needed to convince the U.S. Navy, the Maritime Commission, and the U.S. Lines that a superliner capable of smashing all speed records was necessary and should be built at the very end of the liner era when air travel was on the verge of making point-to-point liner travel no longer economically viable.

To carry the Gibbs thinking a bit further, examine the schedule he offered in this same report. Including the boat train time at both ends of the crossing the service would take 4 days, 9 1/2 hours to deliver a voyager from London to New York. At both Brest and Fort Pond the rail terminals would be on the piers and train connections for all of Europe or all of the United States would be operated from pierside. Comparing the schedule with the *Aquitania's,* there would be a "clear saving between London and New York of one and one half days and this without allowing for any unusual delay at New York." The ferry service to New London would mean "a short route to those bound for New England points who do not wish to stop over in New York." That the capacity to envisage broad new patterns was very much a part of the make up of the two Gibbs brothers is shown by the next blockbuster idea: "In connection with the transcontinental train service projected from the Fort Pond terminal, it is proposed to operate a fast passenger steamer line under the American flag from San Francisco to the Far East. This will enable the United States to offer the traveler from London or continental cities a through service *de luxe* to the Far East, reducing by several days the time by the 'All Red' route of the Canadian Pacific Railroad."

As if to overwhelm all possible opposition, the report added that the direct rail connection from Fort Pond terminal "will enable passengers who are bound for interior points to stop off in New York City more conveniently than is now possible. The passenger would be landed in the heart of the city on local transportation lines instead of at the inaccessible North River waterfront of Manhattan or Hoboken."

The richness of the Gibbs brothers' imagination could be seen in the thoroughness with which they did their home work on the Fort Pond project. The question of crews for the new liners was addressed in the following fashion: "One of the most important problems connected with the operation proposed will be to obtain and retain high class and efficient crews. It should be borne in mind that since the steamers burn oil fuel, low grade labor has been practically eliminated. To operate the ships successfully it is essential that the officers and crew take a personal interest and have a keen *esprit de corps.* To accomplish this is all but impossible in a large community like New York. However, there are many examples which show that it may be obtained to a high degree where there is a small community around one industry. For example, we draw attention to the town of Hershey, Pa., which is built up around the plant of the Hershey Chocolate Company. It is a model community whose interest is centered on the industry which supports it. By this means a higher type of conservative labor is attracted to the industry and the labor turnover is reduced to a minimum. The shores of Fort Pond Bay offer an ideal site for such a town. The Bay on the east and the west is surrounded by high fertile ground and on the south side there is a level stretch sufficient in extent to accommodate the business section of the community. The average temperatures are several degrees warmer in winter and cooler in summer than New York. Each of the steamers would require a crew of 900 men, while there would probably be an extra relief crew to allow a proper relief and layover to the men without delaying the ships. This would mean a body of 2,700 men, the large majority of whom would be skilled workers. Compared with many modern industries, this is but a small number and it would be possible thus to insure a trained body of employees who would have an *esprit de corps* and interest so necessary to insure efficiency in the operation of these steamers."

Just 30 years later Frederic and William Francis would be planning special training schools for stewards for the *United States,* and walking through the new superliner's crew quarters via preliminary blue prints with Joseph Curran, president of the National Maritime Union. The *United States* would always have the reputation among her crew as a "happy ship," and this was no chance happening.

The Fort Pond memo envisaged the Shipping Board giving the management and operation of the express liners to IMM and predicted that this would assure the cooperation of the Pennsylvania Railroad, producing the "most powerful alliance of transportation agencies in the world." The memo shed a few tears for Cunard Line: "It is quite clear what a tremendous disadvantage the Cunard Line, our most formidable British competitor, would be under in attempting to compete for the American passenger traffic." How the railroad would help was the icing on the cake. It would give the steamship company the right to open ticket offices in all of its principal stations and would provide through tickets to London or Continental points with through checking of baggage. The railroad would advertise the service as an extension of its lines. The railroad would offer special facilities in the Pennsylvania Hotel. The railroad would double track the lines to Montauk and "provide the necessary *deluxe* equipment for handling this business." The memo added that "as it will take four years to build the steamers, this rail development can be made gradually."

The in-depth coverage of this plan to dock the 1,000-foot express liners at Montauk is offered as evidence of how thoroughly the Gibbs brothers approached each problem. Here was a brand new idea, a fresh approach that none of the older ship operators had thought about in the near century since 1838 when the *Sirius* began trans-Atlantic steamship travel. And it was researched to a degree and with an enthusiasm that under any normal circumstances would have resulted at least in a good college try. But 1919 and 1920 were most abnormal years for American shipping. The world's greatest shipbuilding effort was disgorging new merchant ships from many yards on all coasts of America. None had been ready in time for the war itself, and no one knew what to do with them. They were offered for sale, but no strong policy was established on prices and so the bottom dropped out of the market. It was no time for the Shipping Board to pursue its announced aim to build twin 30-knot, 1,000-foot express liners. To make matters worse, the Shipping Board suffered from weak leadership and served a sick President. The time was just not ripe for "the big ship." For the second time the Gibbs brothers found themselves forced to breathe deeply and turn to other projects, although not for a moment was the express liner project abandoned.

William Francis was asked to investigate the fuel consumption of the new 16,000-ton *Regina,* built for the Dominion Line by IMM and soon to be shifted to the Red Star Line and named *Westernland.* He contributed much design time to the two new Atlantic Transport Line twins *Minnewaska* and *Minnetonka,* huge passenger-cargo vessels that were to have short lives. He converted another vessel for this company, the *Minnekahda,* making her the first one-class liner. All these assignments were done at the same time as one other project was beginning to assume larger and larger proportions on the Gibbs horizon.

What was the Shipping Board to do with the huge ex-German liner *Leviathan?* Built in 1914 for the Hamburg American Line as the *Vaterland,* world's largest ship, she had been laid up in New York for three years with her German crew still aboard before America entered the war. Upon our involvement, she was seized and turned into the biggest troopship ever, capable of carrying 14,000 soldiers in one trip. Since her transport duties had ended, she had lain idle in Hoboken. Everyone assumed that America's largest shipping company, IMM, would be assigned the management of this vast 54,000-ton vessel and that she would be used on its American Line route flying the American flag. On December 17, 1919 P.A.S. Franklin signed an agreement with the Shipping Board under which he would maintain her while it was decided how to proceed. For the next four years the *Leviathan* was to occupy the time and talent of the Gibbs brothers as no other project had done up to that point. As a training ground for their eventual career-climaxing construction of the *United States,* this work could not have been more helpful ... they had to battle vast disinterest, tearing political opposition, superhuman design challenges, financial handicaps, penny pinching, and a whole new array of situations endling with the government actually turning the ship over to them to operate for her first six crossings after she had been rebuilt.

The *Leviathan* assignment was a superhuman job and Gibbs emerged from it with a reputation that put him in one huge step in the forefront of American naval architects and marine engineers. Although he would continue to casually remark that he was not really a naval architect because he had never had any formal schooling in the field, from then on such comments would be accepted as pleasant jokes. He had more than proved himself.

Record keeping, cost accounting as it came to be called later, was one of the areas that the Gibbs brothers made sacrosanct, another trait that would stand them in good stead for the rest of their careers. Frederic's genius meshed perfectly with that of William Francis on this score. A report dated June 13, 1920, for work on the idle *Leviathan,* is an early illustration of this ultra-precise facility. During the week that ended on that day, 13,966 hours of work were put in on the huge liner. The 13-page report, typed single space, recorded each penny of the $1,734.77 spent in those seven days. For example, it cost $11.66 and consumed 16 hours to empty garbage cans throughout the vessel. The adjusting of rat guards took four hours and cost $2.92. The refilling of fire extinguishers took 8 hours, costing $5.83. The bailing of water from boat covers consumed 9 hours, costing $6.56. The closing and opening of portholes was a 72-hour operation that cost $52.47. Everything done was timed, priced, and recorded.

When the 60 draftsmen were hired to make the plans of the *Leviathan,* the construction department of IMM consisted of only eight people. There were the Gibbs brothers and a Mr. McQuillan, an ex-secretary; a naval architect named Sanders, chief engineer Henry Meyer and his assistant H.L. Culpepper, and two male secretaries: William Bontempo and John Kelly. William Francis needed someone skilled in electricity. He heard of a young man working in the research department of the International Telephone and Telegraph Company, later to become Bell Labs. His name was Norman Zippler and he had worked with the New York Shipbuilding Corp., of Camden, New Jersey. He had high recommendations. Gibbs went at the problem like he did all problems. He offered Zippler twice what he was making and he had his ninth man. Mr. Zippler would remain with the two Gibbs brothers throughout the remainder of his working life, and would play a major part in the creation of the *United States.* His first assignment, in fact, was to write specifications for S-171, the 1,000-foot "high-powered, 4-screw liner."

The 1,000-footer was very much in Gibb's mind, and all his contact with the *Leviathan* just enhanced his awareness of what he wanted. Here, placed in his charge, was the finest liner ever built, bar none. Through this exercise he had superimposed over his dream ship the images of a range of magnificent public rooms the like of which had never before been seen on any ship: from the dark paneled smoking room far forward to the magnificent Ritz Carlton dining room far aft. Grand as they had been, the main saloons and lounges of the *Oceanic, Celtic, Lusitania,* and even the *Olympic* had been nothing compared with the public rooms of the *Leviathan.* No better experience could have been had for one determined to create a new American superliner than the experience with the *Leviathan.*

Norman Zippler was hired not for the *Leviathan,* although he did a great deal of work on her, but for the 1,000-foot superliners Gibbs was still hoping to build for IMM. They would be operated with the *Leviathan* in an American flag service that would be second to none. When both new ships were built IMM would dominate the Atlantic with two weekly services, each with superior ships. One could be operated by the two 1,000-footers. The other would see the *Leviathan* sailing in conjunction with the *Majestic* and the *Olympic,* her British flag companion ships.

Electric drive was vital to the Gibbs concept of the twin 30-knot trans-Atlantic liners to be fast enough to maintain a weekly service. Up to then such a service required three ships. Gibbs would do it with two. In 1920 however, the double reduction gear approach to power in a ship had not been evolved. Electric drive was the only known way to propel a ship with a horsepower as high as 200,000. The Navy had been doing a good deal of experimenting and planned to install electric drive in their giant battle cruisers, whose plans were well along when the war ended. They would be the largest and most powerful warships ever built and their shaft horsepower was listed as 160,000. They were the models Gibbs was watching for his own purposes. He had been shocked to see plans for all but two of the projected battle cruiser

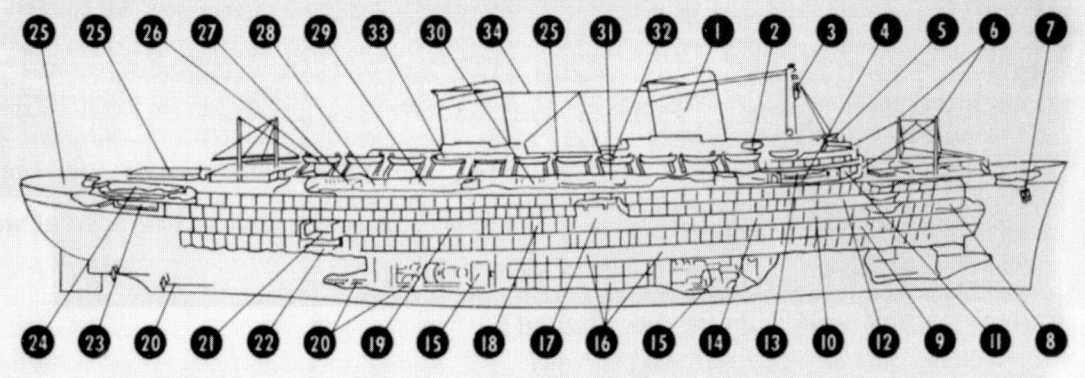

1. **Smoke Stack**—its top is 175 feet from keel of ship, equal in height to a 12-story building.
2. **Navigation or Chart Room**—course and position of ship are figured here.
3. **Radar Mast and Crow's Nest**—radar is ship's eyes at night and in fog; look-out is always on duty in crow's nest.
4. **First Class Observation Lounge**—extends from port to starboard sides with unobstructed view of the ocean.
5. **Navigation Bridge**—the heart of the ship with almost-miraculous navigational equipment and aids.
6. **Kingposts**—with boom is used to raise or lower cargo.
7. **Anchor & Cable Chain**—latest in naval design and electrically operated.
8. **Garage**—space for cars which need no special preparation for voyage.
9. **Hospital**—modern with fully equipped operating room.

A cutout featured in a promotional brochure of the ship.

10. **Tourist Dining Room**—seats 346 people; has modern decor featuring ships, shells and nautical motifs.
11. **Tourist Lounge**—with reading and writing rooms; dancing in the evenings.
12. **Tourist Smoking Room**—extends full width of ship; has bar and is comfortably furnished for relaxation.
13. **Tourist Theatre**—ultra comfortable with a seating capacity of 199 people.
14. **Tourist Galley**—an up-to-the-minute kitchen, providing international cuisine.
15. **Engines**—the powerful high-speed turbines are located in this lower area.
16. **Store Rooms**—would hold enough to care for a full division of troops traveling 10,000 miles non-stop.
17. **First Class Dining Room**—decorated in red and white; the finest American and continental dishes are served here.
18. **Galley**—ultra modern kitchens feature radar stoves.
19. **Cabin Class Dining Room**—a charming setting for gracious dining at sea.
20. **Shafts & Propellers**—powerful shafts transmit power from turbines to the giant propellers.
21. **Gymnasium**—every latest type of gymnastic equipment.
22. **Swimming Pool**—made of monel metal, it is surrounded by beach and lounge area.
23. **Cabin Class Lounge**—decorated with modern motif; has a 17 x 26 foot dance floor for dancing in the evening.
24. **Cabin Class Smoking Room**—its three sides face on the enclosed promenade deck.
25. **Play Decks**—open to the sun for lounging or playing of all types of deck sports.
26. **Life Boats**—one of 22 aluminum life boats, non-sinkable and fully fire proof, which can accommodate 3000 persons.
27. **First Class and Cabin Class Theatre**—seating 352 persons, it is fitted with modern acoustics; shows first-run films.
28. **Shopping Center**—offers wide variety of merchandise to suit every taste and purse.
29. **First Class Smoking Room**—large lounge room featuring huge aluminum maps of the world.
30. **Navajo Cocktail Lounge**—an intimate room decorated with Navajo sand paintings.
31. **First Class Ballroom**—center of social life; afternoon teas and dancing at night to Meyer Davis orchestra.
32. **Kennels**—clean modern kennels for pets; veterinarian in constant attendance.
33. **Play Room**—three play rooms aboard ship provide a liliputian playland for the younger set.
34. **Aerials**—these stretch between the largest smoke stacks of any ship in the world.

THEORETICAL POSITION OF OBSERVER—420+ FEET FROM CENTER OF SHIP AT HORIZON HEIGHT

series cancelled when the war ended. He was happy to see that the two surviving craft would be completed as aircraft carriers. They would eventually become the legendary *Lexington* and *Saratoga*. Fundamentally, the new Gibbs 1,000-footers had power plants that were copied from these carriers. "It was a good thing the liners were never built," Norman Zippler would say a half century later. They would have been too far ahead of their time from the propulsion standpoint. The Navy would learn to their discomfort that electric drive had many problems. It would be many years after 1920 that the high speed turbine with double reduction gears would be developed to make the Gibbs dream really feasible.

With a team like the Gibbs brothers and an experienced management such as IMM there was every reason to assume that the great *Leviathan* was headed for a most successful future under the American flag. And then appeared William Randolph Hearst, known for his antipathy to everything British. He waged a newspaper campaign to prevent the Shipping Board from turning the big ship over to IMM, claiming that the Morgan combine was not through-and-through American. Hearst had uncovered some documents that showed that the IMM's flagship service, the White Star Line, was subject to certain British Admiralty controls in time of war. The newspaper mogul insisted that the *Leviathan* would be lost to America if she were given, as planned, to IMM. He fanned the flames of war-time patriotism under the banner of saving the famous *"Levi,"* the great troopship that had done so much to win the war for us and which was so beloved by all those who had sailed across on her to fight the "Hun."

He instituted a taxpayer's suit and succeeded in his effort. The weak-kneed Shipping Board was confused, didn't know what to do. P.A.S. Franklin, IMM head, was shocked as he saw what was happening to his dream. The Gibbs brothers were up against big time opposition for the first time. As the battle flared the seemingly powerful IMM proved to be something of a paper tiger. Franklin was no match for Hearst. The Shipping Board had neither the guts to support the original decision nor the resolve to denounce Hearst for the yellow journalistic tactics he was using. They allowed the IMM to bow out of the picture and left the whole *Leviathan* situation in one chaotic mess.

It was a classic moment of decision for the Gibbs brothers. It was the time that they were thankful for the independent status they had somehow achieved within IMM. All their painstaking handling of the *Leviathan* now came to the fore as evidence of what had happened. All their memoranda about how the ship could be made to pay, about how successful she would be under the American flag, all the stacks of documents and figuring they had amassed now stood out as a signpost pointing to them as the persons most interested in making the great ship a paying and successful proposition under the Stars and Stripes. The *Leviathan* had become their ship, and in a way that few ships have ever been associated with people. It was the story of the *United States* told in preview.

To put into a few paragraphs what took me an entire volume to relate in my six-volume series on the *Leviathan,* the Shipping Board asked Gibbs Bros. to take over the ship. They were asked to form their own company and to supervise the reconstruction of the huge liner. They were asked, in other words, to separate from IMM and go it alone. Needless to say the matter was one that caused a sharp break between the Gibbs brothers and P.A.S. Franklin. Instead of being the IMM's right hand bower, the two young geniuses in one step became competitors of the first order. Franklin was furious. The enmity lived on to the next generation. P.A.S. Franklin's son, John M. Franklin, would eventually become President of the company and, for years, would carry the memory of the split between his father and the Gibbs brothers. Bringing John Franklin and William Francis Gibbs together for the building of the *America* in the late 1930s was a task that took much fence-mending. The feeling of antagonism had not fully calmed when they were again forced to assume the role of partners for the construction of the *United States.* The decision to separate from IMM was one of the most difficult and crucial moves in the life of William Francis Gibbs; one fraught with most long-range consequences. But he did it, and in February, 1922, he and his brother set up their own independent company which they called Gibbs Bros.

The Gibbs reputation had been made. It had been made at first via the remarkable performance of the brothers in selling themselves to General Electric, to the Navy, to P.A.S. Franklin and to J.P. Morgan with their 1,000-foot express Atlantic liner plan. It had been made over again with the remarkable performance by William Francis in creating blue prints for the *Leviathan* from the inside out, without the help of the ship's original drawings. It had been re-enforced by a series of remarkably able lesser accomplishments with IMM ships in the immediate post-war years, not to mention the continuing evolution of plans to build the S-171 express liners. Finally it had been enlarged even more by their meticulous and dedicated care-taking operation on the idle *Leviathan* at her pier in Hoboken. They were more than ready for independent status. They accepted its burdens and responsibilities with zest!

Even while the Hearst battle was in progress and just before the separation was made, the work with model testing for S-171 continued. Late in 1921 four different propellers were tested, each time with a different pitch. Nine blue prints were prepared following these tests. The horsepower curves from 32 knots and above were shown going off the top of the graph, which indicated a maximum of up to 100,000 effective horsepower. The displacement tonnage of the real ship indicated in these model tests ranged from 51,500 to 62,500 tons. In addition to propellers, the model tested had a spade-type rudder, bilge keels, and shaft bossings (streamlined support structures holding the propeller shafts firmly in position as they extended outside the hull proper). And well after the separation from IMM the S-171 project remained alive. Whenever an engineer or a draftsman had some spare time, he would be assigned to do a specialized study for the express passenger liner project. It can be said that from 1915 to the unveiling of the first blueprints for the *United States,* "the big ship" project was never for a moment out of the mind of William Francis or Frederic Gibbs.

For the years 1922 and 1923, however, the *Leviathan* was on top in their pattern of thinking. They were years of tremendous activity, tremendous publicity, and tremendous success. The election of President Harding had brought a new man in as head of the Shipping Board. His name was Albert Lasker and he was a human dynamo. With a spirit that matched William Francis Gibbs in many ways, Board Chairman Lasker had immediately recognized that action had to be taken with the *Levia-*

than. Helped by the Gibbs brothers, he had secured the needed $8,000,000 to restore her and settled on the Newport News Shipbuilding & Dry Dock Company as the yard to do the job. The Gibbs Bros. were asked to continue handling the ship as agents for the Shipping Board. This meant Gibbs Bros. had to get the crew to sail her down to the Virginia shipyard, another new challenge but one that was surmounted with all the finesse that people were becoming accustomed to seeing when William Francis Gibbs was involved. Although the ship had not moved for over three years and was deeply stuck in the mud of her Hoboken slip, the move and the voyage down the coast were made without incident. Using his own blueprints, Gibbs supervised the restoration over a 14 month period. It was another tremendous effort calling for all the drive he had.

The wide public interest in the ship, plus the great amount of national publicity she had been given during the Hearst campaign, created an atmosphere in which everything that happened was news. The *Leviathan* was so much bigger than any other ship in an American shipyard that the Nation's newspapers were eager for progress reports and pictures. The job was a lifesaver for the Newport News yard, and everyone in the community watched as the great grey-hulled lady slowly was restored to her queenly status as an express passenger liner. Her superstructure and stacks rose high over all the buildings at the yard and she could be seen from many of the surrounding areas. When her stacks were finally painted a brilliant red, white, and blue the spirits of the townspeople reached a new high of enthusiasm and local pride. Just the same feeling would again come to the area 30 years later when the first coat of red, white, and blue would go on the two huge stacks of the *United States.*

Homer L. Ferguson, president of the Newport News shipyard, summarized the project: "I doubt if there has ever been a job that so taxed our utmost resources, patience, and skill." More than that the determination shown by William Francis Gibbs to make the ship the very finest in every particular, and his passion for detail, resulted in the shipyard ending up with a loss of $1,250,000 on the restoration. When President Ferguson took a report of the loss to an owner of the yard, railroad magnate Henry Huntington, he also had with him in his pocket a letter of resignation. The occasion was a dinner party with Mr. and Mrs. Huntington in their home. When he brought the loss up, Mr. Huntington, known for his patriotism and philanthropic approach to things, waived the matter aside saying: "My wife owns most of the stock in the shipyard, and she has not been feeling too well recently, so maybe we should say no more about it."

William Francis Gibbs wanted two honors for the *Leviathan.* He wanted her to be the world's largest ship and also the world's fastest. He knew full well that her sistership the *Bismarck,* renamed *Majestic* by White Star, was slightly larger. She was six feet longer and her tonnage was 56,000. The first of the Albert Ballin trio had been the *Imperator,* and her tonnage was 52,000 She had been taken over by Cunard and renamed *Berengaria.* The *Vaterland* came next and was 54,000 tons. Gibbs knew all this background but he also knew all about gross tonnage, how it was measured, how 100 cubic feet of permanently enclosed earning space was one gross ton, with many exceptions. He knew that the admeasurers who figured out a ship's tonnage had lots of leeway in their determinations. When the *Leviathan's* new tonnage was announced, shortly before her trials, it came to a new and astonishing total of 59,956.65. No one but William Francis Gibbs would take the tonnage to the last hundredth, but he did and that is how it was publicized from then on in virtually every advertisement, every brochure. The White Star Line and P.A.S. Franklin were outraged! They had been calling their 56,000-ton *Majestic* the world's largest ship, but now the *Leviathan* was also claiming the title. Both ships would continue this battle for years.

As to the speed crown, the famous Cunarder *Mauretania* was still the fastest ship on the Atlantic. However, Gibbs devised a way that he too could claim the title for the *Leviathan.* His patriotic verve and his competitive spirit, two prime forces behind his drive to create "the big ship," were very strong here as well. He selected the run from Boston to Cuba and back to New York for the trial trip so that he could come up the coast on the return leg for her final speed test. With her passenger list of cheering congressmen, she set the world's speed record for a 25 hour passage, a time span equal to one-day's sailing for a westbound crossing of the Atlantic. She traveled 687 miles in that period, 11 more than the *Mauretania's* best record. Her average speed for the 25-hour time was 27.48 knots. It was hailed as "the world's speed record" for liners. For many years the

Leviathan would claim in brochures and other announcements that she held the world's speed record. But in reality she never was able to beat the *Mauretania* on an actual Atlantic crossing. The trial trip speed record had been made with the help of the Gulf Stream. She was clearly, and would remain for the next six years, the world's second fastest liner.

Before leaving the *Leviathan* experience, one more remarkable episode should be enlarged upon a little. The Shipping Board had asked three existing American steamship lines to create a new operating agency to run the *Leviathan*. The three companies publicized their new service under the trade name United States Lines. When the *Leviathan* was ready, the Shipping Board was so aware of the many complicated facets of her operation and so proud of her that they did not dare permit her to go directly under the management of the new company. Instead they once again turned to Gibbs Bros., and asked them to run the world's largest ship. William Francis and his brother Frederic had undoubtedly set the stage for this very development. They turned to with a will, working up operating rules, designing uniforms, creating a company insignia and houseflag, preparing management handbooks, stocking the ship with food, and the thousand and one jobs needed for her maiden voyage.

The assignment gave them the fullest possible responsibility, just what they liked the most. For six crossings the ship was operated by Gibbs Bros. To my knowledge, never before or since has such a remarkable situation existed. The experience set in motion one of the few major unrequited ambitions of William Francis Gibbs, the ambition to become a ship operator. For the next six years Gibbs Bros. again and again tried to buy the United States Lines. Generally, their offers were made in conjunction with J.H. Winchester, a well-known New York shipping agent. While these later attempts to get control were being made, the Board had again become a second-level bureaucratic operation, Albert Lasker having moved on to greener pastures. All the Gibbs' offers were rejected largely because they called for various forms of government aid which the Board was unable to guarantee. But the Gibbs' passion for ship operation would never die. When the *United States* was built it would surface again through the maintenance of strict secrecy rules about speed, hull structure, and operating information. It would be seen by all through the Gibbs' custom of being at the pier for every arrival and every departure of "the big ship." And it would be evident in his insistence on calling both the captain and the chief engineer of the *United States* every single day she was in service. It would be called the most celebrated "love affair" ever known between a man and a ship.

Between 1923 when the *Leviathan* saga was finally completed and 1930 when four new *"Santa"* ships were built for Grace Line, the Gibbs Bros. grew and prospered. The major event of this period was the designing of the Matson Line's *Malolo,* the first full-fledged passenger liner ever designed by William Francis Gibbs. She was to prove one of the most successful vessels ever built, lasting until the writing of this work was first undertaken in 1978. A book must be written on this historic liner which embodied so much of the Gibbs' genius. The *Malolo* would have a charmed and highly profitable life, lasting for over 50 years. But on her trials her career might have ended right then and there. She was steaming off the Atlantic Coast with a large party of experts, including William Francis and Frederic, aboard. And then she was struck by a freighter coming out of the fog. Let Admiral David W. Taylor describe his sensations:

"I was in my stateroom when I heard the commotion on the bridge and looking out a porthole saw the ship coming at us. They say she is a small boat, but let me tell you she looked like 20,000 tons. She came up with a bone in her teeth and she looked as big as a snow bank. You can judge how hard she hit us by the fact that she struck on the port side and cracked a plate on the opposite side of the boat. It hit just at the bulkhead partition. An enemy ship seeking to disable her could not have selected a more vital spot. It is unprecedented to see a ship rammed square amidships and still float. The *Empress of Ireland* went down in minutes from a similar injury. The *La Bourgogne* was sunk under similar circumstances. The *Titanic* perished from the same sort of a hit."

Frederic Gibbs makes the crash seem even more real with his personal memories: "My brother and I were standing on the bridge. It was a dense fog. Suddenly there was the *Jacob Christensen.* She came out of the fog straight at us. She struck us just under the bridge on the port side. My brother walked over to the control activating the watertight doors, and then together we went down below to see for ourselves if they worked. We hurried! When we reached the spot the door was still open and the water was pouring in. My brother reached for the manual control, but just at that moment the watertight door slowly began to close. It shut and stopped the inrush of water."

The *Malolo's* two boiler rooms, 32 feet high, were completely filled and the water rose an additional six feet above the ship's E Deck, but her engines proper were undamaged. The gash was 15 feet long, 10 below the water line, and two feet wide. Through it poured 7,000 tons of water, but the ship remained on an even keel, thanks to the Gibbs compartmentation. Towed safely into New York, she was repaired with relative ease and sailed out to the Pacific to enter service.

The marvelous Gibbs' enthusiasm showed through during an interview at about this time. The interviewer was editor of a New York maritime magazine, his name Durward Primrose. His analysis of Gibbs the man is appealingly fresh and complete:

"Physically, Mr. Gibbs has all the earmarks of the careful thinker. He is tall and dark and his complexion has a studious pallor through which, however, glow indications of excellent health. His manner is keen and incisive and he has a way of getting to the nubbin of an argument without undo haste, but with firm finality. On the subject of the new Matson liner he spoke with justifiable enthusiasm. 'She will be the finest ship of her type ever built. It is our intention to incorporate every modern idea that will pass the stern scrutiny of practicability. I believe this ship will far surpass anything of her type afloat.'"

The *Malolo* was a liner of 17,000 tons, American measurement. When put under a foreign flag years later this became 21,329 tons. In contrast to the *Leviathan,* she was a ship with a positive stability, rolling quickly. Her owners did not understand this and she got a poor reputation as a roller because of improper loading on her first voyage. Although this was corrected the reputation never left her. There are those who said that Mr. Gibbs had gone a bit too far in making her stable. The lessons learned in her construction were vital in the eventual design of the *United States.* Another lesson that the *Malolo* taught Mr. Gibbs was how to get his way with the shipyard. William Cramp and Sons, of Philadelphia, builders of the *Malolo,* thought when they won the contract that they would be allowed to make substitutions in the specifications if they thought it desirable, to save money. Gibbs would not permit this and received the fullest support from the Shipping Board and from Matson Line. As a result Cramp lost so much money on the job that they went out of business. It was another example of the Gibbs style of demanding perfection. It would be the same approach he would later use with the Newport News shipyard in building both the *America* and the *United States.*

The accident to the *Malolo* and her survival caused world wide acclaim to come to Gibbs Bros. The reputation of William Francis Gibbs was again confirmed "as was his resolve to maintain only the very highest standards of safety at all times," in the words of Walter C. Bachman, one of his leading lieutenants writing years later for a pamphlet published by the National Academy of Sciences.

In 1930 Gibbs Bros., which by then had become Gibbs & Cox, was hard at work on four new passenger ships for Grace Line. There would be planted during this assignment many seeds that would blossom with "the big ship." Of special interest was the propulsion machinery, for the advances pioneered in with these four small ships led to major contributions for the Navy and, eventually, to the greatest single feature of the *United States* – her high speed. William Francis had abandoned the electric drive, although a number of successful liners had by then been built with such propulsion. Instead he adopted for the new Grace ships the solid rotor impulse turbine which permitted a steam pressure of 375 lbs. per square inch, very high for that day. Double reduction geared General Electric turbines were used, and a number of other innovative engine design features, making these ships true pioneers. There were dramatic new features outside the engine rooms as well. Each First Class cabin had its own private bath, an unheard-of innovation, particularly as the liners carried only First Class passengers, except for a special space for 50 steerage voyagers. The columned dining room designed for the quartette was one of the finest ever built into any liner, large or small, rising 2 1/2 decks and opening up to the sky via a rollback ceiling dome – another new feature. The twin smokestacks bracketed the roll-open dome and it was vital to have a device to prevent the ship's smoke from the forward stack from blowing down into the Dining Saloon. This produced the air suction funnel style. It featured a flat soot deflector "wing" on either side of a rounded top at the after end of the stack. It looked futuristic and it caught on. Many liners, great and small, have followed in this design, modified in various ways, including the *America, France, Michelangelo,* and *United States.* On the *America* it was known as the "sampan design," and was used on both stacks. On the *France* it became the toreador stack. One reason for the striking interior design of these four new Grace Line ships was the team of Anne Urquhart and Dorothy Marckwald, of the firm of Smyth, Urquhart & Marckwald, employed as the interior architects. They would continue to serve William Francis Gibbs with the *America* and then with the *United States.*

The four Grace ships were built at the Federal Shipbuilding & Dry Dock Company yard at Kearny, New Jersey. They were named the *Santa Rosa, Santa Paula, Santa Elena,* and *Santa Lucia.* Originally of 11,200 tons, their tonnage was reduced to 9,100 as a device to save money with Panama Canal tolls. They had 13,000 horsepower each and could make 20 knots. The *Rosa* and *Paula* survived the second World War and were sold to the Typaldos Lines, of Greece, in 1962, being renamed *Athinai* and *Acropolis.*

A major contribution to the U.S. Navy was made by Gibbs & Cox in the early 1930s with the destroyer *Mahan.* The determination by William Francis Gibbs to raise the steam pressure of her boilers to 600 pounds was considered by many as a radical step and there began what was known as the "Battle of High Pressure-High Temperature Steam." It raged for some time, just as the battle a few generations earlier between advocates of steel and wooden hulled vessels for the Navy. Conservatives lined up on one side in opposition and a farsighted few supported Gibbs on the other. Eventually, the performance records of the new destroyer class showed them to be not only more efficient but more reliable and the battle was won by Gibbs. It has been said that this battle was more important than any single naval engagement in World War II. In effect it increased the efficiency of the "new Navy" by more than 25%. The new machinery ideas offered and demonstrated by William Francis Gibbs in this period were used in practically all steam-driven combatant ships in the U.S. Navy built during World War II, including destroyers, cruisers, battleships, and aircraft carriers. Another key benefit that came out of this design experience was the development of a central design and purchasing organization which made possible the large-scale shipbuilding programs of World War II. A summary of the Gibbs brothers contribution was made by Admiral Harold G. Bowen, Chief, Navy Bureau of Engineering:

"As I have repeatedly said and it is in the record in many places, the advent of the *Mahan* marked the most distinctive advance in naval engineering in a generation or more and in reaching this turning point in naval engineering the Navy must be indebted always to Gibbs & Cox."

And another one-sentence accolade came from the Dean of Engineering of Massachusetts Institute of Technology, C.R. Soderberg:

"Gibbs and the Navy Bureau of Ships were probably the most successful team in our history."

This melding of purpose and interests would be carried on with the supreme achievement of the Gibbs career, the *United States.*

In 1934 a disaster took place that helped shape the thinking that eventually went into "the big ship." The virtually new and most luxurious American passenger liner *Morro Castle* burned off New Jersey. Many passengers were lost. Although the ship was built according to the highest safety standards then in force, it was obvious to William Francis Gibbs that the existing rules for fire safety were far from adequate. He testified before the Congressional committee of inquiry and two of his team served on the several study committees set up by Congress. One of these was Norman Zippler. Another was the young naval architect Matthew Forrest. Matt Forrest, who would go on to be a main spring in the *United States* design, was another veteran of service at the famed New York Shipbuilding Corp. yard. He had worked there under Ernest H. Rigg, who had long backed

Gibbs on the 1,000-foot express liner concept. The Matt Forrest contribution both with the *America* of 1939-1940 and later with the *United States* would be enormous. William Francis Gibbs had a way of picking and then keeping fine men.

Charles J. Altenburg joined Gibbs & Cox in 1935. He would become another of the inner team which would design the *United States*. He helped create New York's famous *Firefighter*, the most powerful fireboat ever built. Gibbs designed her as he did the land fire engine known as the "Super Pumper," also the most powerful vehicle of its kind ever built. Firefighting had been one of the earliest interests of the Gibbs brothers and their passion for it remained with them throughout their lives. Mr. Altenburg did surveys, made log books, and was otherwise occupied in the Gibbs & Cox merchant ship division. One of the men he most admired on the Gibbs staff when he was first hired was Edwin Stevens, a grandson of Colonel John Stevens, inventor of the railroad tie and builder of pioneer steamboat *Phoenix*, the first steampowered craft to make a coastal run in American history. Edwin Stevens was a propeller specialist with Gibbs & Cox. His lifetime assignment was to increase propeller efficiency. He worked for many years on various propeller combinations, on the positioning of propeller shafts, on types of blades and the like. He was frequently given time to do studies on the high-speed trans-Atlantic liner which he knew as the "four-screw ship," or the "fast quadruple screw ship."

The *America*, next milestone in the road to the *United States*, was contract No. 1 of the Maritime Commission's new building program. Under Franklin D. Roosevelt, a ship lover of the first order, the old Shipping Board had been reorganized and out of it had come the Maritime Commission. A strong new chairman had been picked, Joseph Kennedy, a man who was known for his ability to get things done, and father of John F. Kennedy. The *America* was his first project, and she was launched on August 31, 1939, the day before Germany invaded Poland to begin World War II. Her design and construction had been another major effort for the Gibbs brothers. Many of the features built into her would go into the *United States,* from the famous "Duck Suite" to the wide use of aluminum. Interior decorator Anne Urquhart remembered the moment of the launch well. She saw tears rolling down the cheeks of Frederic Gibbs. It was doubly an emotional event because the world was on the brink of war and everyone knew that the great new liner would probably not be able to sail on her trans-Atlantic route, might even be used as a troopship instead of a liner. There would be a moment in the life of the *United States* when the decision to complete her as a liner was abandoned and she was ordered finished as a trooper.

The *America's* planning had gone back as far as 1936. Winning the right not only to design her but to supervise her construction was a matter of high priority to Gibbs & Cox. They had been called down to Washington by the Maritime Commission along with other naval architects and shipyard people. In the end it came down to a battle between the Gibbs & Cox design and the blueprints offered by the Newport News yard. The way William Francis prevailed over the shipyard shows another facet of his makeup. He played to win. The two competing "pro-forma" designs were to be reviewed at an all day meeting. William Francis brought his ace young designer Matt Forrest with him. In the morning both sets of plans were reviewed. Gibbs requested a long lunch break. He returned to his hotel with Forrest and set out to draw up a completely new sheet of "pro-forma" designs. His photographic memory enabled him to put down on paper all the better parts of the rival shipyard design. His brilliant designing capacity found ways of incorporating all these things in such a way that they seemed integral parts of his own earlier drawings. When he returned and resumed the meeting at 3 p.m. he unrolled the new plans and explained that those he had shown in the morning were just introductory. He won the contract, and the shipyard was given the task of building to his specifications.

Another member of the Gibbs team was Britton O. Smith, fondly known in the firm as "B.O. Smith." He had come aboard as the *America* planning was getting under way and would remain throughout the construction of the *United States* and for years after that. He never had a title with Gibbs & Cox, just being their machinery specialist. His special part with the *United States* would be her "feed system," the water cycle "to the boilers to the turbines to the ..." His goal was to achieve the "minimum fuel rate" for the ship. A sixth generation native of Canada, he was already well along in a brilliant career when Gibbs found him. In the middle of the first war he had been sent to Britain by the Canadian Vickers shipyard to get "British experience." Joining the British Army he helped build zeppelins. He then served with the De Laval Turbine Company and more time after that with the Moore Pump people, later absorbed by the Worthington Pump Company. He was an experienced and highly specialized talent and that was why William Francis Gibbs spent a full day with him in New York's Carl Schurz Park overlooking the East River convincing him to come to work for him. He never regretted the move.

The *America* design was a major step in the evolution of the Gibbs & Cox dream of "the big ship." She was 723 feet in length with a beam of 93 feet, by far the largest liner built in the United States up to that time and one of the largest in the world. Her gross tonnage under British rules was 33,961. She was an enlargement of the highly successful sister ships *Manhattan* and *Washington*, built for the United States Lines in the depth of the depression to replace the *Leviathan*. In many ways she was a dry run for the superliner *United States*, and much of the design work that had been done over the previous 15 years for "the big ship" was put to good use in her creation.

This chapter will end with a brief tribute to the wartime achievements of Gibbs & Cox, which did much to cement the position of William Francis Gibbs as "Mr. Navy," a spot that helped him greatly in winning the fullest measure of naval support for the national defense features of "the big ship." His experiences in World War I had demonstrated how dangerous it was to permit the nation's shipyards to go on their own separate ways in a wartime building crisis. He was able to set the patterns for design and procurement for the vast shipbuilding program that the war made necessary. In addition to being Chairman of the Combined Shipbuilding Committee, he was a special assistant to the Director, Office of War Mobilization. Under his direction Gibbs & Cox produced the designs or working plans for over 63% of all oceangoing merchant vessels built in the war period and 74% of all naval vessels.

3

She Gets Her Name

Although the actual building of the *United States* would take only a little over two years and four months, the planning went back to 1915. As William Francis Gibbs would say many times, the first ship he designed was a 1,000-footer that eventually became the *United States*. The similarity in overall dimensions between the 1915 design and the final product is eerie! The four-stacker showed to J.P. Morgan in those far off days before America's entry into World War I was just 131 inches longer and 54 inches wider than the final magnificent product which would make her maiden voyage from New York on July 4, 1952. But what went into the 990-foot hull – that was the great difference. The power plant was amazingly new, the aluminum superstructure was utterly different from anything that had gone before, and the safety features were so superior to other ships that, to this writing, they have not been approached in a passenger liner.

It can be said that the span between 1915 and the 1950 keel laying was one long era of gestation. The work done on S-171 was not wasted, it just slowly evolved into the final form, becoming more real, more solid with each evolution. As early as 1940 certain "specification sections" were being done for "the big ship," as Matt Forrest remembered. Newport News was doing electrical specifications based on broad brush treatment from Gibbs & Cox. They were what are known in the trade as detailed design drawings. They followed the basic Navy design rules; for example all auxiliary machinery was designated either as vital or non-vital. Non-essential services such as galley auxiliaries could be cut off so that the power needed for vital machinery like fire pumps and propulsion could be maintained.

Perhaps it was escapism from the horrors of World War II, possibly it was serious planning for the years ahead, but in 1943 and 1944 the talk of superliners was everywhere in the maritime field.

The British magazine *The Shipping World* in November 1944 carried a comment that would make the Gibbs brothers take especial note: "It is a paradox that the United States, a country which does most things in a 'big way' had never gone in for the really large passenger ship." James McNeill, naval architect of the John Brown & Co. yard, where both the *Queen Mary* and the *Queen Elizabeth* were built, was quoted in the same issue suggesting that after the war there would be more superliners. "There is no indication to show that the growth in dimensions will be arrested, although on the grounds of cost the rate of growth might be slowed down over a certain transition period." William Francis Gibbs read all these comments and kept all the clippings. But he, unlike most of the others cited, was well along with his plans for a ship that really would materialize.

That there would be federal support for a new American passenger ship fleet was established with a directive of President Roosevelt issued on October 24, 1944. It authorized Vice Admiral Emory S. Land, Chairman of the War Shipping Administration, to develop a "bold and daring" plan for new passenger ship tonnage. Eleven luxurious superliners were to be built under this plan, one-third faster than the best American ships in service and for use on all important trade routes of the seven seas. On November 15, 1945, details of the first two of these projected ships were announced in Washington. They would be of 37,500 tons deadweight, would have a speed of 29 knots and would cost from $22,500,000 to $25,000,000 each. Anthony Leviero, of the *New York Times*, noted that in the over-all planning the government had kept in mind "to a certain extent" the "looming competition of trans-ocean airlines." It was added that the ships would be the safest in the world, not only from the standpoint of fireproofing "but in radar equipment for travel by night and in fog."

The actual design and construction period for the *United States* may be said to cover ten years: 1943-1952. This period is broken down into two parts, the first from 1943 to the beginning of 1946, when Gibbs & Cox worked entirely on its own on plans. Some $103,770.16 was spent in this period on "the big ship." The second part would begin in March, 1946, when the U.S. Lines would authorize Gibbs & Cox to make plans for the superliner. During the entire ten-year period, the Gibbs involvement was so great that a substantial amount of unauthorized funds from its own coffers would be spent on the project. All this is described in a remarkable compilation of memos and documents now preserved at The Mariners' Museum, Newport News, Va. Inside the front cover is the Gibbs book mark, a colorful design featuring the Latin phrase: "Renax Proposiri," which means "By Their Works Ye Shall Know Them," the favorite Bible passage of William Francis.

Everyone sensed in early 1945 that the war was coming to a close. Gibbs & Cox had 3,200 employees and, if they were to be kept busy, there had to be a substitute for all the Navy procurement and new construction. The old S-171 project number had not been used for some years. A new number was assigned to the long hoped for 1,000-foot liner. It was 12201. At the same time another big liner was under study, not quite as big as the 1,000-footer, but larger than the *America*. She was given the number 11811. She would be able to make 30 knots, and would have a length of 790 feet. Her estimated cost was $34,500,000.

In March, 1945, William Francis Gibbs brought Matt Forrest home from the Pacific. He had been doing work with new Navy destroyers and picket ships in Okinawa, but was now needed back in New York to get to work on "the big ship." This was one of the first signs that William Francis meant business. The government was also hard at work with its "bold and daring" plan. Vice Chairman of the War Shipping Administration, Admiral Harold L. Vickery, met with William Francis and James L. Bates, the Maritime Commission's liner specialist, to review all options for new Atlantic passenger ships. In June, 1945, they outlined four possible ships for future consideration:

Type
A	22 knots	690 feet in length	$22,000,000 Cost
B	25 knots	745	$25,000,000
C	30 knots	790	$31,500,000
D	30 knots	936	$39,000,000
			to $41,500,000

It was decided that the 790-foot ship could not maintain the desired speed with comfort for passengers. A memo by William Francis went still further: "It would be desirable to prepare a tentative design of a ship of substantially the size of the largest Maritime Commission (Type D), *but with surpassing speed,* on the theory that to build a much larger ship than design 11811 and not to increase the speed well above the *Queen Mary* and the *Queen Elizabeth* would, be to overlook a most valuable commercial asset in North Atlantic competition."

The Gibbs memo book contained a short note on its fourth page:

"Design 12201–The undersigned made the first inboard profile sketch personally under date of July 6, 1945. ... This sketch was revised July 12, 1945." The signature, of course, was that of William Francis Gibbs. Below this on the same page was another comment: "These first drawings ... the inboard profile and hold plan revised to July 18, 1945, are the general arrangement of the ship with 19 bulkheads substantially in accord with the current design. ..."

Germany surrendered on May 7 and President Truman ordered an atomic bomb dropped on Japan on August 6, and another on August 9. The Japanese announced their surrender on August 15 and signed their capitulation document on September 2.

On many fronts the way was being prepared for an American peacetime superliner. Quoting facts and figures about how the two British *Queens* carried more than 1,000,000 American soldiers to Europe without the loss of a single man, the *Maritime News Digest* for July 1927 said there was a lesson in this for the United States: "Our future merchant fleet should contain three or four huge liners comparable to the two *Queens*. Such ships are indispensable in time of war." And others were downgrading the possible danger to shipping from air competition. many believed as did Dr. Henry Francis Grady, president of American President Lines, when he said: "Seriously, I am not worried about the competition of the air lines, any more than the telegraph companies need worry about the development of airmail service for letters. There will be increased transportation, there will be increased communication, and so we will all go ahead together." The National Federation of American Shipping was leading a crusade in Washington to permit ship lines to own and operate airplanes so that people might go one way and return the other.

One of the key younger figures at Gibbs & Cox during the designing of the *United States* was Thomas N. Buermann. A passion for ships had guided him since he began carving wooden boat models at the age of five. After graduating from the University of Michigan he joined Gibbs & Cox in 1939 and got badge #177. Hired by Henry Meyer he was assigned to work under Matt Forrest. Tested and proved during the tremendous war effort, he remembered going to William Francis Gibbs after the war ended to ask if he might have something new and different to do. Mr. Gibbs said he had a task for him and told him about job 12201. "I want you to draw a set of lines for this ship," he said. In reply Tom Buermann asked if Matt Forrest knew about the assignment. Mr. Gibbs replied: "Don't worry about him, you are working for me now." Tom went back to his old desk, got his pencils and returned to find that Mr. Gibbs had cleared off a space for him to work near his own drawing board so he could watch. As he worked he had to contend with an almost continuous overseeing by William Francis. He would call for "more freeboard," or more this and that as the design progressed, constantly offering advice and help. One evening Gibbs called for more bow radius, but it was late and Tom Buermann did not have time to calculate it. The next morning he found that Gibbs had gotten someone to re-do the bow radius and had put it into the drawing. The lines were done at an 8th of an inch to the foot, and after they were finished Gibbs said: "Now I want a flooding diagram." The finished diagram showed the ship to be a four-compartment ship, meaning she would stay afloat if as many as four compartments were flooded. The world standard called for a two-compartment ship. American Coast Guard requirements specified that a passenger ship must float with three compartments flooded. The *United States* would be able to remain afloat with four flooded. Next Buermann was told to do a set of lines on aluminum one-half inch to the foot. This time there was no rush and he was given an assignment. The assignment took three months and later Newport News designers would say they had never seen anything so close to perfect accuracy – only at most a half an inch off the real, full-size design. A year later Mr. Gibbs called for Tom Buermann. He said, "You told me that this was a four-compartment ship. Now you have to figure how to operate her as a real four-compartment ship." He did.

The process of convincing the United States Lines to accept the Gibbs plans for a vessel "with surpassing speed" took some time. The company had turned to freight ship operation during the war and was doing very well. The man who had to be convinced was John M. Franklin, who had succeeded Basil Harris as president. During the war he had served in Washington with the Army's transport division, earning the rank of "General." William Francis himself told the story in a speech he gave in 1953 in Philadelphia:

"At the close of the second World War, in which we had done a good deal of work for the Navy, my brother and I sat down with General Franklin on his return to the U.S. Lines. We discussed the possibility of a great ship, and if it was to be built, should be built primarily for the national defense of the United States and we would try to combine in such a design the requirements of a passenger ship. The result was that General Franklin became enthused and he backed us with the millions necessary to force such a ship so far as the U.S. Lines was concerned. But, strange to say, it didn't take much forcing, because when we presented our ideas to the Navy, the Maritime Commission, and the Coast Guard in Washington, they were received with enthusiasm."

The convincing process was not something that happened all at once, as a memo dated February 6, 1946, showed. The memo described a lunch meeting between the Gibbs brothers and General Franklin. The General at that point was pushing for two ships of the 11811 style. He said that two such vessels would be better than three of the Maritime Commission's smaller 25-knot vessels. William Francis chimed in that a "far faster and more outstanding ship" could readily be designed and added that "such a ship could have surpassing speed and qualities." Frederic Gibbs added that "it might be that one ship would place the United States Lines in a pre-eminent position and prove economically sound." General Franklin, the memo concluded, stated that this idea had "great possibilities" and that he would give the whole matter further consideration.

Things were moving. On March 4 and 5, the two Gibbs brothers met again with General Franklin. This time they went to the General's apartment in the Carlton House. Out of this meeting came a memo stating that he had agreed to go ahead with the ship that could make a "sustained sea speed of 33 knots, corresponding to the schedule speed of 28 1/2 knots of the *Queen Mary,* could be designed and built at a figure of about $50,000,000." Such a vessel, the memo noted, would have a trial speed of 35 knots and could carry passengers in excess of 1,650-2,000. The high-speed, quadruple screw, 1,000-foot express Atlantic liner was at long last taking real shape and form. On March 12 General Franklin placed the matter before the U.S. Lines Board of Directors. He was authorized to take the plan to Washington, which he did the next day. And on the day after that, March 14, 1946, General Franklin officially requested Gibbs & Cox "to proceed with the design of such a vessel." Much of the conceptual work for the *United States* had already been done. But now, finally, the brothers were not doing it all for themselves. They were on someone else's payroll – shades of their 1915 interview with J.P. Morgan. And they were charged with developing contract plans and specifications for their dream ship. There was still a long, long way to go but, perhaps, the major hurdle of them all had been surmounted.

Walter C. Bachman in his biographical memoir about William Francis Gibbs called the *United States* "a synthesis of all the experiences gained from the passenger ships such as the *Leviathan,* the *Malolo,* the Grace liners, and the *America* combined with the technical advances made in machinery, structure, materials, and methods developed in work for the U.S. Navy." The new ship had to be the safest afloat, with standards of subdivision and fire resistance surpassing all others. She had to compete with the two British *Queens* in luxury, accommodations and to be much faster – and all this at less fuel consumption. And she had to be at the same time convertible to a troopship. Quite an order, but the Gibbs brothers were ready and eager to move ahead.

On March 26, 1946, General Franklin wrote to the Maritime Commission confirming his verbal presentation of the 13th. The new ship would need a large construction subsidy. She would be capable of a two-week turnaround between New York and Southampton, with a stop at Plymouth and Le Havre. She would be operated in conjunction with the *America,* due to be returned by the Navy to the company shortly, and the *Washington,* giving the line a weekly sailing from New York. General Franklin's letter could have been written by William Francis Gibbs. Its concluding portion rang out loud and strong:

"It is the desire of the United States Lines Company to develop and build the greatest passenger ship in the world. We have come to the conclusion that the progressive, sound position for the company to take at this time is to build the fastest, safest, and greatest passenger vessel ever built, which will place the American Merchant Marine in a sound competitive position on the North Atlantic for the next 20 years."

The company expected that the *Washington* could be used for an additional eight years in her partially restored condition and at that point "consideration would be given to the building of a second fast sistership for the North Atlantic." The U.S. Lines began to take part in the planning, and on April 12, 1946, a letter from them spelled out to Gibbs & Cox that the new ship would make 24 round trips a year. An unusual itinerary was projected: The port of Flushing, in the Netherlands, was selected as the ship's European terminal, with a stop on the way over at Plymouth and a visit to Southampton westbound. The letter also projected that the ship would have to steam at 33 knots average for 4,572 hours in each calendar year. In addition she would go at reduced sea speeds for 576 hours and would consume another 492 hours entering and leaving port for a grand total of 5,640 hours in motion each year. She would be in service for 235 days out of each year, or 64% of the time under such a schedule.

Originally, the U.S. Lines people argued for only two classes, but William Francis Gibbs had his mind made up, and "you don't argue with God," as Matt Forrest put it so aptly. Gibbs demanded and got three classes; he wanted the traditional ship just like the *Queen Mary*. He stressed that she would be carrying many troops and dependents from Europe to home and that they could be carried in Third or Tourist Class. Not only was Gibbs quite accustomed at this point to winning all arguments, but he demanded and received the fullest cooperation in maintaining a tight aura of secrecy around the entire *United States* project. This was based on the Navy implications in the ship's construction and also on Gibbs' determination never to let rival steamship companies know anything at all about the new liner. Some 80% of the machinery that went into the *United States* was a result of developments during the second World War. Her power plant would embody the key advances in high pressure and high temperature that went into the Navy designs. It was only natural that such things would be kept secret, but no one dreamed to what lengths Gibbs would go on this score. One of those who was caught up in the trap of secrecy obsession would be the author, who at this time had just become a shipping reporter for the *New York Herald Tribune*. Matt Forrest, interviewed on the subject 32-years later, characterized the Gibbs penchant for secrecy as a highly developed competitive sense which paid off. He said that other superliners built after the *United States* such as the *France,* the *Queen Elizabeth 2*, and the two Italian *Michelangelo* sisters, were "just new versions of the *Queen Mary.*" Their designers never discovered the key design secrets of the *United States*. The basic secret was, he added, the placing of a "colossal amount of power" in the ship. John Kane, of the Newport News Shipbuilding & Dry Dock Company, expanding on this same theme, came up with another conclusion. To him the secret of the *United States* was her light displacement due to her naval type construction, "her very light construction" as he put it.

There was a major structural difference between the *United States* and all other liners, Matt Forrest explained. She was longitudinally framed (except for the side shell), not transverse, as were the *Queen Mary* and other major liners. Her strength came through a combination of her long longitudinal beams and her plating. The ordinary ship was built with ribs spaced several feet apart as the chief strength skeleton. In the final analysis, it must be stated that since the *United States* was constructed to meet the standards of the American Bureau of Shipping, her structure was not significantly lighter than her contemporaries, although her longitudinal framing made her stronger for the same weight of structure. Her real secret was that she had a relatively light displacement and a great amount of horsepower, i.e., more horsepower per ton than any of her competitors.

The use of aluminum for the ship's entire superstructure was another way that Gibbs pioneered in the *United States* design, and contributed substantially to the light displacement of the ship. In order to be able to use aluminum a way had to be found to link it safely and permanently to the steel hull. In creating the *United States* design, Gibbs made a major contribution in this field by discovering that this connection could be made by using stainless steel rivets. It was also learned that for the link up to be lasting the aluminum had to be riveted on the outside of the steel, over-lapping it so to speak. On an Italian ship built later the overlapping was done in reverse and there was continuous trouble from spray and rain entering the unprotected crevices and creating havoc. Stainless steel does not have any reaction when next to aluminum. Although after years of testing, Gibbs was virtually certain on the stainless steel rivet linkage between steel and aluminum, he would continue for years after the *United States* entered service to make frequent checks on how his system was holding up, Charles Altenburg remembered. Needless to say the use of aluminum was a well kept secret.

Another concept that was a key to the strength of the *United States* and which was evolved from Navy experience in this early planning period was the cardinal rule about openings in the ship's main or "strength deck." A basic decision made at the start was that there would be a minimum number of openings in this deck, and that all such openings would be made close to the center line, and away from the sides, where cracks usually start. The projected large, two-deck high Dining Saloon for First Class caused a great deal of difficulty. It required special strength girders. Twin uptakes for the smokestacks like those on the *Leviathan* and the *Normandie* were not permitted. They would have weakened the ship. The placing of all stairwells, elevators, and other deck openings were carefully planned from the earliest stages in the design period. A large model of the strength deck was made and stood in the large design room at the Gibbs & Cox, 21 West Street headquarters. With the keel below and the strength deck above, the hull was not unlike a great steel beam. These two structures, acting like a girder, reduced sagging and hogging. Needless to say this insistence on girder strength for the hull brought many complications to Barton O. Cook, the Gibbs & Cox specialist assigned to the work of interior layout supervision. He was a veteran of his field, having drawn the passenger spaces for the' never-built superliner designed by Theodore Ferris for U.S. Lines several years before World War II began. And the passenger people of U.S. Lines had fits when their plans ran contrary to considerations of safety and structural strength as espoused by William Francis Gibbs.

Vincent A. Moynihan, senior staff engineer for electronics at Gibbs & Cox, was one of those charged with making the *United States* safe against fires. The electrical system was completely insulated from the hull. The hull, in other words, carried no current, as it did on virtually all major foreign liners. Safety had become Mr. Gibbs middle name. Every phase of the ship's construction was viewed from the standpoint of safety. The electrical system was designed so that in the event of disaster with flooding, it would continue to function, although first one, then two, then three, and so on of her compartments between water tight bulkheads were flooded. Gibbs told Moynihan to create a system of emergency lights backed up by storage battery power that would come into service instantly. The *United States* was the first design that included all electrical lighting systems, where "we had motor generating systems that charged automatically." As a result there would be power on an uninterruptable basis, with temporary emergency power sources called on if regular power was cut off and ready to come on instantly, after which the Diesel system would pick up and carry the load. The emergency generators were on the top side of the ship, Diesel-driven, entirely independent of the steam system. They would remain operative up to the very last. Not only safety considerations were involved in the ship's lighting. Staterooms always had overhead lighting to permit the stewards to clean corners better. She would be the first big ship with all electric galleys, and here Gibbs & Cox had great difficulty attempting to anticipate what the peak load would be. This meant they had to do a lot of guessing as to what size power cables had to be installed to handle the power needed for the 10 electric ranges and the microwave ovens. The ship would also have the first really first class air conditioning system. The system was designed to cool the air first, remove all its moisture and reheat to the temperature set by the individual control panel. The great number of fan rooms needed proved a terrible problem to Barton Cook and Matt Forrest.

Another key point was the extra freeboard that Gibbs wanted forward, a weakpoint on the *Queen Mary*.

During all the design period, and for that matter right through the construction of the ship, William Francis Gibbs "was all over the place," as Matt Forrest remembered. Although the various divisions of Gibbs & Cox had learned to work together well, Gibbs never relaxed. He made it a point to at least seem to be continually in motion. More than that, he looked over everyone's shoulder. He continually needled. He brow beat, demanding more effort, better and quicker solutions, and more intense zeal. There would be an impassé once in a while and then Gibbs would call all the differing parties together in a conference room and hash it out. But, with him always as the judge and jury!

Well aware of the battles ahead about the cost of the superliner, the Gibbs brothers uncovered everything they could about what great liners of the past cost. A table in their memo book showed the following:

Liner	Her Cost to Build
Normandie	$28,000,000
Queen Mary	24,000,000
Rex	$15,500,000
Empress of Britain	$10,500,000
Manhattan	$10,500,000
Pres. Hoover	$7,350,000

On the matter of insurance Frederic Gibbs discovered that the *Queen Mary* was insured for $23,856,000 in 1936. He learned also that the *Queen Elizabeth,* only partly completed, was covered in 1940 for $22,596,000. Somehow he unearthed annual fuel and crew costs for the *Queen Mary* and compared them with the anticipated costs for the new American ship:

Cost	Project 12201	Queen Mary
Annual wage costs	$3,700,000.00	$2,136,048.50
Fuel costs	$3,152,000.00	$5,753,000.00

More input from U.S. Lines – a letter to the Maritime Commission giving the total capacity of the new liner should she have to be used as a troopship came to Gibbs & Cox. There would be space for 13,864 troops, with an additional 400 bed hospital and a crew of 1,444. It was noted that the two *Queens* each had a maximum capacity of 11,000 troops. The U.S. Lines also made studies to show how costly it would be for them to operte a vessel built with special national defense features. She would need two enginerooms, so her propulsion capability would have back up in a torpedo attack. This would require 155 engineers instead of 95 needed for a normal ship, at an added annual cost of $200,000. The maintenance of her defense features would cost an additional $100,000 per year. Despite these extra expense items, Frederic Gibbs on July 15, 1948, submitted for the record a memo estimating that the vessel would have a net profit after taxes of $11,153,146.90 for her first six years of operation. A more modest estimate of $8,457,393.65 annual profit was offered at the same time by U.S. Lines.

Two important new people became part of the team at about this time. Several major American yards were hard at work preparing estimates for bids on the new liner. The yard with the inside track was Newport News, and they assigned their John Kane to work on their bid proposal. He was an assistant to Mark Ireland in their engineering technical department and had been with the yard since 1936. He had gone all through the America project, and had come to have a high regard for William Francis Gibbs. Eventually it would be he who would become the yard's liaison man with Gibbs & Cox. The other new team member was Nicholas Bachko, who had graduated from the U.S. Merchant Marine Academy, Kings Point, N.Y., and had served during the second war as an engineer on U.S. Lines ships. In 1945 he had come ashore as Port Engineer. He was being groomed to be the principal liaison for his company with Washington and Gibbs & Cox.

The Gibbs brothers had a big day on April 5, 1948. Their offices at 21 West Street, overlooking the Hudson River, were the scene of a momentous announcement, and, for the first time, a finished model of the new superliner was unveiled. At the meeting were top officials of the Maritime Commission and General Franklin. Pictures of William Francis, the General, and others examining the glistening new model were carried in newspapers and magazines throughout the world. The ship's gross tonnage was revealed as to be 48,000 tons, and her passenger capacity would be 2,000. It was also made known that she would have 48,000 cubic feet of refrigerated cargo space as well as an additional 100,000 cubic feet for automobiles and other express cargo. She would be able to carry 14,000 troops as a transport in times of national emergency and would be built to the most stringent Coast Guard safety regulations. William Francis announced that the American Bureau of Shipping had approved the new ship's specifications. Maritime Commission Chairman, Admiral William W. Smith, said he would send the complete plans to the Navy and his own technical staff for study.

In mid-July, 1948, the U.S. Lines made an offer to the Maritime Commission to put up $25,000,000 toward the building of the new express liner. Estimates for the total cost had by this time risen from $65,000,000 to $70,000,000. It was hoped that the $25,000,000 would be enough in view of the building subsidy and the national defense allowances. The government was explaining to all and sundry at this point that it had two alternative ways to finance the new ship: (1) pay for it all itself, or (2) find a steamship line willing to put up perhaps a third of the cost. It was noted that the second route seemed wiser, but there would be many who would object to this course in the months ahead. Editorial support for the government's stand was developing. On July 23rd, 1948, the *New York Times* spoke out. It said the call for an American superliner had been made many times. It concluded that if one was to be built, it would be judged not so much for its peace time speed potential but as a defense asset.

A memo in the record book showed that Frederic Gibbs had further documentation comparing great liners of the past with the new ship:

Ship	Number of Bulkheads	Height of Bulkheads	Height above Waterline
#12201	19	55 feet	24 feet
Leviathan	13	50 "	11 "
Queen Mary	15	55 "	16 "
Normandie	11	63 "	26 "

Three major yards were invited to bid on the U.S. Lines superliner in mid-August. They were the Newport News Shipbuilding & Dry Dock Co., the Bethlehem Steel Corp., and The New York Shipbuilding Corp. They were the only yards with facilities capable of building a ship of this size. The weekly news bulletin of the American Merchant Marine Institute hailed this call for bids and noted that editorial writers throughout the nation were "talking up the idea of the new ship with enthusiasm." The *New Bedford* (Mass.) *StandardTimes* said that the expenditure of a subsidy of $50,000,000 would be "justified on security grounds." The *News-Sun,* of Waukegan, Ill., agreed, adding that troop transports "are essential to any U.S. defense plan." The *Columbus* (Ohio) *Dispatch,* also stressed national defense, concluding: "It is to be hoped that the decision of the Maritime Commission will be based on military requirements more than commercial, in spite of the attractive possession of a ship holding the North Atlantic speed record might have." Gibbs hoped, and he would be proved correct, that this somewhat negative tone of the nation's editorials would change into a more enthusiastic one as the ship came closer to reality.

On October 5, 1948, the firm of Eggers & Higgins proposed a budget of $124,000, for doing the interior architecture work on the new liner, later raised to $151,000. In due course they would get the contract. When the firm of Smyth, Urquhart & Marckwald first learned about the new Gibbs superliner they began making proposals and budgets. Their smallish offices at 821 Madison Avenue were already crowded with desks, sample shelves, and cabinets. They needed more space and one of their budget items was for renting some rooms nearby where they would work exclusively on "the big ship." Competition for the contract was so severe that they had to eliminate this budget line and content themselves with the crowded office they already had. Their estimated three-year budget of $157,010 was submitted November 15. They had the inside track because they were well-known both to U.S. Lines and to Gibbs & Cox. A team of women interior decorators was favored by the ship line because they knew that 80% of all passage tickets were sold upon the recommendation of the woman in the family. They wanted colors and designs that would appeal to women.

Shipyard bids on the express passenger liner were opened at 2:30 p.m. on December 1 in Washington. The New York Shipbuilding Corp., builders of the *Manhattan* and the *Washington,* submitted no bid. Bethlehem's bid, made for their Quincy, Mass., yard, was for $75,649,000 and the company pledged to finish the ship in 1,430 calendar days. The Newport News bid was for $67,350,000 with a 1,218 day delivery. The story on the bidding carried in the *New York Times* said the vessel "will be a mystery ship in many of the features incorporated for military purposes." It added that "there have been hints in official quarters that the new ship actually will far exceed the normal size of a 48,000-ton ship because of lighter metals used, without sacrifice of strength and that its speed will be far greater than the listed requirements."

In order to find out the cost of the national defense features, the shipyards were asked to give bids for constructing the vessel minus these special characteristics. Vice Admiral William Smith said on December 3 that he hoped the second set of bids would be in within two weeks and that a decision might be expected by the first of January. Unfortunately for everyone, the Maritime Commission was at a low ebb in its reputation in Washington. It would be over four months before a decision was reached. In the meantime another spate of editorials appeared. The *Raleigh* (N.C.) *Times* echoed the common sentiment that the ship would have real military value. The *Elgin* (Ill.) *CourierNews* noted that "in peace time the great luxury liners have seldom been good business investments in their own right, but they have great advertising value for the lines operating them and are considered a distinctive credit to the nation whose flag they fly."

Anne Urquhart and Dorothy Marckwald were called down to 21 West Street one day early in 1949 and William Francis Gibbs took them into one of the many conference rooms, with neatly framed pictures of the ships designed by the firm on all four walls. He said he would back them for the contract to do the interior decoration, which in effect was all they needed. They knew they had the assignment of a lifetime! Later he would joke about having taken on a pair of women for this most important job, saying: "I prefer known horrors to unknown ones." Their contract covered all the interior decoration for staterooms and all public spaces, but not crew areas. For a while the two women would work together on all the general planning, furniture designs, color schemes, choice of materials, and decorations. Then they realized that specialization was in order to get the job done on time. At this point Dorothy Marckwald took the general work as her responsibility and Anne Urquhart concentrated on getting the artists and supervising the decorations. Throughout the three-year project they made all major decisions as a team. While they did the superliner job, Miriam Smyth, the senior partner in their firm, kept the office going and worked for private clients.

Some memories from Anne Urquhart:

"We would get preliminary sketches from Eggers & Higgins and then we would make our preliminary drawings, suggesting colors and styles. Every month we had meetings in the overcrowded quarters at 821 Madison. People had to sit on desk tops, to stand and there were layouts and designs spread out over all the desks and everywhere. B.O. Cook, from Gibbs & Cox, used to attend many of these meetings. He loved cigars and his passion for smoking would have made it impossible for anyone who did not smoke at all. This was how I began to smoke. It was a defensive mechanism."

Eggers & Higgins was represented at these meetings by A.L. Congdon, "a most cooperative and friendly person," Miss Urquhart remembered. The interior decorators continually asked for revisions of the architectural proposals from Eggers & Higgins, but these were given and the responses made in a "very fine spirit of cooperation." The most persistent "nit-picking" developed over the colors of paints and materials. Each block of staterooms, for example, would have a different scheme of coloring, so that a passenger walking down the corridor who might look into his neighbor's cabin would never see the same colors as in his own. And the fireproofing regulations created great difficulties. The ordinary paint samples proposed by Urquhart and Marckwald had to be duplicated, to their satisfaction, in fire retardant paint. All curtains and furniture covering materials had to be tested for color changes when they were made flame proof. "We were tremendously appreciative of the unending patience of Gibbs & Cox and of the shipyard in helping us get the results we wanted," Anne Urquhart said.

A cardinal rule for the ship was that no material which could burn would be used in its construction. Wood was the enemy – and was to be kept out of the ship at all costs. However, William Francis Gibbs had to make an exception very early in the planning and permit some wood aboard. The concession was kept so secret that it was virtually forgotten, except by an inner few. Needless to say it was never mentioned in publicity about the ship. The bilge keels, which would be 210 feet long, had to have some kind of filler. William Francis pressed Matt Forrest to find something other than wood that could be used, but, eventually, in a memo contained in the record book, the following conclusion was reached: "It was agreed that there was no satisfactory substitute." And so the twin bilge keels, designed to keep the ship from rolling, were filled with Oregon pine.

As the year 1949 opened there was tremendous activity on a dozen fronts. Although the award to build the liner had not as yet been announced, the Newport News yard made public early in January the fact that it had assigned one of its "two giant drydocks for the construction of the American superliner." This would mean that the two largest vessels ever built in the country would rise side by side, for the other drydock was already earmarked for a 65,000 ton flush-deck aircraft carrier. One of the earliest decisions made by Gibbs was to build the liner in a drydock instead of on the conventional slanted ways. This meant a tremendous saving in calculations and added an element of security. Ships built on ordinary ways were constructed at an angle of 1/4 to 5/8ths of an inch to the foot. The fact that Newport News had a graving dock large enough for the new ship was a big plus in its favor.

On January 4 the first of a series of meetings between Frederic Gibbs and Joseph Curran, president of the National Maritime Union, was held. William Francis was ill and could not attend. To get the union leader into the proper mood Frederic showed him the model of S-171 hanging on the wall of the conference room where they were, explaining how it had been tested in 1916 in Washington. Joe Curran was the big, burly, and most able leader of the largest union of unlicensed seamen in the merchant marine. He was a remarkable person, a specialist in shattering the calm of the nation's leading shipowners at bargaining sessions. He went to the attack immediately. He had looked over the deck plans, he said, and had found that certain showers were too far aft. What's more, he didn't approve of rooms for six – there were some in the plan. But the good impression created by Frederic kept Curran's usual sarcastic and brow beating manner under control and he was cooperative and understanding, according to the memo Frederic wrote that evening for the record book. As the chief representative of the majority of the 1,030 men and women to serve aboard the new ship, it was vital that Joseph Curran be cooperative. Frederic's memo noted that he observed that "in every ship you always had undesirable locations of this sort and that these conditions usually led to complaints on the part of crew members." Despite this somewhat cold comment, Frederic's memo concluded that Curran was "tremendously enthusiastic over the appearance of the ship and said he had never seen such a beautiful form." The following day the NMU leader wrote to General Franklin:

"We are gratified to note that in spite of the difficulties that occur in allotting space on this type of liner, that special thought has been given to providing good ventilation in the form of air-conditioning similar to that to be provided for the passengers. We were also impressed by the fact that in this liner, unlike those built in the past, due consideration was given to providing large messrooms for the Stewards Department. The messroom for this department on this liner will accommodate practically one-quarter of the steward staff. Since this has been one of the main difficulties in the past, we were happy to see the improved planning in this connection. Mr. Gibbs pointed out that 30 square feet or more would be available per room, a substantial improvement over any quarters on any vessel in the past. After carefully examining the plans with respect to crew quarters, mess rooms, toilet facilities, and recreational facilities, speaking in behalf of the union, I can assure you they are satisfactory and she should prove a happy ship!"

Over the next 10 months the number of crew proposed for the vessel would be changed six times, going up as high as 1,093 and ending back at 1,030. During this same period the total number of passengers to be carried was changed frequently as plans were worked over and over again. As of November 22, 1948, for example, there were to be 907 in First, 564 in Cabin, and 510 in Tourist. As of February 7, 1949, this had changed to 913 in First, 558 in Cabin, and 537 in Tourist. There would be many later changes as the different departments fought over each cubic foot of space.

Under the government's construction differential subsidy legislation up to 33 1/3% of a new ship's cost could be paid by Washington, and even more if special conditions warrant. A liner in foreign trade would also receive an operating differential subsidy to permit her to compete with lower cost foreign competitors. From the outset one of the main problems facing the Gibbs brothers and the Maritime Commission was finding additional money beyond the company's contribution and the building subsidy. They knew the U.S. Lines could not be counted on to provide much more than one-third of the total cost, if that much. The subsidy could be stretched up to a point. Where was the rest to be found? It would amount to many millions and a new formula had to be created to justify it in the eyes of Congress and the public. The evolution of the idea that it was reasonable for Washington to pay for the cost of the "national defense features" of the new ship was the answer. The high speed beyond what could be used commercially was one key item. The twin engine room design was another. A special industry, Navy and Maritime Commission committee was created to decide these features and to cost them out. It was headed by Huntington Morse, of the Commission. Others on it were James L. Bates, brought out of retirement for the work; Frank C. Nash and Rear Admiral C.D. Wheelock, representing the Navy, and William Francis Gibbs. Their assignment was not an easy one, and right up to the day the liner was to be delivered there would be battles over the formula they would devise. After much thought they came to the conclusion that the cost of the national defense features would be $25,398,000.

As part of the problem, they had to try to convince the U.S. Lines to make a larger financial contribution. The company was asked to recognize that at least a part of the high speed built into the ship would have commercial value. General Franklin accepted their thinking and on April 1, 1949, convinced his Board of Directors to offer $28,087,216 instead of the original, $25,000,000. Of this a quarter was to be paid from the company's capital reserve fund during the construction of the ship and the remaining 75% was to be covered by notes secured by a preferred mortgage on the vessel payable in equal installments over a 20 year period. It would never be paid in full, as the balance of the mortgage was accounted for when the Government purchased the *United States* for $12,000,000 with a net payment to U.S. Lines of $4,600,000. On April 7 this agreement and many other details were announced by the Maritime Commission. The vessel would have a length of 980 feet and a beam of 101 1/2 feet. She would cost $70,000,000 and Newport News would build her. The difference between the original Newport News bid and the final figure was explained as designers fees and other such charges. The new ship would take 1,218 days to build. Her top speed was not announced "for security reasons" but it would be about 30 knots it was "unofficially stated." On April 8 the Newport News yard announced that the new superliner would be their hull #488. No name had as yet been chosen.

A series of problem stories followed the April 7 announcement. How could insurance be found to cover the $70,000,000 liner? Was the $25,398,000 ascribed to national defense costs too high? The *New York Journal of Commerce* editorialized that "there are grounds for believing that the actual cost of these features to the Government is considerably lower. Probably less than half." And what would happen should the company and the Government decide to build the ship without the extra defense features? William and Frederic Gibbs knew more than anyone else what was involved and these newspaper attempts to penetrate the carefully worked out formula for finding funds caused grave concern at 21 West Street. It was not a question of what was really right, but what had to be.

The question of what to name the new vessel came up. Some wanted her called *Mayflower* and others suggested the name *Columbia*. The magazine *Science Illustrated*, in an article that was far from entirely favorable, proposed that she should be called *American Engineer*, "for the new ship was sure to be a floating monument to U.S. engineering ingenuity." The article's title hinted at its basic conclusion: "White Elephant or White Hope – A U.S. Super Ship." It called her small size the "most amazing of the liner's features," adding that "anyone can speculate on the kind of miracle that would make it possible to put all the 81,000-ton *Queen Mary*'s passengers in a 48,000-ton ship and carry them across the ocean in quarters as commodious as the *Queen's*." The magazine went on by answering its own question: "It is a safe bet that Gibbs will put many passengers in the space ordinarily needed for engines and oil." Obviously written by a very bright outsider who had only casual contact with the shipping industry, the piece hit the nail on the head in some ways: "The Gibbs organization operates in an air of mystery and Gibbs won't say, but the shipping industry believes he is planning to use new and lighter metals, possibly aluminum, proved during the war, in decks, cabins, and other structural work. No one wants to put his chin out with any positive prediction, but it is no secret that Gibbs and the U.S. Lines as well as the Navy, will be surprised and disappointed if she fails to show a clean pair of heels to Britain's *Queen's*. The smoke of hot fight still lingers over the drafting

John M. Franklin (Courtesy of Laura Franklin)

boards in a downtown Manhattan skyscraper where the final details are being worked out. Are superliners really a good idea for the U.S.? Can they really make money, or are they costly props to national prestige?"

Despite these questions and critical comments, the steamroller was in motion. Nothing could stop it at this point! On May 3, 1949, three signatures were put to a sheaf of contracts in Washington – THE Contract. The signers were Grenville Mellon, Vice Chairman of the Maritime Commission, which was ordering the ship; J.B. Woodward, Jr., president of the Newport News yard, and John M. Franklin, president of U.S. Lines to which the Maritime Commission was going to sell the ship. "There is much that is represented in this ship that is undisclosed for some time to come," Mr. Mellon said. "It is far more than a luxury liner. It embraces every component that a big ship needs in wartime. The need for troopships will never be obsolete," he said, with more wishful thinking in his comment that he probably realized.

Charles Hurd, a *New York Times* reporter at the contract signing had a good writer's sense of the dramatic in his makeup. He spotted William Francis Gibbs "standing quietly to one side." He asked him how long he had planned this vessel. "He replied that he began jotting down notes for a superliner in 1916, but, he added, two wars interfered."

A small box below a picture of Mellon, Franklin, and Woodward looking at the Gibbs model of the new liner, added one more very important bit of information to the news of the day-a shocker to many:

"UNITED STATES EXPECTED
TO BE SUPERLINER'S NAME"

The box added that this had for some time been the favored name, but had been put aside because the Navy had assigned the name to one of its new carriers. Two weeks before the Navy had cancelled work on the carrier and the name was freed. The last Atlantic liner to be so named was a little 10,000 ton Danish passenger ship operated for the Scandinavian America Line. Built in 1903 and scrapped in 1935, she had earned a fine reputation and had brought many thousands of immigrants to America. A number of early American passenger steamers had also borne this same name. To many in the industry, however, it was very much a surprise and took quite a lot of "getting used to."

4

From Keel to Launch

The June 9, 1949, issue of Britain's famed maritime magazine *Fairplay* reviewed what information was available about the new American superliner, coming to the conclusion that she should more likely be compared to the *Bremen* and *Europa* in size instead of the *Queen Mary*. It held that "the time is not propitious for building a superliner, for there are developments ahead in the way of gas turbines and the like which may render such a ship obsolete before her time."

Little bits of new information seeped out from under the news blackout from time to time. On June 6 the Welin Davit Boat Company made known that the new ship would have 20 of the most modern lifeboats ever designed. They would be of aluminum instead of wood or steel, meaning, it was said, a saving in weight and permitting much easier handling in time of emergency. They would be double-ended craft 37 feet in length. Each would be able to carry more than 140 persons. Two would have radios and would be Diesel powered. All the others would have hand-operated screws.

Another superliner project was announced in June. Paul Wadsworth Chapman, the Chicago financier who had bought U.S. Lines from the government in 1929, proposed the building of two very large liners capable of carrying 10,000 passengers each. They would cost $100,000,000 apiece and would be chartered by the government to Chapman's company – Liberty Liners, Inc. They would be "cafeteria-type" ships, with the passengers paying for their own meals. The fare on the proposed new vessels would be only $100. Chapman had projected two such ships as replacements for the *Leviathan* in 1935, but his plans did not get very far. They would make not much more progress this time.

The "bold and daring" plan for new passenger liners had seen six ships begun or contracted for at this point. In addition to the *United States,* there were two 29,000 gross-ton liners for American Export Lines' service to the Mediterranean, the *Independence* and the *Constitution,* and three medium-sized liners for American President Lines' round-the-world service. This trio of 13,000 ton ships was building at the New York Shipbuilding Corp. yard in Camden, New Jersey. They were named *President Adams, President Jackson,* and *President Hayes.* The two Export ships were building at Bethlehem Steel's Quincy, Mass., yard. It was an excellent beginning for a new passenger fleet and the Maritime Commission had followed what it thought was a presidential directive in getting these ships started, but the Roosevelt era was past. With President Truman the emphasis was on "go slow."

Following a Presidential directive, the Maritime Commission had been "bold and daring" in its effort to induce private lines to build new passenger tonnage. In order to get American Export and American President to build at all, the Commission had been forced to offer more than the customary 33 1/3% construction subsidy. As in the case of the *United States* it had offered additional funds as payment for national defense features.

On July 11, 1949, Comptroller General Lindsay C. Warren sent a report to Congress attacking the Maritime Commission for "maladministration and excessive expenditures" of public funds. The crux of the issue in all six new ships was the proportion of private investment vs. the government's contribution. In round numbers the six ships were costing the nation $150,000,000 in public funds and the three private lines were paying $70,000,000 to get title to them. This issue would harass William Francis Gibbs and everyone else involved for the next two years.

The shipping editors of New York's two leading newspapers were strong supporters of the Commission and the new ships. Both had watched step by step as the three shipping companies and the government had struggled to produce new liners for the merchant marine. Both came out on July 19 with articles defending the construction subsidy and national defense feature theory. George Horne, of the *Times,* began: "The case for the superliner is being hotly debated pro and con in shipping and government circles, heightened by the disclosure last week that the nation's first such ship was threatened with cancellation." Many had feared that the Comptroller's report might actually bring about the abandonment of the new superliner project. The *Times* editor continued by noting that a Congressional inquiry into the whole subsidy-for-new-ships question had begun and warned that the critics of the superliner "will take this opportunity to frustrate" her construction "if they can possibly manage it." Noting that Comptroller Warren was charging that the U.S. Lines' contribution was only 40% of the new ship's cost and asking why the public should pay the remaining 60%, the *Times* specialist in maritime matters explained: "Advocates reply that the proposed ship will be the most valuable naval auxiliary in the country's maritime history, or in any other country's, for that matter. Its urgent need as a naval auxiliary has been thoroughly attested by naval experts." Mr. Horne noted that some opponents had charged that the new superliner would be too easy a target because of her size. He countered by quoting one marine engineer who said: "Build a ship half the size and you will have twice as many vessels and you face twice the submarine menace."

Walter Hamshar, of the *Herald Tribune,* went back into recent history to note that when the Maritime Commission first announced its plans to build the superliner "more than 15 months ago, the project received the approval of the entire industry. During negotiations leading to the contract for the vessel in April, no opposition was voiced, in or out of the government, until the Comptroller General announced his opposition last week." He quoted shipping men as saying that "only a big ship such as the contemplated superliner could have the tremendous cruising radius, high speed, and high resistance to attack that the Navy wanted built into the auxiliary that the superliner will be. Advocates of building three liners like the *America,* rather than 'putting all their eggs in one basket,' found these facts difficult to refute because it was demonstrated that ships of the *America*'s size could not carry the machinery and armament for the superliner's speed and defense equipment." Mr. Hamshar also noted that the operating expenses of three ships would be much greater than for one "without increasing the passenger capacity over a year's time."

An editorial in the *New York Times* was published July 27 supporting the superliner. "The United States must have passenger ships," it said. "It will be unfortunate if the building program is now thrown into confusion just as it is getting under way after long effort and careful planning."

The Merchant Marine Subcommittee of the House Committee on Expenditures in the Executive Departments was chaired by Porter Hardy, Jr., from Virginia. Although it would have been thought that he would defend the superliner's construction, since it meant so much to his state, the opposite was the case. He began hearings on the subject. On August 13 he stated that he was convinced that Maritime Commission personnel "pulled figures out of the air" in granting subsidies of $70,373,000 on the superliner and the five other ships. He added that his hearings were building up a record of "extremely poor administration" in the Commission, but "is making no charge of dishonesty." Defending the subsidy grants, Maritime Commission member David J. Coddaire testified that the law empowered the agency to go as high as 50% with a building subsidy "upon receipt of convincing evidence that the differential between foreign and domestic building costs is greater than 33 1/3%

An additional inquiry was begun in the Senate, but the general public seemed to respond defensively to the charges of the Comptroller General. A few weeks later George Horne had another article in which he said that the shipping industry was awaiting developments "but its leaders were inclined to doubt that Congress would halt the program started after long debate and intensive study." As if to start some constructive thinking on the subject, the newspaper writer began his story by noting that "the procurement program for the country's first superliner, the *United States,* is already well advanced and vast quantities of materials are either moving toward the giant drydock selected for building or are in the process of manufacture." This was, it is believed, the first public reference to the new name as if it were an accomplished fact. Quoting a Newport News spokesman, probably Robert B. Hopkins, the shipyard's public relations director, he reported that parts received at the yard so far were for the main propulsion machinery, the boilers, turbo-generators and "a substantial quantity of steel of various forms." He added that sample staterooms had been built and furniture, bedding, and hardware for them had been acquired. "Much experimentation and alterations are involved in the selection of cabin designs, but this phase of the construction is getting underway early."

During the construction of the *United States* it was the custom of William Francis Gibbs to get in his long, gray limousine and be driven down to Newport News each Friday afternoon. Promptly at 7 a.m., he would call John Kane at his home and spell out what he wanted to do that Saturday. At first Kane would leap out of bed and comply with "Old Iron Hat's" every wish; that was a nickname that dated back to the *Leviathan* days at the shipyard. Then one Saturday after this custom had gone on for some time, John Kane "blew his top," in a modest way. Couldn't Mr. Gibbs at least wait until 9 to call on Saturday morning. Gibbs was most apologetic, John Kane remembered, and never called again before 9 a.m. But this did not reduce his passion for detail. As Mr. Kane recalled: "He was everywhere, constantly looking over your shoulder."

In September Mr. Gibbs sent Matt Forrest to Europe. He asked him to sail over on the *Queen Elizabeth,* the largest passenger liner ever built, and return on the *Queen Mary.* The *Elizabeth,* which then had served only three years on the Atlantic after her long period of transport service, averaged 27.35 knots on her eastbound crossing. The *Mary* averaged 26.80 knots. A memo to this effect, with copies of the souvenir logs of both crossings, went into the Gibbs memo book.

At this point I entered the scene with a story in the *Herald Tribune* bearing my by-line. I had been confounded with the problem of how a ship could be 980 feet long and only have a gross of 48,000 tons, so I went to the Custom House at Bowling Green, in lower New York, and reviewed the whole system of computation with the Chief Admeasurer, Joseph P. Godby. I learned that there was a substantial difference between the American gross tonnage and all other measurement systems. The American rules were based on a law passed in 1865. The law specified that a ship's gross tonnage was to be a measurement of only those areas encompassed by the ship's hull and the first deck attached directly thereto. A law such as this was only natural in 1865 because at that time ships had to use sails, and therefore there could be no tier upon tier of superstructure atop the hull. But with the development of the twin screw some time after this, the shipowner became fully confident in his steam plant to bring the ship home and sails were abandoned. The dramatic change in the liner silhouette from 1890 to 1914 resulted. Two, three, four, and even five decks were piled up upon the hull, all of which added to the space being used for commercial purposes and therefore meant a higher grow tonnage. One gross ton is the equivalent of 100 cubic feet of permanently enclosed earning space, with many exceptions and variations. Foreign nations changed their tonnage measurement rules to fit the outline of the liner at the turn of the century, but America did not. Mr. Godby, therefore, projected that the new American superliner would measure 60,000 tons by British measurement if she were 48,000 gross by the American system. And this became my story. Its headline read:

"NEW SUPERLINER IS 48,000 TONS
BY U.S. RULE, 60,000 BY BRITISH"

Mr. Godby supported his reasoning by citing the difference between the American and British tonnage of the Moore-McCormack Lines liner *Argentina*. By American rules she was 20,707 gross tons. Her registry papers, however, included an appendix showing her British-measurement gross as 23,476 tons, for when she went into a South American port, the port authorities would tax her on the basis of the British system, since it meant a larger port tax. My story appeared on October 16, 1949. It gained wide circulation and would ensnare me in a personal confrontation with William Francis Gibbs.

Walter H. Jones, U.S. Lines publicity director, told me he would from then on use the 60,000-gross ton figure for all future references to the new ship. He also liked my suggestion that the *America* should be described as a 33,532 gross ton ship instead of with her American gross, which was only 26,314 tons. He said he would use this new tonnage in all future company publicity and would also use 29,627 for the *Washington* instead of 22,846 as she was currently measured under American rules. All this made a new news story which I wrote and which was used in the December 11 *Herald Tribune*. The following headlines were used:

"STROKE OF PEN
ENLARGES LINER
BY 12,000 TONS
U.S. Lines Weighs New
Ship by British Method"

The headline writer didn't understand. Weight had nothing to do with the gross tonnage, however, the idea behind the headline was right.

The stacks of the new superliner would be one of her most striking characteristics. They started out to be considerably smaller on the first blue prints, and were steadily increased in size by design changes. A December 14, 1949, memo in the record book determined that because the forward stack would be slightly taller than the after one, the red, white and blue bands would have to be of slightly different width in order to give the proper impression. The forward stack would have these proportions: the blue band at the top would be 15%, the white band next would be 10% and the red part would be 75% of the total height. In order to maintain the same appearance for the aft stack, the color proportions would be as follows: 17.5% blue, 11.7% white and 70.8% red.

Another bit of new information was revealed in mid-December by the York Corporation, makers of the York turbo compressor water-cooling system. Their John R. Hertzler, vice president and general manager, announced that the *United States* would be completely air-conditioned with their equipment. She would be the first ship in the world with real climate control. The air would be chilled to about 52 degrees and then reheated as desired, giving a nice low humidity rate.

Things were humming at Newport News with raw material from many parts of the country arriving to go into the superliner. I wrote another story which was used in the *Herald Tribune*. It covered the huge mock-ups or patterns for various parts of the liner. Four 50,000-pound wooden patterns were built for the 'spectacle frames,' or struts, which would emerge from the hull at the ship's stern. These struts, which would form the streamlined endings of the bossings, would be subject to a tremendous strain. About 28,000 board feet of lumber was used to make them. The finished metal frames would weigh 360,000 pounds and would be made in a way described as "entirely new to the yard and possibly new to the entire shipbuilding industry," according to the yard's publication *Shipyard Bulletin*. In past jobs the entire frame had been cast. With the superliner the barrel portion (i.e. barrel plate) through which the shaft would pass was to be of welded, rolled-plate 21" thick construction. Such a method would be quicker, cheaper, and easier to examine. The new frame castings would be made by the General Steel Casting Company, of Eddystone, Pennsylvania, and would be shipped by barge to the yard.

The year ended and U.S. Lines was optimistic in its annual report: "The increase in operating profit from $2,286,206 in 1948 to $5,604,197 in 1949 resulted from numerous factors ... Passenger business was good in 1949 and promises to be even better in 1950."

Anne Urquhart had a memory many years later of this period. She visited the factory of the General Fireproofing Company with Dorothy Marckwald. This was where the furniture they had struggled so long and so hard to create was being made. "We would draw a picture of the chair and they had to make it work and, of course, it all had to be completely fireproof, from glass stuffing, aluminum frame, etc." She and her partner entered the factory that afternoon and saw, to their delight, long assembly lines of nice new bureaus, chairs, etc. moving along in orderly procession. A sudden thrill came over them. Here was the reality. Up to then everything had been in their heads or on paper, but it was now really happening. For her the superliner assignment was a once-in-a-lifetime thing. Her firm consisted of 12 women. To be partners in such a great effort as "the big ship" with such a substantial company as Eggers & Higgins, the even larger Gibbs & Cox, the monster U.S. Lines and the vast Newport News shipyard was quite something! "We often felt somehow as if we were the comic relief."

On January 19 1950, a 40-line piece of copy from the *Associated Press* came into the *Herald Tribune's* ship news desk as it did all over the nation. It was an announcement from the Maritime Commission that the keel of the superliner would be laid on February 8 and that the new ship would be completed in April, 1952. My interest in the ship was mounting and I regularly scoured every new publication and release for more information about her. The next day I found three important pieces of news casually listed in the monthly *Merchant Vessel Register,* a mimeographed monthly publication of the Military Sea Transportation Service, the Navy's ocean cargo branch. The new superliner was listed and so were her horsepower, her speed, and her deadweight tonnage. This was definitely worth a news story and it was carried the following Sunday. The horsepower shown in the MSTS register was 118,500. The speed projected for the new ship was 31 knots. Her deadweight was given as a mere 12,810. For purposes of comparison I listed also the horsepower of other famous superliners: 158,000 for the *Queen Mary,* 160,000 for the *Normandie,* 120,000 for the *Rex,* 110,000 for the *Conte di Savoia,* 96,800 for the *Bremen,* and 68,000 for the original *Mauretania.*

Shortly after this story appeared, I received an invitation to visit with William Francis Gibbs. Mr. Gibbs smiled and complimented me on my book, *Lives of the Liners,* which had come out in 1947, and then dropped a bombshell. The *United States* would be about 50,000 gross tons. She was much like the *Bremen* in size. This would be both her British and her American tonnage. There was no difference in her case. I mentioned the *Rex,* which was only 879 feet long but had a gross of 51,062 tons and asked how could a ship over 100 feet more in length have a smaller gross tonnage. Mr. Gibbs merely smiled and said she could. The interview ended, but neither party could put the matter of the new ship's tonnage out of his mind. I wrote to President Woodward of the Newport News yard asking the same question, but received no answer.

The *St. Louis* (Mo.) *Globe-Democrat* hailed the new superliner in an editorial on January 23: "Construction of the 60,000-ton ship, the largest ever built in this country, is scheduled to begin next month." Other newspapers dug for more news. The *Times* interviewed Joseph Curran just before the keel laying and came up with an exclusive: "There will be a training program for the personnel. We plan to do everything possible to make this the finest, smoothest-running ship afloat. We can't afford to do otherwise. At the same time, of course, we expect to get good conditions for the men; you can't have a perfectly run ship without suitable working and living conditions for the crew."

I was one of the press party invited to witness the keel laying. Although no ceremonies were held the nation's two leading wire services each sent out long stories. The *United Press* began theirs: "A 170-ton crane arched over a drydock and gently laid a 55-ton keel today for the biggest passenger liner ever built in the United States." Spotted after the keel laying by one of William Francis Gibbs' assistants, I was told that there was to be a press conference given by the noted naval architect. Most of the other press had scattered and as it turned out I was the only one present when the tall figure of William Francis and his equally tall brother Frederic came into the room. Spotting me sitting on an easy chair, William Francis smiled and patted his pocket, saying: "So you don't believe me, young man." He lifted a letter from his pocket and showed it – it was my letter to President Woodward about the new ship's tonnage. There was a twinkle in his eye, and the general excitement of the day prevailed, although there was not much "hard news" at that press conference.

The whole question of news and statistical information about the ship had for long been a matter of real concern to the Gibbs brothers. They were determined to protect Navy secrets and keep the competition from knowing any of the key design features of the superliner. As John Kane remembered what happened at about this time, Gibbs & Cox sent telegrams to the chief executive officers of Newport News and all vendors instructing them that thereafter all publicity having anything to do with their part in the building of the liner had to be cleared by Gibbs & Cox. Mr. Kane recalled that the telegrams were sent to the homes of these executives and that instructions were given to have them delivered at midnight, for effect. The memo book contains a brief comment on the subject dated March 20, 1950. It cited a letter received by Gibbs & Cox from the Maritime Commission "imposing a close news security system." The letter had undoubtedly been initiated by William Francis Gibbs. It contained this sentence: "All plans, specifications, letters, and other information, verbal or written, shall be considered as confidential and restricted, and all matters of publicity are to be cleared through the design agent."

Still another memo from this record book noted that the new liner would have 14 suites as compared to 20 on the *Queens*. There was a further breakdown:

Type of Suite	Queen Elizabeth	Queen Mary	#12201
4-room suites	2	2	0
3-room suites	8	6	10
2-room suites	<u>10</u>	<u>12</u>	<u>4</u>
	20	20	14

The old Maritime Commission, probably in part because of the adverse Lindsay Warren report, was reorganized and came out in two parts, the Federal Maritime Board, charged with rate making supervision, and the Maritime Administration, which would handle subsidies and all the rest. Fortunately for the superliner a most able man was selected to be the Maritime Administrator, Vice Admiral Edward L. Cochrane. He was named by President Truman on July 28, and took a leave of absence from his position as head of the department of naval architecture and marine engineering, Massachusetts Institute of Technology.

The story of the *United States* was coming to one of its most crucial turning points. The Korean War had begun on July 25, 1950. An invasion of North Korean forces moved at will southward, as the United Nations voted to create a defense force for South Korea. The capital city of Seoul fell before American forces arrived and first met the enemy. By early August the Americans and others from the United Nations had been forced back to the Pusan area, where they began a successful last stand against the troops of the North. It was with such an atmosphere of discouragement and determination that an article appeared in the August 14, 1950 *Daily Press* of Newport News. The piece reported that the Department of Defense had asked the Newport News shipyard how long it would take to convert the *United States* from superliner into a transport for troops. The paper's Washington correspondent added another chiller: "Another idea being kicked around by Washington officialdom, and it's just an idea at this point, is to abandon the superliner and revive construction of the supercarrier in its place, under another name, perhaps a flush-deck carrier." A memo from William Francis Gibbs to his brother carried in the record book noted that it cost Gibbs & Cox $150,000 to make plans for possible conversion into immediate troopship service.

In the late afternoon of September 16, 1950, I came into the large city room of the *Herald Tribune* and took my accustomed seat next to Walter Hamshar. Walter was hunched over his typewriter writing with a grim determination. He motioned for me to read over his shoulder: "The 48,000-ton superliner and three 13,000-ton combination passenger liners under construction for U.S. Lines and American President Lines will be completed as Navy troopships, the government announced yesterday. The change-over is being made at the request of the Defense Department on 'recommendation of the Joint

Keel Laying February 8, 1950. (Courtesy of Bill DiBenedetto)

Forward looking aft from low level. (Courtesy of Bill DiBenedetto)

Stern looking forward from high level May 5, 1950. (Courtesy of Bill DiBenedetto)

41

*Stern looking forward from low level April 7, 1950.
(Courtesy of Bill DiBenedetto)*

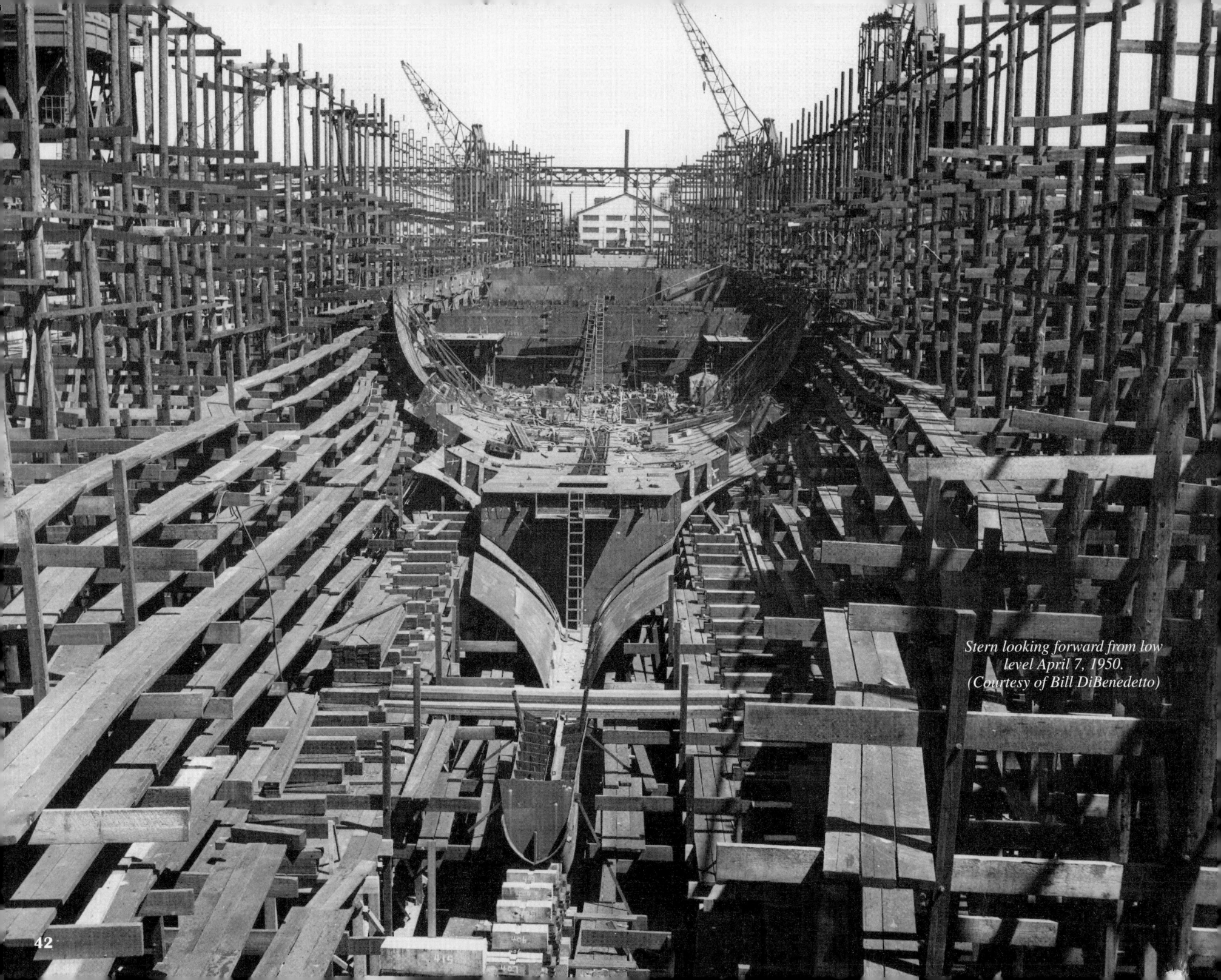

Chiefs of Staff,' according to the announcement by the Maritime Administration of the Department of Commerce. Vice-Admiral E.L. Cochrane said the four vessels were selected for conversion into troop transports because 'the work could be done on them with the greatest economy by initiating it early.'"

Walter groaned and put another sheet of paper in his typewriter.

"The superliner, tentatively named the *United States,* is about 32% completed in a huge drydock in the yards of Newport News." He read and reread the *Associated Press* story by Charles Molony from Washington. The *United States* "will get a new name for military usage. It will carry 12,000 troops. The three 'President' liners will also be renamed. They will each carry from 2,500 to 3,000." He finished his story.

The *Quincy* (Mass.) *Patriot Ledger* ran a lengthy editorial September 21 hailing the wisdom of the government for building the superliner and praising the Maritime Administration for the suggestion that more high speed ships be constructed capable of conversion to troopship use. Another response to the order to complete the new superliner as a troopship came from the pen of George Horne of the *Times*. He was unable to talk directly to William Francis Gibbs about "the taking of his prize ship by military authorities," but did find someone in the firm who said that Mr. Gibbs' attitude could be summarized in half a dozen words: "That's what she was built for."

But to those on the inside, things were different. The Navy's decision to take the ship as a troopship had sent shock waves through all those working on the superliner. The Urquhart-Marckwald team came to a dead halt. Then they were called down for a conference with Frederic Gibbs. He calmly reassured them: "This will not happen." He added that the pause would be most useful to everyone, for they could spend the time doing catch-up work with all loose ends.

A critical Senate report came out in late September. Subsidies for the construction of future superliners should be determined by direct action of the Congress, the 400-page report stated. It advised against any such future construction without the advance approval by Congress, and supported the highly critical House Expenditures Committee report. But both reports were academic because of the order to finish the liner as a troopship. The sting of their negative criticism was no longer newsworthy because of the ship's changed status.

On September 29, Walter Hamshar of the *Herald Tribune* reported that the completion of the superliner as a transport would probably mean a reduction of "several million dollars from her estimated construction cost of $70,300,000, but the saving will not benefit taxpayers." He pointed out that the "abrupt order last month to complete the big ship as a naval auxiliary will cost the taxpayers much more than they would have contributed in the form of construction subsidies. This is because the government will now have to pay the entire building cost, whereas the U.S. Lines would have made substantial contributions if the vessel had been completed as a merchant ship." He added that the order was considered a severe blow to the nation's merchant marine. "It has cut short a liner building program and left the shipping industry in confusion on whether to go ahead in planning new ships." The article went on to detail the many changes in the interior that the completion of the vessel as a troopship would mean.

Forty-seven days after the order was given to complete the new superliner as a troopship, it was rescinded. Secretary of Defense George Marshall on November 1 informed Admiral Cochrane that the Joint Chiefs of Staff had "reconsidered their previous recommendation and now recommend that the ship be completed as a commercial passenger liner." In reporting the happening the *United Press* credited the "swift improvement of the Korean situation," as the cause of the change of heart. Apparently Admiral Cochrane had aggressively led the effort in Washington for the change. This was hinted at in General Marshall's letter making known the decision of November 1 The General concluded: "We are grateful for your wholehearted cooperation in this matter and wish to assure you that we shall endeavor to keep our requests as modest and reasonable as the international situation will permit." The three American President Line ships were not returned, however, and were to continue with long careers as transports. They were renamed, the *Jackson* becoming the *Barrett;* the *Adams* being renamed the *Geiger,* and the *Hayes* becoming the *Upshur.* The last mentioned was renamed *State of Maine* in 1973 as the Maine Maritime Academy schoolship.

In the *Herald Tribune's* city room, ship-news editor Walter Hamshar was so excited at the good news that he

Welding the keel February 8, 1950. (Courtesy of Bill DiBenedetto)

couldn't get started with his lead story for the next day's paper. He wrote and tore out of his typewriter five different opening paragraphs before he finally was satisfied with the sixth. I gathered up all five rejects and saved them along with the copy sent to the desk by the *Associated Press* and the *United Press*. Mr. Hamshar noted in his story that "the reversal will not affect work on the liner which is a third completed." Work had progressed steadily, he said, under original plans "because the vessel had not reached the stage where drastic alterations in design were necessary." The *Tribune* story also noted that while the original order got wide publicity, the reversal order was announced in Washington late in the afternoon after "the attempted assassination of President Truman made it unlikely that it would receive much attention in the press and radio." It was further pointed out that using the superliner as a trooper in the Far East would be costly, dangerous, and inefficient since she would be too large to go into most ports and would have to debark the troops and transfer them to smaller ships. General Franklin, reached in his hotel in Washington, said: "We're delighted to have our vessel back."

Meanwhile the new U.S. Lines superliner continued to rise on her graving dock. The point in time is remembered particularly by Anne Urquhart. She was with a party being given a chance to walk around the hull. J.A. Christofferson, of Gibbs & Cox, was conducting the tour. When they came to the bow, she paused for a moment and put her hand on the cold steel stem. It sent a shiver through her.

On January 15, 1954 William Kaiser, famed veteran of the *Leviathan* and life-long friend of William Francis Gibbs, was assigned to the shipyard to familiarize himself with the machinery plant of the superliner. He was sent by U.S. Lines "as an observer."

On January 19 the subject of what the ship's name was to look like on the finished bows of the ship and on the nameboard atop the pilot house came up for review. Apparently there was no question at this point that the name would be *United States*. For the next three months this matter would require the attention of a number of people for, to the Gibbs brothers, such a matter was a most important detail. William Francis asked that a survey be made and pictures taken of the way the name appeared on the *Queen Mary*, the *Liberté* and the *America*. It was found that the Cunarder had letters on her bow that were 30" high and 24" wide. They were made of mild steel. The *Liberté*, formerly the *Europa*, had bronze letters 36" high and 27" wide. The *America's* name was painted on in letters 27" high and 24" wide within a welded-bead outline. With the *Queen Mary* the letters were welded on. The *Liberté* name was riveted on. Stanley Rosenfeld was employed to make photos of all these names and of the nameboards as well. Eleven pages of single-spaced typing were devoted in the record book to this subject, replete with designs, tables, and the like. In due course it was decided that the nameboard was to be 11 1/2 feet long and 1' 5" high, to be made of 3/16th mild steel plate, with the "inconel letters" 10 x 1/8th of an inch thick welded on. The memo's final page noted that approval was given to buy the bow and stern letters for $3,285. They would weigh 485 pounds. Approval was given by Capt. Jones F. Devlin, operations manager for U.S. Lines. However something must have happened to this plan for in due course the name was painted on the bows and the stern in large white letters.

Admiral Cochrane and William Francis Gibbs held a press conference on February 13 and released a number of photographs of the new ship under construction and a few new facts. The hull was finished and workmen were erecting the superstructure up to the Sun and Sports decks. The two "towering funnels will be emplaced before the launching," which was to be sometime in the summer. No date was given. Construction was well ahead of schedule, but Mr. Gibbs bemoaned the delay caused by the brief troopship inter-

Starboard side looking forward August 9, 1951. (Courtesy of Bill DiBenedetto)

*Aft from high level looking forward
October 5, 1951.
(Courtesy of Bill DiBenedetto)*

ruption. The boilers were installed, the shafting was in place, and many of the auxiliary power units were fitted. "It is an amazing progress in one year," Mr. Gibbs said. "I have never known a ship of such dimensions to go so well, and we are very pleased." Mr. Gibbs said that 2,500 men were employed at the yard on the construction work, adding that many others around the country were prefabricating interior work and equipment. He noted that many details of the ship "never will be made public because she is one of the Navy's principal auxiliaries."

Despite the restrictions on publicity Walter Jones and the U.S. Lines public relations staff began to gather information and work up stories about the superliner. A 26-page memo for Mr. Jones was prepared March 8, 1951, about the new vessel. Several new points were brought out. A few of them follow: The Newport News yard was the largest in America, covering an area of 225 acres. A model of the new ship's bow with the three anchors she would have in place was built and tested in New York. It was used to discover the exact angle and shape that the three hawse pipes should be. Most ships have only two anchors, one on either side of the bow, but some of the very largest like the *Leviathan, Normandie,* and *Queen Elizabeth* had a third at the very stem, in case of emergency. The new superliner would have one there also. Samples of all types of paint were tested for their fire-retardant qualities. Wind tunnel tests were made with smoke piped into the stacks of a model of the superliner to observe the exit velocity to make sure that no smoke would drop on the after decks. The stacks would have the same sampan-like wings as the *America* for this same purpose. Full-size sample staterooms for each of the three classes were built to check not only construction details but the color of furniture and interior decorations. The ship's hull consisted of 152,000 individual steel plates. The steel used in the superliner was pickled to remove the mill scale and to provide a good bond for the priming coat of paint. The largest single "weldment" for the ship was the stern frame. A specially fitted car was required to move it from the stress-relieving oven to the pier where it was loaded on a barge for transport to the shipway. The new liner was the first ever built in America with high tensile steel used extensively for shell plating. The eight boilers were the largest marine boilers ever built in the United States.

The swimming pool was in reality a 28-foot long box, 20 feet wide and 8 feet deep. Built of monel clad steel it was lighter and less susceptible to damage than an ordinary tiled pool. Above the promenade deck the majority of the structure was aluminum riveted to the steel transverse structural members of the superstructure.

The new ship would use Pier 86, on the Hudson River, as her New York terminal, the same pier that had been used for so many years by the *Leviathan*. A $1,400,000 renovation was begun on this 1,000-foot structure by New York City's Department of Marine and Aviation to get it ready for the maiden arrival of the new liner in mid-1952.

The Gibbs memo book contained a brief and revealing memo dated March 26, 1951, as to the ship's gross tonnage. Matthew Forrest reported to William Francis that the ship would measure 39,900 gross tons under American rules and 51,500 under British rules!

On April 4, another long memo on facts about the ship was prepared. It was worked up by Mr. Jones after a visit to see the ship. Some of the new facts he uncovered were: The drydock in which the ship was being built was 35 feet deep and the keel was laid on blocks five feet high from the dock's floor. The propeller shafts were hollow, which would lessen their weight but they would be just as strong as solid shafts because the outside diameter was increased. The ship would be the first ever to have a flake ice-making machine that could turn out seven tons of ice a day for chilling foods.

I telephoned U.S. Lines on April 18 and learned that the date had been set for the launching. It would be Saturday, June 23. I was asked not to use this information as it was scheduled to be released to the press on Monday, April 30.

On many different fronts things were happening involving the new ship. A memo dated April 25 listed the owner-furnished supplies for the *United States,* and the name was now being used regularly by everyone. Put out by V.C. Short, the general purchasing agent, it showed that a mammoth job of furnishing was in store for the company. A few sample items that the U.S. Lines was being asked to provide were as follows: 2,200 white and blue aprons, 900 cook caps, 600 cook neckerchiefs, 3,000 laundry bags, 7,000 bedspreads for passengers and 3,600 for crew members, 2,200 crew blankets, 4,800 passen-

Bow looking aft from high level April 4, 1952. (Courtesy of Bill DiBenedetto)

ger blankets and 1,500 steamer rugs, 125,000 pieces of chinaware and 6,000 of crockery, 15,000 waiters coats of various types, 57,000 pieces of glassware, 9,300 bath mats, 10,000 coat hangers, 170,380 napkins, 6,000 pillows, 44,000 pillow slips, 44,000 bed sheets, 29,000 table cloths, 65,024 bath towels, 81,024 face towels, 5 service wagons and 7 caskets for the hospital.

The building of the *United States* drew on suppliers in every state of the Union. A list of principal vendors was issued May 4 and ran single-spaced for six pages. A John Masefield might have been inspired to turn the list into poetry. There were structural steel plates and shapes, forgings, hot rolled steel, steel hex nuts, and steel heads from the Bethlehem Steel Company. And brass flat bars, brass tubing from the Chase Brass & Copper Company. And from Johns-Manville Sales Corp. came rubber gaskets, marinite panels, magnesia block insulation, asbestos packing, marine furring, magnesia pipe coverings, copper-asbestos gaskets, and mineral wool insulation. The Formica Company provided plastic tubing, sheets, and angles. Otis provided electric elevators. More copper-nickel alloy tubes and sheets came from the Revere Copper & Brass Company, founded by Paul Revere. And so on down to Westinghouse Electric Corp., which provided the main propulsion machinery, turbines, heaters, fans, forced draft blowers, and instruments.

There were other lists. Four of them were collector's items. They were timetables for the construction of the *United States*, the *Queen Mary*, the *Queen Elizabeth*, and the *Caronia*. These were prepared by Allan Philips from the personal scrap books of William Francis Gibbs. They were prepared so that interesting comparisons could be drawn with the new U.S. Lines ship. The *Caronia*, while of only 34,000 gross tons, had been used as a model for cost comparisons to enable the Maritime Commission to establish the construction subsidy.

A three-way press release from U.S. Lines, the Maritime Administration, and Newport News issued May 9 announced that the launching would take place on June 23. Although it was nowhere stated in so many words, the name of the new ship was now certain – she was the *United States*. One striking change was made, also with no spotlighting announcement. The new ship would have an overall length of 990 feet, not 980 as previously stated. She would be only 28 feet shorter than the 81,000 ton *Queen Mary*. Her gross was now listed as to be 51,500 tons. The *America,* which was mentioned in the announcement, was shown as being of 33,532 tons. Virtually no details of the launching were announced except that there would be a ceremony and that the waters of the James River would be let into the drydock to float the new vessel.

On May 15, 1951, Frank Reil, of the American Merchant Marine Institute, wrote to famed *International News Service* columnist Bob Considine reminding him that May 22 was coming, that it was National Maritime Day, and that this year with the launching of the *United States* the merchant marine finally had something to be really proud about. He noted some details of the original steamship *Savannah,* whose voyage in 1819 began on May 22 and in whose honor National Maritime Day was created. A few days later Mr. Considine devoted an entire column to the little 300-ton *Savannah* and her historic voyage and led off with a few paragraphs about the new superliner, her importance, and her upcoming launching. The country was beginning to awaken to the fact that things were happening on the maritime front.

Frank Reil also knew Bob Ripley, whose famous "Believe It or Not" cartoon series was known and read by millions. He asked Walter Jones for some interesting facts about the number of blueprints needed to create the *United States.* Walter replied in a letter on May 21 noting that Robert B. Hopkins had told him that up to the time of the launching the shipyard would have made 8,400 different working drawings with a total of 1,200,000 blueprints being made from these drawings. If put end to end these prints would stretch 510,000 miles. He suggested also that Frank Reil try to get the same kind of material from Gibbs & Cox and then expand both figures with estimates of the total number of blueprints to be necessary up through the completion of the ship. It could be, he added, the basis "for a terrific story on paper to say nothing of ink." Many minds were now working to insure that the public became aware of the new superliner.

May 22, National Maritime Day, came and there were celebrations in many port cities. Photographs of the forward stack of the *United States* were released and sent around to hundreds of leading newspapers throughout the country, Many used one illustrating how huge the stack was. The photo showed the stack on a shipyard pier with 10 automobiles parked face out from its forward end to its after edge – a distance of 68 feet. Comparisons like this had been used for decades and were familiar to ship lovers since 1906 when a Cunard Line publicity photo was taken showing a procession of cars, two abreast, being driven through the four smokestacks of the new *Mauretania* laid end to end on a pier next to her rising hull in Wallsend-on-Tyne. The shipyard did some research on the size of the stacks and pronounced that they were the largest ever built for any ship. Certainly they were the longest, fore to aft, and they were probably the highest on any ship at that time. However, they were not the tallest of all time, as that honor probably should be given to the *Imperator* as first built. Her three towering yellow-buff stacks rose to a height of 69 feet and were 29 feet fore and aft and 18 feet wide. After her maiden voyage, when she showed definite signs of being top heavy, about 10 feet was cut off each stack, but they still would have been higher than the 55 feet of the forward stack on the *United States*. But the massiveness of the stacks on the new American liner were not so much in their height but in their length. As was noted above, the forward stack was 68 feet bow to stern and the after stack was 64 feet lengthwise. The largest stack on a modern liner before the *United States* was that of the *Caronia,* which was 46 feet high, 53 feet long, and 26 feet wide. As originally built in 1939 the French South American liner *Pasteur*'s huge single stack may have exceeded these dimensions, certainly in height, but her stack's particulars were not available at this writing. She carried a smaller stack as the North German *Lloyd Bremen,* a name she acquired after the war. The *Herald Tribune* on that Maritime Day showed the forward funnel of the new ship being placed in position. It was colored a light green at this point and when it went into place there was a cheer heard for miles around. The *Times* Maritime Day story threw in a few new facts about the ship's gross tonnage. It was given as 51,000 tons and that figure was said to be the British measurement "which includes some passenger spaces not counted in this country."

More details about the new ship's lifeboats came out on May 31 when the Coast Guard began testing them at Perth Amboy, New Jersey. The craft were made entirely of aluminum, with no wood or other combustible material in them. Their thwarts, hand-propelling levers, tillers, and rudders were all made of metal. There was so much interest in this event that even the *Associated Press* sent a writer down to watch the tests.

The launching, trial trip, and delivery voyage and the maiden voyage of the *United States* were heralded with one of the finest publicity efforts ever mounted in the history of American shipping. It did not just happen. There were four different publicity groups all working toward the same goal. Gibbs & Cox had Arthur Colton and Allan Philips. Within the strict limitations of their positions they did their best to provide accurate and interesting information. Newport News had a good staff headed by Robert B. Hopkins. The Maritime Administration had their able and experienced Stephen C. Manning in Washington and "Gus" Gill in New York. But the real team push came from U.S. Lines with Walter Jones at the helm. His staff included the charming veteran of three decades with the company, Miss Carla Dietz, and her assistant Constance Barnard. There were also Jim McDonald and Frank Reil, not to mention a most able photographer named Sam Shere. Walter Jones also had the professional help of two top men from the company's public relations agency – J. Walter Thompson: Gaynor Collister and Wilson Lloyd. A series of memos dated May 19-21 were put out by Walter Jones. The first was in connection with "all future news releases and photographs concerning the *United States.*" It began:

"After copy for the release or caption for photograph has been obtained, a clean copy should be sent to Mr. Lloyd who will arrange for the volume production of the release or caption as well as complete distribution to our total list of newspapers, magazines, radio and television stations, special news commentators, and newsreels. Where photographs are included, we will endeavor to supply Mr. Lloyd with three negatives of each photograph so that he might give a negative to each of the photo services with a caption. For the distribution of photographs we will have Sam Shere make as many prints as are required by Mr. Lloyd as well as additional prints for our use at 1 Broadway in making distribution to our District Offices, Europe, general agents in foreign countries, as well as our offices in the Far East. Mr. Lloyd should arrange to take care of South American coverage."

Careful instructions as to labeling envelopes containing negatives and for filing photographs were the subject of another memo. Still another suggested that for the next year all the chief public relations people should arrange to "take three or four press people to lunch aboard the *America* while she is in port each time. I would suggest that when any one of the group plans to invite some one they first talk with me so that we can avoid duplication and set up a plan that will cover all branches of the publicity field and make the maximum use of our time." Another memo instructed Sam Shere to work with Mr. Sumner Besse, of Newport News, on a story line for a moving picture on the *United States*. A good deal of footage had been taken and it had to be reviewed and given some "intelligent and interesting continuity."

As the date of the launching approached William Francis thought more and more about the tonnage situation. A memo in the record book signed by him noted on May 23, 1951, that Mr. G.F. Ravenel, U.S. Lines Vice President for Operations, had suggested that the gross be made as much as possible. Two days later William Francis replied that this would be considered by the shipyard. On May 31 he visited the shipyard and chatted with the local tonnage admeasurers, Messrs. Hogge and Wise. His memo written that evening to his brother read: "After discussions, it was agreed that the undersigned would meet with Mr. Sweet, the senior admeasurer in Washington, so that appropriate instructions could be issued with respect to measuring the subject vessel." Mr. Gibbs was taking no chances. He would see that the top man in the nation's capital knew the situation and gave the proper orders. A few days later Mr. Gibbs met with Mr. Sweet. His memo for the record book recorded the points made at the session:

"1. I went to see Mr. Sweet and he was extraordinarily pleasant.

"2. I pointed out to him in connection with the data on the *Europa* that the original figure for the *Europa* gross tonnage was 49,746, and after reconditioning by the French, the gross tonnage was stated to be 49,850, and that now I am informed that the French are claiming the tonnage to be 51,850.

"3. I pointed out that the *United States* is the third largest ship in the world and that under these circumstances the Lines and the Government, the Maritime Administration (whom we represent), feel strongly that the gross tonnage should measure more than the French claim for the *Liberté*.

"4. Mr. Sweet inquired over the telephone of various of his people whether they had any tonnage measurement yet and he was informed that they did not. He said that he was completely in sympathy with the suggestion that he would be very glad to communicate with Mr. Watts, at Newport News, and issue the necessary instructions to him to measure the ship so that the gross tonnage will be as great as possible, in consultation with Newport News.

"5. My meeting did not last more than 10 minutes, as no argument was required in this instance, and the course suggested was sound." Slowly but surely the gross tonnage of the *United States* would go up, but nothing like as dramatically as would that of the *Queen Elizabeth 2* a few years later. When she was first planned it was announced that she would measure 55,000 tons gross. Later her tonnage was raised to 65,863 tons, making her almost the same as the *France,* out just before her.

Every effort had been made to get Mrs. Harry S. Truman to christen the *United States*, but on June 1 she declined, saying that she would be in the East at that time. A three-color magazine type folder was put out at this time by Walter Jones. Entitled "Latest News About the Great New American-flag Superliner *United States,*" it contained pictures and stories touting the vessel and telling of the upcoming launching. It was made known that the folder would be a monthly publication of the "*United States* News Bureau."

On June 2, (they hadn't wasted any time), it was announced in Washington that Mrs. Tom Connally, wife of the well-known Texas Senator, would christen the *United States.* Asked whether it would be her first such experience, she replied: "Well, no, but the other experiences aren't to be compared with this. One was a Victory ship launching out in California, the other a Mississippi River boat christening in New Orleans." On the same day in Newport News, William Francis Gibbs and William E. Blewett, Jr., executive vice president of Newport News, took a small gathering of press around the ship for a prelaunching showing. Among those attending were George Horne of the *Times* and Walter Hamshar of the *Tribune*. It was said then that the ship was 66% finished and would be 70% complete on the day of the launching. The party saw her twin stacks in place, but they had not yet been given their red, white, and blue coat of paint. They were still green and there was considerable scaffolding around them. The hull was shiny black with its white "boot-top" and red underbody. George Horne's story carried the next day noted that "from a distance she appears to be almost finished. But inside the cavernous hull, 2,900 shipyard workers are swarming daily in three shifts. The deafening clangor of rivets and powered machines keeps the mass of steel, aluminum, and other metals vibrating." The inspection party began their tour at the bottom of the graving dock under the sharp stem: "This bow section appears to be as thin as a knife blade, and in fact can just be spanned at the center by a human hand. From the stem the hull flares back and out in graceful lines into the broad midsection. The visitors crawled the entire length of the ship. About a third of the way back, in the bottom plates, was a large barred opening through which the ship will scoop sea water for the condensers and her fresh water plant. A little further aft was a similar opening, the exit for exhaust water to return to the sea. On either side, sticking out laterally, were the fin-like bilge keels. Back aft the party could see the weird conformations of the hull where it flared to house the propeller shafts, and beyond these were the massive propellers – 'wheels' to the professional shipyard man. The design and weight of these huge blades are among the many secret factors that the builders and the Navy have placed under security 'wraps.'"

Walter Hamshar noticed and reported in his story that the name *United States* had been painted in white letters on her bows and stern. He added: "The upper decks, where the grand ballroom, lounges, smoking room, and other public places will be located, are mere steel shells. But in the lower reaches of the vessel all is in final stages. The principal task of the next year before

Launching day for the SS United States.

the vessel goes into service will be installation of the appurtenances that will make the *United States* the world's most luxurious liner. To William Francis Gibbs, the superliner's creator, she is already a dream come true. He designed into his ship all the safety and defense attributes of a naval vessel, all the comfort of a luxury ship and all the speed of an express liner."

Harry Nash, of the *Associated Press,* was also in the same inspection party. His long story was sent over the wires for use Wednesday, June 6. It began: "Two cranes hoisted the 30-ton navigating bridge from the ground and swung it gently into place aboard the ship. With this addition the ship began to look less like a lost weekend and more like the superliner she is to become by next spring. Let's go aboard, says your escort, an official of the Newport News yard... So you go aboard. But you don't stay long, because your ears just can't take much of the deafening thunder set off by the riveters who swarm over every deck. You take a quick tour and see hundreds of men – electricians, welders, shipfitters, pipefitters, and all the other craftsmen – helping to build the biggest ship in America's history. And this is the ballroom, your escort tells above the ear-killing noise, pointing to a big, bare enclosure. But instead of strapless gowns you see three men in sweat stained overalls, each one driving rivets like mad."

I was invited to attend the launching and went, with a special U.S. Lines train providing transportation down and back. Walter Hamshar asked me to prepare a story for use the day after the launching in Sunday's *Herald Tribune*. He made a date with Theodore J. Young, partner in the firm of Eggers & Higgins, for an interview. This company, under another name, had designed both the Jefferson Memorial and the National Gallery in Washington, but doing the interior of the *United States* was even more complicated, Mr. Young said. Also interviewed was Alfred L. Congdon. "Even now," Mr. Congdon said, "we run into ducts that turn up unexpectedly to surprise us." Eggers & Higgins were responsible for the design of all interior details of passenger space such as bulkheads, ceilings, walls, and placement of lighting and windows. The *America*, also their assignment, had some wood aboard, but the *United States* would have none except in the pianos and the butcher's block. This brought up the story of the encounter that William Francis Gibbs had some time earlier with Theodore Steinway, during which confrontation the naval architect tried to persuade the piano mogul to build

49

an aluminum piano. Those who heard the battle said the language was "horrific." Swearing on proper occasions was one of Mr. Gibbs' best known traits. Another joke on William Francis was published in the *Daily Press.* "One wag has written that even the ship's orchestra leader will wield an aluminum baton, but that as yet Gibbs has devised no method of rendering the musicians themselves incombustible."

On June 11 Frank Reil sent Robert Hopkins a draft of the U.S. Lines two-page launching release, asking for his approval. The release was based on a detailed launching memo prepared by the shipyard and distributed to 27 key shipyard officials who would be directly involved, and copies sent to 32 top officers of the yard for their guidance. This memo was signed jointly by G.D. Cole, superintendent, hull outfitting division, and P.F. Halsey, superintendent, steel hull division. It detailed each step that would be taken in the 53 hours and 41 minutes before the moment of christening. The launching actually would begin at 7 a.m. on Thursday, June 21, with the removal of 14 "A" frames aft and the painting of the places on the hull that they had rested against. Step by step each crib, each shore, each link with the land would be knocked loose or taken away and the proper places on the hull smoothed and repainted. A final inspection of the bottom and the shipway was scheduled for between 2 and 4 p.m. on Friday. On the morning of the launching, things would begin to happen at 4:30 a.m. with the removal of the two last gangways at frame 160 (one on either side) and the moving of the remaining mooring lines to wall cleats. Flooding would be started at this same hour and the ship would be afloat at 5:05. At 8 a.m. the inclining tests would be started.

All this was summarized in the release written by Frank Reil and put out for Sunday, July 17. Both the *Times* and the *Tribune* had long stories. The *Tribune* carried a two-column photo showing the twin stacks painted red, white, and blue for the first time. The inclining test was described in the press release, but, after it was in the hands of the ships news reporters, it became the embarrassing duty of Walter Jones to call each of them and ask him to cross out all reference to this part of the press release. It had been censored. And everyone crossed it out. This is the paragraph that had to be deleted: "This test to determine stability is required of all new vessels by the Coast Guard and the American Bureau of Shipping. In the case of the *United States,* it consists of placing a weight of more than 50,000 pounds on one side of the ship, checking any list and then moving it to the other side for a similar study of incline. As it will be necessary to move the liner 15 feet out of its dock in order to perform the inclining test properly, the vessel will then be returned to its position for christening, forward in the dock with the bow towering over the land end directly in front of the sponsor's stand." The inclining test was a most important and highly scientific problem for Gibbs & Cox, as witness the 200 pages of graphs, charts, and studies that resulted from the two-hour effort that were later placed in the ship's record book.

The day of the launching dawned and, as fate would have it, a four column picture of the *United States* was run on the front page of the *Herald Tribune* just below a large five-column headline: "SHIP STRIKE ENDED BY MARITIME UNION." The juxtaposition of this "ship strike" headline directly above the picture of the magnificent new American superliner was pure chance, and few probably gave a second thought to it. But, in retrospect, it foretold the doom of the liner at one glance. The strike had lasted one week. "The accord was a smashing victory for the National Maritime Union," Walter Hamshar wrote. Among the reasons for the unconditional surrender by the shipowners was the maiden departure of the new liner *Constitution* that was set for June 25. As had happened so often and would continue to happen, the industry gave way on wages and benefits that would be disastrous in the long run and got in return a few short-term objectives. The conditions imposed by the unions in this and other similar contract settlements would prove the undoing of the *United States.*

The U.S. Lines outdid themselves with their launching press packet. It contained 14 separate releases describing all phases of the great day's event. One release was devoted to the "flotation" launching. Another was given over to Mrs. Connally, and listed her matrons of honor and the others to be on the launching platform. Strangely absent was William Francis Gibbs and his brother Frederic. There was no room for them, and they stood just to the right of the five-foot high platform.

Ten thousand people crowded into the shipyard to see the christening and many others saw it from the surrounding roof tops. It was hot, with a temperature near 100 degrees. The yard clinic treated 20 people for heat prostration. Senator Tom Connally hailed the peaceful nature of the liner: "The *United States is* not a mighty battlewagon like the *Missouri,* nor is it a death-dealing aircraft carrier. It is a passenger ship built for operation by a privately owned American company." Admiral Cochrane also highlighted the commercial side of the liner, adding, however: "But she will always be ready at hand like a pioneer's flintlock over the fireplace, ready for immediate use in an emergency."

The "flotation" went like clock work. There were no high winds and the 990-foot hull painted a shimmering black and crowned by its two mammoth smokestacks in their red, white, and blue dress was moved without incident out of the graving dock and around to the north side of the yard's Pier 10 bow inboard.

An editorial in the *Herald Tribune* called the *United States* a superliner "in every sense of the word, ranking with the greatest merchant ships of the world today, taking second place to none for dependability, modernity, and luxuriousness." Three days later the *Liverpool Journal of Commerce* had a two-column story about the new liner, with an air view showing tugs moving her out of the graving dock. Their headlines were:

"SEVENTY PER CENT COMPLETE
AT LAUNCH
Claimed Equal to Any Other Ship in
Speed and Safety"

In New York the *New York Journal of Commerce* also had a big spread on the superliner this same day, June 28, 1951. Written by Jacques Nevard, its headline read:

"SUPERLINER AIMS AT ATLANTIC
RECORD"

The article stressed the many untold features of the ship, saying: "There are so many secret features about the giant new liner that her designer, William Francis Gibbs, who regards the vessel as the crowning achievement of his career, finds himself in the position of an artist who has created a masterpiece and cannot talk about it."

5

An Attack from the White House

Of all the many words broadcast at the launching of the *United States,* two brief stanzas quoted from a John Masefield poem stood out. Both were part of the speech by shipyard president J.B. Woodward, Jr. Strange to say, Mr. Woodward did not mention that the poem had been written especially for the launching of another ship – the *Queen Mary!* The phrases quoted:

"...a rampart of a ship,
Long as a street and lofty as a tower,
Ready to glide in thunder from the slip,
And shear the sea with majesty of power.

"May shipwreck and collision, fog and fire,
Rock, shoal and other evils of the sea,
Be kept from you; and may the hearts desire
Of those who speed your launching come to be."

Despite the fact that the new *United States* was designed from keel to mast tip as a challenger for the *Queen Mary's* speed crown, no more fitting words could have been found by anyone to honor the occasion. And Mr. Woodward did not need to apologize for the fact that the new liner would not thunder down the ways. Her christening in a graving dock was just one more example of the depth of planning that had gone into her from the beginning.

The keen rivalry between the Cunard *Queens* and the new *United States* was the theme of an editorial in *Marine Progress* for July: "It is possible that the British have held a tight rein on their *Queen Elizabeth* – that she can outstrip the *Queen Mary,* which now holds the mythical Blue Riband of the Atlantic – but the 'Lizzie' is going to have to strain her every rivet to keep up with the sleek looking *United States.* Those in authority flatly refuse to discuss her speed beyond one of those 'more than 30 knots' answers, but they never appear to be much concerned about the possibility that she won't be the speed queen of the seas, and more than likely their faith is well merited. At any rate, another year will tell the tale."

Another editorial, widely syndicated, was carried July 15 in the *St. Louis* (Mo.) *Globe-Democrat*. It began: "The largest passenger ship ever built in this country, and one of the largest in the world, is now afloat. *Life* magazine called this new flagship of the merchant marine 'a proud present for the nation on her 175th anniversary of its independence.' This is not an exaggeration."

The *New York Times* in an article published the next day made known the embarrassing fact that the ornate Hales Trophy, emblematic of the Blue Riband of the Atlantic, was lost! It had been turned over to the French Line in May, 1935, when the *Normandie* crossed the Atlantic at an average speed of 31.37 knots on her eastbound maiden voyage. When the *Queen Mary* had beaten this record, the Cunard Line announced that it would not accept the trophy, pointing out that their new liner was not out to establish new speed records, but only interested in maintaining her schedule. The *Times* continued: "The French Line's records pertaining to the trophy were destroyed in the war. No one recalls whether the trophy was on the *Normandie* when she burned in 1942, and no trace of it was discovered during the dismantling of the 82,799 ton liner."

Another bit of information squeezed through the security curtain surrounding the new superliner in mid-July. A press release about the ship's deck chairs was issued by Johanns & Keegan, which was making them. It said virtually nothing and the *Herald Tribune* decided not to have any story after being unable to get more facts from Gibbs & Cox. The *Times* was more clever. Richard F. Shepard, one of their ship news reporters, ran a short box with the following headline: "Liner's Steamer Chairs 'Declassified' – A Little." The text began: "Security authorities cleared information yesterday about the steamer chairs that will be placed aboard the superliner *United States.* With some hedging, it was conceded that the 2,000-passenger ship would carry 'over 1,000' steamer chairs when she enters service next year. Gibbs & Cox declassified many of the details on the chairs. They will have aluminum frames, in colorful harmony with the promenade deck. Resilient webbing, which is also fire-retarding, will ease the lot of the voyagers. The angle of recline, however, was still a top-drawer secret."

The record book for July 21, 1951, disclosed some policy thinking by William Francis Gibbs. A memo for

First class lounge and tourist class theater on Promenade Deck. (Courtesy of Bill DiBenedetto)

Swimming pool area starboard looking forward. (Courtesy of Bill DiBenedetto)

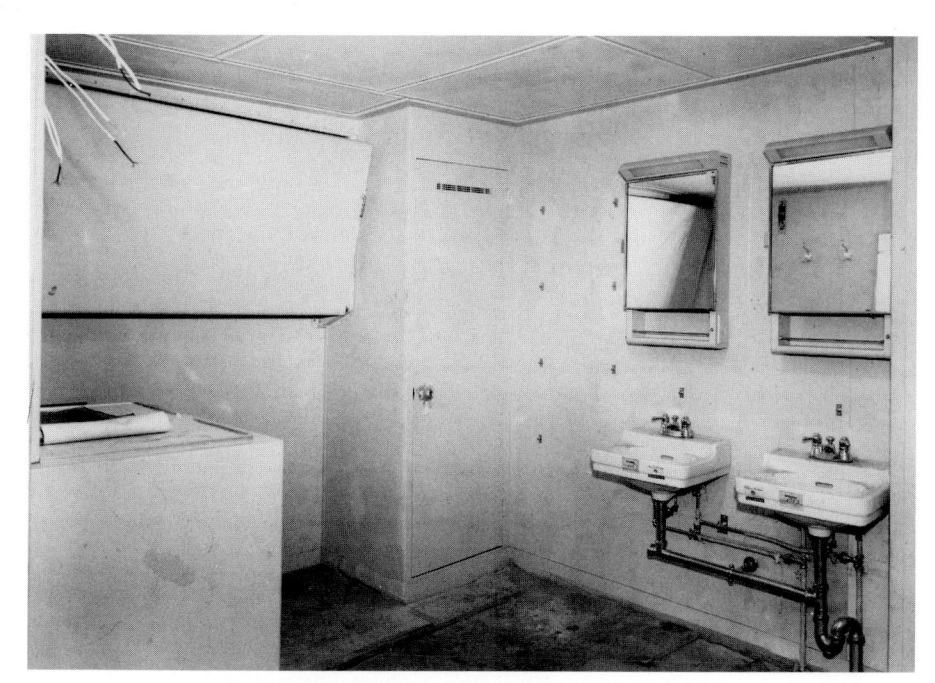

Stateroom A-24. (Courtesy of Bill DiBenedetto)

Ballroom on Promenade Deck. (Courtesy of Bill DiBenedetto)

that date described a meeting attended by the Gibbs brothers, Commodore Harry Manning, William Rand, John Brennan, and Newbold Lawrence. Mr. Rand was a rising star in the U.S. Lines, having married General Franklin's daughter. The meeting was held in Captain Manning's cabin aboard the *America*. Its purpose was to review the routes and schedules of the *United States*, but it turned to the subject on everyone's mind—breaking the speed record. William Francis warned against operating the ship at high speeds for the first few voyages. He said in the memo that all were in agreement. He went on: "I warned them that in my opinion no attempt to operate at high speed should be made until they had several crossings at midspeed and the crew had been thoroughly broken in." And then on the subject of the record, Mr. Gibbs told U.S. Lines vice president Brennan that "under no circumstances should they beat the record by very much." He added: "I said they could beat it by a reasonable amount, or make the average 32 knots but that they should under no circumstances indicate to the British by performance what the ship's power is." He told them that Cunard Line was designing another ship and to hold back until she came out and then beat her. Mr. Brennan said the *United States* could make a new record by a few minutes each year and continue to get good publicity. The memo indicated that an intense study and documentation of the voyages of the *Queen Mary* and the *Queen Elizabeth* was underway.

A new and highly automatic system of steering was being designed for the *United States*, it was reported by the Sperry Gyroscope Co. on August 2, 1951. With the addition of something called "electronic rate control" the new system "can direct a vessel automatically to its proper heading from a small to large course rapidly, positively and with no overshoot. The new device takes care of such variables as speed, ship's turning momentum, wind and sea conditions, and calls for just the right amount of rudder."

Intense interest in Europe in the speed of the *United States* was reported by David P. Brown, vice president of the American Bureau of Shipping, when he returned from a tour of foreign shipyards early in August. The wide publicity received by the new ship had created much curiosity among shipping men, he said. There is considerable "coffee shop talk in England of building a new superliner to compete with the *United States* should the latter wrest the Blue Riband from the *Queen Mary*." Mr. Brown emphasized that such talk was mostly of the rumor variety, but that it was indicative of future events. He said a new British superliner "would be built along the lines of the *United States* with emphasis on speed and power in the engine room." He added that he found "no ambitions to build a 'national pride' ship in France, Italy, and Germany." He noted that the once great Blohm & Voss yards in Hamburg "stand unused since World War II."

The rivalry between the ship news staffs of the *Times* and the *Herald Tribune* was keen, and my personal satisfaction can be imagined when I discovered the whereabouts of the Hales Trophy. The earlier *Times* story about it being missing had sent me to digging. On August 12, I had a by-line story with this headline: "Atlantic Speed Trophy Found After 10 Years – The Hales Cup Located at Silversmith's." All sorts of quaint facts about the late Harold Keates Hales, one-time member of Parliament who had created the trophy, were also discovered. His chief boast in life was that he was the only driver who had never once blown his automobile's horn. As a Conservative member he was remembered for the occasion when he had interrupted a debate on herring in the House of Commons by pulling a dead herring out of a bag and waving it at his opponents. He was also known for having flown an airship around St. Paul's Cathedral in 1908, and as a survivor of one of the first airplane crashes in 1910. His trophy was designed for the Cunarder *Queen Mary*, and he was crestfallen when the line had refused to accept it. When he first had it made he had intended to give it to the Italian Line's *Rex* for her recordbreaking crossing from Genoa to New York. The *Normandie* broke the Italian ship's record before he had the chance to have a presentation to the *Rex*, so he changed the rules to permit each holder to have the trophy for a minimum of three months. This made it possible for him to have two gala presentations, one in Genoa and one in New York. Such events were much to his liking and he generally began his "few words" with: "The Haleses never amounted to much before, but now. . . ."

The search for the ornate trophy had begun after a British newspaper report had surmised that it had burned with the *Normandie*. This alerted both the U.S. Lines and French Line to the fact that it was missing. A company known as Facts, Inc., was hired to search it out. A French Line representative in England remembered that it had been sent to London when the *Queen Mary* broke the *Normandie's* record. Since Cunard refused to accept it, it was returned to its donor. He gave it back to the silversmith who had made it, and they were in possession of it in August, 1951, when my story appeared. The trophy consists of a globe resting on a winged figure of Victory, in turn standing on a base of yellow onyx. Around the middle is an enameled blue ribbon. Festooned with models of old galleons, modern vessels, and statues of Neptune and Amphitrite, it is topped with a figure depicting Speed with a three-stacked liner in her hand. Speed is lunging forward pushing out of her way a figure called Force of the Atlantic. At this writing the trophy is in the American Merchant Marine Museum at the U.S. Merchant Marine Academy, Kings Point, New York.

The speed record talk continued on all fronts. Britain's maritime magazine *Shipbuilding and Shipping Record* for September 6 devoted an entire column to the "Anglo-American competition" for the Blue Riband. Their feature began: "The interest which the American people are taking in the new *United States*, and their hope that she will rival the *Queen's* in the matter of speed, is a reminder of the keen competition between the Collins and the Cunard lines a century ago." The article highlighted the high financial cost and great operating losses of the Collins Line in their review of how for a brief period American steamships had wrested the speed supremacy from Great Britain back in 1852.

An extensive crew training program for the new superliner was reviewed by William Francis Gibbs on September 8, 1951, at a meeting with Captain Devlin and Admiral Lee. Chief Engineer Bill Kaiser was said to have expressed an eagerness to attend the planned training sessions for engineering officers. A series of publications was projected. The course of lectures was to run from February 7 to May 6. Special emphasis was to be put on damage control, fire fighting, machinery, air conditioning, electrical systems, and deck safety.

The question of a high gross tonnage came up again in the memo book. A memo dated October 8, 1951, from William Francis to John Brennan included the following new information. Mr. Brennan was worried that a high gross would cost U.S. Lines money in greater port taxes, to which William Francis replied: "You could not eat your cake and have it, but if you wanted the maximum gross tonnage, you had to be prepared to take any disadvantages that came from it, but such disadvantages are entirely minor in a big ship running the trans-Atlantic." Talks with Mr. Christoffersen at the shipyard showed that by installation of a manhole of the requisite size the cubic measurement of the forepeak could be included in the ship's gross tonnage. Mr. Christoffersen noted that he had taken up the matter with the yard. Six months of such study and effort would eventually produce a gross tonnage of over 53,000 tons for the new ship.

The first travel page advertisement for the *United States* appeared on October 9, 1954 in many newspapers. It featured the *America* and her six sailings. At the bottom, however, separated by a line of stars was a small artist's conception of the original *United States* model. It showed a mainmast, which would never be on the real ship, and it did not show the stem anchor. The stacks were slightly smaller than the real thing. The text was brief: "In the summer of 1952 – joining the *America* in trans- Atlantic service ... the greatest passenger liner ever to fly the Stars and Stripes ... the superb new *United States*."

The last stretch had begun for those deeply involved with the building and decorating of the new liner. Two stories from the memory bank of Anne Urquhart came from this period. Finding the artists to do the decorative work on the ship was one of her assignments. On one occasion she was shocked when it developed that one of her choices was not a citizen. Mr. Gibbs called her in and explained the seriousness of the situation. How the Federal Government was paying so much in construction and operating subsidies, how only American artists should be used, and how this was clearly stated in the contract. There were some bad hours for her over this. In the end the artist's contract was bought back and another was found to do the small carved glass panels in the sitting room of one of the suites.

One of the most striking rooms on the *United States* would be the forward "Observation Lounge" for First Class. Its basic color scheme was a remarkably exciting combination of greens and blues. While the bulkhead decorations for this room were being worked out, Rachel Carson's book *The Sea Around Us* was a best seller. It was only natural that someone would propose two major mural decorations about the Atlantic Ocean. One would have the currents and the Gulf Stream. The other would be of the underwater topography. They would be done on large floor-to ceiling concave bulkheads as three-dimensional maps. They had to be made in panels, because of their size. The one of the undersea topography actually had a small door in it that led into the Tourist Class cinema. The artist Ray Wendell was selected to make these paintings. He was a youngish man, very talented, and he lived with his mother in Flushing. Their apartment was not large. When he was hired, William Francis Gibbs had given him some highly secret Navy charts of the Atlantic as a guide. Gibbs had stressed how secret they were and how vital it was that no one, positively no one, else see them. The work on the murals progressed and finally, when it was half done, Ray asked for his 50% payment. Anne Urquhart and Dorothy Marckwald had to go out to see the work to verify that it was, in fact, half finished. They told William Francis they were going, and, to their surprise, he said he would like to go, too. That meant that Frederic would also go and at least one other from the company. So on the appointed day a huge black limousine made its way from 21 West Street out into the narrow streets of Queens. The artist's mother, overwhelmed by the presence of such a distinguished party, hurried around and seated everyone and then made tea. William Francis was at his most charming best. The marine artist brought out one panel after another. He had no table large enough to show them off on so he had to lay them out on the floor. Storage was a tough problem in the small apartment. He had the panels stacked under his bed. Fortunately for all hands, Mr. Gibbs liked the work and said so. Then he paused and asked if Ray had taken good care of the secret charts. Ray was quick to answer and most emphatic: "Oh, yes," he almost shouted, "and I keep them under my mattress."

The spirit and never ending drive of William Francis Gibbs was all pervasive. Not only did his enthusiasm and zeal provide inspiration for all those in highly responsible places in Gibbs & Cox, but his passionate zealotry stretched out to everyone he met and to every occasion. He made a life-long custom of attending as many weddings of company workers, or anniversary parties or retirement banquets as he possibly could. He would always have the same toast: "All you want, doubled, and the big ship!"

On November 3, 1951, "the big ship" was 85% completed. She looked virtually ready to sail from the outside, but inside 2,500 men still labored to complete her public rooms and cabins. Steam heat was piped aboard from the ship yard's plant to keep them warm and to expedite the drying of the thousands of gallons of fire-retardant paint that was being used. The delivery date was still scheduled for the summer of 1952. It was said that if sufficient metals for all her fire-resisting furniture were "immediately available," she could be delivered even sooner. A U.S. Lines press release described what was going on aboard her: "Bulkheads, electrical equipment, complex systems of piping and ducts for fresh water, salt water, steam, and ventilation are going into place. Prefabricated shower enclosures, for quick and easy installation, are going into passenger spaces. Galley equipment, which includes cooking ranges operated on radar principles, ovens, peelers, shredders, griddles, batch mixers, and dish washing machines, is being snugged into place. Great care had been taken to avoid waste action. For instance, the marble counter on which pastry is prepared is actually the top of a refrigerator where the special pastry dough will be kept. Constant cool temperature is especially desired in the handling of this kind of dough."

On Monday, January 7, 1952, it became known that the *United States* would sail on her maiden voyage on July 3, a Thursday, at noon. Her sea trials would take place in May, and she would be delivered to U.S. Lines in June. She was scheduled to make 12 sailings from New York over the remainder of the year. *Sailing Schedule No. 1* showed her route. She would stop first at LeHavre, arriving there on the morning of July 8 on her first crossing, then steam on to Southampton that same day. Her maiden westbound trip would begin July 10 with her return to New York scheduled for July 15, a Tuesday. The schedule listed her gross tonnage as 52,000 and showed the *America* as 33,532 gross tons. Minimum rates for the new liner for the summer season were listed in the No. 1 rate schedule as being $360 in First Class,

$230 in Cabin and $170 in Tourist. The top rate for suites on the Upper Deck was $930. The U.S. Lines had hoped to give special names to these suites, which included a bed room, a sitting room, a trunk room, tub bath, two showers, and two toilets, but the idea had been vetoed and they were known simply as U-87-89, 90-92. The old liner *Washington* was not on the sailing schedule, having been retired.

Three "preliminary deck plans" were issued by U.S. Lines in January, one for each class. All showed artists' conceptions instead of photographs of the public rooms, cabins, and deck scenes. All were printed in Navy blue. They folded out to a maximum width of 48 inches. The top or Sports Deck plan showed 11 single cabins, identified by letters from A to L, the children's playroom and two game decks--one aft and the other between the funnels. Later the deck between the funnels would be given to Tourist Class. Next came the Sun Deck, devoted entirely to First Class staterooms and an open promenade under the lifeboats. The promenade went completely around the superstructure. Below the Sun Deck was the Promenade Deck – entirely devoted to First Class public rooms, except for the Tourist Class Cinema and Lounge far forward. The Observation Lounge came first, with a small writing room and library fitted into port and starboard of its most forward portions. Then the Main Foyer with the top of the main staircase and two elevators right in the center. Next the Ballroom, arranged to give the appearance of being circular. Abaft that came the bar, athwartships. Then, on the port side, there was a small and exclusive Restaurant, while on the starboard the deck plan showed a "Cocktail Lounge." This later would be known as the Navajo Room because of the beautiful copies of sandpaintings done in vitreous enamel on copper by Peter Ostuni. Abaft these two little rooms was another foyer, with another pair of elevators and a second stairway. Then came the Smoking Room, two shops, and finally the Theatre. There was plenty of luxury here, certainly far from a troopship! Two more decks were devoted to First Class cabins, the Upper and Main Deck. The main Dining Saloon, which with the Theatre and the Swimming Pool were the only two- deck high rooms on the ship, was on A Deck. The Gymnasium was on B Deck and the Pool on C Deck.

The folder was far from modest: "Never before has so much ingenuity and skill ... all in the highest American tradition ... gone into the construction of a passenger vessel. The staterooms are particularly noteworthy. They are extraordinarily large and have been designed in collaboration with a famous firm of women decorators. And so, women especially will appreciate the extra closet and drawer space, the downy beds, comfortable chairs, full length mirrors, dressing tables, chests of drawers and other furnishings. Colors, fabrics and fittings blend in delightfully."

Cabin Class used areas on six different decks, sharing the Theatre and the Swimming Pool with First Class. Their deck space was the after end of the Promenade Deck, the Upper and the Main Deck. A good-sized Lounge, a Children's Play Room and a combined Library-Writing Room were on the Upper Deck. A Smoking Room was on the Main Deck, along with spaces for hairdressers and manicurists. One elevator for Cabin Class linked these decks. Cabin Class staterooms were aft on Main, A, B, and C Decks. The Dining Saloon for Cabin was on A Deck, just abaft the First Class Saloon. All Cabin Class staterooms had showers and toilets.

Tourist Class accommodations were forward and were spread over eight decks. There was an open promenade area on either side of the forward stack on the Bridge Deck, and more deck space on the Promenade Deck forward of the superstructure. A Tourist Lounge occupied the extreme forward end of the Promenade Deck and gave access to the Tourist Theatre. Two stairways and two elevators served this class. Other public rooms included a children's playroom on the Upper Deck, a Smoking Room/Bar just below it on the Main Deck, and the Dining Saloon, divided into two parts by a bulkhead, on A Deck. Most cabins had upper and lower berths and there was none with private showers and toilets. Showers, baths, and toilet facilities were located in the center of the ship. There were no portholes on C and D Decks, the deck plan noted, "but all staterooms on these decks are provided with the same ultramodern air-conditioning ventilation as all other staterooms throughout the ship."

The *America* and the *United States* were side by side again at Newport News over New Year's. The smaller vessel needed repairs to her boilers and machinery. She sailed January 15, and many pictures of the two sea queens, each with their twin red, white, and blue stacks, were taken. The next day reporters from many of the leading wire services and newspapers of the country were given a tour of all 12 decks of the new superliner. Yard Executive Vice President Blewett explained that the work force completing last minute details was the highest it had ever been, about 3,100 men. He said that there would be two trials in May, the first the regular builder's sea trials and the second a special trial to test power and speed. He described the ship as a "joint venture of the steamship line and the Maritime Administration," adding that the Navy "is exercising broad powers because of the ship's value as a naval auxiliary." This concept of a "joint venture" was a device to explain the very large subsidy needed to build the superliner. As events would soon show it should have been stressed much more than it was as a defense against those who were attacking the size of the government aid required.

Reporters were told that the ship's boilers were given their first firing earlier in the week allowing residents of the James River area to see for the first time smoke pouring from the two massive stacks "which dominate the waterfront rising 175 feet above the keel." The fact that the ship had two engine rooms, widely separated, was explained. This almost doubled the ship's ability to retain power even though torpedoed and one engineroom put out of service. It was a most costly feature. Similar double engine rooms had destroyed the peacetime value of the government's large fleet of 20-knot, 600-foot transports built during World War II. Many had thought that the P2 troopship would be useful after the war just as the 535-foot transports built for the first great war did become the backbone of America's liner fleet in the inter-war period. A ship with two engine rooms, however, required nearly double the normal engineering staff, and at the same time had just so much less earning capacity.

Some of the ship's Tourist Class staterooms were complete even to their wall-to-wall carpeting "which is covered with protective canvas." As each room is finished, the reporters were told, "it is locked and checked off the work lists." The crew quarters were described as "the finest on any ship." Mr. Blewett was candid about the problems: "We are coming now to the frill and gingerbread phases, and this brings headaches. Architectural doors, fixtures, furniture, illuminated signs, bars, and decorations will be going in."

A major new point brought out in the interview was the increase in cost. The price was no longer $70,000,000. It was reported that the final cost "will exceed this sum considerably, some of the estimates going as high as $78,000,000." Escalator clauses in the contract covered price fluctuations and rising costs of labor. No one asked and no opinions were ventured as to who would pay the extra $8,000,000.

An editorial syndicated throughout the nation resulted from this press preview. It did not mention the controversial cost development but concentrated on the innovative use of light metals. Its concluding paragraph read: "The vessel represents a United States bid to get into the competition of superliners by the use of aluminum in great quantity throughout the ship. The use of this metal saves weight and makes the superliner practically fireproof. The processing of the aluminum includes complicated technical processes, in which the United States excels, and if the use of this light metal becomes accepted, may become an advantage in shipbuilding competition for U.S. builders."

Rumors that the U.S. Lines had agreed to operate the new ship at well below her service maximum speed of 28 knots "as a contribution to amity between America and Great Britain," were the subject of a lengthy article by George Horne in the *New York Times* for February 10 1952. The basis for the rumors was a "distortion of the rules of the Trans-Atlantic Passenger Conference." These rules set three factors as the standard for establishing a minimum First Class passenger fare: size, age, and speed. In submitting its proposed minimum First Class fare of $350 for off-season, the U.S. Lines had stated that it planned to operate the *United States* on a four-and-one-half-day crossing schedule, calling for an operating speed of 28 knots, roughly the same as the British *Queens*. The rates for other great Atlantic liners for this same off-season were: $365 for the *Queen Mary* and the *Queen Elizabeth;* $325 for the *Ile de France;* $300 for the *Caronia,* and $295 for the *Nieuw Amsterdam.* Raymond M. Hicks, Executive Vice President of U.S., Lines called the report "absolutely untrue," adding that it was "absurd to think we would enter into any such bargain." The *Queen Mary's* record passage from Ambrose Lightship to Bishop's Rock was made in August, 1938, and took 3 days, 20 hours and 42 minutes at an average speed of 31.69 knots.

And more trouble over the subsidy in Washington. On March 3 Representative Hardy said that the Maritime Administration should insist on the renegotiation of the construction subsidy for the *United States.* He cited a recent action by the Federal Maritime Board in which it had reduced the government aid toward the building of the two American Export ships, saying that he saw no reason why the same thing should not be done in the case of the U.S. Lines superliner.

An even more unexpected blow came March 11. There was a gale blowing early in the morning in the James River and the Panamanian-Rag freighter *Shakin* dragged her anchor and crashed into the cleanly-painted stern of the *United States.* The upper portion of the hull was damaged slightly. The Main Deck rail was smashed and an *Associated Press* wire story went around the nation with the headline: "Ship Hits Liner *United States.*"

On March 12 the nation's newspapers had a more pleasant story. The new master of the superliner was named – he would be Captain Harry Manning, Commodore of U.S. Lines, famed rescue skipper and one of the nation's best known master mariners. Harry Manning had begun his career as an able seaman on the barque *Dirigo,* after graduating from the New York state schoolship *Newport* in 1914. He had risen to his first command at the age of 31 in 1928. He had been an officer aboard the *Leviathan* and later served as captain of the *Manhattan, Washington,* and *America.* He was well known as an outspoken critic of maritime labor unions and had consistently refused to become a member of the Masters, Mates & Pilots organization. For his strong stand on this issue he was admired by some but hated by others. His most famous rescue took place in 1929, during a January storm at sea when he was chief officer of the old *America* (ex *Amerika).* He commanded a lifeboat which rescued all 32 crew members aboard the sinking Italian freighter *Florida.* In 1937 he had taken a leave of absence from U.S. Lines and joined Amelia Earhart as her navigator on her first attempt to circle the globe at the Equator. She crashed during the take off at Honolulu and he thought better of continuing on the flight, having become alarmed at her "aggressive" handling of the plane. When Miss Earhart continued her trip she was lost in the far Pacific and never heard from again. During the early days of World War II, before America's entry, Captain Manning was stopped by a German submarine while bringing 1,000 Americans home from Europe on the liner *Washington.* The sub threatened to sink the liner, her captain refusing to believe she was a neutral ship. Manning ordered his passengers into the outswung lifeboats and continued a sharp repartee via blinker with the German until the latter finally allowed him to proceed. Manning was 55 when his command of the *United States* was announced. It was noted that he had been in Newport News for some time observing the final stages of the ship's construction.

As the time for completion came closer, more parties of VIPs made tours of the new supership. Secretary of Commerce Charles Sawyer and Maritime Administrator E.L. Cochrane came on March 30. Vice President Alben W. Barkley came April 7. The shipyard scene was a busy one.

A new issue of the U.S. Lines "clipsheet" about the *United States* came out in early April. It contained stories about the first *United States,* a wooden paddle wheeler built in 1848, which took 13 days on her first trip between New York and Liverpool, and about the 10,000 keys that were needed for all the cabins, lockers, vaults, and other spaces needing locks aboard the new superliner. There was also a story about famed Chef Otto Bismarck and the ultranew radar ranges in his galley aboard the new liner.

Early in April the engines of the new liner were given their first trials with the ship firmly moored to the yard pier. Photos carried in newspapers of April 6 showed the propellers churning up a white wake around her stern. On that day it was announced that her trials would begin on the morning of May 14 and that they would take two or three days. Spokesmen for the yard said she was 90% finished, with carloads of additional furniture arriving daily at dockside.

Sculptress Gwen Lux had been given a choice decorative assignment. It was to design something appropriate for the two-deck high bulkhead at the after end of the First Class Dining Saloon. She was given orders that the decoration had to be large, impressive, and of very light weight. She decided on four figures, each about five feet high, with sun beams linking them together. If done in plaster each figure would have weighed about 200 pounds, much too much. Metal would have been even heavier. Then she heard about foam glass, a dark grayish lightweight material that came in block form. She experimented at length with adhesives to hold the basic foam glass blocks together. Successful in this she turned to the problem of carving the forms from the blocks. Chisels would shatter the glass, but she found she could do the trick with a number of metal files of different sizes. Filling the seams between the blocks so that they could not be seen was her next challenge. She did it. Finally she applied fire retardant paint to give lustre and suggest solidarity. It went on beautifully. Each figure weighed only 35 pounds and the whole ensemble was the first major decoration to be installed on the ship.

By April 15 the pool was just about finished. Relatively small in contrast to the three-deck high pool on the *Leviathan,* it had, nevertheless, some appealing features. The *United States* news clipsheet noted, somewhat over enthusiastically, that "when the swimmer wearies after one or more trips from end to end, he won't have to drag himself (or herself) out over a cold tile edge or a rough matting. The pool will be surrounded by a synthetic 'beach'-a strip which simulates sand in color and which by its texture as well as appearance invites the bather to sit at the edge for a while with his feet dangling in the water." A display of colored code flags on the after bulkhead facing the pool would say: "Come on in, the water's fine!"

A formal announcement that William Kaiser was to be the Chief Engineer was made April 16. His biography noted that he started at the bottom, rising to the rank of Second Assistant Engineer on the *Leviathan* in 1933. He first became a chief in 1941 aboard the *Manhattan,* on which he served as a naval reserve officer during the war. After the war ended, the Navy sent him to be Engineering Officer aboard the captured German superliner *Europa* for the voyage that brought her to the United States as a war prize. Later he was chief aboard the same ship when she was sent back to Europe to be reconverted as the *Liberté* for the French Line. He took the place of Patrick Brennan as Chief aboard the *America* when the latter retired. His brother Charles was a U.S. Line's master.

On April 22 the annual report of U.S. Lines disclosed that the firm had made a profit of $7,489,812 during the calendar year 1951, more than double the profit made in the previous year. In addition to the *America,* the line operated 46 cargo ships with a total deadweight capacity of 484,912 tons. It also operated an average of 14 ships on charter from the government. The report noted that Bremerhaven had been made the company's European terminus for the *America.*

A week later the ship's engines were again put through trial "spins" at dockside, while navigational and other equipment was tested in preparation for the trials then only two weeks off. The ship's 24 lifeboats were in their chocks, with their davits tested. The ship's cargo booms were rigged and ready. All cabins and public rooms on seven of the 12 decks were finished and sealed off. Workmen were rushing to complete the last interior finishing work on the three top decks. Involved were 34 different kinds of floor covering and rubber tiling and 99 different shades of paint. Soundproof paneling was in place throughout the ship and tests were being made with the concealed loudspeaker system. Within a few days the ship was scheduled to be moved from her pier and to return for a brief final visit to the drydock in which she was built to have her bottom cleaned before her sea trials. After all she had been afloat for nearly a year.

The Westinghouse Electric Corp., of Pittsburgh, put out a one paragraph news announcement about the new liner's propulsion plant. All that they were permitted to say were the basic facts that everyone knew about the ship and that the trials would begin May 14. A photo of the virtually completed liner was shown and editors were offered a glossy print upon request. Three short paragraphs were offered in another release by the Raybestos-Manhattan Company, Passaic, New Jersey, on the "partial rubber covering" they had provided for the propeller shafts. The story noted that "a crew of men was sent from the Passaic plant to do the work at the yard." A line at the bottom of the release stated: "Cleared for publication by Gibbs & Cox, Inc."

Anne Ruggles of the *World-Telegram and Sun* interviewed Dorothy Marckwald and Anne Urquhart. She brought out some of the difficulties in the superliner's interior design work, for example the question of a light, sheer fabric that was proposed for curtains in one of the lounges. It was handsome and non-flammable, but after some discussion it was rejected because it would sway with the ship's motion and might induce seasickness. The drapes used had to appear light, but be sufficiently heavy to resist moving with the ship. Among the tough, long-wearing and non-flammable materials used on the ship were wool for soft floor coverings, rubber tile for hard surfaces and upholstery, and drapery materials in leather. The Ruggles story appeared May 1. There were stories every day now, and the marine magazines were bursting with features and advertisements about the *United States.* Statistics of all kinds abounded. For example, the ship's 69 electric toasters, if used to their full capacity, could turn out 15,250 pieces of toast an hour.

On the much more serious side, Secretary of Commerce Charles Sawyer declared on May 11 that he would abide by the Maritime Administration's contract with U.S. Lines and would not follow the proposal of Comptroller Warren calling for a redetermination of the subsidies. The Secretary disputed the Comptroller's contention that the contract was not binding: "My own solicitor and the general counsel of the Federal Maritime Board had reached an opinion exactly opposite to the one indicated by you," he wrote Mr. Warren. "There is no suggestion that the contract was affected by fraud of any kind, and to me the opinion of my counsel that it is a valid and binding contract is persuasive." Fortunately for the U.S. Lines, Secretary Sawyer was a man of great common sense and practicality. He was also not one who would run away from a fight. His conclusion follows: "I prefer not to strain at a gnat and swallow a camel. From the standpoint of the taxpayer and his ultimate situation and from a practical common-sense standpoint, it seems to me more important for the United States to carry out its contract already entered into than that the Government be saddled with a ship it cannot run and a lawsuit which it cannot win."

Would that there had been a forceful voice in Washington like Secretary Sawyer's to answer the 1921 lawsuit of William Randolph Hearst that kept the *Leviathan* from being run by the International Mercantile Marine and forced her under government operation. The two situations had much in parallel.

A new oil painting of the liner by marine artist William Aylward, of Port Washington, New York, was com-

United States *with tugs alongside.*
(Courtesy of Bill DiBenedetto)

DATE ?

58

pleted and put on display. Strange to say it showed the main mast, a feature long-since dispensed with in the actual ship.

A rash of news stories heralded the day of the sea trials, when the *United States* would first leave the shipyard and head out into her natural element. Edward Tastrom, shipping editor of the *New York Journal of Commerce* was at Newport News with many other ship news editors for the trials. His stories and those by George Horne of the *Times* and Walter Hamshar of the *Herald Tribune* make the first trial trip come to life as if it had happened yesterday. A large number of government officials and shipyard and U.S. Lines executives were aboard, along with several members of the House and Senate, a total of 1,600 in all. When the ship first moved at 9 a.m. on May 14, 1952, and began to slip stern-ward from her fitting out berth, she dramatically sounded a three-blast salute to the thousands of shipyard workers all around. They paused and interrupted their respective tasks to watch. The saluting continued for others, the thousands of spectators who lined the shores as the new *United States* got under way under her own power for the first time. Captain E.D. Edwards, of the Virginia Pilots Association, was on the bridge with Commodore Manning. Two escorting tugs pushed through the waters on either side. Shadows from their smoke and from the clouds of white steam and smoke pouring from the monster stacks of the *United States* darkened the sunlit waters around the slowly progressing superliner. Both the *Herald Tribune* and the *Times* would have front page photographs of this scene the next morning. The *New York Daily News*, which rarely had anything about ships or shipping, would devote an entire center spread to the event. Their news airplane was overhead and snapped the *United States* as she regally steamed past the battleship *Missouri*, making the war craft look like a small boat. The *News* also carried a striking bow view from the air, showing the liner's bow anchor out at the ready and with only faint whisps of haze coming from the two stacks. As the ship moved she paid tribute to her hull design by churning up very little white water or foam around her hull.

A 32-page booklet on the trials was published by the shipyard. With a striking tinted drawing of the new ship on its cover, it gave an hour by hour account of what was to happen from 9 a.m. Wednesday, May 14, to 11 a.m. Friday, the 16th, when the ship was due to return to her shipyard pier. The booklet was designed for the convenience of those aboard and also covered the second trials, which were set for May 22 and 23. Descriptions of the many public rooms, the decorations, the telephone system, and the program for meals were carried. Both the First and Cabin Class dining rooms were to be used and there were to be two seatings for all meals. Quite unlike an Atlantic crossing, the meal times were set to permit the best use of the working hours. Breakfast was from 5 to 7 a.m. Lunch was from 11 to 1 p.m. Dinner was from 5 to 7 p.m. An item in the booklet warned trip guests: "Please be careful – the company is required to make delivery of the ship with all furnishings in perfect condition. Your co-operation in preventing damage to carpets, furniture and other equipment will be much appreciated. Please be particularly careful of lighted cigars, cigarettes, and liquids." The ship's Slop Chest on B Deck (port passage, frame 196) was open at all hours and sold soft drinks, candy, cigars, and the like. Room service was not offered and the pool was not open, but moving pictures were to be shown nightly and there was a refreshment bar in the First Class Smoking Room, where at certain hours, food and drink might be obtained.

Admiral Cochrane again stressed at an informal press conference that the ship was "a joint venture of the Government and the U.S. Lines and one of which the country can be proud, since it will help reestablish our position in world maritime affairs." Yard President Woodward summed up his thoughts: "If the people of this country could just understand what a remarkable ship this is, what lies behind the painted bulkheads in safety and stability, and what she will mean to the country in carrying power and speed, they would truly be proud of this American achievement." Admiral Cochrane added that he expected the speed trials to "best any ocean liner or any large naval vessel." George Horne, commenting later on this statement, said it was the first time that any high official connected with the building of the superliner had said openly that she was going out for the Blue Riband of the Atlantic. Richard P. Cooke, who represented the *Wall Street Journal* on the trials, noted in his story the next day that Admiral Cochrane described the new ship as "not a luxury liner in the usual sense." He wrote that the builders "have avoided lavish outlays for lavish decorations but that the ship would be a money maker and is already booked solid for the coming season."

As the *United States* slipped down the James River and headed for deep water the first steam rate tests were begun at 10:45. These were to determine the efficiency of the turbines by measuring the pounds of steam needed per horsepower in an hour. At noon she reached the Chesapeake Light Ship and swung around for calibration of her radio direction finder and magnetic compass adjustments. At 3 p.m. she began her first builder's economy trial to measure fuel consumption. Two hours later she reached the first of the Raydist buoys. The Raydist System was a special measuring device for the high speed tests. It had been created by the Hastings Instrument Company, Hampton, Virginia, and was being used for the first time. It worked by placing two small buoys with their Raydist equipment in the water on the course the ship would follow on her trials. The buoys sent out impulses which would be received on the ship. As the ship moved away from the buoys a measurement would be made of the distance gone that was thought to be as accurate as one part in 5,000. As night fell the ship began her first endurance trial at normal shaft horsepower.

On the following day at 4 a.m. the Coast Guard tender *Conifer* joined the superliner and placed the Raydist buoys in the trial course area. At 5 the ship began her first speed run at 15 knots. Other runs were made up until about 4 p.m. The day was a dramatic one with nature combining to make a magnificent setting for such an historic occasion. There were rough seas and winds increasing to gale weather, but the sky was brilliantly clear. Photographers on the *Conifer* were overjoyed at the opportunities for superb shots and, some of them, driven to despair by seasickness and bruises from being thrown around as their tiny ship bounded up and down in all directions. One, The Mariners' Museum photographer William T. Radcliffe, got some particularly impressive scenes that would make his name famous. Overhead, a plane provided by Thomas Airviews, of Bayside, New York, took some extraordinary views showing how the ship's wake was something to talk about. It stretched out as a thin line, with virtually no side waves or fan effect-just a long, narrow, thin line.

George Horne wirelessed his second story home that evening from aboard the ship. He noted that she was remarkably free of vibration despite the "confused sea and high winds." And he also reported something that brought frowns to many faces. The reduction gear bearings in two of the four engines had given a slight indication of overheating. B.O. Smith was there and the problem was a minor one, and yet it cast something of a shadow over the entire trials. B.O. Smith "tipped all the bearings and that cleared it all up," Norman Zippler said years later. But it was necessary to postpone the final full-power tests until the Official Trials. Pressed by newsmen for comments about the highest speed attained, Admiral Cochrane would only say that he was more than ever sure that the ship could beat all Atlantic speed records. Reporters wrote for the next day's papers that the ship had reached and maintained a speed "well over 32 knots for long periods" during the trial. Yard President Woodward summed up the performance by saying that the trials had shown the "economy and superb sea-going qualities of the *United States* conclusively under full gale conditions."

A round up of opinions after the first set of trials showed three general conclusions: (1) that the ship would certainly take the speed record, (2) that she was remarkably free of vibration despite high winds and rough seas, and (3) that she had superb sea-riding qualities and would be a very comfortable ship to ride in bad weather.

On May 22, Maritime Day, the U.S. Lines put out a release comparing the new superliner with the *Savannah* of 1819. The Maritime Day banquet in New York at the Waldorf Astoria had on its menu cover a full-cover reproduction of the Aylward painting of the *United States*. The enthusiasm and tempo were rising. The Official Trials had been scheduled for May 22-23, but it became known that they had been postponed until June 4-5. William Francis Gibbs was taking no chances. Activity continued on many varied fronts. Some 400 stewards due to serve on the liner were in training at the Maritime Administration's center at Sheepshead Bay. Two hundred more would join them shortly, it was announced, May 25. The National Maritime Union and U. S. Lines had instructors at the center as did the government shipping agency. Deck and engineering officers were already aboard the ship. Both groups had begun their training in late April. Early in June many unlicensed seamen would begin to board the ship at the yard to familiarize themselves with her and to attend lectures on their duties. Of the 1,036 persons in the crew, 761 were to be in the steward's department, 138 in the engine room staff, and the remaining 137 would be deck personnel. This compared with 511, 85 and 94 on the *America* in these same three categories.

More syndicated editorials appeared hailing the *United States* and predicting that she would break the trans-Atlantic speed record. Such towns as Monroe, Louisiana, and El Dorado, Arkansas, whose readers rarely saw a line about a ship, were treated to this "Queen of Atlantic" editorial via their local papers.

On May 29, with the delivery date only three weeks and two days off and the maiden voyage barely one month and five days ahead, it was again announced that the Official Trials would be put off. The new date was not indicated.

One of the many well-known artists employed to decorate "the Big Ship" was Seymour Lipton. He did many of the aluminum sculptures that provided a continuity of decor in the ship's foyers and public spaces. In the Tourist Dining Saloon one of his works featured a bull. The bull had a most obvious male organ and, on the first trial trip, this caught the eye of the somewhat sedate *New York Times* ship news editor George Fox Horne. George, possibly in a casual moment, questioned the taste of the decoration. His comment was taken quite seriously by a number of people and the shipyard's public relations director Bob Hopkins found himself in the center of a growing storm. The matter went all the way up to William Francis Gibbs. Some weeks later in his third floor office at 229 West 43rd Street, Mr. Horne was surprised to receive a large package from Newport News. Opening it he found the offending male member affixed to a polished plaque, a gift from the shipyard. The bull had been, in effect, castrated. This emasculation brought a storm of protest from artist Lipton, who objected most strenuously to his work being altered. Years later when he retired to move back to Oklahoma, George gave the plaque to me. Still more years later I loaned it to friends in the American Bureau of Shipping to be copied as a farewell "joke" retirement present for their Ralph Christiansen. Mr. Christiansen had been most active for the ABS in connection with the building of the *United States*.

The Gibbs passion for safety and no wood aboard the new ship was becoming something of a national joke, as a line in a *Readers Digest* article by Fillmore Hyde indicated. The line was directed at those superstitious voyagers. It was: "If you want to knock on wood, take it aboard with you."

The conflict between Secretary Sawyer and Comptroller General Warren flamed up again, on June 1 when the Commerce Secretary rejected another proposal made by the Comptroller. Mr. Warren had sent him a 41-page letter insisting that the government was paying too large a share of the cost of the *United States*. The word in Washington was that Mr. Warren was emboldened because he knew that he had the backing of President Truman. There would be much more on this unfortunate business in the next few weeks.

A pleasant interlude into the non-controversial world of history is offered at this point by Alexander Crosby Brown, Newport News maritime historian and former newspaper man. He wrote a letter on June 5 to General Franklin noting that the last American ship to win the Atlantic speed record was the *Baltic*, of the Collins Line. Her 9-day, 13-hour passage, which won the mythical Blue Riband took place in August, 1852, and stood for 11 years. Her average speed was 13.34 knots, and she was the last American-built ship to hold the record up to the moment of his letter. "It would almost seem prophetic justice if in the month of August, 1952, the *United States* might be successful in returning the Blue Ribbon to this side of the Atlantic," he added. As a final note, historian Brown pointed out that his great grandfather, John Brown, had been "your century-old opposite number as president of the New York and Liverpool United States Mail Steamship Company, more familiarly known as the Collins Line." Three weeks later the U.S. Lines president replied: "I am very much interested to hear that your great-grandfather was the President of the Collins Line at the time the *Baltic* made her record, and I do hope he didn't have as many headaches as I have had over the *United States*. "General Franklin was immersed in the Sawyer-Warren controversy when he wrote.

Captain Sherman W. Reed, of the Maritime Administration, who years before had been Second Officer on the *Leviathan*, took his wife to Sheepshead Bay early in June to observe how the NMU steward-training courses were progressing. They were photographed being served a bowl of clear oxtail soup by waiter Marcel Delasio, for a feature article that ran June 6 in the *Herald Tribune*. Waiter Ralph Toledo was pictured deciding which of four wine glasses he should serve Rhine wine in. Another shot showed bellboy Bill Krudener practicing how to tie a bow tie on bellboy Ronnie Nicholl. A fourth photo showed seamen training for the *United States* going through lifeboat drill in Monomoy lifeboats. The six-week program would end June 19. On June 7 the *United States* was opened at her shipyard berth for public inspection for the first time. Over 25,000 people took advantage of this chance to see her.

The announcement finally came. The second trials were to commence June 9. The day arrived and a bevy of reporters was on hand again to make the two-day trip 150 miles out to observe the ship make her full power tests. On the same day in New York City's Central Park, with the fullest possible help from the U.S. Lines publicity department, ship model enthusiast Frank Cronican tested his new 50-inch scale model of the superliner. Photographs of his model, which had won the approval of William Francis Gibbs, were carried in most New York newspapers. Members of the Maritime Administration's official acceptance board were among the 1,704 persons who boarded the real ship that morning at the shipyard. She left her berth at 9 a.m. Reporters were promised by Captain Rex L. Hicks, chief of the Maritime Administration's office of ship construction, that they would be informed if the ship surpassed the Queen Mary's record speed. They also learned that the contract called for a horsepower rating of 158,000. Finally they were informed that there was a new gross tonnage – 53,290 tons.

The first day passed quietly. The big moment came around noon on June 10. The *Times* story built up the excitement: "During a sustained power run last night at 158,000 horsepower the new liner steadily maintained speed that 'considerably exceeded 34 knots,' according to an official announcement. just before noon, building up her power again beyond 158,000 horsepower, the ship raced through deep water and attained an even higher speed. But it was kept a secret. There was a surprising absence of vibration, and when full rudder tests, crash stops, and full-speed astern were carried through the persons aboard were astonished at her stability." Walter Hamshar, in the next day's *Tribune*, was even more sensational: "The speed burst was the most dramatic incident of the two-day trip. When the engines were fully opened, a tremendous surge of power could be felt throughout the ship. Everyone knew he was witnessing a display that probably never will occur in the vessel's normal usage. The awesome wake churned up by the four huge propellers rivalled the Niagara River Whirlpool, according to several passengers." Both newspaper editors noted that the ship traveled backwards at 20 knots, "which is faster than most merchant vessels can go forward." When the *United States* returned to Newport News she boasted an outsized broom riding on a mast high above her decks. Later, photographers snapped pictures of this huge broom, emblematic of a clean sweep in her performance trials, with Commodore Manning, yard president Woodward, and William Francis Gibbs.

The exact speed that the *United States* made on this full power run on June 10 1952, was not revealed except to a very limited number of persons until November 3, 1977, when John R. Kane read a paper before the Society of Naval Architects and Marine Engineers. His paper was entitled "The Speed of the *SS United States*." It began with a review of the Gibbs dream of a four-day record breaker. It reviewed the basic Gibbs concept behind the superliner's speed in this way: "The formula for speed of the *United States* was one that would scarcely have come as a surprise to Donald McKay, William Webb, or any of the other master builders and designers of the clipper ship era who were the first to apply it so spectacularly. It is, in simple terms, to combine the maximum driving power you can achieve with the lightest displacement compatible with the work the ship must do, and with the longest, finest, and cleanest lines that will serve to make a good wholesome seakeeping ship." Gibbs called for the very latest steam plant with 925 pounds per square inch steam pressure and 1,000 degree F temperature at the boiler superheater outlet. This plus the use of high-speed geared steam turbine machinery permitted a reduction in the weight and space of the machinery and increased the maximum shaft horsepower to 60,000 SHP per propeller. This gave the ship a total of 240,000 SHP, as compared to 158,000 maximum of the *Queen Mary* and the *Queen Elizabeth*.

Gibbs gave "great attention to the compact arrangement of the ship without sacrificing unduly the elegance and luxury of staterooms and public spaces which are necessary to a premium passenger liner," Mr. Kane noted. He did this in order to get the lightest displacement possible and his use of aluminum "in all of the deck-house structure and decks above the main deck" was a key to this effort. This resulted in a ship that could carry almost the same number of passengers with a maximum loaded displacement of 47,300 tons. The *Queens*' displacement was 77,400 tons. The *United States* had a much higher ratio of installed horsepower to displacement (240,000/47,300) or 5.074 shaft horsepower per ton, in contrast to 2.0 shaft horsepower per ton for the British *Queens*. When Mr. Kane delivered his paper, this power to displacement ratio had not been exceeded in any large passenger or cargo liner "and indeed is approached by few if any naval capital ships larger than destroyers and light cruisers."

The Kane paper delved into the remarkable ability that Gibbs had that permitted him to ask for criticism of various design features, study and accept the best and take the final responsibility for all decisions. His selection of a modest bulbous bow instead of a larger one was based on his fear that a large one might cause pounding or lateral hull vibration. The extreme care and depth of study he gave to hull design, propeller placement, and design all contributed to his final success. Mr. Kane revealed in his paper that the *United States* had gone 38-32 knots while developing 241,785 total shaft horsepower and at the trial displacement. His concluding paragraph: "William Francis Gibbs was happy. The vessel had exceeded his expectations in most every respect, and he was ready to take on anyone who wished to challenge for *the* speed supremacy of the North Atlantic."

A Liverpool Journal of Commerce editorial published June 12 commented on the trial trip announcement that the *United States* had attained a speed which "considerably exceeded 34 knots" by noting that the new liner, because of her defense features, "is not exactly comparable with the two *Queens*, which, whether or not

61

they improve on past performance, have as their primary purpose the maintenance of the existing weekly service." While not closing its eyes to the prestige of the ownership of the fastest liner in the world, the publication noted that the Cunard Line has "consistently deprecated the names of any of its ships being coupled with attacks on trans-Atlantic speed records." Successive Cunard chairmen, it added, "have explained that the company is not interested in speed for speed's sake, and is primarily concerned with the safety, regularity, reliability and economical operation of its fleet of trans-Atlantic liners, and the comfort and convenience of passengers." And as a final conclusion the editorial said: "It was almost incidental that the maintenance of a weekly service by two ships, instead of three, resulted in the fastest Atlantic crossing achieved to date."

Also on June 12 it became known that the *United States* had struck a submerged object on her most recent trial and suffered damage to a propeller. It was not serious, but she would have to be drydocked again before sailing for New York for delivery to her owners. Yard officials said they did not expect the damage to delay delivery.

The battle between the Comptroller General and the Secretary of Commerce was now front page news. On June 13 the U.S. Lines held a news conference in Washington to put their position on the record. General Franklin pointed out that it was not fair to say that his company had purchased a $70,000,000 ship for $28,000,000. "The fact is," he explained, "that the U.S. Government will receive from the U.S. Lines a contribution of $28,000,000 for the building of this great troopship." He said the company would not renegotiate its contract and expected delivery to take place "next Friday" for the agreed price of $28,087,000. To enforce his point that the contract was reviewable, Comptroller General Warren had held back about $13,000,000 in operating subsidies due U.S. Lines for freighter operations. General Franklin made note of this and said he hoped the Government would

Control panel of one of the two engine rooms.

pay this "very soon." He proposed that the ship be delivered and that "the orderly American way" would be to settle the controversy over the company's right to retain the liner in the courts. Cletus Keating, U.S. Lines counsel, explained that it would cost about $43,000,000 to build the ship for purely commercial purposes, adding that her cost if built in Great Britain would have been about $25,000,000 under these conditions. The cost of the added naval features would come to about $27,000,000 and the building subsidy would come to $18,000,000. All the construction costs will be paid by the Maritime Administration to the Newport News shipyard. Should the *United States* eventually be sold, the terms of the contract preclude the U.S. Lines from making any profit on the sale. The excess must be turned over to the Treasury.

President Truman was known to be supporting the Comptroller General. An appeal to him by the NMU called upon the White House to back the transfer of the *United States* to U.S. Lines. NMU President Curran challenged the right of the Comptroller to deny the validity of the Maritime Administration's subsidy contracts. He insisted that the new liner be delivered on schedule.

In between the battle of the giants little things were happening, too. Mayor Vincent R. Impellitteri, of New York City, and Edward F. Cavanagh, his dock commissioner, were joined by General Franklin in a tour of renovated Pier 86 on June 16. On the same day Walter Jones memoed reporters that "one or more Moran Towing Company tugs would be available to the press to meet the arriving superliner down the Bay and escort her to Pier 86 on Monday the 23rd. The tugs would leave Pier 1, Hudson River, at 10 a.m. and those wishing to be aboard were asked to telephone Bob Monroe." On June 18, Commissioner Cavanagh wrote to the American Merchant Marine Institute asking the trade association's assistance "in rendering an ovation and salute to the vessel *United States* as she goes up the Bay and the North River."

More harsh words from Comptroller Warren sent chills down the backs of Franklin and Gibbs: "If Secretary of Commerce Sawyer deliberately turns over this ship at the thoroughly repudiated price fixed by the former Maritime Commission, he will be giving away the money and property of the U.S. Government without the authority of law to the unjust enrichment of the U.S. Lines. Under these conditions the buyer will get nothing more than a tainted title. That, gentlemen, would be the latest chapter in a long and sorry story of maladministration and disregard for the law and the public interest." He was addressing a House Merchant Marine subcommittee. The date was June 17, just three days before the projected delivery. The story was again front page news.

As if to make things more exciting the *United Press* released an inflammatory wire service story on June 19, with an amazing almost mirror-image of the saga of the *Leviathan* 31 years earlier. Harried William Francis and Frederic H. Gibbs, with a thousand other worries on their minds and driven to the end of anxiety by the Comptroller General, must have turned gray when they read the opening paragraph of the UP story:

"The U.S. Lines has arranged a lavish junket for Congressmen and high government officials aboard its sleek new $70,000,000 superliner, the *United States,* it was disclosed today."

Three decades before, almost to the day, the same kind of story had dubbed the trial trip of the *Leviathan* a "million dollar joy ride" and had so frightened invited Congressmen that many turned down the invitation of the Shipping Board to go along. The *Leviathan* had been reconditioned at the Newport News shipyard to plans prepared by Gibbs. At issue this time was the delivery trip to New York. In reality only a very few Congressmen had been invited, and it was certainly a stretching of things to call it a "lavish junket." The *United Press* played down the number of Congressmen invited, casually mentioning the matter in a bottom part of the story as follows: "A reporter's check revealed that invitations have been sent to well over a score of Congressmen, including mem-

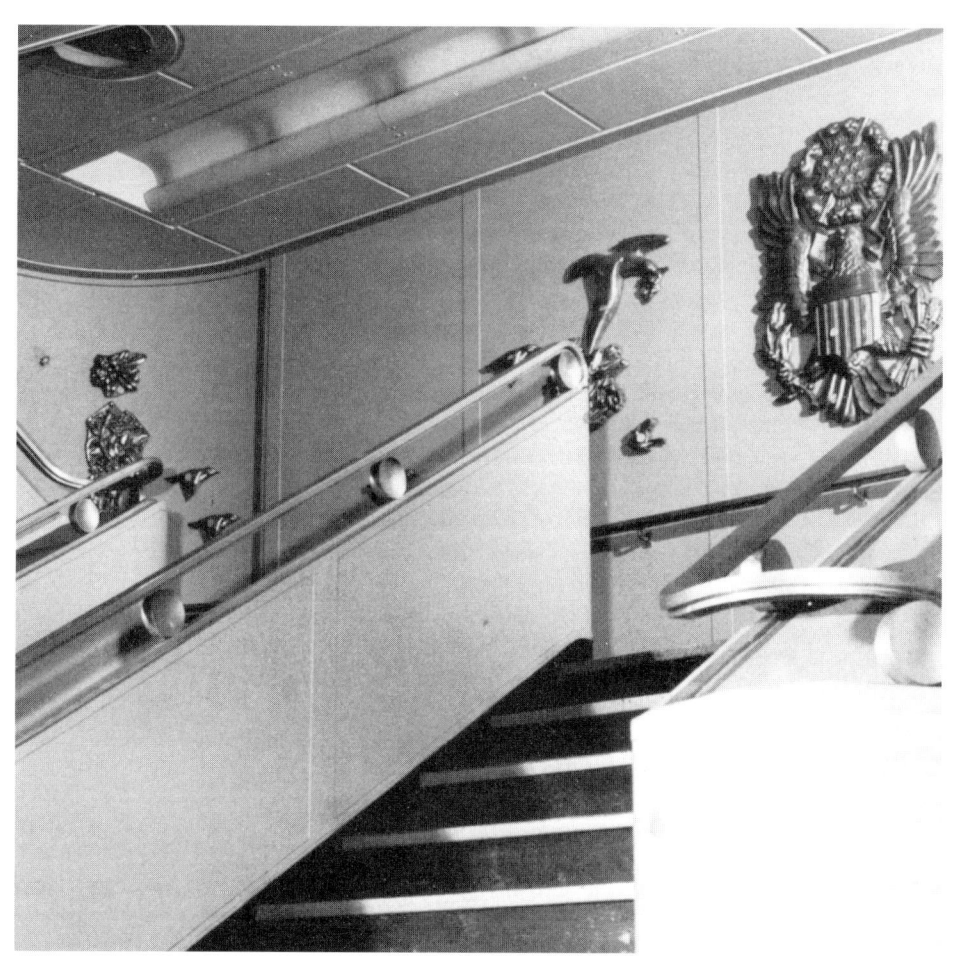

Stairwell showing an example of artwork exhibited throughout the ship's interior.

bers of committees which handle ship subsidy laws or appropriations." The story noted that one Congressman, Rep. Clare E. Hoffman (R., Mich.), had "promptly rejected his invitation." A member of the House Executive Departments Expenditures Committee, he said: "There is no reason why that company should ask Congressmen to go on this trip, but it's always a question of a person's ethics." He added that the taxpayers were being "taken for a ride anyway."

The *United Press* built up the Sawyer-Warren controversy to get added mileage for their story: "The government is scheduled to chip in $43,000,000 in subsidies to help pay for the luxury liner. Comptroller Warren is trying to block the deal. He claims the taxpayers are getting a rooking. At least one member of the House subcommittee which is investigating allegedly excessive ship subsidies has accepted the cruise invitation. A list of the Congressmen invited appeared to be a closely guarded secret. Spokesmen for the line in Washington and New York said their plans were so 'confused' they didn't know exactly who or how many were invited."

The question of how to get insurance coverage for such a costly ship had plagued the world's insurance market for some time. The total insurance needed was $31,000,000, or less than half the anticipated cost of the liner. On June 19, the British magazine *Shipbuilding and Shipping Record* had a long article on the subject, showing how the insurance industry had grown over the previous 40 years. The *United States* coverage amounted to £11,000,000 in terms of sterling. The British market covered over half the total required, or $17,250,000 of it. In 1912 the *Olympic* and *Titanic* were insured for £1,150,000, a sum that was regarded as the limit of the capacity of the market at that time. Owen C. Torrey, president of the American Institute of Marine Underwriters, said the insurance on the *United States* was the largest amount ever written anywhere on one vessel.

Commodore Manning was on the cover of the issue of *Time* which came out Thursday, June 19 It was dated June 23. A painting by Ernest Baker showing him in uniform with a porthole behind him suggested the joys of travel to England and France tied together with colored streamers. The caption: "Commodore Manning of the *United S*tates – For a Blue Ribbon contender, hushhush features." Some superb color shots of the new superliner were offered along with a review of the ship's great speed as demonstrated on the trials. Calling the new vessel "the dreamboat of William Francis Gibbs," the article in typical *Time* fashion skipped and hopped with striking anecdotes and interesting comparisons through the life of the superliner up to that point: "Because of her long, slim prow, she is racier-looking than most ocean liners ... the hull is as sleek as a shark ... the First Class dining room seems chopped up, because the Navy demanded extra reinforcing stanchions." Happily for U.S. Lines very little attention was devoted to the Sawyer-Warren brouhaha except to say that the ship might have to sail under lease. Most of the piece was devoted to Manning, "by his own admission, a stubborn, bullheaded, tactless introvert." Among the exploits that he was given credit for was the shaming of British port authorities into improving the channel into Southampton. He had been provoked into this by being held up aboard the *America* for six hours one time when the *Queen Elizabeth* was aground in one of the hairpin turns in the old channel. "Manning saw the British press, stomped up and down his cabin berating the Admiralty for Southampton's 'primitive and disgraceful' harbor." A better channel was dug.

This was the time I was asked to draw a large "cut-away" of the *United States* for the *Herald Tribune*. It was to show the location of the public rooms in relation to each other and was used in a special section devoted to the new liner for Sunday, June 22. The drawing was quite a challenge because no conventional deck plans had been issued and much had to be done from imagination and guess work.

On Friday, June 20, 1952, the *United States* was formally delivered by the government to the U. S. Lines, with the transfer of title taking place at Hoboken, New Jersey, and formal acceptance of delivery from the builders at Newport News. In making the transfer Secretary of Commerce Sawyer defended his action and said it was "the proudest day in our maritime history."

Two hours later the White House released a letter from President Truman to the Attorney General "making it certain that the great ship would sail on a sea of controversy," as reported by the Washington bureau of the *New York Times*. The President followed the full line of reasoning of the Comptroller General. He asked Attorney General James P. McGranery to take legal action to determine whether the building subsidies paid had been excessive. He quoted a report by Representative Hardy's House subcommittee as "largely substantiating" the Comptroller General's contention about "errors of calculation and possible misconstructions of the law." He deplored the refusal, as he put it, of U.S. Lines to discuss "possible adjustments in the contract." President Truman also noted that the ship would probably cost "almost $78,000,000." Both Secretary Sawyer and General Franklin immediately announced their willingness to cooperate with the Attorney General, but the U.S. Lines President denied that his company had refused an invitation by any officer of the government to review the contract on an exploratory basis. The question, he said, had been thoroughly explored. The company refused to agree to renegotiation. The General also said it was "unfair" and an "untruth" for anyone to charge that taxpayers would foot the bill for guests being brought from Newport News to New York on the delivery trip. He said it was not a "junket" and that its cost would be borne by the company. I was one of those invited to be aboard and was looking forward to it with eagerness.

It was indeed a most unusual situation to have the President and one of his Cabinet members on directly opposing sides in a national controversy. Secretary Sawyer did not hold back because of this new and direct White House involvement. He released a five-page, single-spaced letter to Congressman J.F. Shelly, Chairman of the special subcommittee of the House Merchant Marine and Fisheries Committee, which had been assigned the review of the subsidy arrangements for the *Independence* and the *Constitution,* of American Export Lines. It set forth in a most direct and spirited way the full defense of the Maritime Administration and the U.S. Lines on the whole subsidy question. And it denounced the Comptroller General in no uncertain terms, saying that he was attempting to make the public think that he was "a knight in white armor defending the taxpayers from some nefarious plot to which I and the Maritime Board are parties." He hailed the part Admiral Cochrane had played and said he had never known a "more devoted, honorable, hardworking or competent group of public servants" than Admiral Cochrane and his associates. He concluded: "In my opinion the public interest referred to by Mr. Warren required me not to withhold but to deliver this ship. Mr. Warren has by his statement in effect dared me to turn this ship over to the U.S. Lines. Well, I have turned it over. He claimed that it was within his power to tell me that I could not go through with this contract. 'Upon what meat doth this our Ceasar feed, That he is grown so great?'"

The whole amazing battle between a member of the Cabinet and the Comptroller General backed by the President was one more illustration of the climate under which this supreme achievement of the world's passenger steamship era was built. The cards seemed stacked against the *United States,* and yet, with each new crisis there arose a man to defend her. So great was the initial thrust and desire of William Francis Gibbs to produce his dream ship, that despite all obstacles he found the way and the backing to do it. He wanted her to be the finest of luxury liners, but because of the changing competitive scene he had to bill her as a troopship in order to get the financial backing to pay her cost. She was entering service just as a new surge of American tourists were making the travel business boom, but it was also the year that air carriers took 40% of the trade.

It was probably impossible for the Gibbs brothers, and for most others in that summer of 1952, to realize that before the *United States* would reach middle age even the strongest argument in their stock of reasons for building the superliner would be taken away. It would not be too many years before the Defense Department would once-and-for-all abandon the concept of the transport of troops by sea in favor of air. But this was the last thing on the minds of the Gibbs brothers on this fabulously exciting greatest moment in their lives. It was Friday night, June 21, 1952, and the entire 990 feet of the great new U.S. Lines flagship *United States* was illuminated. All 53,300 gross tons of her were ready and waiting for her special guests to board the following day for the short trip to a gala welcome in New York.

[Handwritten note at top: "THE YEAR IN WHICH ALL THE EVENTS IN THIS CHAPTER TAKES PLACE IS FIRST MENTIONED ON THE END-TO-LAST PAGE OF THE CHAPTER."]

6

The Blue Riband

[Handwritten note: "WHAT DATE? WHAT YEAR?"]

"Kindly present this card at the Train Gate, Pennsylvania Station, New York, to obtain Reservation Card showing Pullman assignment on the Special Train and stateroom assignment on the *SS United States*."

So read the guest card sent me and many of the 1,200 others who were invited to make the delivery run from Newport News to New York. "Dress will be entirely informal," the program said. "Gratuities for all service on the Special Train will be taken care of by the U.S. Lines ... guests are requested to print their names on the appropriate space on the enclosed baggage tags and affix the tags to their baggage before arriving at the Train Gate." Walter Jones and his 10 assistants had done their job well. Along with the guests were 162 newsmen, one of whom was making copious notes. His name was Ray Erwin and he would do a special piece entitled: "Press Works, Plays Aboard Superliner" for his publication: *Editor & Publisher*. I had just resigned from the *Herald Tribune*, with keen regrets, to become Director, Bureau of Information, of my old trade association, the American Merchant Marine Institute. My old employer there, Frank Reil, had suffered a heart attack and died, partly because of overwork in the interests of the *United States*, and I had been asked to return to take his place.

There were actually two special trains, with "frequent diners and lounge cars interspaced" between the Pullmans, Ray Erwin noted. Reporters considered the assignment "one of the most important in marine history." The trains left at 10:20, stopping at Newark, Philadelphia, and Baltimore to pick up more guests. My seat was in Car 4 and my packet of instructions showed that my cabin was B143, an inside Cabin Class room with four berths. It was forward on the starboard side. We reached Newport News and were taken by bus to the pier. There was an air of great excitement as we climbed the long gangplank up to a sideport and boarded the ship. She was wonderful to see, to smell, and to relish! The Meyer Davis Orchestra was playing in the Ballroom, resplendent with its curved glass panels and their beautiful designs. The Adrian Rollini Trio and other performers entertained. The schedule of events showed that a new MGM moving picture called "Pat and Mike," and starring Spencer Tracy and Katherine Hepburn would be shown at 10:30 p.m. The evening was balmy, the shipyard sounds and lights were a most unusual setting, and the expectations of the morning to come were high.

The next morning at 6 we sailed. Many hundreds of the guests were up and about, walking the composition-covered aluminum decks and peering out of the curtained windows. The gigantic red, white, and blue stacks were breathtaking! Every craft in the area tied down her whistle in salute as the new liner slowly slipped out of her berth and headed for sea. Holy Mass was celebrated in the Observation Lounge between 7 and 8 and breakfast began in both Dining Saloons on A Deck right afterward. There were no women aboard except two in the crew, a matter of keen disappointment to several female reporters. General Franklin had three cabins assigned to him: U8I-83-85. The Gibbs brothers were aboard, but were not shown on the cabin list. Secretary Sawyer, about a dozen Senators and Representatives, and many Admirals were also on the guest list.

Press headquarters with facilities for writing and wiring were on B Deck in the Purser's Administrative Office. Members of the Fourth Estate were asked to register their wishes re the use of these facilities. A press conference was held at 2:20 Sunday afternoon with General Franklin as the spokesman. A whole schedule of sports, cinema, and musical events was given out to the passengers. The movie for Sunday was "Walk East on Beacon." Clocks were to be set ahead one hour that evening. The first issue of the ship's newspaper *The Ocean Press* came out. One story from Washington noted that Senator Taft was saying that he had enough convention delegates to win the Republican presidential nomination. The Brooklyn Dodgers had defeated the Pittsburgh Pirates.

Paul C.C. Friedlander, travel editor of the *New York Times*, described his sensations that day during lunch. The ship was riding on a smooth sea, very steady and without vibration. For a straight hour, while everyone ate, the power was increased. When the hour had passed it was announced that the liner had been making between 33 and 34 knots. Mr. Friedlander later would write in a column: "This landlubber, a notoriously poor sailor, was able to stand steady before the cold buffet table, both to

65

admire the display and make a generous selection. There was no pitch, and just enough roll to be discernible, but not enough to bother any but the most squeamish traveler." His comments about the public rooms and other passenger areas were friendly but not overly favorable. A handsomely printed red, white, and blue passenger list for the trip gave the full complement of the principal officers. After Commodore Manning there was Frederick Fender as his Executive Officer, Chief Engineer Kaiser, Executive Assistant Engineer Robert J. Jones, Chief Purser John A. Lock, Executive Purser John J. Wilkinson, and Chief Radio Operator Thomas Cerio. Dr. John E. Sheedy was Chief Surgeon. The Chief Steward was Herman Mueller and the Assistant Chief was Andrew Malmsea. The Sunday dinner menu showed 79 items and *Times* ship news reporter Arthur Richter made an heroic attempt to try them all.

In New York stories of the superliner filled most newspapers. The *Herald Tribune* had a 14-page section with many advertisements and feature articles hailing the new ship. The *Daily News* had a centerfold of color and a full-page feature article with more colored shots. Their piece was entitled: "Our New Queen of the Seas ... Out To Recapture Atlantic Blue Ribbon." Millions eagerly awaited the maiden arrival in the port. It would be another welcome like those accorded the *Leviathan, Normandie,* and *Queen Mary.* Captain John A. Meseck put his excursion boat *Americana* at the disposal of the Propeller Club, and several thousand lucky people, including my wife Doris, had tickets to sail out on her to meet the incoming *United States.* The notice to Propeller Club members offering tickets, first come, first served, showed the enthusiasm of the hour: "We are going to experience a great thrill which should fill us with pride. ... The 53,300 gross ton liner will be welcomed by top city, state, and federal authorities, and a tremendous reception will be accorded the ship. No more than 3 tickets can be allowed to each member. Please cooperate with us." The last sentence was underlined. The Moran Towing Company, which sent out a superb arrival photograph whenever a new liner they handled docked, was swamped with requests to be on the photo list for the superliner. A total of 1,856 names were on this list, including 111 to be sent by courier to Washington. According to the famous tug company's policy, the photo had to arrive on each favored person's desk within 24 hours of the time that Moran's Jeff Blinn snapped the picture. This meant an all-night work assignment for Bob Monroe, Jeff Blinn, and the well-paid photo house that made the prints. Two Moran tugs were earmarked for the press and some 60 reporters had asked permission to go out aboard them. One was Brooks Atkinson, famed drama critic of the *Times,* a liner buff from way back. Two smart McAllister Brothers tugs were chartered by the National Defense Transportation Association's New York Chapter, and many other "candy stripe" tugs would be on hand for the welcome. New Yorkers knew McAllister tugs as "candy stripers" because their stacks were decorated with red and white stripes.

Eight varieties of eggs were on the breakfast menu for Monday, June 23, as the liner steamed along the coast of New Jersey. One could pick from nine kinds of cold cereals. From the grill you could order pork chops, bacon, Yorkshire Ham, or sausages. The menu was stylish with a red, white, and blue ornament at the upper left over which was printed the famed American eagle design of the old American Line houseflag in gold. For those who could sit down and eat while the harbor welcome was taking place there was just as elaborate a luncheon menu.

Four Navy destroyers met the ship an hour before she reached the Narrows and took up escort positions. Two women boarded the liner far down the Bay from a Customs vessel, Jeanne Toomey, ship news reporter for the *Brooklyn Eagle* and Carla Deitz, smiling veteran of the U.S. Lines publicity department. Mayor Impellitteri and a group of VIPs boarded the ship in the Upper Bay and were duly photographed on the Bridge with Commodore Manning. First dozens, then hundreds of small boats joined in the procession and the welcomes began in earnest. Whistle salutes, plumes of hissing steam, sounds of cheering, bands playing, and the splash of great white fans of water from a dozen red fireboats added to the exciting din. I was almost deafened, repeatedly, because I picked as my place to watch the arrival the top of the pilot house. It was pandemonium. The one memory that stands stark out in my mind was one of concern, for I saw the *Americana* following us listing over at what seemed at least 40 degrees; everyone was on one side cheering. And right behind her, charging up fast, was a destroyer. All I could think of was that the wash of the destroyer would swamp the low-hulled excursion craft and throw her thousands of passengers, including Doris, into the harbor. It didn't happen.

Brought aboard from small boats were stacks of the various Monday newspapers, including an 8-page special section about the superliner printed for the *Journal of Commerce.* A full page ad of welcome opened this special section. It was sponsored by eight other American ship lines and Todd Shipyards, a classy example of intercompany goodwill. The *World Telegram* came out with a front page five-column picture of the arriving superliner under the heading: "Hi, *United States!* Welcome to New York!" Directly above it were eight-column headlines telling of a strike by 500 American war planes in Manchuria. The Korean war was going better, and the new ship would not be needed as a troopship. The *Telegram's* story read: "Scores of harbor craft, flying colored pennants, criss-crossed crazily around the majestic liner, tooting furiously. But the roar reached a deafening peak as the *United States* moving at a slow stately pace so all could see, passed the skyscrapers at Manhattan's tip at 12:10. Lunchtime crowds lined the waterfront cheering. A snowstorm of ticker tape fluttered down from the buildings. Veteran tug skippers called it the greatest reception they could remember." There were many signs on buildings on Manhattan, but the largest by far was a huge "WELCOME UNITED STATES, Gibbs & Cox, Inc." hanging from 21 West Street. The word "welcome" covered eight windows, stretching the entire width of the building.

Under a five-column air photo of the superliner surrounded by small craft, Jack Tait of the *Herald Tribune* described the welcome as "glorious, heartwarming." Full page advertisements, half- page photos and innumerable short items deluged the public with information about the new ship. She would be open to the public on Saturday from 10 a.m. to 4 p.m. One spectator of the arrival commented: "Every American should see this ship."

At a ceremony aboard after her arrival a silver bowl, done in the style of the celebrated 18th century silversmith Paul de Lamerie, was presented by Owen C. Torrey, president of the American Institute of Marine Underwriters. A little booklet commemorating the presentation was issued by the trade group with a picture of the bowl on the cover, Frank Farrell, *World-Telegram* *colum*nist who had come up on the ship, opined that there should be nine more ships like the *United States*. Then, he wrote, the 500,000 Americans who would be touring Europe in 1952 could all be within 4 days of home should "Soviet legions decide to roll across the rest of that continent." Another ceremony aboard saw the new liner receive her Naval Reserve pennant, proof that the master and at least half her officers were members of the Merchant Marine's Naval Reserve. A dinner was held for the press with a speech by General Franklin. He thanked everyone for their coverage of the maiden arrival and went on to say that the ship could not have been built as a commercial venture.

Perhaps the most elaborate document put out in connection with the first visit of the *United States* to New York was a 120-page magazine produced by the West Side Association of Commerce. Called *The Westsider,* it was entirely *United States* from first to last page, and included an insert with the deck plans for the three classes. I contributed an article on the *Baltic,* the last American built liner to hold the Blue Ribbon, and also a double-page drawing showing the evolution of the American ship from the Indian canoe to the *United States.* Anne Urquhart and Dorothy Marckwald had an article entitled, most aptly, "Decorations DeLuxe" and beautifully illustrated. The May-June issue of the Newport News shipyard house magazine, *Shipyard Bulletin,* offered even better photographs, particularly a double-page spread of the new liner taken on her trials by William T. Radcliffe. It would become a favorite photo of William Francis Gibbs and he would have large blowups made, framed, and available to give special friends. The U.S. Lines distributed many new pieces of literature, perhaps the finest of which was a 24-page full color brochure designed by Lester Beall. Even the fancy-letters which began each paragraph were two-colored. The brochure featured excellent water color impressions of the ship's interior overlaid atop full page impressions of happy passengers just hinted at by a few artistic light blue lines. A fold-out centerspread 33 inches long and done in red, white, and blue, gave a sweeping artist's impression of the superliner, with stacks that were raked too much and actually too small. Until someone actually saw the stacks on the *United States* it was impossible to conceive how large they really were.

The Post Office Department issued a story from Washington on June 27 noting that it expected 150,000 pieces of philatelic mail to sail on the *United States.* A cachet had been designed for all covers sent to the Postmaster at New York. Those for delivery in the United States might also be sent on the first voyage and they would be backstamped on receipt at Southampton or Le Havre and returned to the addressee in the United States. Another cachet was prepared for the maiden voyage by the Seamen's Church Institute of New York. The trip would be well documented philatelically.

The *United States* was the cover picture of *Newsweek* dated June 30 and out June 26, with the caption: "Fastest, Toughest, Most Beautiful." Their story began: "The man who has grabbed the initiative again for the U.S. is William Francis Gibbs, 65-year old, bespectacled, publicity-shy head of the New York firm of Gibbs & Cox, world's biggest independent ship designers. Hardly known outside the shipbuilding industry, he has been described as the 'greatest influence on naval design since John Ericsson.' When attempts are made to give him full credit for the *United States,* however, Gibbs replies testily that 'about 50% of the marine engineering brains of the country have been applied to this ship.' Swiftness is only one of the new ship's defense features. Below her waterline alone, there are so many secrets that the locks had to be opened and the drydock had to be flooded the night before the crowd arrived to watch her christened." The story stressed her bulkheading: "No single torpedo could sink her as one did the *Lusitania.* She could survive a collision like that which sank the *Titanic.*"

Saturday, June 28, finally arrived, the day when the public was allowed aboard, and it produced one of New York port's most remarkable spectacles. The crowd began to line up early, although the ship was not open until 10 a.m. More and more police had to be called, there were so many people. The line stretched from Pier 86 at 46th Street, three abreast, all the way down to 37th Street, turned with a "U" and extended back to Pier 86, the equivalent of 14 blocks in length. The year before 13,000 people over several days had seen the new *Independence*. In 1932 the *Rex* had drawn 17,000 paying visitors. But in this case 70,000

Cover of the U.S. Lines 24-page full color brochure designed by Lester Beall.

*The 24-page full color brochure designed by
Lester Beall distributed by U.S. Lines.*

people showed up to stare, 19,696 were permitted aboard and many others who had stood in line were turned away. The Travelers Aid Society earned a record of $12,654 in fees from the lucky ones who got aboard. Mildred Tross, of the Broadmoor Hotel, was asked why she stood in line so long: "I wanted to see the boat. I just wanted to see it. It's the only way I'll ever get on it. One puffing woman asked a policeman how long the line we to the south and he replied: "I can't see that far, lady. The Lord didn't give me such good eyes." The viewing was to end at 4 p.m., because an evening VIP inspection had been scheduled, but the crowd was so vociferous that John Brennan extended the time to 5 and then to 5:30. Still the police estimated 4,000 had to be turned away.

On Monday, June 30, Jeanne Toomey, who because she was a woman had been denied the privilege of sailing up from Newport News on the delivery trip, devoted a column to the fact she had been invited on the maiden voyage. "Of course Margaret Truman and the Vincent Astors are going too," she quipped. "Don't know whether I'll be anywhere near them, but even if it's only a hammock in the engineroom, it'll be air conditioned."

A list of 1,700 persons was scheduled to sail on the maiden voyage, the U.S. Lines announced in their first press release for a *United States* sailing issued July 1. Heading the company was Margaret Truman who had Cabin M-66. General Franklin was in Suite U-83-85. The Astors were shown occupying Cabin U-87-89. William Francis Gibbs had U-124. Frederic was staying home. Other passengers included Dorothy Marckwald (U-139) and Anne Urquhart (M-143). Miss Gwenn Lux, sculptress who had designed the large wall decoration in the Main Dining Saloon, was in S-15. Metropolitan Opera conductor Fritz Reiner and Mrs. Reiner were aboard. General David Sarnoff, who had made the controversial trial trip of the *Leviathan* in 1923, was a passenger, along with three Senators and two Congressmen. Federal judges, business leaders, society, and the press were liberally represented. A special 16-page maiden voyage booklet, in red, white, and blue, was published by U.S. Lines. The company also produced a little flyer the like of which to my knowledge was never done for any other ship. It gave the square foot area for every First Class stateroom. Also provided was the depth (thwartships) and the width (fore and aft) measurements, the area of the shower, the area of the cabin's foyer when there was one, and the areas of the bath, the trunk room, and the dressing room. The largest of the double cabins had 364 square feet together.

Rumors of what high speeds the *United States* had made on the trials were circulating. The *Missoula* (Mont.) *Sentinel* ran an editorial on July 2 entitled "Great New Ship" that showed what the public was expecting. "The American challenger, though five-eighths the size of the *Mary* and *Elizabeth,* has exceeded 40 knots, though officially she admits to a speed of only 34. At 40 knots, the crossing could be cut to a flat three days, which would make naval history. May her big red, white, and blue stacks become the symbols of inspiring achievement on the seas."

Some of the foodstuffs taken aboard for the maiden crossing included 123,811 pounds of meat, 59,450 pounds of poultry, 12,468 quarts of fresh milk, 7,935 quarts of ice cream. Fish eaters could choose from 24,458 pounds of smoked, fresh and chilled fish, including lobster, shrimp, frog legs, shelled crab, and clams, and 500 pounds of caviar. The 70,000 spectators on the previous Saturday had so alarmed pier officials that only guests of passengers were to be permitted aboard during the hours before the noon sailing on July 3. Each passenger in First Class got three passes, and those in Cabin and Tourist got two each. Word from Southampton and Le Havre indicated that big preparations for welcoming the liner were underway. At the British port rockets would be fired from the training ship *South Hill* by cadets of the Southampton School of Navigation. The *Liverpool Journal of Commerce,* in a cordial article about the liner, bemoaned the fact that its editor had not been invited by U.S. Lines to be aboard on the crossing. The reason, it was added, was "easily appreciated-the long list of American journalists who have prior claim." However U.S. Lines has offered space on the crossing from Le Havre to Southampton. More than that, the Liverpool paper had arranged "for a passenger on board to send messages to this newspaper during the voyage." Their article noted that airplanes were already taking 40% of the trans-Atlantic traffic, "most from the highest fare-paying group," and expressed the opinion that speed was not important any longer in ship travel.

Sailing day came and everyone but Commodore talked of little else but the Blue Ribbon. The Commodore was asked about this and, with a broad grin, replied: "I have been ordered to observe the schedule. The main thing is a safe passage." Privately, however, it was known to a few that he was hoping to be able to "cut the corner," as it was said in the marine world. He wanted to steam closer to the Coast Guard iceberg patrol ships than was allowed to save time by reducing the distance on the great circle course. The weather ships were used to this. It was done by all big ships when they wanted to make a fast crossing. It must have been a frightening experience to serve on one of these weather craft and to see a great hulk appear out of the fog going 27 knots! The *Herald Tribune's* story ran under a headline that expressed everyone's thoughts: *"SS United States* Sails, May Try for the Record." Its lead sentence surmised that "there was every indication that she was out to win the trans-Atlantic speed record on her first trip."

Some 8,000 invited guests of the 1,600 passengers gave a festive feeling to the sailing, keeping stewards running for ice, champagne and other wants. Another 5,000 onlookers clustered about the street end of the pier stopping traffic on 12th Avenue. At 12:07, flags and bunting draped from her masts, the great new superliner began to ease into the current of the Hudson. Colored confetti and streamers were thrown from the shore and from the ship. The band played "Anchors Aweigh." At 12:20 she cast off from her Moran tugs and blew three deep-throated blasts as the white water churned at her stern. Two hours and 16 minutes later, at 2:36 to be exact, she passed Ambrose Light and was pouring on the oil," according to ship-to-shore telephone reports from aboard. Her wake was boiling under her stern. Possibly this was why no reply was made to a whistle and a signal flag and a radio signal from the incoming Cunarder *Mauretania*. When this two-stacker inheritor of the great *Mauretania's* name docked at 5:30, Captain Donald W. Sorrell said he was neither miffed nor disturbed. He said the vessels were a mile apart and the *United States* might easily have failed to hear his whistle or see his flags signaling "Good voyage." As for the radio message, he noted that she was probably so swamped with messages that she could not reply. This most friendly attitude was to be repeated a thousand fold when the ship reached Southampton.

"If the ship makes a record, I can't help that," Harry Manning told reporters at noon on the first full day out. The *United States* set a new world's record for that first 20 hours and 24 minutes since passing Ambrose. She traveled 696 nautical miles at an average speed of 34-11 knots, but again Commodore Manning denied that he was trying to make a record. Asked whether he was satisfied, William Francis Gibbs replied: "My expectations are rather high, and the ship is running them hard." George Horne would later call this "an expansive statement for the laconic Mr. Gibbs," and would say "that he was experiencing what for most people would be excitement and exultation." That first day out the weather was clear with a mild southwest wind and a slight to moderate sea. The forecast ahead was for good weather. Members of the steward's department were kept busy delivering what Purser John Lock described as a record volume of bon voyage gifts and messages. There were 5,000 packages, 5,000 Pieces of mail, and 12,000 telegrams. Walter Hamshar would jot down in his notebook for transmittal that evening by wireless that there were some complaints of vibration in the aft Cabin Class spaces "but seasoned travelers report that it is minute compared with high-speed voyages of other ships." Commodore Manning said his own hand was trembling more than the ship as he stood at a point not far from one of the two engine rooms. The *Tribune's* story joked: "One of the complaints that the passengers themselves are taking steps to meet is that there is a superabundance of men in First Class, while women are more abundant in Cabin. It is expected that the shortage of dancing partners in the two classes will be adjusted by the time Independence Day festivities get under way." Mr. Hamshar, a specialist in square dancing, was keen on this subject. The *Associated Press* noted that on the first day of her record run in August, 1938, the *Queen Mary* had gone 685 miles at an average of 31-13 knots.

There was a straw in the wind that reared its ugly head on Saturday, July 5. Arthur LeBarge, assistant business manager of the Marine Engineers Beneficial Association, asked a negotiating session for a 15% increase in wages and an increase in the manning scale from 43 engineers to 60 on the *United States*. He had made a survey of working conditions on the new ship, he said, and maintained that she had such an intricate power plant that the "extremely high degree of skill" required of her engineers demanded more money. The demand for a one-third increase in personnel was also justified as "essential to safety, efficiency, and decent working conditions." The harried U.S. Lines offered a 10% wage boost for the three first-assistant engineers and suggested further discussions on the manning scale demands. Mr. LeBarge called this reply inadequate and unfair, but agreed that no action would be taken until after the maiden voyage. Throughout her life the *United States* would be a marked ship from the standpoint of labor disputes. As will be seen the almost continuous series of work stoppages and strikes that would shock her later days were responsible in good part for her relatively short career.

While Eisenhower and Taft battled for the Republican Presidential nomination, the story of the maiden voyage remained front page news. On Sunday, July 6, the wireless accounts of the previous day's steaming were read by millions of Americans. The stories were about how on the night of July 4/5 she had continued her record-setting pace despite blinding fog and bumpy seas. After two days and 1,497 miles of ocean her average was close to 35 knots. Deck chair experts were predicting that she would pass Bishop's Rock off the English coast before dawn on Monday to break the *Queen Mary's* record by six to ten hours. Commodore Manning got only three hours sleep over the night of fog. With her two giant radar screens as his eyes the ship was reported to be hitting 36 knots. By morning of the 5th, Saturday, the fog had lifted, but a strong wind whipped the waves into what seamen called "moderate sea." Commodore Manning received a message from Captain Harry Grattidge of the *Queen Mary:* "Welcome to the family of big liners on the Atlantic," it said. The famous Cunard racer, 81,000 gross tons, was eastbound. There was no word from the *Queen Elizabeth,* 83,000 tons and the world's largest liner, which had left New York 35 hours ahead of the *United States.* Many representatives of the British radio and newspaper world were aboard the new superliner giving their readers in England a day-by-day account of the crossing. BBC commentator Douglas Willis was saying: "This ship has got it. She'll win the Blue Ribbon by 10 hours." The log would show that she made 80 miles on her second day, at an official average of 35.60 knots.

Sunday was filled with excitement for those aboard the *United States.* Just before noon the 53,000-ton French liner *Liberté,* which as the *Europa* had been a holder of the Blue Ribbon of the Atlantic, was diverted from her course toward New York so she could pass fairly close to the new superliner. There was great cheering and waving as the two huge ships steamed past each other. An even more dramatic moment occurred moments later when a voice from the heroic past of Commodore Manning came out of the ether to remind him of one of his most heralded feats of bravery. It was a message from Captain De Marzo, an Italian who had been a crew member 23 years before aboard the Italian ship *Florida*. Commodore Manning, then Chief Officer of the old *America,* had skippered the rescue lifeboat which took De Marzo and all others safely off the sinking vessel in one of the year's worst gales. Now he was master of the 8,929-ton student travel liner *Arosa Kulm* somewhere beyond the horizon. His wireless reminded Commodore Manning of their association and added: "Please accept my best wishes to you and all aboard. God bless you." In reply Commodore Manning said: "Many happy remembrances." Something that was not mentioned in the news accounts from the *United States* that day was that the *Arosa Kulm* was formerly the U.S. Lines passenger-cargo ship *American Banker,* only one of her class of former World War I transports to survive World War II. She had been rebuilt by the American Merchant Line to carry nearly 100 passengers in the interwar period between New York and London. After the war the Arosa Line, a Swiss-owned company, had again rebuilt her with space for 900 students.

Still another warming note from that eventful day aboard the *United States.* It was made known in the morning that the new liner, when she entered British waters, would specifically refrain from displaying the sailorman's traditional symbol of a clean sweep – the broom. This cachet of nautical supremacy was being withheld out of courtesy to English seamen, who were known to be sensitive about such a gesture. The tradition had begun in 1652 when a Dutch naval commander, Admiral Martin Harpertzoon Tromp, had paraded the length of the British Channel with a broom at the masthead of his flagship in defiance of the English fleet. His gesture signified his intention to sweep them from the seas. Since then no one had approached the British coast with such an insult. When the *Queen Mary* won the Blue Ribbon she was careful not to use such a display in her home waters. On the advice of the London office, U.S. Lines decided to forget the broom.

At noon the loudspeakers once again announced a new record for the previous 22 1/2-hour day. The ship had gone 814 miles at an average speed of 36.17 knots, the equivalent of 41.64 land miles per hour. "Only an unexpected fog could now stand between this liner and an Atlantic record," George Horne wrote for the next day's *New York Times.* Eastbound on the *United States,* going against the path of the sun, the days were 22 1/2 hours long and the clocks advanced 90 minutes each night. Commodore Manning said he expected to pass Bishop's Rock between 4 and 8 a.m. on Monday, ship's time, and promised to blow the whistle regardless of the hour. Many were planning to stay up all night to wait for the moment of victory.

The day's most dramatic and never-to-be-forgotten moment, however, came as the late afternoon was nearing its end. A smudge of smoke appeared on the distant horizon to the south, just a dot at first, but obviously moving at great speed. It was another liner and it had to be a big, fast one. The two ships approached on parallel courses, closing the gap at a rate of almost 80 land miles an hour. They were the two fastest ships in the world. The great vessel to the south was the sleek *Queen Mary,* her long black hull and full white superstructure topped by her three distinctive red/orange smokestacks, each taller than the one before from stern to bow. What a magnificent sight she was to those aboard the *United States.* And for those on the British superliner, what an exciting picture the new *United States* made. The churning of the American ship's wake seemed about one-fifth of her length, a passenger on the Cunarder said. She was obviously moving through the water at about 36 knots, another said. There was much excitement on the British liner and even the movie was emptied when her loudspeaker announced that they were in sight of the new American superliner. "What a thrill," another *Queen Mary* passenger was quoted the next day in the press as remarking. "If we couldn't be aboard her on her first crossing, at least we passed her on the high seas." The British liner lowered her colors in courtesy and the *United States* replied in kind. They were past and separating all too quickly.

The *Queen Elizabeth* docked at Southampton Sunday night, and her master, Commodore George E. Cove said: "You can take it for granted that there will be no attempt to beat the *United States.*" Although his ship was thought by all to be faster than the *Mary,* she had never attempted to outdo her slightly older companion ship. Another related story from that same Sunday night: "Well it looks as if we are going to lose the old Blue Ribbon," said a hat check man in one of London's big hotels. A *New York Times* reporter overheard him and used the line as his lead in his London-datelined story for the following day. The reporter's name was Clifton Daniel, who would some time later marry Margaret Truman, the best known passenger on the new superliner.

At dinner that night aboard the new ship, Walter Bachman sat next to the sculptress Miss Lux. They were at the Captain's table, just beneath her huge piece of sculpture. Mr. Bachman had been at the same table on the delivery run and remembered hearing William Francis wax eloquent about the meaning behind the four figures in the large wall decoration. He had asked yard president Blewett, who was sitting with him, if he had ever heard the real meaning behind their creation, what they were meant to depict. Then he called the whole piece by some long German name, meaning the four seasons, and went into great length about which figure depicted Spring, which was Winter and so on. Bachman was impressed. He turned to Miss Lux and told her how Gibbs had obviously been very keen on the story behind the work. She smiled and said: "Mr. Gibbs was making it all up. The four figures represent the four freedoms, and he knows it perfectly well!"

Monday, July 7, was the day of days for those aboard the *United States.* For many the day began at midnight. The weather was bad. It was rainy and miserable outside but cheery inboard. There was one continuous long all-night party for many simply would not go to bed. Everyone knew that the ship would reach Bishop's Rock sometime around dawn, but the thrill of anticipation kept them awake. Walter Jones was a wreck, barely able to keep his eyes open but he postponed sleep for a few more hours, knowing that the key moment of the trip for him and for the company was just ahead. Margaret Truman wisely got in a few hours rest. Commodore Manning forced himself to spend a couple of hours in his bunk, just after midnight. William Francis Gibbs had gone to bed early with a call to be awakened at 4 a.m. He, perhaps above all others, knew when the moment of moments would happen. He had planned it all. He had ordered Commodore Manning not to exceed 150,000 horsepower on the maiden voyage. It had been this order that led Commodore Manning to casually comment that she was "just cruising." He knew that she was not using her full power, but he could not explain his comment. This led later to charges that he had been boasting, and produced some unfortunate publicity. The official horsepower of the *United States* was set at 158,000, the same as the *Queen Mary*. This was what the official building contract had called for, but there was a one-page addendum to the contract of which only three copies were made. This addendum called for 240,000 horsepower for naval purposes. The three copies were in the hands of the Maritime Administration, the Newport News shipyard, and Gibbs & Cox, according to Walter Bachman.

At 5:16 a.m. Greenwich time, 6:16 ship's time, 2:16 New York time, the *United States* broke the *Queen Mary's* record. She passed Bishop's Rock. The exact time of her crossing was 3 days, 10 hours and 40 minutes. The average speed was 35-59 knots. She had upped the Cunarder's average speed by 3.90 knots, the greatest margin since the little British channel steamer *Sirius* had raced the *Great Western* across the Western Ocean in 1838. A 25-knot wind was blowing at the time. The Rock was eight miles away and could not be seen in the early morning mist. But it was clearly visible on radar. The passing was marked by a single blast on the whistle. Pandemonium broke out on deck and was carried by chain reaction into the Observation Lounge, the Bar, and everywhere. Many passengers were still wearing the colored paper hats that had been passed out the evening before at a premature Victory party. The ship's band struck up the "Star-Spangled Banner," and cheer after cheer echoed from bow to stern, the crew joining in with unabashed enthusiasm. One choice photograph taken by a passenger showed a conga line of exhausted but happy passengers winding around the enclosed promenade forward.

As radar showed the Rock to be falling behind, the tension on the Bridge relaxed. Margaret Truman added her congratulations to the many that were offered to Commodore Manning. He said he felt like a pitcher who had just struck out the last batter in a no-hit game. William Francis was surrounded by an adulatory crowd who looked at him for an historic pronouncement. He had spent almost the entire voyage making notes on the vessel's performance, and everyone expected a phrase they would always remember. "A fine performance," was all they could get out of him. Back in his cabin there awaited his perusal a radiogram from New York:

"The outstanding unprecedented performance and record of the *SS United States is* surely a reward for your extraordinary knowledge, skill, and foresight, plus years of your great and constant enthusiasm. I know this better than anyone else and in addition I believe destiny and divine providence smiled upon us. My sincere admiration and congratulations go out to you. Freddie."

His reply was prompt: "Many thanks your message. We share equally in our participation in the result. Had hoped to communicate by telephone but this appears impractical. The performance of the ship is in line with our hopes. Operation excellent. Many, many thanks for your invaluable assistance and cooperation. Concur divine providence made possible result which should enthuse our fellow citizens well. Willie."

More telegrams came over the wires, including one from President Truman. Although the speed run was completed, the liner drove on at an undiminished pace as the weather cleared. At noon, when she was only 57 miles from Le Havre, the order was given to diminish speed. She was so far ahead of schedule that all sorts of complications could be expected. She had not been due to dock until the following morning and boat trains for Paris would not be ready until then. The official French welcome was also scheduled for the following morning and could not be changed. Passengers were told that after the ship docked they could debark if they chose, but most preferred to remain aboard for the night. The French harbor master informed the ship by wireless that no pier space was ready and that she would have to anchor off the entrance to the port. But nobody worried. Everyone was joyous; everyone was exhausted. But more was to happen before that day would be over.

The noon announcement Monday showed that another record, the fourth in a row, had been made in the previous 22 1/2-hour day. The ship had gone 833 miles at an average of 36.21 knots. Commodore Manning's scheme took form, each day a little more power, a little faster. The day's runs had been 696 miles, 801 miles, 814 miles and finally 833 miles. The speed had edged up slowly from 34.11 knots to 35.60 to 36.17 to 36.21. Pressed for more comments Commodore Manning praised the work of his radar. "I'd rather be without my right arm than radar." He predicted that the new record might not stand for a very long time, adding that "atomic developments may produce faster ships." He said he would try for a record on the westerly crossing "if the opportunity is there" but said the "prevailing winds will make the crossing slower."

Word reached New York radio stations of the record and was broadcast Monday morning. I telephoned a press release to all major news services pointing out that the new speed record had been won "by a wider margin than ever before in the history of steamships on the Atlantic." The release was widely used. Elizabeth Toomey, writing for the *New York Daily News,* noted in her July 7 release from the ship that the high speed had prevented most passengers from enjoying any deck chair reading. The winds "bowled over deck chairs and overturned ping-pong tables, but the smooth-riding ship itself betrayed none of the turmoil on deck." She was no relation to the *Brooklyn Eagle's* correspondent aboard, Jeanne Toomey. Commodore Manning, in one of his rare jokes, said about the ship's stability that the only roll aboard was on the breakfast table.

The passage to Le Havre ended at 12:24 p.m. British Standard Time. The liner would have to lay at anchor for four and one-half hours awaiting permission to enter and space to tie up. It was still another record. The passage from New York to Le Havre had taken 3 days, 17 hours and 48 minutes. The average speed had been 35-53 knots. Perhaps the most rousing welcome, as the *United States* entered French waters, had come from what everyone thought to be an American warship. Her crew lined up on the decks and cheered, a band played "Anchors Aweigh" and her siren blared a continuous greeting. To everyone's surprise she turned out to be the British carrier *Indomitable.* The enthusiasm of the British press and television people aboard the *United States* had also surprised many and was an omen of what was to come. They had been up on the Bridge on Monday morning with their American colleagues when Bishop's Rock had been passed and they were the first in the radio room with hurriedly written pages of copy telling that England was no longer mistress of the seas, at least as far as speed was concerned.

One ship at the entrance to Le Havre did not salute. She was the sleek pre-war liner *Batory,* of the Gdynia American Line. She had left New York service some months before never to return after taking home Gerhard Eisler, a Communist who had jumped bail and was a fugitive.

Finally, as her passengers were entering the Dining Saloon for dinner, the two Le Havre pilots assigned to the *United States,* Albert Guerrier and George Dubois, gave the signal for up anchor and the progress into Le Havre began. The ship, "wearing her laurels like an aristocrat," as George Horne of the *Times* put it, received a tumultuous welcome. Whistles tooted, fireboats pumped water into the air, thousands of onlookers along the beach and on the quays cheered as she was escorted into the harbor and to her berth. It was the same pier, much rebuilt, where the famous *Paris* had burned and where the *Normandie* had docked.

More messages of congratulations came aboard. F.A. Bates, chairman of the Cunard Line, sent one to General Franklin and another to Commodore Manning. Commodore Cove sent a "generous message to his old friend, Commodore Manning," as one report noted. Don Iddon, reporter from the London *Daily Mail,* who was aboard the *United States,* telegraphed to his readers these lines of consolation: "It is true we have been beaten in speed, possibly in lack of vibration. But in comfort, size, food, service, and dignity we are still supreme." A writer for the British news service *Reuters* reported along this line that "the service on board is not quite up to the remarkable speed, but the purser is confident that it will improve." Several British newspapers reported that a considerable number of the crew of the new American supership were Britons, trained aboard Cunard ships. Clifford Thomas, of Kingston-on-Thames, won the final ship's pool, having made the best guess on her record speed. Pocketing about $4,000 he was overheard saying: "Well the British have won something."

Barbara Jo Allen, born on the maiden voyage, with ship's doctor, Frank Ciparelli, at her christening. (Courtesy of Emma Elisabeth Arbenz – the former Barbara Jo Allen)

As France honored the *United States* for her record breaking passage, they also paid tribute to one of their own – M. Jacques-Yves le Toumelin, who returned home on the same day from a round the world voyage alone in his 32-foot sloop named *Kurun*. He had sailed from the Breton port of La Croisic and it was to that point that he returned after a 34-month, 30,000-mile voyage.

Although the formal French welcoming ceremonies for the *United States* were set for the morning of Tuesday, July 8, many port dignitaries came aboard the night of the 7th and there were gay parties from one end of the liner to the other. Among the visitors were a number of the officers and crew from H.M.S. *Indomitable*, which had moored just ahead of the American liner.

A champagne breakfast was held aboard the *United States* to start the festivities of welcome Tuesday. While officials were making speeches and bands were playing, the first new life was ushered into the world aboard the new ship. A 5-1/2 pound daughter was born to passengers Dr. and Mrs. Milton J. Allen, of Madison, New Jersey. She was named Barbara Jo. The Allens were enroute to England.

The Channel crossing began at 12:46 p.m. on July 8 and the 75 miles to Nab Tower, off the entrance to Southampton, took only 2 hours and 51 minutes, at an average of 26.31 knots. Aboard was the *Liverpool Journal of Commerce* reporter who regularly wrote a column in the style of Samuel Pepys' Diary. His comments: "Apart from the ship herself, I were most impressed by two things – the modesty with which those responsible have assumed the laurels her performance hath gained, and the warmth of the reception accorded at Southampton. Commodore Manning, her commander, did express himself to me as really proud and happy to have gained the Blue Riband, but he did feel a tinge of sadness in taking it from the *Queen Mary,* with years of tradition and service behind her. He did remark that the latter had the chance to gain it back, but added with conviction – 'Not if I can help it!'" Bearing in mind British skill in shipbuilding, William Francis Gibbs said: "We submit our effort with humility and friendliness for kind sympathy and consideration, We honour you for your achievements in ships. We have tried to emulate you." He noted in particular the appearance off Le Havre of the new French liner *Flandre,* which "does possess an impressive profile, suggestive of power, but be not, of course, designed for records." Her seamen and trial crew "did cheer and wave to the big American liner." The Liverpool writer also noted with some satisfaction that as the *United States* began her departure from Le Havre the band of the *Indomitable* played "Britannia Rules the Waves," something of a "gesture of assurance, even defiance."

There is no question that the welcome in Southampton was an ovation. It was described by many different sources as the greatest reception ever given to any ship at any port in the world. It was warmer and on a larger scale than any of the ship's company or officials of the U.S. Lines had anticipated. Even the British passengers aboard were astonished. As the *Liverpool Journal's* correspondent put it: "We be regarded as nationally phlegmatic and unemotional." Many scores of small craft and thousands of people were on hand to shout and whistle and wave their welcomes. Walter Hamshar's story began: "The British people gave a dramatic display of international sportsmanship today by greeting the superliner *United States* with one of the greatest spontaneous welcomes ever tendered to any ship in any port. The festive welcomes began even before the British coast was sighted. Jet planes flew overhead and a number of British and American destroyers and other naval craft took up positions to serve as escorts. Off the Isle of Wight a flotilla of pleasure craft and sightseeing vessels joined the entourage, crowded to the gunwales with passengers. The welcoming fleet grew even larger as the superliner neared the inner harbor. Jam packed sailboats, ferries, and tugs filled with cheering people tried to keep up with the slowly moving superliner." Over 6,000 had applied for tickets to enter the Southampton docks, but only 2,000 could be accommodated. The ship's orchestra on the crowded Promenade Deck played both the British and the American national airs, as did the Southampton Police Band on the pier. Alderman E. Burrow led a host of 150 dignitaries and newsmen up the first gangplank. He brought an official welcome to Miss Truman and escorted her ashore. Brief ceremonies were conducted in the Smoking Room on board. The Mayor and Mayoress of Southampton presented a telegram from Prime Minister Winston Churchill. There were several speeches. William Francis Gibbs was his most gracious best with his comment: "I hope she will never be used in war, except to defend the cause of English-speaking peoples."

James Edmund Duffy, *World Telegram* ship news reporter, was aboard helping with the ship's newspaper. The welcome so overcame him that he sat down and dashed off a seven-page article which he entitled: "Who Said the British Hate Us." It was so emotional that it was almost hard to read at this writing. A few lines will illustrate: "Do the people of England really hate us? Is there any truth in the charges frequently heard in the last few years that England is jealous of our world position, and that if the occasion arose she would line up with Russia and her satellites against us? Ridiculous! The reception given this great American ship by the British press and people not only thoroughly dispelled these beliefs, but evoked a demonstration of good will for us that could never have taken place if there had been enmity, or even the slightest ill feeling in the hearts of the British or the American People. Crew and passengers aboard the *United States* were so amazed at what occurred on their arrival in England that they found it difficult to control their emotions." And this from a veteran, hard-as-nails New York City reporter. He quoted the *London Daily Mail,* which said: "Southampton that has welcomed nearly every great liner in the world gave her greatest welcome last night to the new *United States.* It could not have been any noisier, gayer nor more sincere if the new liner had been British. It was even more boisterous than that given to the *Queen Mary* when she made her maiden voyage in 1936. Throughout the afternoon crowds had gathered on the quay side until at five o'clock – more than an hour before the ship was due – they stood 20 deep. The roof of the Ocean Terminal was crowded six hours before she arrived." And Jim Duffy concluded: "The writer is a witness that when the Americans aboard, so far from home, finally became conscious of what was happening they could no longer suppress their choked up emotions. Tears were in the eyes of many, and be it to their credit they were unashamed of them and felt better for the experience."

William Francis sent another telegram to Frederic: "Arrived Southampton 6:10 after most satisfactory voyage. All enthusiastic and very complimentary. Prime Minister sent warming congratulations. I am remaining on ship as must attend VIP luncheon tomorrow. Extraordinary enthusiasm and receptions Le Havre and here."

In Washington Secretary of Commerce Sawyer sent a radiogram to Commodore Manning: "I knew you would do it. Congratulations on the marvelous run. All of us at home have followed the amazing performance of the *United States* with growing excitement." He praised William Francis Gibbs and said: "His prophetic vision of the possibilities of a great superliner, backed by your initiative, courage, and persistence have produced something of which all America is very proud."

Surrounded by small craft sounding their horns, the SS United States *enters Southampton Docks at the end of her maiden voyage.*

In a jeweler's shop in the town of Hanley, near London, sat the Hales Trophy. The shop's owner, Eric Pidduck, was wondering that July 8 whether U.S. Lines would want it. He had heard nothing from them. The trophy had been in his shop for 11 years, having been returned by the French Line after Cunard had rejected it. The Pidduck company had made it in 1935. It had cost $2,500 when made and Mr. Pidduck thought it would cost about $7,000 as of that moment. The prize was under the authority of a board of trustees headed by England's Duke of Sutherland. They had asked Mr. Pidduck to get it ready for the arrival of the American superliner and were eagerly awaiting instructions from 1 Broadway.

A flurry of editorials throughout America and England hailed the new liner and her record. Newspapers in the Middle West that had never mentioned a ship carried such comments. William Francis Gibbs and his "dream boat" became common topics of conversation, especially whenever ships were discussed. Commodore Manning became a citizen of the world. Little did he or anyone around him realize that his period of supreme fame would be short, and that within less than a year, he would leave the sea never to return.

At the VIP lunch aboard the *United States,* Viscount Runciman, chairman of the General Council of British Shipping, gave credit to the "whole body of American taxpayers" in his reference to the government subsidy that made the ship possible. He stressed that competition "need not be inconsistent with cooperation." General Franklin illustrated this theme by saying how grateful U.S. Lines was to Cunard for altering its schedule so that Southampton's new terminal would be available to the *United States.* Commodore Manning recalled that more than 2,000,000 men and women of the U.S. Military forces had landed at Southampton in World War II. Mayor Edwin Burrow stressed the port's role in the "glorious association of our peoples" since the *Mayflower.* U.S. Ambassador Walter S. Gilfford said he hoped the new ship would never be called to perform the kind of services her companion vessel, the *America,* had to do in the second war. While all these speeches were going on a procession of launches and tugs crowded with sightseers went past the new liner. They waved and cheered. One man on one of those boats was heard to shout: "It won't be long!" He meant that Britain would soon regain the symbolic maritime speed trophy. Shipping men, however, were doubtful that the *Queens* would ever be replaced. Back in New York after the *Queen Mary* had docked, one of her passengers, Vice-Admiral C.C. Hughes-Hallett had been quoted as saying that neither the *Queen Mary* nor the *Queen Elizabeth* would be able to regain the trophy. He was head of the naval section of the British Joint Services Mission.

The *United States* sailed from Southampton to Le Havre on the afternoon of July 10. Her return voyage would be something of an anticlimax – more of the same, more records, more congratulations, and another gala welcome. Among the 1,617 passengers was the Duke of Sutherland. The U.S. Lines had decided very quickly that they did want the Hales Trophy and had invited him to come over with it to present it at a dinner aboard the superliner on July 15. He had to come across anyway as he was heading for Nassau for the season. After a brief stop at Le Havre the liner set out for New York, leaving the Le Havre Lightship behind at 2 a.m. on July 11. She passed Bishop's Rock at 9:17 British Standard Time and headed out into a glassy sea with 5-mile-an-hour winds. At noon on her first full day of sailing (this way, with the sun, a day was 25-1/2 hours), another new record was announced. She had covered 902 miles at an average speed of 36.08 knots. Chief Engineer William Kaiser said the record eastbound trip and the start of the return crossing had revealed no mechanical defects in the two giant engine rooms. He predicted the *United States* would be the world's foremost ship for the next 50 years. Commodore Manning congratulated his crew via a message posted in crew quarters along with copies of the messages received from President Truman and Prime Minister Churchill. Plans for New York City's welcome were well along, it was announced by Grover Whalen, chairman of the Mayor's reception committee. A Broadway ticker-tape parade was scheduled.

The *Illustrated London News* for July 12 featured two pages on the new liner, with a specially-drawn map of the Atlantic spelling out day by day the mileage traveled and speed made by both the *United States* and the *Queen Mary* on their record runs. This day aboard ship saw moderate seas and slight fog force a slight reduction in speed. At noon on Monday, the 13th, Commodore Manning announced that only 865 miles had been made over the previous 25 1/2 hours, at an average of 33.92 knots. The ship was entering an area of heavy traffic and precautions would have to be taken despite the desire to attain another record crossing. There was not the same tenseness and air of expectancy among the passengers as on the eastbound crossing. Whatever her time of arrival, the liner would conform to her planned 9 a.m. Wednesday docking schedule, anchoring at Ambrose Light overnight if necessary. At noon on Tuesday, Commodore Manning reported the previous day's run of 872 miles at 34.19 knots. Only hours away from Ambrose a record was now virtually certain.

At 4:29 p.m., July 14, 1952, the *United States* reached Ambrose, completing her maiden voyage. The red lightvessel gave her three blasts on her whistle, to which she responded with three deep whistle bursts, the last of which being a prolonged signal to the passengers that the race was over. Several planes flew overhead and a destroyer lay off to starboard as an escort. Other welcoming craft tossed in the haze-covered ocean. The passage from Bishop's Rock had taken 3 days, 12 hours, and 12 minutes at a speed of 34.51 knots. The Meyer Davis orchestra aboard played "God Bless America" and a new song dedicated to the big ship: "First Lady of the Sea." Paying tribute to Commodore Manning, the band then played "I'm Just Wild About Harry." Slowly the sleek new liner moved through the evening waters. She was making only 10 knots or so as she approached her anchoring place for the night. A pilot came aboard and there was another round of congratulations. A plan to fly a specially-made Blue Ribbon contributed to the ship by the newspaper men aboard was announced and drew cheers. It would be brought out the following morning and presented during the trip up the Bay. At an interview with correspondents on board William Francis Gibbs indicated that persistent rumors of a 40-knot speed were not excessive. He noted that the *United States* had set another record – a total of 5,844 nautical miles at an average of better than 35 knots for her historic round trip between Ambrose Light and Bishop's Rock. No naval or commercial vessel ever had sustained or even reached such a speed for more than a brief period. Asked for a final word, Commodore Manning said his first goal after dropping anchor off Quarantine was to take a bath and get some sleep.

The Bridge of the SS United States.

The next morning at 6 Mayor Impellitteri and the rest of the City's official party boarded two Coast Guard cutters at Pier 9, East River, and headed down to Quarantine. They climbed aboard the new liner through a sideport at the Narrows. Shortly after 7 she lifted her hook and began the two hour trip up the Bay, surrounded by a fleet of welcoming craft, large and small. Her bow bore evidence of the fierce wave friction endured on the passage home, many square feet of black paint had peeled off from her cutwater aft for one hundred feet. As she advanced, the 40-foot blue banner was hoisted from her modernistic aluminum mast. She flew the Blue Ribbon.

General Franklin announced to the press that the ship would not attempt soon to better her speed records, but would be throttled down hereafter to maintain her published five-day schedule. Cadet Midshipman Albert Hertenger kept the rough log as she moved majestically up the Bay. He estimated that her whistle responded with some 400 blasts to salutes from 130 small boats. Two fireboats waited off the Statue of Liberty, joining the parade as it moved up toward Pier 86. Six helicopters buzzed here and there and the Staten Island and New Jersey ferries joined in the procession. Aboard the City tug *Brooklyn,* the Sanitation Department Band did their best, but could only occasionally be heard over the continuous din. The parade passed the Italian Line's motorship *Vulcania,* which shouted out her welcome. Four blocks above, the great *Queen Elizabeth* called down a greeting. The Fire Department Band played on the pier end in front of masses of American flags. The ship docked at 9:12.

Comments about the maiden voyage ranged from the sublime to the ridiculous. *The Herald Tribune* in a lead editorial intoned: "From now on, she will be a familiar and cherished sight in the Hudson.... all New Yorkers join in twin salutes of welcome and 'well done.'" Jeanne Toomey joked in her column "Harbor Lights" that the round trip could have been dubbed "Operation Hangover." She called it a "gold-plated junket," and said that the bartender in the First Class Ballroom had remarked that he would be happy to take the cost of liquor consumed instead of his annual salary. Steve Manning, no relation to the Commodore, of the Maritime Administration, was chosen unanimously by reporters aboard as their candidate as dark horse for President.

The liner was scheduled to remain at her berth until July 23, when she would coordinate her schedule with the *America*. Great plans for the Broadway parade were announced. In addition to marching groups from the Air Force, Army, Navy, and Coast Guard, the 700 cadets from the U.S. Merchant Marine Academy, Kings Point, New York, would participate. Chief Engineer Kaiser, interviewed just after the docking, asserted that had it not been for the fog on Saturday and Sunday the ship would have excelled her eastward run.

"I believe the new records will stand for good," he added.

7

Subsidy Feud Continues

A superb cartoon drawing in black and white appeared in the July 16, 1952, issue of *Punch,* world famous British humor magazine. It summed up the cordial and yet competitive attitude of Britain to the winning of the Blue Ribbon by the *United States*. It was signed by an artist named Illingworth, who obviously had more than a taste for the sea. To the lower left foreground was an excellent air view of the *United States* at full steam in mid-Atlantic. Crossing her bow in the upper half of the picture was an airplane – the *Comet,* Britain's bid for air supremacy. In the wake of the *Comet* are two words, drawn as if made by some mysterious kind of sky writing: "Congratulations – Sister." An editorial in the *Shipping World,* published on this same date, was equally generous: "The reception accorded on her arrival at Southampton to the new passenger liner *United States* was without precedent for any foreign ship, in truth, it might be said that the ordinary Briton, always excepting that tiny minority which consistently works for disruption among the English-speaking peoples, does not think of America as a foreign country, but as one allied, far beyond the ties of written agreements, with the people of the British Commonwealth of Nations. As one American remarked in the new ship, 'Only the British having lost the Blue Riband, would give so freely an ovation rivalling that of the home port.' This imaginary and over-publicized Blue Riband has caused a good deal of wrong thinking in regard to the *United States,* and there have been not a few who thought that the new American liner was a freak ship designed somehow to do 40 knots or more, even if the boilers burst in the process. This is very far from being the case, and the true position should be clearly stated. Let it be said at once that the *United States is* one of the finest feats of naval architecture, ship construction, and marine engineering that has ever been seen. Without disrespect to the captain, Commodore Harry Manning, and his officers and crew, it may be said that the greatest tribute should be given to William Francis Gibbs, the designer of the ship, and indeed, the father of the whole project. ... We must say, as was so well said by so many in Southampton: 'Welcome to the *United States.*'"

The same publication had a lengthy article with pictures. Where facts were not known, the editors drew conclusions that were very close to the real situation. Their estimate as to the ship's total horsepower was 250,000 or barely 10,000 above the actual. Their only criticism was on the mixing of steel and aluminum alloys in the superstructure. And Gibbs took their concern to heart and insisted after each voyage of the new liner that a complicated series of tests be made to be sure that no electrolytic corrosion was happening. His method of linking aluminum to steel was not generally known at that time and the fact that in the ship's lifetime there were no problems on this score is further evidence of his depth of initial research.

An equally generous salute was made by the Pan American Airways in an advertisement. It showed their new Boeing B-377, known as the Stratocruiser, which had entered service in 1949, flying over the *United States.* The text proclaimed: "Pan American dips its wings to the new *SS United States.*" One of the same type aircraft as that shown was named *Clipper United States.*

A more scholarly British review of the new American superliner came from the pen of A.C. Hardy, noted British maritime author. His comments were carried in the July 17 issue of the *Liverpool Journal of Commerce,* and he mixed a little humor with his analysis: "Few will quarrel with her hull form, firstly because so little is known about it, and secondly because it has obviously proved itself by performance." Mr. Hardy continued: "Few new ships have been commissioned in such an atmosphere of controversy as has pervaded the liner *United States.* Differences of opinion about her even extended to her shape and general appearance. Many disagree about the enormous funnels, which, by reason of their dimensions could be of no other than light material."

An unnamed correspondent for the *Shipbuilding and Shipping Record,* another British magazine, writing in the first person, included some interesting observations: "I was surprised to find the upright upholstered chairs in the Cabin Class public rooms rather hard for sitting, in marked contrast to most of the other pieces of furniture I tried on board." He also noted that, "There is not the same falling off in the quality of the decorations and fittings of those tourist spaces compared with the First and Cabin public rooms, which feature is so characteristic of the vast majority of passenger ships." This writer had a large imagination which was evident when he described the new liner's troopship capacity of 14,000 men. "It is believed that the necessary fittings are concealed behind the linings of the pillars, shipsides, and bulkheads." He discovered little facts about the new radar ranges: "Perhaps to the layman the most interesting piece of equipment in the galleys was the electronic ray cooker, which cooks steaks in one minute, 14 seconds, and baked potatoes in one minute, 16 seconds. I am told that lobster takes a few seconds longer. These dishes are cooked on special type plates which remain cool and can be handled immediately they leave the cooker."

The American reaction to the new ship was more unrestrained: "Our Gal' the *Journal American* headline shouted: "In all of her great fresh beauty she came up the Bay and up the Hudson, moving with such easy grace as would fill your heart with pride to look at her, moving up the Bay and up the Hudson in all the glory that was hers." Poetry! Unabashed panegyric. And the parade up Broadway was seen by 150,000. Among those marching were 100 cadets from the *Statsraad Lehmkuhl*, Norwegian square-rigged sail training ship. At City Hall the Mayor welcomed the officers and crew and all those who had paraded in their honor under the large blue banner that the press had contributed to the ship to be her Blue Ribbon. And after it all the VIPs went up town to the Starlight Roof at the Waldorf-Astoria for a fancy luncheon, with music provided by the Police Department Band.

Horace Sutton, writing for the *Saturday Review of Literature*, poured a little cold water on the otherwise unanimous paean of praise: "Judging her as a transport for tourists, which is more in the purview of this department, her decorative scheme seems unimaginative, unrepresentative of a national or an individual personality." Not all the public rooms, however, met with his disfavor and he cited as "sprightly exceptions" the Observation Lounge, the Navajo Room, and the *a la carte* Restaurant. On the subject of fire prevention and safety at sea, Mr. Sutton found amusement in the boast that even the orchestra batons on the *United States* would be made of aluminum. He quoted columnist Robert Considine as saying that "some mighty nasty fires had started in batons." And he hinted darkly that it may have been a spark in a baton that had started the blaze aboard the excursion steamboat *General Slocum*.

On July 23 the *Scandinavian Shipping Gazette's* correspondent hailed the superliner: "Few ships have received greater attention from the general public than the new $80 million dollar flagship of the U.S. Lines. Her completion marked a red-letter day in the life of Mr. William Francis Gibbs, her designer. Is the *United States* a phenomenon? At a guess I would say that no one would attempt to build a ship of this size and power. The Americans are known to be very far ahead in their water-tube boiler design and it would be interesting, if it were possible to find it out, to know if they have succeeded in bringing down the specific fuel consumption to less than half a pound of oil per horsepower per hour. I do not think that others interested in the trans-Atlantic liner business will be greatly impressed from the point of view of passenger accommodation and the layout of public rooms. The First Class Dining Saloon is too small. The Observation Lounge is broken into as far as area is concerned by a trunk hatch and a large boiler-uptake, but then it should be remembered the *United States* is intended to be a quasi-warship. She is likely to retain the fastest merchant ship title for all time. She is an inspiration rather than a challenge and nothing could be more unfair than to compare her with some of the old trans-Atlantic ships."

During the ship's first layover period at New York, Mr. Gibbs ordered that samples of the fuel be taken for careful analysis. He would do this after each voyage from then on, and would also carefully review all voyage maintenance data. He was paid by U.S. Lines for performing this function, but he would have done it anyhow. He also began the custom of being on hand for each arrival and each sailing. Voyage 2 began July 23 and 1,710 passengers were aboard, including Admiral Cochrane. The following day in Washington the National Federation of American Shipping, a lobbying group, presented U.S. Lines with its second Distinguished Service Citation for its "courage, vision, and initiative" as contributing to the advancement of the merchant marine by incorporating into the *United States* unparalleled standards of speed, safety, and comfort. The trade group's previous citation had gone eight years before to Captain Henrik Kurt Carlsen for his display of courage in trying to save the freighter *Flying Enterprise*.

A slightly jaundiced perspective was used by editors of US. *News & World Report* in their July 24 issue. They described the new ship as "giving the country the thrill of having the best ship afloat and a lesson in the high cost of a modern merchant marine." She is, they added, "a storm center of controversy," and has "cost the taxpayers $48,000,000 to build, may cost them another $4,000,000 a year in operating subsidies and can cost both the country and taxpayers still other millions before it goes to scrap." On the plus side the magazine did note that the United States had paid about $100,000,000 during World War II to transport soldiers on the *Queen Mary* and the *Queen Elizabeth*. It concluded that "a sistership for the *United States* is already more than a gleam in the Navy's eye."

As the month ended the American Merchant Marine Institute's public relations committee sponsored a lunch to honor Walter Jones. A hand-done scroll with lots of colored letters and gold leaf was presented to him for his handling of the public relations during the introduction of the new superliner – "the First Lady of the Seas." The lunch was held aboard the *America*.

During the first and second voyages a large number of Gibbs & Cox specialists were aboard to help when occasion demanded. Norman Zippler, the electrical wizard who had come with Gibbs Bros. way back in 1922 to start planning for "the big ship," was one of these specialists. He had many minor problems because the stewards were still not familiar with the many new features of the ship. At midnight, for example, he had to go throughout the vessel and show them what lights to cut out. It had all been most carefully planned in advance, but the crew had to be told and told again. Special night lighting circuits were to be used for the public rooms. There were more special circuits for the corridors so that there would always be one light at least burning in every area all night. Teaching the stewards was the main problem. But it was not only the stewards who were having difficulties getting to know the new ship. Mr. Zippler remembered that he was continually being called night and day by Chief Engineer Kaiser. The Chief knew nothing to speak of about electrical matters, according to Mr. Zippler. Another of the specialists was B.O. Smith, and he was also very busy during these first crossings. He pointed out that the ship's turbines were not stopped while at foreign ports. It took six hours to "turn them off," and just as long again to get them started, so they were allowed to rest only while the ship was in New York.

The Gibbs brothers had great respect for the quality of work produced by the Newport News shipyard. They were also great admirers of the Bath Iron Works who built many destroyers to their designs. William S. Newell, Chairman of the Board at the Maine shipyard, was asked to summarize his thoughts about the *United States*. "Magnificent is the only word that can be applied to her and to her performance. The whole conception of the vessel, her design, construction, and operation place her on a plane apart. Having no part in her construction, I cannot speak for her designers, the builders, nor the Line, but I can speak as an American, proud of the achievement of fellow Americans; as a passenger who has witnessed her performance; and as a member of the shipbuilding fraternity. I can testify to the fact that in her role as a deluxe passenger liner she is comfortable to a remarkable degree and very easy at sea. As for vibration, the very lack of it-even when making knots at a pace previously unheard of-approaches the unbelievable. Finally, from a professional viewpoint, I am bound to state that not only was the *United States* wonderfully conceived but superbly executed. Not only is there no finer ship afloat, there is none her equal."

On August 4 the *United States* reached New York at the conclusion of her second round trip. Once again a full passenger list was aboard, 1,725 persons, including Mrs. William Francis Gibbs. Albert V. Moore, President of MooreMcCormack Lines and Mrs. Moore were also aboard, as was David Gimbel, son of the president of Gimbel Brothers, with his family. Rumors were flying that it would be Harry Manning's last trip. Although there was no company announcement his replacement was known by many to be Captain John W. Anderson, of the *America*. Commodore Manning said he hoped to be able to take a vacation for "a couple of months." He explained that he had lost ten pounds on the first trip and had averaged only four hours sleep a night. On the second he had managed to average six hours sleep, but he was exhausted, ready for a rest. He would not make the next voyage.

Captain Anderson was a complete opposite in temperament. Tall, quiet, gentle, retiring – John Anderson was, like Harry Manning, a life-long seaman. He had, again like Manning, graduated from the New York State Schoolship. During the second World War he had been master of the famous Swedish liner *Kungsholm*, renamed *John Ericsson*. All newspaper reports said his taking command of the *United States* would be temporary. Others were convinced that the Commodore was retiring for good to take a shore job. His lifelong ambition had been to return the Blue Ribbon to the United States. He had achieved it. And there had been rumors of a rift between the Commodore and U.S. Lines over Manning's blatant antagonism to organized labor. When he had been appointed many had thought it was only for a few trips. Still others heard stories of a battle between Manning and Gibbs. As Matt Forrest remembered, Manning's stubborn streak ran straight into Gibbs' determination to do things his way and there could be no compromise. William Francis Gibbs was particularly concerned over the loading of liquid ballast and the consumption of fuel. The maintenance of proper stability was a fetish with him. It meant a well thought out and strictly adhered-to routine. He was determined to be sure that the ship always maintained the highest standards of stability. He wanted to keep her intact stability excessive so that if she suffered a collision or damage there would be a great margin to prevent capsizing or sinking. The great importance of such adherence to a strict stability plan would be attested to in 1956 by the loss of the Italian Line's *Andrea Doria,* whose captain had failed on this very count. Commodore Manning would have had great difficulty fitting into this mold. He didn't want to be told, step by step, what had to be done. And he hated being checked up on to make sure he had done exactly what was required, step by step. Although Mr. Gibbs had been his most ardent supporter when he was first appointed, it would be this conflict of personalities that would limit Commodore Manning's time aboard the *United States,* and seemingly cut him off in his prime. When he left the ship on August 4 it was, in effect, the end for him. He would make a few more crossings, but never on a regular basis. It was the beginning of a sad and even tragic ending to a great career.

Historically, the question of Commodore Manning's future was the key development of August 4, but a much more important event for most reporters became known when the ship docked. The superliner had sailed from Le Havre about 30 minutes after the *Queen Elizabeth,* with 2,142 passengers aboard had left Cherbourg, her French port of call. At 10 that morning, the American vessel spotted her larger British rival just ahead. They had both just passed Bishop's Rock. Commodore Manning judged the *Queen* was making her normal cruising speed of 28 or 29 knots. He was averaging 31. The two ships were about a half-a-mile apart, or even less, judging from a photograph taken by a United Press photographer aboard. He had carefully posed two *United States* passengers, a Mr. and Mrs. Howard Hailey, of Atlanta, on either side of one of the ship's life preservers. He waited until the *Queen Elizabeth* was visible through the life preserver on the horizon. Then he snapped the picture. The *Elizabeth* appeared with a large bone in her teeth, but her average for the first day out showed clearly she was not making her best possible speed. Commodore Cove on the Cunarder ran up some signal flags to say "Pleasant voyage." Commodore Manning replied: "Thank you." Within four hours the British vessel had disappeared to the stern of the *United States.* She docked nine hours behind the new American racer.

Later both Commodores denied emphatically that they were racing, but Commodore Manning's denial was a bit sarcastic: "There wasn't any race, we just raced away from her," he said upon docking. "It was like standing still," he added. The log showed she had covered 776 miles at an average of 31.04 knots on her first day out. The *Elizabeth* averaged 27.84 knots and covered 720 miles on her first day. Later Commodore Cove said: "Commodore Manning and I merely exchanged greetings off Bishop's Rock." But many of the passengers and crew on the two ships knew the ships were racing. Meyer Flax, a Los Angeles businessman aboard the *United States,* said he felt "as if I was at a prize fight and looking at a champion who'd been knocked out." The colorful *maitre d'hotel* on the American ship, Archie Mundy, a veteran of the *Leviathan* and the *America*, was even more competitive. He had often received scoffing radiograms from Arthur Fagan, head bartender on the *Queen Elizabeth,* he said, when the Cunarder passed the

America. When the *United States* steamed past the British liner, Mr. Mundy radioed to Mr. Fagan: "You look so stately and so slow." A passenger aboard the *Queen* who did not become involved in the "race" was Aly Khan, on his way to seek a reconciliation with his wife, Rita Hayworth.

It was raining when Bob Hope boarded the *United States* on Friday, August 8, for a trip to Europe. Followed by news photographers, the comedian reacted quickly, draping his raincoat over his felt hat and extending his hand to feel for the rain, he spoofed Little Red Riding Hood. His photo was used in many of the next day's papers. Vera Ralston, actress, also made the papers with a big smile. There were 1,650 passengers aboard, including Secretary Sawyer and his wife, Lawrence Rockefeller and his family, George Jessel, and three Senators. The sailing marked the beginning of Captain Anderson's long association with the *United States.*

A very negative editorial appeared August 20 in the *Scandinavian Shipping Gazette,* which, on several counts, showed that not all the welcomes to the new ship were as warm as those in Southampton. There was much jealousy in the European shipping world. The piece began by ridiculing a request made by a member of Parliament from Glasgow, asking that the Government give quick early consideration to building a troop-transport liner capable of recapturing the Blue Riband (the British always called it Riband instead of Ribbon). The request "may get a lot of support on Clydeside, but it got none from the Government and certainly will not appeal to the shipping industry." The editorial was written by the magazine's British specialist. It continued by noting that people who were in a hurry "now go by air." It added: "No doubt a certain number of people will choose the *United States,* generally in the tourist class, in order to be able to boast that they have travelled in the world's fastest ship, but far more people will consider the standards of attention and comfort in the Cunard and Compagnie Générale Transatlantique liners." The piece went on to predict that Cunard "certainly does not want such a ship." The *Queen Elizabeth 2* was still hardly a dream in Cunard's mind. The editorial added that "a lone ship on the Atlantic has never yet paid her way and the *United States* has yet to show

Bob Hope, Alfred Hitchcock, and quests enjoy a meal aboard the ship. (Photo by Andrew Malmsea, Chief Steward, SS United States, courtesy of Sven Olefeldt)

whether she will be a success." It concluded by looking back, almost hopefully, at the sad record of the Hamburg American Line's *Deutschland,* which held the speed record for a short time, "but proved an absolute failure commercially and after a few years had her boiler power reduced by half in order to make her a cruising yacht of moderate speed." Would the *United States* be another *Deutschland,* was the unstated question left in the reader's mind.

Another negative situation emerged at home. The *United States* was smoking too much, and William G. Christy, director of the Smoke Control Bureau, held a press conference aboard her after she docked on August 19. The next day's papers had small stories on the meeting. Captain Devlin told Mr. Christy that the ship's smoking had diminished with each crossing. "I ask the city to have forbearance while we explore every possible means to alleviate the situation," he pleaded. The U.S. Lines pledged to do "everything humanly possible to eliminate excessive smoke from the stacks of the new ship" steaming in and out of the harbor. Mr. Christy meant business. Only a few days before he had cited the *Queen of Bermuda* with a smoke violation and given her owners a summons. Two tugs had also been cited.

On Friday, August 22, the *United States* took out 1,575 passengers. The eastbound season was over and fewer people were going to Europe, but it was a near capacity list and included such names as Perle Mesta, the Ambassador to Luxenburg, Senator Estes Kefauver, and Alexander Hamilton, a descendant of the first Secretary of the Treasury. The U.S. Lines announced on August 24 that the new liner would make five winter voyages to Bremerhaven. Her sailing schedule through May was made known, along with that of the *America.*

The American Merchant Marine Institute on August 27 sent out a press release hailing the speed record of the *United States* as "symbolic of the rebirth of the American Merchant Marine." Walter E. Maloney, AMMI president., stated that the ship, her owners, and crew have "placed the entire merchant marine in a new position of importance to the country at large."

An editor of Britain's *Shipbuilding and Shipping Record* carried in full the list of "Suggestions for the Avoidance of Accidents" published by Purser Lock's office on the *United States.* His story noted how common it was for passengers to be bumped about and jolted particularly in the winter months, adding that it was "more commendable therefore" to see the new *United States* issuing such a warning to passengers. The 10 points covered began: *"Never let go of the hand rails when proceeding up or down companionways. Always hold on to safety ropes. ..."* Possibly the editor was attempting to show obliquely that even the *United States* was subject to bad weather. His conclusion was humorous: "With vivid memories of me and my chair being catapulted some years ago across the foyer of a famous liner and crashing into the then President of France, who was writing a letter at a table which came adrift, with him and his chair, I would strongly recommend that such advice be sent out with every passenger ticket issued."

A happy editorial from the September *Holiday* magazine hailed the new ship. Calling her the "dream craft" of William Francis Gibbs, it said she was "doubly blessed in the public mind as not only the largest, exclusively American vessel built on domestic ways, but as the hugest single entity built for peaceful, pleasurable purposes at sea for many a weary year." The editorial predicted that the *"States"* would certainly handle her share of the 750,000 Americans engaged "in making this the biggest European travel year ever."

A Britisher wrote to *The Syren and Shipping,* another outstanding English shipping magazine, to state that if the designers of the new American superliner had really wished to they could have found an alternative to wood for the ship's butcher's block. The writer had seen one made from a whale's vertebra by a man who was ship's cook in the Glasgow-owned bark *Pass of Killiecrankie.*

Captain Anderson noted casually upon his arrival September 3 that he had made an eight-mile detour to avoid overtaking the *Queen Elizabeth* and avoid embarrassment to the British liner's crew and passengers. "I'm sure any Cunard captain in the same position would do the same thing," he said. The *United States* docked at 8 a.m. and the big British *Queen* came in two-and-a-half hours later. She had 2,244 passengers aboard. The *United States* brought in 1,750, including Margaret Truman. Miss Truman and other passengers praised the performance of Captain Anderson and the liner in a storm that had hit them the previous Sunday night. Captain Anderson said he had reduced speed "as an experiment but not a necessity." General George C. Marshall and Mrs. Marshall were among the 1,650 passengers who sailed September 5 with the *United States* on Captain Anderson's third voyage. It was made without incident.

The Society of Naval Architects and Marine Engineers heard Matt Forrest give a talk about the *United States,* listened to U.S. Lines Vice President Newbold T. Lawrence review "operating problems with trans-Atlantic liners," and saw a moving picture about the construction of the superliner at their September 7 meeting in New York. A highlight of the day was a tour of the ship in the afternoon. The cost of the dinner, including tips, came to $2.50.

The tremendous publicity given the new superliner brought continuing large passenger lists and many famous names. On September 19 she sailed with Rita Hayworth, Buster Keaton, and Adolph Menjou among her passengers. De Witt Wallace, owner of the *Readers Digest,* and Mrs. Wallace were also aboard, as were the Contesse De Limure and her spouse, Ivan De Limure. Nat Holman, well known baseball coach, was sailing. So was Senator Elie Beauregard, speaker of the Canadian House of Commons. This was the superliner's sixth eastbound crossing and she had been sailing at virtual capacity every crossing.

Another lengthy article in the *Shipbuilding & Shipping Record* reviewed all the publicly-known facts about her tonnage and speed. The writer fell into the same gross tonnage trap that I had become involved with when he said: "It should be observed that the gross tonnage of American vessels is about 20% less than corresponding British tonnage, accordingly the 52,000 given might become 62,000 under our tonnage laws." He carried his conclusion a step further: "If it be assumed that the displacement of the *Queens* and of the *United States* bear the same ratio as do the tonnages, then the 77,500 tons of the former becomes 58,000 tons in the latter vessel." The comment concluded that the light weight design was the real secret of the new ship.

The U.S. Lines had originally planned to ask the Duke of Sutherland to present the Hales Trophy following the maiden voyage, but had changed their minds at the last minute. Plans were made for a much larger event. In late September it was announced that the trophy would be officially presented at a dinner aboard the liner on November 12. A press release about the ornate object was put out by U.S. Lines. It was noted that Mr. Hales had spelled out his purpose in an autobiography: "One of my life's ambitions was to present a trophy which would serve as a stimulus to the craft of speed and mechanical perfection which I have loved so well. In my early days I had visions of ocean greyhounds of revolutionary design, cleaving their paths to New York and back again in as few hours as the *Great Western* had needed days. Before I die, I thought, I will present a trophy to be held by the country whose liners hold the Atlantic record." The trophy was made in 1935 and Mr. Hales died on November 7, 1942.

Made of solid silver, heavily gilt and weighing approximately 100 lbs., the trophy's total height, including its onyx plinth, is nearly four feet. The release explained: "It has two finely modeled figures surrounding the globe, the uppermost figure being symbolic of speed overcoming the forces of the Atlantic and urging forward a modern liner. The Atlantic Ocean is depicted by pale blue enamel, the liner's route from Fastnet to New York being indicated by a red line in enamel. The four winds are symbolized by four sailing ships of some 450 years ago. The blue girdle contains four enamelled panels illustrating the evolution of the steamship, the *Great Western,* of 1838; the *Mauretania,* which held the record for the longest period of time; the *Rex,* which was holder of the record at the time when Mr. Hales' gift was accepted in 1935, and the *Normandie,* which wrested the

Hales Trophy

red ink, the *United States* in blue in the printed schedule. There were six occasions during the year when the *United States* made two voyages to one for the *America,* although the fact that the *America* was going all the way to Bremerhaven was partly responsible for this.

A Finnish shipping journal called *Suomen Merenkulku* denounced Commodore Manning in a most unusual editorial at this point. Blaming him for actually speeding up when his ship entered a fog bank during the maiden eastward crossing, the journal called his performance "irresponsible," and compared it with the action of Captain Smith of the *Titanic,* when he failed to reduce speed while passing through the ice belt in 1912. Radar does not nullify the rules of navigation, which order that in fog all vessels shall proceed at moderate speed, the editorial reasoned. "Captain Manning will get no praise from us. It was not to his credit that nothing else was 'crossed' than the Atlantic, but it would have been his fault if anything had happened. On the radar screen there may be a highly insignificant point which, in relation to the onrushing Atlantic giant, may be a very low fishing vessel, a point which an observer, 'firmly determined to keep the schedule,' as Captain Manning said, might easily treat like the historic spot of dirt on the chart of the careless skipper of proverbial fame. Drawing attention to this is neither peevish nor pedantic."

Commodore Gerald Norman Jones, a retired Cunard master, had equally strong opinions about the Blue Riband. He was quoted in the *Shipbuilding & Shipping Record.* Speaking of his old company, he said: "We know nothing about the Blue Riband in the Cunard offices. The Cunard Company, after the *Queen Mary* was built, was offered a rose bowl as a symbol of superiority, like Van Tromp with his broom. We needed no broom or rose bowl. The service we gave was all the reward the company asked, and reward has come to them by the continued success wherever the ships have sailed." He had been Staff Captain of both the *Queens.*

The National Maritime Union's newspaper *The Pilot,* ran a picture of William Francis Gibbs chatting with NMU President Curran on October 2. It described how Mr. Gibbs had praised the NMU crew and said that the ship could not have broken the Atlantic record without the excellent union men. Mr. Gibbs said that the deck, engine, and stewards departments all "worked diligently to operate the ship as a unit" and he turned toward Mr. Curran and said "he deserves a vote of thanks."

Commodore Manning was on the bridge again on October 3, 1952, when the *United States* began her seventh voyage. She took Out 1,720 passengers including motion picture producer Harry Popkin. Mr. Popkin's newest film, starring Ray Milland, was scheduled to have its world premiéré in mid-October in New York City. A preview took place on the crossing. Apparently the rift between Manning and Gibbs, plus all the other difficulties that the famous skipper's obdurate make-up caused, were too much. After this voyage he again left the ship for a protracted vacation.

On the vessel's next three crossings she carried 1,500, 1,669, and 1,100 passengers. The passenger department people at 1 Broadway were getting to feel like old hands with the new ship. Despite the airplane, liner traffic was booming. New ships were being planned by a number of companies. The Italian Line would introduce the first of a pair of 29,082-ton luxury liners the following year; her name was *Andrea Doria.* A second new French Line 20,419-ton liner, the *Antilles,* would make her maiden voyage in May, 1953. The 22,071-ton *Kungsholm* was also due out in 1953 and another even larger Swedish American Line ship was projected. As yet unborn were four more ships of the superliner class. The age of the liner was far from over; in fact, in many ways, the 1950s would be the high point in trans-Atlantic passenger service. The picture was a good one for the *United States,* at least so many felt it was reasonable to think.

The November 6 crossing included a very special inanimate passenger along with the 1,617 regular customers. It was the Hales Trophy. Brought aboard quietly at Southampton in a wooden box, it attracted little attention. Only 200 yards away as it was carried up the gangplank lay the *Queen Mary,* which had spurned it many years before when she had first broken the speed record. Escorting the trophy to New York was the Duke of Sutherland, chairman of the committee of trustees set up by Mr. Hales. The Duchess of Sutherland was also aboard, as were two women performers, each renowned in their quite separate fields: opera star Lucretia Bori and actress Yvonne de Carlo. They were given equal billing in the U.S. Lines press release telling of the ship's arrival.

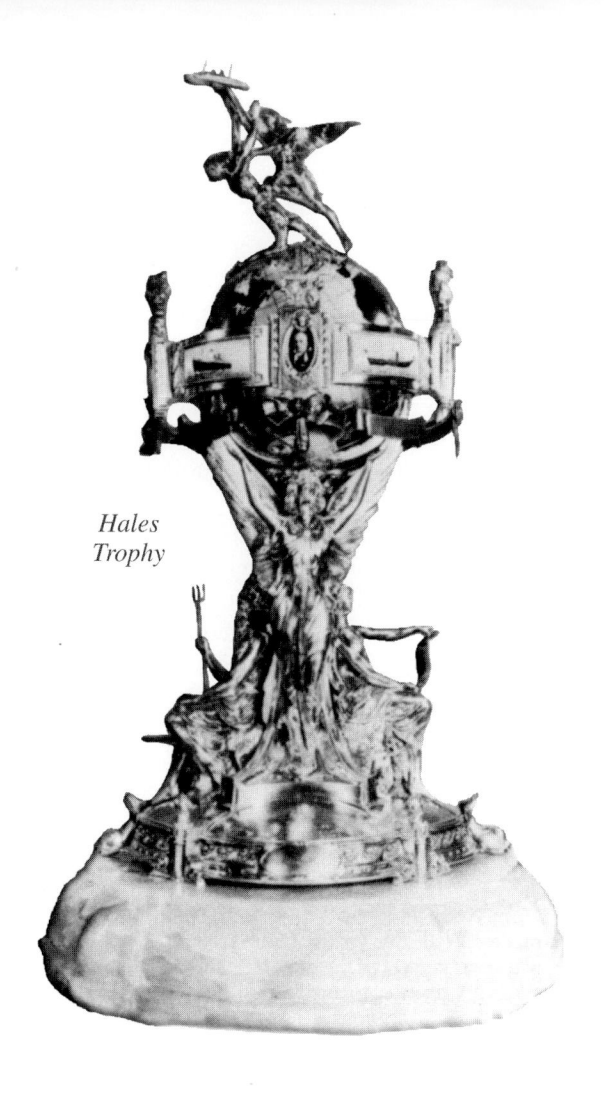

record from the *Rex.* The Blue Riband is supported by two winged figures of Victory standing back to back. The seated figures represent Father Neptune, the god of the sea, with Trident, and his wife, Amphitrite, these two figures being seated on an ornamental onyx base."

The *United States* brought Senator Tom Connally and his wife home on the passage that ended September 30. A new sailing schedule listing crossings up through the end of 1953 was put out by U.S. Lines at this time. The tonnage shown for the *United States* was 53,330 and for the *America,* 33,532 gross. Twenty-two round trips were scheduled for the newer vessel, while the *America* would make 16. The *America* was shown in

A new trifle of news about the ship's power plant came out in November, 1952, in the Westinghouse Electric Corporation's stockholders' quarterly. For the first time the cost of the "mighty machinery" that helped the new superliner set her records was revealed. The four Westinghouse geared turbines cost $3,250,000 and required over two years to design and construct at the company's South Philadelphia steam division plant.

News photographers snapped pictures of the Hales Trophy at 7:30 p.m. in the First Class Dining Saloon on November 12 as the distinguished guests were gathering for the formal presentation ceremonies. General Franklin posed with the Duke of Sutherland and Commodore Manning before the large award. The Commodore had been called back for the occasion. William Francis Gibbs and his brother Frederic were on hand but kept away from the cameramen. Also on hand was W.E. Blewett, Jr., of the Newport News yard. Five separate press releases for the occasion were put out by Walter Jones. There were three speeches, each quite lengthy, and the dining room was filled with politicians and "big wigs" of the armed forces.

General Franklin once again felt called upon to hammer away at the proposition that the *United States* was built with use as a Navy troopship in mind as well as a passenger ship. He praised the service of the two *Queens* in particular and British liners in general, saying that of the 7,000,000 troops that embarked from the United States during the war, over 1,500,000 traveled on British vessels. He thanked the Duke of Sutherland and all the British people for their kindness in presenting the Hales Trophy to the *United States* and called for a toast in the Duke's honor.

Edward Tastrom, writing in the *New York Journal of Commerce,* November 14, gave his impression of the Hales Trophy dinner and stressed the possibilities of atomic power for ships of the future. Noting that the Society of Naval Architects and Marine Engineers was meeting in New York for its 60th annual convention, he said that papers were being read at their sessions suggesting that nuclear energy "will be available for ships within the next four years."

Stephan Gmelin, a fellow member of the Steamship Historical Society of America, and a collector of ship photographs, asked me to get him a pass to see the *United States* sail Saturday, November 15. Later he wrote of his experiences: "There's one thing I wish I had done. As the ship backed out, I noticed a man sitting near me on the bulwark (there were only about two dozen people on the lower level, ideal conditions for picture taking). This man, with a wide brimmed hat pulled low over his head, watched her back out, with his head in his hands, with a sort of dreamy expression. Well, a little later, as he moved away, I realized that it was none other than Mr. Gibbs himself. What a picture it would have been with the *United States* in the background and her creator looking at her from land."

The Gibbs legend was taking form. Not only would he be at each sailing and each arrival of the *United States* at her home port, but he would frequently be driven in his long, grey Cadillac down to the area of Fort Wadsworth on the Brooklyn side of the Narrows to see the ship leaving or arriving. It was in every sense a love affair with a ship. Some years after this 1952 experience by Mr. Gmelin, a famous *New Yorker* writer would concentrate pointedly on this subject in a personal interview with William Francis Gibbs.

"Only heaven could be better," was the way two shipyard engineers described their five months spell on the *United States*. They were Malcolm Christie and J. Lester Cooper, and they would be leaving the ship shortly. She was about to complete her 10th voyage and was going to Newport News for a nine-day survey. The builder's guarantee on the ship expired in December, 1952, making the survey necessary. Others who had been aboard representing the U.S. Lines and Gibbs & Cox included Nicholas Bachko and J.A. Christoffersen. The general opinion of all these specialists was that the ship had performed remarkably well. Chief Engineer Kaiser was said to be frustrated because he would have liked "to open the turbines to their top capacity to see what they really could do." But it was not thought likely that he would ever have such an opportunity "unless there is a war emergency or unless a new foreign express liner is built such as the British are said to be considering," wrote Walter Hamshar in the *Herald Tribune.* "Completion of the guarantee period will mark the end of an ideal existence for the visiting engineers. Although they have had many duties while riding back and forth across the Atlantic they have lived as passengers enjoying all the luxuries of first class accommodations."

On Wednesday, November 26, the *United States* debarked her passengers at New York. She found a longshoremen's strike in progress and was prevented from unloading her mail, cargo, or baggage, except that baggage that her passengers could carry off by themselves. It was a mess, just the beginning of a long series of labor difficulties that would so mar the magnificent ship's career. Many passengers had brought their cars back with them and some of these people decided to sail down with the ship to Newport News to be on hand when their autos were unloaded, all of course at the expense of U.S. Lines. She was brought into an outfitting pier at the shipyard. A string of mail and express cars were backed onto the pier and shipyard cranes rapidly unloaded the mail and baggage. The cars that had drivers were also unloaded and taken away by their owners, who had enjoyed the fun of a short coastal cruise to boot. The other cars were parked for later delivery to their owners, another added expense to the ship line. By early afternoon the ship left the yard and headed for the Norfolk Naval Shipyard where she was to be drydocked. The two Newport News drydocks large enough to handle her were both occupied with naval work. Her underwater hull and parts were found "as good as new," despite the fact she had traveled 65,000 miles at high speed. It was said she could have gone another six months without drydocking. On December 2, she left the drydock and returned to Newport News for five days of touching up and the myriad of adjustments that such a ship as the *United States* under the overall supervision of such a man as William Francis Gibbs needed. At the time the yard announced that not one major change was necessary nor had any failures been reported. The luster of the event is reflected in the enthusiasm of the shipyard's publication which described the completion of this first overhaul as follows:

"Late Sunday afternoon the sun made her freshly painted stacks shine as the shipyard workers began disconnecting cables, hose, etc., preparatory to sailing. U.S. Lines officials and their guests were coming aboard and the necessary tugs were assembling at the outboard end of Pier 10. By 6 o'clock she was ready to sail and slowly backed out into the stream. Escorting the ship downstream

84

*Company advertisements featuring the SS United States.
(Courtesy of Bill McBride with McBride Publishing)*

were numerous harbor craft and in answer to their whistles, three-note blasts from the *United States* echoed across the water to the thousands of watchers lining the shore and occupying every vantage point. She made a beautiful sight as she moved through Hampton Roads with her great stacks and gleaming white superstructure floodlighted. After an overnight voyage the *United States* arrived at her pier in New York at 8 a.m., Monday, December 8, 1952, and was ready to resume trans-Atlantic service."

U.S. Lines put the Hales trophy in its main floor passenger booking office at 1 Broadway, a room of remarkable beauty and glamour, second only to the magnificent Cunard lobby at 25 Broadway. A press release announced its new location and for days large crowds of noontime viewers came to stare at the ornate "Blue Ribbon" statue. A large water-line model of the *United States* was also on display. Years later it was discovered that it was actually a full hull model of the ship, but for security reasons the ship's underbody had been carefully hidden by a plaster-of-paris ocean.

The subsidy battle came to the surface again. Attorney General McGranery announced on December 11 that the U.S. Lines subsidy contract could be voided and that the government could collect as much as $10,000,000 for the superliner. What action he, as the Attorney General, or President Truman would take was not made clear at the time. His statement was made in the form of a report to the White House: "I am convinced that the contract of sale is voidable at the election of the United States; that it reflects violations of the Federal statutes, and that it contains numerous errors and miscalculations to the financial detriment of this government. In an effort to avoid a lengthy litigation with its concomitant serious damage to those good relations between the company and the government so desirable to America's position in world maritime affairs, I personally, and officials in this department under my instruction have conferred with representatives of the U.S. Lines. We have asserted a willingness to settle the dispute on a reasonable basis. The generous spirit prompting this offer has not, I am sorry to say, been reciprocated. The Company had taken the irrevocable position that it will not even discuss an amicable settlement; that it is prepared to concede nothing. In view of this obstinate attitude in the face of the inequity of the contract of sale,

I feel that the Government must take appropriate action to recover the amount properly owing to it."

At this point some $14,000,000 in operating subsidies for U.S. Lines freighter routes was due the company. The Attorney General ordered the Department of Commerce to forward to him a voucher for $10,000,000 of accrued operating-differential subsidy earned by the U.S. Lines to pay the claim of $10,000,000 for excess construction-differential payments.

John Lardner devoted a column in *Look* magazine to the new song: "The *SS United States,* First Lady of the Sea." He compared it to the ballads written about the time that one Floyd Collins had perished in a cave and when Lindbergh crossed the ocean, and said it was no worse "and maybe faintly better than the average specimen of its school." He quoted a part of the chorus:

"She's got New York style, California's grace, The Midwest's strength, And Texas space, The Southland's charm, And the Nation's pace."

He noted that the words were by Emery Davis and the music by Meyer Davis, and added that the output of topical songs had slowed down in "recent years." His conclusion: "It may be that great events are succeeding each other too fast."

The December 17 departure from Southampton produced the first major accident story about the *United States*. It was a big story but, fortunately, not a big accident. With gusts of up to 100 miles an hour the new liner was slammed up against her pier as she attempted to pull away from the passenger terminal with 600 voyagers bound for America. Paint was scraped from the starboard bow as she was dragged 200 yards along the quay with seven tugs battling to keep her under control. The port side of her bridge was slightly dented as it jammed between two dockside cranes. After an hour of maneuvering the ship was brought back to her berth where she waited until the wind died down. The *New York Post* story was accompanied by a three-column photo of the ship leaving New York some time before. It was interesting because it showed towering columns of billowing black smoke coming from both stacks, enough to send any smoke-control official into delirium. A radio photo carried in the next day's *Times* showed the towering bow of the new ship brushing against a tall Southampton crane.

A strong defense of the U.S. Lines position in the brawl over subsidies was given December 19 by Edward Tastrom in the *New York Journal of Commerce*. "The *United States* basically is an auxiliary naval vessel operating as a passenger liner. If U.S. Lines had not agreed to undertake construction the Navy was prepared at the time to build a similar ship as a fast troop transport. We venture to say it would have cost considerably more than the final $78 million figure, since the Navy never bothers too much about expense, would have been paid for entirely by the Government and probably be laid up in moth balls for more than half its active life. That is the other side of the shield which is always overlooked. Both parties to the contract for construction of the superliner – the U.S. Lines and the Commerce Department – say it is a firm commitment. But this does not free the $10 million due the company on an entirely different account, that the GAO had ordered withheld. This financial blackjacking is something which cannot be viewed lightly. It is coercion pure and simple on the part of the GAO to force the company into a price redetermination that could not be effected in any other manner. This last minute, strong-armed attack by the GAO does that office no credit and the U.S. Lines would be justified, it seems to us, in resorting to any legal means available to upset this questionable tactic."

The *United States* lost 21 hours because of the gale at Southampton. She made it up on her return trip, arriving on schedule after a crossing of three days and 23 hours. She brought in a total of 1,385 passengers, including the 7th Earl of Warwick and opera star Jan Kiepura with his wife. She docked at the company's downtown Pier 61 in the Chelsea area, but was moved up to her regular Pier 86 for the Saturday, December 27, sailing.

An excellent description of the bunkering of the *United States* was carried in *The Lamp* magazine published by Standard Oil of New Jersey in December, 1952. It began with a listing of the flags the ship flew as she came in past Ambrose. There would be the red and white "H" of the International code, the pilot flag. Also flown would be the blue flag with "USM" in white, the mail flag. The blue and white "M" code flag also flew, a request for Customs inspectors to come aboard. Also flown was the "J," another blue and white code flag, which called upon the services of Immigration officers. Great liners no longer flew the yellow "Q" flag, which meant they were waiting for Quarantine clearance at the Narrows, as they got permission to dock by radio and could pass Quarantine without stopping. While the largest of liners such as the *Leviathan* and the *Queens* had to dock within the half-hour on either side of slack water, the *United States* could dock without regard to the tide because she drew only 30 feet. She regularly sailed at noon on a Friday, after having arrived 76 hours earlier at 8 a.m. on a Tuesday. Brought in from Ambrose with the help of a Sandy Hook pilot, the ship would be directed into her slip by a Moran-tug docking pilot. When the ship was secure he would "sound the cheerful wolf call on his mouth whistle which meant 'finished with tugs,'" and the debarking would begin. A dozen gangways would be brought into place and the baggage "begins clicking down the belt conveyors to the pier where the porters sort it out under the owners' initials to await examination by 150 to 300 customs inspectors." The article continued:

"Preparations for departure have already begun. Two oil ports low down in the off-pier side are opened. Big Esso oil barges on the far side of the slip are brought alongside by more tugs. The oil and steam lines are coupled up and the liner's engineers gauge the heated oil in the barges' tanks. While an Esso man discusses the details of the bunkering plan with Chief Engineer Kaiser the black six-inch oil lines stiffen up under the throbbing of the pumps. Pumping continues for 20 to 24 hours, stopping only to remove an empty barge and pull up a full one. Coming aboard is the heavy black oil, burned in the booming dazzle beneath the boilers, which produces the steam that drives the liner across the North Atlantic. It also heats and lights the ship, runs the blowers, elevators, telephones and radio, provides refrigeration for the butcher's storerooms, hot water for the bathrooms, and steam for the steam tables in the galleys." Esso's record delivery up to that date had been 54,933 barrels to the Cunard Line's *Berengaria* on October 12, 1936. The *Queens* and the French Line's *Ile de France* and *Liberté* took on thousands of gallons of fresh water during their turn-arounds at New York, but the *United States* evaporated all her water requirements from sea water.

The December 27 sailing of the *United States* marked her first voyage all the way to Bremerhaven. Kenneth Gautier, Vice President for Passenger Traffic, and other dignitaries were aboard because important welcoming ceremonies were scheduled. Among the 1,350 passengers were four U.S. Lines employees from offices in England and Europe, who had won a trip to New York for the Christmas holidays. Two were telephone operators, one was a secretary, and the fourth was a typist.

A remarkably thorough look at the U.S. Lines and its continuing dispute with the Attorney General was taken by Richard P. Cooke, of the *Wall Street Journal* on December 29. "You can't talk about U.S. Lines without making it sound like some sort of a national institution," Mr. Cooke began. He listed the company's two passenger ships named *America* and *United States*. He noted the company's name and the fact that its office was "at the impressive address of No. 1 Broadway." He then went into the battle over the construction subsidy, adding that the *United States* would probably need an annual operating subsidy of about $4,100,000. He quoted Vice President Brennan of U.S. Lines as saying that winter bookings "are running quite heavy." Mr. Brennan added that "There have been some breaking-in troubles with the new *United States,* but no more than expected and nothing pertaining to the mechanical operation." Some 5,000 military dependents going to Europe over the winter season and some winter excursions were helping to "pad out the lean winter season," the newspaper man learned. Also quoted was Captain Devlin, who smiled and said there had not been any unsuspected problems popping up in connection with the new superliner: "There's just twice as much of everything to look after." Captain Devlin was enthusiastic about Joseph Curran's National Maritime Union: "They were VERY HELPFUL," he emphasized in getting together the crew of 1,000 for the liner.

The *United States* carried 36,044 passengers on her 23 sailings in 1952, a company year-end report made known. An additional 29,092 were carried by the *America* on her 29 sailings and 3,218 passengers made crossings on the line's 46 cargo ships.

The year ended and a somewhat confused future was in prospect for the new superliner. While the ship accomplished everything that was expected of her and more and was known the world around, there were dark spots in her future. All around her the spectre of greedy men was tarnishing her magnificence. Her owners would not pay one cent more for her than their original contract required. In order to defend their position they were damaging her reputation as a liner by overplaying her potential as a troopship, a role that was more demeaning than enhancing. She was a great liner, not a troopship used as a liner. It was the Gibbs passion for structural safety, stability, and security from fire that made her public rooms smaller than those on the great liners of older days, not Navy requirements that she be suitable for conversion into a troopship. The Comptroller General was using the new superliner as his ticket to the front pages of America. He was playing politics with her. And the howls of various labor leaders, who often were fighting to keep their own positions more than to help their members, were beginning to be heard. More money, double and quadruple overtime, penalty overtime, and all the other featherbedding techniques developed at that time were the order of the day.

The ship moving alongside an aircraft carrier at Southampton, England. (Courtesy of Bill DiBenedetto)

8

The Honeymoon Period

Ten Dutch bulb shippers were among the 1,349 passengers brought into New York January 10, 1953, aboard the *United States*. They were mentioned in the U.S. Lines press release along with a Countess, a Princess, and a General. They had interesting names: one was Cornelius Veldhuyzen van Zanten, another was Hendrikus P.G. de Cler. They traveled First Class and had four cabins between them. On January 14 the liner took out 1,600 passengers, including Vincent Astor, a director of the company. Her 1953 season had begun and it would be a good year.

A new set of deck plans was issued February 1, still using the artists' conceptions for the interior views, but otherwise unchanged except for one new paragraph of type. Added wording boasted of the ship's speed records: "The new *SS United States* is the world's fastest and most modern liner. Never before has so much ingenuity and skill ... all in the highest American tradition ... gone into the construction of a passenger vessel. She has been constructed to meet and even exceed the exacting standards of the U.S. Navy ... the highest construction standards in the world today ... insuring high speed, great stability, and the very utmost safety." For some reason the tonnage, which had up to then always been shown as 53,330 gross, was given as 52,000 tons.

The arrival of the new superliner on February 15 with 1,243 passengers gave the *New York Times* an excuse to do a story about how the Moran docking pilot brought her in. It was written by Ira Henry Freeman and was run on the following day with three photos. It was a crackerjack story: "Berthing a colossus such as the *United States*, 990 feet long and weighing (sic.) 53,300 tons, alongside a pier only 997 feet, 10 inches long, remains a labor at once herculean and delicate, requiring five or six tugs and years of specialized experience on the part of the docking pilot." The story began at the beginning on the 25th floor of the Whitehall Building, 17 Battery Place, New York City, the dispatching office of the Moran Towing & Transportation Company: "The seascape of the Upper Bay, framed in the big windows, has just faded from black to the battleship gray of a rainy morning. When the legend, 8:05 SS UNITED STATES PASSING IN QUARANTINE, appears on tape from the Western Union maritime ticker, Joe Finnegan, dispatcher, alerts a cluster of tugs waiting in 'Tugboat Alley' at Pier 1. 'She's on time, Bill,' he says over the short wave radio to Captain Frederick W. Snyder, docking pilot. 'You got the *Carol, Barbara, Grace, Doris,* and *Peter.* Want any more help.'"

From there on it was a delightful minute-by-minute account of how Captain Snyder and his five Moran tugs did their thing. It read true, for during my 10 years with Moran, I had enjoyed such marvelous experiences hundreds of times and knew all the excitement and drama that an early morning docking of a great liner could produce. And to make the story even better it ended with a special twist: "While Captain Snyder was bringing the *United States* in, the pilot who had taken her out of Le Havre was enjoying himself among the First Class passengers. George DuBois was still aboard because big seas had made it impossible for him to leave the liner outside the French port. It was the first time such a thing had befallen him, he said, in his 14-year career. He is flying back to his wife and two sons."

Commodore Manning was back on the bridge for the February 18 sailing. There were 1,575 passengers aboard including Her Royal Highness Queen T. Pahlavi, of Iran, with her daughter and grandson, and also His Royal Highness Prince Axel, of Denmark, with Princess Margareta. General Franklin's daughter Laura was aboard, along with Miss Betsey Palmedo, his niece. The General was still having trouble with the Comptroller General. The U.S. Lines on February 24, 1953, sued the U.S. Government in the Court of Claims for $8,697,115.74, representing the unpaid operating-differential subsidy that the Comptroller had ordered withheld, although the Maritime Administration had certified it was due for payment. It would be a long and tedious battle and the less said about it the better.

One of the passengers returning on the *United States*, March 5, was Lord Ismay, secretary general of the North Atlantic Treaty Organization, and son of Bruce Ismay, head of White Star Line and survivor of the *Titanic*. Commodore Manning had three days ashore and then again sailed as master on March 7, a Saturday. It would be his last trip. Booking was done right up to the last minute and the company press release was forced to say "over 1,500" passengers when giving the total number on the passenger list. Aboard was Captain G.T. Atkins, president of the Masters, Mates & Pilots Association, whose ranks Commodore Manning refused to join. The trip was made without incident and the Commodore left for good upon the ship's return to New York on March 21. The company put out a press release announcing his retirement. It explained that he had requested "early retirement so that he might devote more time to writing and lecturing concerning his many and varied experiences during his 40 years at sea." He was retained by U.S. Lines as a consultant. It was a sad and much too early end to a remarkable career. There must be a book written about Commodore Harry Manning.

A photograph that would become known the world around was made March 21 from the air. It showed the inbound *United States* passing the outbound *America*. Since the *America* was in the foreground, she appeared to be virtually identical in size to the new superliner. The picture went out over the International Soundphoto wire service and was used in thousands of publications. It was picked up by U.S. Lines and used repeatedly on calendars and other printed items. Both ships looked in the peak of condition. Four Moran tugs were on the port bow of the *United States* and she was moving slowly in the water. The *America* was getting on headway, as shown by her bow ripple in the otherwise mirror-smooth water. It was a classic photograph!

Four days later Captain Anderson was back in the Pilot House, a place he would not relinquish, except for vacations, for the next decade. On his return trip he would have among the passengers Chancellor Konrad Adenauer, of the Federal Republic of Western Germany. Also aboard would be Admiral Giles Stedman, of *Leviathan* fame, who was serving at the time as vice president Pacific Operations, U.S. Lines. This particular arrival was fixed in photographic history by a shot made by the *New York Post's* veteran photographer Barney Stein. It showed the new liner just turning to enter her slip, with a Moran tug at her bow. She was framed by a heavy wooden structure along the inner bulkhead and the reflection of her white superstructure and two huge stacks filled the open foreground perfectly.

On May 5 the U.S. Lines announced to all, stockholders a special series of inspection days aboard the *United States:* "Many of our stockholders have expressed a desire to inspect our new passenger liner, the *SS United States,* particularly after reading the press notices about this fine vessel and its (sic.) record-breaking trips across the Atlantic in both directions," a U.S. Lines memo to stockholders read. The company set up a series of 11 days between May 20 and December 2 for stockholders to tour the new ship. The hours were from 1:30 p.m. to 3:30.

Large passenger lists with a goodly number of important people aboard marked the superliner's crossings as she neared the end of her first full year of service. Two events set the May 22 departure apart from the ordinary. One was that Captain Anderson had a new title. He assumed the title of "Commodore." The other was the extraordinary passenger list. Topping it were His Royal Highness the Duke of Windsor and his wife the Duchess. They had Suite U87-89 and it was to have been given to them at no charge until Kenneth Gautier objected. He went all the way up to General Franklin to make his point and won. He was concerned with the press and public reaction as well as possible adverse comments on the part of his colleagues in the Trans-Atlantic Passenger Conference. General Franklin accepted his viewpoint and time would prove him right. It further developed that the fares were paid by Buckingham Palace. Also aboard on this May 22 departure was Grover Whalen and his wife. Mr. Whalen had made his reputation as the official greeter for New York City, a position he had held since the days of the *Leviathan.* Whitelaw Reid, editor of the *Herald Tribune, was aboard,* as was Sol Hurok, famed impresario and Lee Shubert, head of the Shubert Theatre Corporation. CBS television newsman Walter Cronkite was also sailing. It was a near-capacity list of 1,675 passengers. The day was National Maritime Day, and that evening the Propeller Club, Port of New York Chapter, held its 31st annual banquet at the WaldorfAstoria. The Aylward painting of the *United States,* the one with the mainmast, was on the cover of the banquet program.

The departure on June 5 saw even more passengers sailing – 1,725 in all, including George S. Kaufman, playwright, and Tennessee Williams, who was identified in the press release as "producer of 'A Streetcar Named Desire,' and other plays." Ten more people were squeezed into the ship for the next sailing on June 26, a total of 1,735. The July issue of a publication put out by Captain Devlin's office on Pier 60 and called "Excerpts and Gleanings" featured the picture of the *America* and the *United States* passing. Inside an article showed that the *America* was not doing quite as well as the *United States* from the standpoint of crew accident frequencies. On her 20th voyage the *United States* had no reportable injuries while the *America* had two on her 111th voyage. Because of her very large crew, the *United States* had by then just surpassed the "crew man days" total for the *America.* The new liner had 14,644 crew man days in her career, while the *America* had 14,259 since she returned to U.S. Lines operation after troopship service during the war. The average accident frequency rate for all the ships of the company was 5.57.

Junius S. Morgan, vice president of J.P. Morgan & Co., and son of the late J.P. Morgan, Jr., made the return crossing on the *United States,* arriving July 7. Also aboard as a guest of the company was Albert E. Gibbs, doorman of the American Club in London for over 34 Years. He had retired recently. For years he had wanted to visit America and an executive of the U.S. Lines London office, T.A. Monroe, had arranged for him to make the trip.

It was just one year from the day that the superliner had passed Bishop's Rock and broken the trans-Atlantic speed record, and Walter Jones put out a release announcing the completion of her first year in operation. She had carried 70,514 passengers, 35,400 eastbound and 35,114 westbound. This spoke well for her reception by non-Americans, because American ships generally carried more passengers eastbound than on the homeward crossing. Her 46 crossings (23 round trips) had seen her travel 146,959 nautical miles and her propeller shafts "have never been stopped or slowed due to a machinery derangement." Since July 3, 1952, she had been under steam at sea for a total of 233 days, or 67% of the total period. Of this period, she had been operating at high speed for 190 twenty-four-hour days. To operate the new ship for one year had cost $18,175,000 and of this total $7,375,000 was paid in wages to her officers and crew.

Gary Cooper

Gabor Sisters – Magda, Eva, and Zsa Zsa

Duke and Duchess of Windsor

Barbara Stanwyck and Robert Taylor

President Dwight Eisenhower

Jackie Gleason

(Photo by Andrew Malmsea, Chief Steward, SS United States, courtesy of Sven Olefeldt)

91

The passenger total carried worked out to an average of 1,533 passengers per trip for each of the 46 crossings, something of a record when it is recalled that the ship's normal capacity was considered to be from 1,650 to 1,700 and that the period covered not only the peak summer but the dull autumn and winter seasons. On July 10, starting her second year of service, she sailed with 1,725 passengers, including General Franklin. She had a new master, Captain Frederick Fender, who was elevated from his previous post as Executive Officer to give Commodore John Anderson a little rest. The Commodore began his vacation in a happy mood. Before leaving the ship for his home in New Jersey he was presented with a new red and cream six-seater Ford car. The 1,060 crew members had banded together and bought it as an expression of their regard for him. Many of the crew had served under Commodore Anderson on the *America*.

Famous names who were passengers in July, 1953, on the *United States* included golfer Ben Hogan, news reporter Edward R. Murrow, the Count and Countess Alain Costa de Beuregard, Mrs. Joseph E. Davies, Ludwig Bemelmans, and Mrs. Joseph P. Kennedy, to mention a few. A new sailing schedule came out early in August, which again showed the tonnage as being 53,300. Sailings through early June, 1954, were included. Once again the *United States* was scheduled all the way to Bremerhaven during the winter months and through April. The schedule of fares was as follows:

	Off Season/Summer Southampton	*Off Season/Summer* Le Havre	*Off Season/Summer* Bremerhaven
First	$350 $365	$360 $375	$375
Cabin	$220 $230	$227.50 $237.50	$240
Tourist	$165 $175	$170 $180	$185

Rates for the *America,* while only $5 less in Tourist Class, were $20 less in Cabin and $55 less in First.

The Coronation of Queen Elizabeth II produced a magnificent Naval Review in the waters off Southampton and the *United States* on one of her summer sailings passed through a long double row of British Royal Naval ships and vessels from many other nations. Among them was the American cruiser *Baltimore*.

A 14-year-old lad who was a passenger with his mother on the westbound *United States* crossing which left Southampton August 13 would play a part in the ship's later life. He was Michael Shindler. His passion for the ship began on this crossing. It made him one of the most vociferous letter-writers in her behalf 20 years later when her fate was being pondered in Washington. Young Michael saved the passenger list from his crossing. He was in Cabin U-100. There were 1,705 passengers aboard. Michael also saved the "Gala Dinner" menu, a magnificent red, white, and blue affair with the Aylward painting on its cover. The three principal meat dishes offered were Southdown Lamb au Jus, with Mint Jelly; Stuffed Maryland Turkey, Giblet Sauce, Cranberry Jelly, Sirloin Steak, and Mushroom Sauce. A letter written in his childish hand to Chief Engineer Kaiser began: "I would like to respectfully request that I be allowed to visit one of the ship's engine rooms. I have long been interested in ships and especially the *United States*. . . . "He got his tour!

While passenger lists sparkled and enthusiasm for the new ship grew, several publishing events took place which continued the process of making the *United States* a ship that would always be remembered. The Viking Press in October, 1953, published a little 128-page book, primarily for children, about the new liner. It was written and illustrated by Henry Billings, who had also done books on the Tennessee River Valley and the TVA, on the highways of America, and on the Diesel-Electric locomotive No. 4030. A red, white, and blue paper jacket showing a sketch by Mr. Billings of the *United States,* bow on, gave a most attractive look to the book. Its title: "Superliner *SS United States*" left nothing to the imagination. The author's illustrations were black and white pen drawings that looked as if they were woodcuts. Excellent style was evidence that Billings not only knew how to draw but loved his subject.

The preface quoted William Francis Gibbs when he had said that the new superliner was the equivalent of "a large cantilever bridge covered with steel plates, containing a power plant that could light up any of our larger cities, with a first-class luxury hotel on top." Mr. Billings added: "For a long time now we have been experts in building all three of these (bridge, power plant, hotel), and it has certainly been within the capabilities of the United States to combine them in one vessel. Why, then, did we wait so long? Part of the answer is that during these past hundred years we Americans have for the most part given up being a seafaring people and became a nation of farmers and landsmen. And so this book is not addressed to the veteran ocean traveler or to those experienced in nautical matters. Rather, the attempt here is to answer the more general questions that naturally arise in the mind of an inland person." And he succeeded. Among his sketches was a page devoted to showing how the *United States* was built like a steel girder, with her strength deck as the top part and the keel as the bottom. Another explained the difference in tonnage measurement, what gross and net were.

In a summary of the special qualities that set the *United States* apart from other merchant ships, Mr. Billings listed five points: her strength and hull design, her aluminum superstructure, her lack of vibration at high speed, her superior safety standards, and her most-complete air conditioning. On the safety question he did not know the most important single safety feature, which at this point had still not been revealed. Most passenger ships would sink if more than two compartments were flooded. The *United States* went far beyond this; she was a four-compartment ship, that is she would remain afloat even with four adjacent compartments flooded.

The Rand McNally publishing company of Chicago also came out with a little book for children about the new superliner. Its name was identical to that of the Billings book. Written by J. Duncan Ford, it was a much smaller work and very much for the younger child. With large, gaudy colored illustrations by A.K. Bilder, the book's opening paragraph showed its purpose and style: "Riding across town from the hotel in New York City, Frank and Judy were so excited that they could hardly sit still. They were going to sail all the way across the Atlantic Ocean to visit their Daddy, who was in France on business. And, best of all, they were going on the superliner *United States,* the biggest and most beautiful ship ever built in America, and the fastest in the world." Enough said.

A rather sad little anecdote involved the marine artist Logan U. Reavis. He managed, with tremendously painstaking work, to put together on his own a master deck plan of the *United States,* with the appropriate areas of each deck on top of those of the decks below. This was difficult because the company had not been permitted at that point to issue a single-sheet deck plan. But Logan Reavis perservered, and from this he was able to make a 10-foot long, cutaway painting of the ship. It showed every deck, each public room, countless cabins, automobile and high price cargo stowage holds, the swimming pool with people swimming, and the dining saloon with people eating. It was very well done from the overall standpoint, although the artist had been forced to use his imagination when it came to what the engine rooms looked like. He sold it to Walter Jones of U.S. Lines. After much discussion it was reproduced in full color under the title "Let's Look Inside the World's Fastest Luxury Liner – *SS United States.*" Unfortunately no credit was given in the folder to Mr. Reavis and his signature shown in the original under the bow of the ship was eliminated to make room for a caption explaining the areas shown. Thirty-four numbered places were identified with white numbers on black circles and guide lines were drawn over an outline sketch of the painting at the bottom of the folder. It was a grand piece of publicity and millions of copies were distributed. One day some months after the folder was first put out, Mr. Reavis came to me in my office at the American Merchant Marine Institute. Softly he mentioned, in quite a casual way, that he had never been paid by U.S. Lines and what should he do about it. It had been a clerical oversight. Walter Jones and his department were being driven crazy by the great public interest in the new ship, by demands for new brochures, moving pictures about the ship and all the other projects generated by her success. Mr. Reavis was paid. The "look inside" folder was re-issued and re-issued under half a dozen different formats right up through the end of the ship's trans-Atlantic career, probably being the most widely distributed piece of literature ever put out for the ship. On one of its last issues published in 1968 the Aylward painting of the ship was shown on the cover. The mainmast had finally been painted out.

Another publication featuring the *United States* was the October issue of *The Lookout* magazine, published by the Seamen's Church Institute of New York. Its lead article was about all the things that had to happen during a turn-around of the *United States.* Written by May Stoke it had many excellent photographs. The opening and closing paragraphs show the fun Miss Stoke had in her writing: "It's 7:30 a.m. and a series of thunderous booms roll heavily in over the waterfront, thudding dully against the taller buildings. Tug whistles shriek; ferryboats cough hoarsely and sharply, like wheezy old elephants. Cars pull to one side and people clamber out to stand at the river's edge. The *United States* is in. Her sharp, slender prow noses around the end of Pier 86. Two Moran tugs nudge her gently as they perform the delicate business of warping her around the pier end. She slides silently forward into her berth, her immense bulk inking a quivering shadow on the water. ... The tugs steam about importantly, guiding the big ship out into midstream. She rides the water regally and her court of riverboats shriek, wail, and toot in proper homage to the Queen."

On October 21, 1953, the tall, lean, gaunt figure of William Francis Gibbs stood before a distinguished crowd in Philadelphia to accept, with a few words of "requital," the Franklin Medal. His speech was later published in the journal of the Franklin Institute, and reprints were made. The six-page printed document stands as one of maritime history's most humorous of human documents. Mr. Gibbs began: "I am laboring under considerable difficulty tonight – beyond that which normally accompanies my feeble effort to talk in public. ... " After a half a dozen opening sentences, he noted that Franklin Institute's President Rolph, during the banquet, had said that he was doing his best to keep the program on time. He had looked "furtively at his watch and pointed out that we were behind." Asked how long he should talk, the same official "with a note of sadness in his voice" asked William Francis if he would need more than 10 minutes. At that point Mr. Gibbs promised that when he noticed that a majority of the audience was snoring he would come to a conclusion – all this was part of the speech.

"I have a brother who is here present. We have been associated ever since we went to work. Everything that I have done he has provided the sinews of war for. I think the most important, or one of the most important, things to me is that he pays my salary. But seriously, he has contributed a good deal more than half of everything that I have done in the world and received credit for. But he is a modest man and he stays in the background, and he gives me extraordinarily good advice. When he heard I was coming over here and I was to make this address, he gave me a very good piece of advice. He said: 'Say nothing.' And I can tell from the blithe look on your faces that you completely agree with him. ..."

"Mr. President, I accept this medal not for myself, because in my mind's eye I see hundreds and thousands of people who have contributed to this ship that you honor me for tonight. ... And the extraordinary thing about this particular endeavor is the fact that ... the people who actually did the building of the ship and also all those who contributed to the components – all these people knew what they were doing. The basic understanding was that for once we were aiming at nothing but perfection. Perfection, Mr. President, is an extremely hard task-master. Perfection in the arts and sciences does not come easily. It comes hard. To get perfection you have to demand perfection and the people who demand perfection are rarely popular." At this point, Mr. Gibbs brought down the house! "Beneath this rough exterior beats a heart of granite, and the only function I performed in connection with this ship was to demand perfection from everybody who had anything to do with it. And when it comes to perfection I believe that I am implacable."

Mr. Gibbs went into the ship's power to survive adding: "And that, Mr. President, is the difference between the *United States* and all other merchant ships and all other auxiliaries for the Navy. The ship has an enormous reserve of flotation and is absolutely fireproof-the first time that that has ever been done. The ship is entirely different from any of the ships of the past. It had to be different. You couldn't accomplish these two simultaneously – what has always been regarded as antithetical conceptions – unless the whole method of design were changed. That had to be done in the *United States.* ... Now, all that I have said to you and the fact that I have studied the arts in college, that I have a law degree, that I have a Master of Arts degree, that I am a member of the Bar, and that the naval architectural societies to which we all belong allege that I am a naval architect and an engineer-all this indicates to you that I am a jack of all trades and a master of none. My sole contribution in this performance is the fact that I took the responsibility for failure, and when you realize that a great ship like this is the most complicated structure that a man puts together, you can see that it is not much of an encomium on my intelligence."

Mr. Gibbs concluded: "I think it is appropriate that we should draw a generalized lesson from this amazing cooperation of a vast number of people in a common project. And the people who did this job understood what they were doing. They knew that they were trying for the greatest ship in the world."

The Franklin Institute's gold medal was awarded to workers in the physical sciences or technology who had done most to advance scientific knowledge or its application.

The original claim that the *United States* would carry 2,000 passengers was not accomplished in reality. The ship invariably sailed with up to 250 or so empty bunks in rooms that were occupied. While the actual number of berths totalled 1,995, from a practical standpoint her capacity was 1,650 to 1,700. The additional berths represented upper bunks in First Class rooms which were only used when families or groups desired to travel 3 or 4 in a room. Otherwise First Class space was sold for 1 or 2 passengers in a stateroom. In First Class all of the upper berths were literally hidden in the ceiling when not in use. Her glamor attracted the top names in society, business, sports, and the world of entertainment. King Paul and Queen Frederika of Greece took her on the October 23 sailing from New York. The crossing was not entirely a comfortable one. She ran into what one passenger described as her first really bad weather. A crewman broke his leg and several passengers suffered bruises. Barbara Hutton, then the Princess B. Troubetzkoy, sailed with 1,698 other passengers on the return crossing that left Southampton on November 7. The November 17 eastbound crossing saw the ship's 100,000th passenger come aboard. She was Mrs. Margaret Rhodes of Flint, Michigan, and she was going to visit her husband in Europe.

On Friday, December 18, the *United States* reached New York to complete the year's service. She had a passenger list of 1,724 persons, including two motion picture stars (Jeanne Crain and Dane Clark) and an Ambassador (Winthrop W. Aldrich). She arrived 11 hours behind schedule "after a tussle" with a 70-mile-an-hour storm on the way over. Commodore Anderson had been forced to reduce speed to 11 knots for 8 hours. He said she took maximum rolls of "about 25 degrees" at the height of the storm. Her first full calendar year of operation had been "most satisfactory," as the U.S. Lines annual report modestly put it. She had carried 70,589 passengers on 23 round trips during 1953, 34,842 eastbound and 35,747 westbound, for an average of 3,069 per round trip. The *America,* in 15 round trips, carried 26,220 in all for an average of 1,748 per round trip. On December 19, the new superliner sailed for her annual overhauling at Newport News. More than half her crew remained in New York with a deserved time off.

The year 1954 began with a set of new deck plans boasting excellent color interior photographs. They showed that Tourist Class had been given the large and very fine open deck space between the funnels, previously assigned to First Class, a much-needed area for this class. The Tourist Deck plans featured a photo of the forward stack with a caption boasting that the stacks on the *United States* were "by far the biggest funnels afloat." The colored photos did much to show off the best qualities of the various public rooms. The curtains and excellent decorative wall hangings were graphically shown. For example, the red-legged chairs with black backs and seats in the Cabin Smoking Room looked striking, as did the dark blue walls and blue columns in the Cabin Dining Saloon. Needless to say the photos of First Class were even better and belied the deriding comments made by some that the ship was more troopship than luxury liner. At long last a regular deck plan was issued, although it came out in so-called miniature form. For the first time all the ship's ten passenger decks were shown in sequence, five on one side and five on the other. They were called: Bridge, Sports, Sun, Promenade, Upper, Main, A, B, C and D. The Tourist Class was not shown as having the deck area between the funnels in this first miniature plan – an error.

In order to get the annual overhaul finished so the ship could be back in New York in time to sail Friday, January 15, 1954, work had to be done round-the-clock at the shipyard. A night view of the vessel brilliantly lit up was widely published. Although it was the peak of winter, 1,500 passengers sailed out on the *United States* on her first trip of 1954. Among them was Harrison Salisbury, Moscow correspondent for the *New York Times.* On the next departure from New York one of the passengers was Austin Purves, Jr., the sculptor who had done many of the aluminum figures as decorations throughout the ship. Also aboard was Hugh Gallagher, national president of the Propeller Club and vice president of Matson Lines. A new sailing schedule was put out in March taking the ship through the end of 1954. Commodore Anderson left the liner when she arrived March 4 and was given two round trips to rest up, his place being taken by Captain Fender.

On March 15, 1954, the government answered the U.S. Lines suit and asserted a counter claim. It conceded that it owed the operating-differential subsidy to the company, but counterclaimed against it charging that the price of the *United States* was too low. The U.S. Lines instructed its lawyers to prepare a reply.

Descendants of two famous Frenchmen were among the 1,639 passengers arriving April 7 at the end of Captain Fender's second consecutive trip as master. One was Dr. Francois J. Emile Zola, grandson of the famous author. The other was Count Rene de Chambrun, descendant of General Lafayette. On the April 8 departure there was another interesting passenger pairing: Sisters, Mrs. Reginald C. Vanderbilt, who was starting her 116th Atlantic crossing, and her sister Viscountess Furness. Several of Mrs. Vanderbilt's crossings had been on the *Leviathan.* She would have remembered the new purser of the *United States,* who had been Chief Purser on the *Leviathan.* Purser John Lock had unfortunately died at sea on March 27. His duties were assumed by Clarence P. Gehrig, known to his many friends as "Bob." Born in Brooklyn, he had spent 32 years at sea and had most recently been Chief Purser aboard the *America.* During World War II he had been a Navy commander for five years, seeing duty in the Atlantic, Pacific, and South Pacific. In 1943 he became finance officer at the U.S. Merchant Marine Academy, Kings Point.

Not all the distinguished passengers were listed on the press releases that were put out several days ahead of each sailing or arrival by Walter Jones' shop. One such individual wrote to William Francis Gibbs on April 19, to thank him for the "consideration you showed to the writer upon the occasion of my trip aboard the *United States.*" Mr. Gibbs had sent him a book and a box of cigars. He was James A. Farley, former chairman of the Democratic National Committee and then head of the Coca-Cola Export Corporation. Mr. Farley explained that he had to return to attend a meeting and so came home on the *Queen Mary* "otherwise I would have returned on the *United States.*" He said she was "the finest ship that sails the seas," adding "you have every reason to be proud of that great ship."

The U.S. Lines announced a drop in its dividend rate from the previous year's 81 cents per share of common stock to only 5 cents a share in a statement dated April 20, 1954. The slowness of the Department of Commerce in paying its operating subsidy was one reason, the company said. An amount of $31,500,000 was due the U.S. Lines for accrued operating payments. The dispute over the cost of the *United States* was the basic cause for this bad report, and pressure was mounting for a settlement. It came May 18 and the company agreed to add $3,400,000 to the original purchase price for the *United States.* This brought the total U.S. Lines share, after a final price had been established and escalation agreements had raised their original contribution slightly, to $32,900,000.

The arrival of the superliner at New York on May 25 produced a human interest yarn that many papers used. It involved the coming of the Emperor of Ethiopia, Haile Selassie I, on his first visit to America. Both NBC and CBS TV had decided to cover the arrival and had sent camera crews to Pier 86 to get pictures as the little monarch debarked. There was slight hope that he would consent to be interviewed, but it was assumed that he would at least have to pause while the Fire Department Band played the national anthems of his country and of the United States. The producers of CBS's "The Morning Show" were dubious, however, as to their chances of even a fleeting interview, so they worked out another plan. All details were cleared in advance with the State Department and the Ethiopian Embassy. They hired a tug and sent her down the Bay with a TV camera crew aboard. They sent another CBS reporter down the Bay with other reporters aboard the early morning cutter. There were no TV cameras on the cutter and the couple of NBC men aboard suspected nothing. As soon as the CBS reporter boarded the *United States* at the Narrows he sought out Emperor Selassie and persuaded him to give a rail-side interview. He was taken to a good open spot on the starboard side in full view of the approaching tug with the CBS TV cameramen aboard. It was all described later as "an ingenious television scoop." The tug's camera had a long-range lens and the CBS reporter on the *United States* had a portable "mike" with a two-way audio "feed" to the picture on the nation's TV screens. With the good-natured cooperation of the Emperor the TV audience at 7:45 a.m. got a close-up view of the little monarch gazing at the Manhattan skyline. At one point Walter Cronkite, talking from the CBS studio, asked Haile Selassie if he would wave to the television audience. The Emperor heard the cue from the amplifier and gave a vigorous wave and a smile to the camera on the tug. The NBC men aboard were stunned when they learned what was happening, but took it in good nature. After the interview one of them was seen to go over to the CBS man and silently hold out his hand in congratulation.

The *Cleburne* (Tex.) *Times Review* carried a syndicated picture story featuring Otto Bismarck, *chef des cuisines* on the *United States* on June 4. Used as well in many hundreds of other papers it was a coup for Walter Jones. It described the famous Chef's plans for Father's Day at sea, June 20. He had scheduled as a treat roast chicken with a special kind of stuffing. A photograph of Bismarck's special roast was shown under a picture of the *United States* leaving New York. Superimposed over the right skyline was the smiling face of Otto himself. The Chef had conducted a survey, the story added, which showed that people aboard ship eat more chicken than do landlubbers. And so his *"Poularde a la S.S. United States."*

On June 11, 1954 the *United States* sailed with 1,735 passengers, said, at the time, to be her largest passenger list up to then. This was not so as she had brought in 1,750 on September 3, 1952, but it certainly was an excellent list. Among those aboard was screen star Robert Montgomery. Upon her return the ship would complete her second full year in service and statisticians were busy working up figures to show how successful she had been. George Horne, of the *New York Times,* who had come home aboard the *United States* May 11, wrote a lengthy account about her anniversary. Its headline: *"United States'* 2-Year Operation Proves Speed Record Is No Fluke." He noted that when she was commissioned it was estimated that she would have to carry 65 to 70% of her passenger capacity during her 20-year lifetime expectancy to permit her owners to break even financially. "Thus far she has bettered this mark," he wrote. He added that she had beaten the *Queen Mary's* record run of 3 days, 20 hours, 42 minutes several times without gaining particular notice. "One quality that has attracted the attention of naval architects and engineers is her extraordinary stability," he continued. "It is understood that during the stormy winter months between November and March she averaged better than 30-46 knots, faster by two knots or more than any competitor in the big luxuryclass field." The story pointed out that studies then being made would show that this record was made with remarkable fuel economy: "It is known that the engineering advances represented in the liner have made possible unequaled fuel economy, even at high speed." On the subject of a sistership, Mr. Horne was not optimistic. "Industry leaders doubt that the idea will go beyond the talk stage. Commercial shipping men and Navy men, whose enthusiasm made the liner possible as a potential naval auxiliary, agree that the ideal is a team of two express vessels. But both Congress and the Administration are economy-minded."

When the *United States* docked she was the center piece in a row of six major Atlantic liners. The *Herald Tribune* had a front-page photo showing from top to bottom: *Queen Mary, Flandre, Olympia, United States, America,* and *Independence.* Her departure on July 8 saw Vincent Astor and Mrs. Astor heading the passenger list of 1,700 persons. Among the others aboard were Joseph P. Kennedy, the former chairman of the Maritime Commission and ex-Ambassador to Great Britain, and Harold Gray, originator of the Little Orphan Annie cartoon.

The second half of 1954 was largely uneventful, with one exciting exception-a docking during a major hurricane. The *United States* continued to carry good passenger lists, although at one point she dipped for the first time well below 1,000 persons on one crossing. The honeymoon period was still in effect with labor, at least on the surface. A mid-year hull check-up was thought to be necessary and, instead of going to Newport News, the

Passengers boarding the liner. (Courtesy of Bill DiBenedetto)

superliner was drydocked at the Navy drydock at Bayonne, New Jersey. It was a routine inspection after her first two-years of service. Her propellers, rudder, hull, and underwater gear were all found in good shape. She sailed at noon, Saturday, July 24 with 1,575 passengers. A new sailing schedule was issued three days later taking her up through May of 1955. It was said that heavy advance bookings indicated that 1955 would be "another banner year for European travel."

Many articles had been done on the turnaround of the *United States* at New York, but none on the turnaround at Southampton. *Nation's Business* for August filled in the blank with a beautifully illustrated story by Vernon Pizer. He had boned up for his piece by making an eastbound crossing and staying aboard during her turnaround. "It was an incredible display of efficiency, speed and teamwork." The picture sequence began with views of officers on the bridge passing up the Solent, a view of Captain Fender and the sixfoot uniformed Channel pilot on the wing of the bridge passing Nab Tower, and a tugman's view of the docking at Southampton. Another pair of shots showed a steward moving baggage down the highly-polished rubber floor of one of the ship's miles of alleyways, and seamen handling one of the 20 hawsers, ten fore and ten aft, used to moor the ship while in port. Another picture page showed (1) Kennelmaster Euvrard watching as two mink-clad women passengers come to take their dog, one of nine brought over, and (2) Chief Steward Henry Mueller checking the ship's wine stock, and (3) officers inspecting a long line of white-coated stewards standing in line ready to greet oncoming passengers. The late Chief Purser Lock was shown in another picture, with two assistants, balancing the books for bar sales, deck chair hire, and other voyage receipts. Next Otto Bismarck was snapped carefully making a spot check of an incoming case of fish, with two very British looking men watching intently behind him. The article noted that most stores were bought in New York except for specialties. The final view, a stern shot, showed the ship 19 hours and 49 minutes after arriving in port, homeward bound, "restocked, refueled, refurbished, and completely shipshape." The article was a minute-by-minute, person-by-person type account-detailed and delightful!

Commodore Anderson took the *United States* out on August 6 with 1,700 passengers. For some reason he did not make the westbound return crossing, but turned the liner over to Captain Fender. The ship brought back 1,758 passengers, her largest list up to that point. The total number of passengers carried on the round trip was 3,458-a record. The return was uneventful, but the actual arrival and docking was one of the most hectic ever experienced in the annals of great liners at New York. The storm is remembered as "Hurricane Carol," and the peak of the hurricane just happened to be the moment of docking. Captain Frederick W. Snyder, senior Moran docking pilot, was on the bridge with Captain Fender as the ship came up the Hudson approaching Pier 86. It was August 31, 1954. Let Captain Snyder tell his own story in his own words, as related to me while I worked for Moran as editor of their house organ *Tow Line:*

"As we proceeded up the river it was already blowing a strong Northeast gale. The hurricane was imminent and predicted. In view of this Captain Fender and I began laying our plans for docking and landing on the fender. Five tugs were ordered inlight of the storm, where only three are normally used. We decided to use the port anchor and bring the wind 15 to 20 degrees on our port side to make a lee for the tugs which couldn't come alongside because of the seas running five and six feet high in the Hudson River. We moved up past the pier about 1,000 feet off shore in order that the anchor led well above the pier and well off the pier and began falling in towards the pier with the lee provided for the tugs. The tugs all on the starboard bow and the side were having difficulty getting head on and not pounding into the side of the ship, damaging the hull plating. It is now about 0815 – the storm now at top intensity, force 9 and 10. The anchor and tugs are not holding the ship. It is obvious the ship is falling in and not under perfect control. The *United States* has a stem anchor and that was immediately dropped and brought up. It was now necessary to let up on the tugs or reduce their speed to allow the ship to land gently on the special landing fender and float. The ship now landed and resting on the fender, the bow anchor was hove up, the port anchor cable shortened, two tugs shifted to the port bow, the other three placed on the starboard side aft. In this maneuver the ship was turned around the end of the pier, the two port bow tugs and anchor dragging the bow and the ship was kept under perfect control. At 0900 at the top wind velocity, the ship was all secured." An *Associated Press* wire photo showed this difficult maneuver in the process of completion, with the rarely-used stem anchor out and holding and the port anchor also out and taut.

A new sailing schedule, No. 3, was issued in September, taking the *United States* up through the end of 1955. Her books were open for her fourth year of service.

On Friday, September 3, eleven-year-old Eugene Hart left his home at 18 Schaeffer Street, Brooklyn, with 17 cents in his pocket. His grandmother warned him not to go far and to be back in good time for lunch. He would violate both these commands. As he remembered, his original plan was to go to a movie, but he saw in the morning papers that the *United States* was sailing at noon and he hurried over to Manhattan's West Side to look her over. "I was still looking around when I found the ship was out at sea," he said later. "I wasn't exactly scared, but I didn't know who to tell or whether I should tell at all." Boat drill that afternoon found him without a life jacket. A watchful stewardess spotted him. He was

*Life boat drill on the Promenade Deck aft.
(Courtesy of Bill DiBenedetto)*

97

Burt Lancaster

Joan Crawford

Cary Grant

Marlon Brando and Salvador Dali

(Photo by Andrew Malmsea, Chief Steward, SS United States, courtesy of Sven Olefeldt)

Judy Garland

98

placed on 24-hour guard in the ship's hospital. The ship's surgeon, Dr. John Sheedy, reported later that he was a model traveler, washing out his shirt and dungarees each night." His mother Hildegarde and grandmother, Mrs. Mamie Deckert, were informed that he was in Southampton, but, apparently, they were unable to pay his passage, so he returned in the ship's hospital. Talking to reporters when he reached New York he said he had always loved to travel. He said he had run away because his grandmother had thrown a knife at him. Later his mother denied this, and explained that if the grandmother had ever thrown a knife, it was only a rubber knife and it was done only in fun.

A full page picture of the *United States* arriving after her maiden voyage was carried in the *Times* on September 22 as an advertisement for *Newsweek* magazine. The main headline shouted out in large type: "It would take the SS *United States* 918 trips to carry all the *Newsweek* families with incomes of $7,500 or more." The lower caption noted that the new superliner's passenger capacity was 1,982 persons and that more than 505,000 *Newsweek*-reading families had incomes of this size. The ad was used on several other occasions.

In October a 24-page schedule of passenger fares was issued. With the famous old American Line's eagle in white on the blue cover and with red lettering it offered an attractive format. The second and third pages showed large colored pictures of the *United States* and the *America*, with red and blue decorations and fancy lettering. Rates in all classes were shown, cabin by cabin for off-season and for summer season. The booklet ended with six pages of general information about such things as pregnancy: "The Company reserves the right to refuse passage to women in advanced stages of pregnancy. Prior notice should be given the Company of all such cases." For servants traveling with their employers in First Class, the rate was 20% less than the minimum and "space will be assigned at sailing time." For children under one year the rate was $20 in First and $10 in Cabin and Tourist classes. Automobiles as baggage cost from $250 to $525, depending on their weight one way, or $300 to $575 round trip — quite an inducement to take the car both ways.

Although most passenger lists remained above 1,500 there was one crossing in the Fall of 1954 when only 750 persons were carried. It was the October 29 eastbound sailing. There were 1,659 coming home, however, so the average was not too bad. Captain Fender gave Commodore Anderson another trip off in November. One of his passengers on the return crossing was Marlon Brando. Salvador Dali was also aboard. The last crossing before the ship's visit to Newport News began on December 1. A Bishop, an Ambassador, an Admiral, and the famous lecturer Dr. Julian Huxley were on the "commend list" for special treatment. On the return crossing the Duke and Duchess of Windsor were again aboard. They were given Suite U-87, 89 and 91, a three-room Suite on the Upper Deck. The area included two twin-bedded cabins, a large sitting room with sofa and four easy chairs, a trunk room, and three baths. There were 1,740 passengers coming home for Christmas. Right Honorable the Viscount Furness and famed circus mastermind John Ringling North were also aboard, along with Emanuel Mercer, English racing jockey and William Forsyth, associate curator of medieval art at the Metropolitan Museum of Art in New York.

The schedule for 1954 permitted the *United States* to make only 22 round trips compared with 23 in 1953, so her overall carryings were slightly less: 67,577 compared to 70,589. But her average per round trip was up slightly, 3,072 in 1954 compared to 3,069 in the year before. The *America* continued to do well also with a total of 28,879 passengers on 33 crossings.

William Francis Gibbs' Christmas card for 1954 was a painting of the *United States* at night done by the well-known marine artist Theodore Ewen, whose brother, William Hopkins Ewen, had been president of the Steamship Historical Society of America several times. It was a superb piece of work, with a dark foreground of blue-black waves contrasted with the full hull of the superliner in black but illuminated by hundreds of orange porthole dots and long stripes of bright orange along the promenade and boat deck areas. The whole was capped with the brightly illuminated red, white, and blue stacks standing out against an upper background of moonlit whitish cloud formations. I had taken Ted with the painting to meet Mr. Gibbs, and to have that painting picked by Mr. Gibbs for his Christmas card was a marvelous feeling.

The winter overhauling was an annual junket to those who joined the ship for the ride down to Newport News or the sail back to New York. But it was intensive and sometimes very hard work for the specialists who had to be ready around the clock to do their part. B.O. Smith remembered being called at 2 a.m. one winter morning to check the shafts as the drydock water receded. Going up on the wet scaffolding in the bottom of the cold drydock while it snowed in zero weather was no fun. The *United States* arrived at the yard December 28 and returned to New York January 12, 1955, to begin her new season the following day.

The year 1955 would be an exceptionally good year for the *United States,* one of her very best. Her season started in the worst of winter, January 13, but her passenger lists rose steadily. Better yet there was not the big difference between eastbound and westbound crossings on a seasonal basis, low one way and full the other, that had been so common in 1953 and 1954. The steady rise in passengers carried can be seen for the first six months in these consecutive lists: 1,250; 1,620; 1,325; 1,414; 1,600; 1,608; 1,673; 1,575; 1,467; 1,514; 1,597; 1,675; 1,725; 1,698 and 1,750. And famous names kept sailing: Cary Grant; the Prince and Princess Chula of Siam; Mrs. Clyde Harris, grand daughter of Kaiser Wilhelm; tennis star Victor Seixas; Louis B. Mayer, of MGM; actress Hermione Gingold; ex-Ambassador Joseph P. Kennedy; George Meany, and Burt Lancaster.

When the ship returned from her winter overhaul she had aboard the first cinemascope screen ever installed aboard a North Atlantic liner. She was carrying on the tradition of the *Leviathan,* which had a dozen such firsts to her credit including the first use of television aboard a ship. The two cinema theatres aboard the new superliner were both equipped with 18-foot wide and 9-foot high screens, especially built to conform to the ship's rigid fire regulations. The screen in the 352-seat First and Cabin class theatre rolled up and down so that a regulation screen could be used behind it for conventional films. In the 200-seat Tourist Class theatre the new screen was permanent, but could be masked with aluminum strips for the smaller projection. Two Cinemascope feature films were scheduled for the ship's first trip of the year: "There's No Business Like Show Business," and "Bad Day at Black Rock." The four conventional films taken aboard were: "Country Girl," "Young at Heart," "Far Country," and "Bridges of Toko-Ri."

BACK TO 1955 AGAIN?

In January 1955, the U.S. Lines began an advertising campaign that would prove so successful that it would be continued in the same format for the rest of the ship's Atlantic career. It was designed to overcome the troopship stigma, which had been attached to the ship as part of the effort to justify her building subsidy. The new advertising effort stressed actual people who had sailed on the new ship. It showed photographs and even gave their names and often their home towns. The first such ad was carried in *Holiday*. Its lead headline, carried in blue script, very casual, very "society," read: "Just time for the time of your life." The full-page advertisement had five colored photographs under a dashing colored wash drawing of the new ship. One photo showed Mr. and Mrs. E.R. Cook playing shuffleboard between the two huge stacks in the area later turned over to Tourist Class. The next showed Mr. and Mrs. George S. Farnsworth, of New Orleans, in their suite. They were quoted as saying: "The service is just one of the things that has made this our most enjoyable crossing." Another picture showed Mr. and Mrs. George S. Kaufman and Tennessee Williams eating in the *a la carte* dining saloon. Its caption: "Dine in Paris, London, New Orleans – the menu, studied here by ... is a gourmet's guide to Continental and American cuisine ... caviar from Iran, Dover sole, juicy, inches-thick American steak." The final picture was an indirect slap at air travel – it showed luggage being piled up on deck to be off loaded. Its caption noted that you "can take 25 cubic feet free."

Advertisement for United States Lines featured in the magazine Holiday. *(Courtesy of Bill McBride with McBride Publishing)*

The U.S. Lines announced on January 12 that the *United States* had sailed at "better than 90% utilization of her normal passenger capacity" during 1954. The *America* had done the same, the statement added.

Both the *America* and the *United States* had deck-to-ceiling windows on their glass-enclosed promenade decks. Cleaning the outsides of these was a matter to which considerable attention had been given. An issue of the company's internal house organ, "Excerpts and Gleanings" explained how it had been worked out. An all-metal "trolley" was devised to do the work safely. It was a platform suspended from the lip of the deck above, the Boat Deck, which could be moved from window to window. With two rails around it, the trolley was a strong and safe place to work.

A special telecast was produced aboard the superliner on March 6 and World Telegram columnist Harriet Van Horne was there to cover it for her column. With a bit of sarcasm she began: "I went aboard the liner *United States* last night for a special telecast of the NBC Comedy Hour and all I can say today is – she's a lovely ship." She went on to praise the ship and damn the show: "The Comedy Hour appears to be another victim of NBC's traveling mania. In some plush rookery, high in the towers of Radio City, sits a wanderlusting executive surrounded by travel folders and timetables. It is his notion, I fancy, that TV shows take on glamour in proportion to their distance from welllighted, technically perfect studios. Last night's shipboard shuffle did give viewers a few tantalizing glimpses of the interior of a great ship. But at what a cost! The picture blacked out, the audio came and went, and the singers on deck sounded as if they were yodeling from a diving bell. Still, the technicians, laboring under trying conditions, should be congratulated for managing these remotes at all."

The *New York Herald Tribune,* which had pioneered in such things as the original line-o-type machine, came out with a new-style camera in April, 1955. Called "camerama" it permitted the newspaper to show wide-angled pictures that "shoot rings around standard photographic equipment," the paper said. The introductory picture used to display the ability of this new camera was of the *United States.* Her April 27 departure from New York was spread over 16 columns at the top of two facing pages of the newspaper the following morning. The remarkable view covered New York's skyline from 138th Street to Greenwich Village – a 160 degree sweep. Photographer Luis Azarraga was the inventor and photographer. An ordinary photo of the same scene was carried in four columns below the 16-column picture – and made quite a contrast. Passengers on the liner waved at the helicopter in which Mr. Azarraga was taking his photographs. To keep his secrets from prying eyes, he had encased his special camera in an aluminum "bread box." He compared it to the new widescreen movies then being shown and said that he hoped to adapt his special lens to the taking of motion pictures. The field of vision of an ordinary wide-angle-lens camera was about half that of the Azarraga camera. While in his helicopter he also saw the *Queen Mary, Ile de France,* and *New York* sail. The newspaper offered 29" x 8 1/2", copies of the *United States* 160-degree photo on heavy stock suitable for framing for $1.

An interesting advertisement for U.S. Lines published in *Marine Progress* for May showed models of

An advertisement similar to the one published in Marine Progress *for U.S. Lines. It is showing models of the* United States *and the* America *surrounded with models to scale of the company's 46 freighters. The advertisements featured different copy. (Courtesy of Bill McBride with McBride Publishing)*

the *United States* and the *America* surrounded with models to scale of the company's 46 freighters. The caption: "United States Lines offers the world's fastest superliner and direct cargo service to world ports!" This perfectly illustrated the philosophy of many American shiplines of that day: liners were important prestige ships to bring publicity to a company whose earnings came primarily from freight ships.

Countless groups had visited the new speed queen during her visits to Southampton and her stays in New York. On June 8 I helped one such group, 60 people from Teachers' College who came under the direction of their instructor, Ward D. Whipple. It was always a pleasure to escort groups over the great ship and to hear their "ohs" and "ahs" as they went from one elegant public room to another.

The months of July and August 1955 saw the *United States* carry more passengers than ever before. Of her nine crossings in this period all but two saw over 1,700 passengers aboard. She broke her own mark on the westbound passage reaching New York August 30, bringing in 1,763 persons. For all liners serving the United States and Canada this was a banner year, with 942,245 passengers making trans-Atlantic crossings one way or the other. This represented an 18% increase eastbound and a 21% increase westbound. Involved were 1,239 cross-

101

SS United States *sails in Europe*
March 16, 1953.
(Courtesy of Bill DiBenedetto)

ings by 55 companies or services, according to Joseph Mayper of the trans-Atlantic Conference. In these two months the *United States* carried more passengers than the *Queen Mary* and slightly less than the *Queen Elizabeth*. The following table shows what these three outstanding liners did in July and August, 1955:

Arrival or Sailing Day	*United States*	*Queen Mary*	*Queen Elizabeth*
July			
5	1,714	1,656	
6		1,975	
7	1720		
12			1,915
13			2,214
18	1,704		
23	1,691		
26		1,774	
27		1,734	
Aug			
2			2,098
3	1,743		1,964
5	1,711		
9		1,863	
10		1,548	
16	1,728		2,190
17			1,609
19	1,626		
23		1,934	
24		1,395	
30	1,763		2,192
31	---------	---------	1,666
	15,400	13,861	15,848

The slightly greater operating speed of the *United States* enabled her to gain three days on each of the *Queens* during this 60-day period, and permitted her to fit in one extra crossing. The two *Queens* averaged considerably more passengers than did the *United States,* but made one fewer trip. These three ships were far and away the most used during this period. Neither the *Ile de France* nor the *Liberté* approached them in regard to size of passenger lists. In a sense the original assertion that the *United States* could carry the same number of passengers as the *Queen* liners was being vindicated, for her greater speed permitted her to make more crossings.

A U.S. Lines announcement made at mid-year, 1955, noted that the new superliner had carried 207,807 passengers in her first three full years of service. She had crossed the Atlantic 134 times and traveled 427,752 nautical miles, a distance equivalent to approximately 17 times around the world. During this voyaging she had averaged 30.63 knots, about 35 land miles per hour. And her owners and designers were particularly proud of the final statistic. She had been under steam at sea for a total of 726 full days, or 66% of the three year period. Several other pleasing bits of information were passed out at this time: "During her three years of service the vessel's shafts have never been stopped or slowed down at sea due to machinery derangement. The ship's tremendous air conditioning system which services all staterooms, public rooms, crew's quarters, and all working areas and is in use on every voyage throughout the year, had functioned perfectly for three years without interruption. The exceptional maneuverability of the *United States is* such that she can dock or sail from her piers in New York, Le Havre, or Southampton at any stage of the tide. Her maneuverability has resulted in most favorable comment by all the harbor pilots who have handled the ship in narrow channels."

William Francis Gibbs received two particularly cordial letters from important men in the Fall of 1955, both of which were written while they were passengers aboard the *United States.* Apart from the content of the letters, it was interesting to note that both these distinguished personages had very ordinary handwriting. In each case, obviously, they had decided to write while en route and without benefit of secretary or typewriter. For his own record, Mr. Gibbs had typed copies of each letter made to go in his scrapbook. One was from Senator Leverett Saltonstall. Mr. Gibbs had sent him a copy of James Dugan's book *The Great Iron Ship,* about the historic *Great Eastern;* he had also sent a bunch of red roses, his trademark. The Senator admitted that he had never heard of the *Great Eastern* and likened her to the famous, or ill-famed, seven-masted schooner *Thomas W. Lawson.* He congratulated William Francis for designing the *United States:* "She has speed – comfort – luxury, and no vibration." Mrs. Gibbs had been a passenger on the same trip and Senator Saltonstall mentioned what a pleasant time he and his wife had had chatting with her in Captain Fender's quarters. The other letter, with even worse handwriting, was from Louis S. Rothschild, Maritime Administrator. "The *United States* is indeed all that you told me and more," he wrote.

Declaring the *United States* to represent "the greatest advance in the worldwide field of transportation," the Elmer A. Sperry Board of Award decided in September, 1955, to elect William Francis Gibbs as the first recipient of a new award for distinguished engineering contributions to the world of transportation. The award was announced by Robert B. Lea, son-in-law of Dr. Sperry, noted inventor and founder of the Sperry Rand Corporation. It was presented in Chicago on November 17 at the diamond jubilee meeting of the American Society of Mechanical Engineers.

Many different social events, memorial services, and ceremonies were held aboard the *United States* in these hey-days of her career. One delightful little happening involved the Seamen's Church Institute and one of its fund raising drives. Four hundred and fifty children were asked to write messages to be stuffed inside bottles and dropped overboard in mid-Atlantic from the new superliner. The first of the bottles to be found and returned would insure a prize both for the finder and for the sender. Russell Skillman, of Manasquan, New Jersey, was the lucky message writer. His note and bottle were found in Donegal Bay, Ireland, by Patrick O' Byrne, of Glen Columbkille. Both received original seascapes painted by artist Linwood Borum, of Baltimore.

In December, 1955, the internal house organ of Captain Devlin's office on Pier 60 finally dropped the picture of the *America* which they had used for years as a masthead decoration atop the front page. Instead they put the painting of the *United States* by Aylward, the same one that showed a main mast where there never had been one. Apparently nobody noticed.

9

Labor Troubles Begin

The *United States* carried more passengers in 1955 than any other ship on the Atlantic. Her total of 70,104 voyagers made an average of 1,593 per sailing. It represented a 95% utilization of the ship's "normal passenger capacity," as the company put it. The *America* also did very well, carrying 27,472 persons with better than 90% utilization. Famous names and interesting people continued to book space on the new superliner. On January 28 her list was topped by William Willis with his wife. The press release put out by U.S. Lines began: "From raft to superliner. ..." Willis had recently completed a 6,700 mile, 115-day Pacific voyage alone on a raft from Peru to Samoa. His only companions were a parrot and a canary. He had written a new book entitled: "The Gods Were Kind," and was going to Europe to publicize it.

With one striking exception the passenger lists over the winter months of 1956 were under what had come to be thought of as normal for the *United States.* The exception was the arrival on February 24 with 1,823 persons. A large number of military dependents filled up the Tourist and Cabin classes on this crossing. By mid-April the lists again began to be close to operating capacity. An interesting party sailed from Southampton for New York, arriving on April 21, with suitable ceremony. The Right Honorable Lord Mayor of London and the Lady Mayoress, also known as Alderman and Mrs. Cuthbert L. Ackroyd, were aboard. They were accompanied by William T. Boston, O.B.E., swordbearer, and 1st Esquire to the Lord Mayor; Charles F. Glenny, M.V.O., The Chief Commoner of London, and Alderman Bernard N. Waley-Cohen, sheriff of the City of London, with his wife. I was invited to luncheon aboard the liner on April 24 and saved the menu. Among the specialties was kangaroo tail soup.

The next particularly notable personage to travel on the *United States* in the Spring of 1956 was Harry S. Truman, whose status as a former president gave him almost the same prestige as when he had occupied the White House. Mrs. Truman was with him. A special press advisory about arrangements in connection with his sailing May 11 was issued. A large area on the open Sports Deck between the stacks was provided for photographers, newsreel men, and TV cameras. A 25-minute interview was arranged for two hours before sailing, with the port side of the First Class Observation Lounge forward on the Promenade Deck being reserved for the press. A special area next to the First Class gangway was also roped off for photographers desiring to take pictures of Mr. and Mrs. Truman boarding. The press was asked not to go to the Truman suite, which was U-87-89, usually used by the Duke and Duchess of Windsor.

The sailing was notable for one other thing. Meyer Berger, ace human interest reporter for the *New York Times,* carried a short note at the bottom of his column a few days later. He pointed out that no crewman or officer aboard the superliner "gets more thrill out of that vessel's smooth harbor entries and exits than William Francis Gibbs." Apparently he had spotted Mr. Gibbs at the departure and talked with him. He reported that William Francis had watched 83 of the ship's 84 sailings. The one he had missed was a time when he was sick in bed. "He likes to follow the shore road as she moves in or out, in rain or mist or in a storm," he said.

It was amazing how the Aylward painting got around. A copy of the New Haven Railroad's "Menu & Travel Guide" for June, 1956, had it in full color on the cover. The main mast was there, in full glory. The guide was a 12-page publication with colored liquor ads and a listing of theatre, opera, and other events for the month in New York City, in addition to an elaborate double-page menu for the train's elegant diner.

The June 8 sailing saw another fine passenger list of 1,776 persons. Mary Pickford and her husband Charles ("Buddy") Rogers were among those sailing. The ship was shaken as she approached Southampton by an underwater explosion. Commodore Anderson said upon arrival that "a mine was detonated as the ship passed near a mining ground and caused some disturbance to the passengers." A British Admiralty spokesman, trying to down-play the episode, later stated: "Routine test explosions of depth charges are taking place within a restricted area near Ryde, Isle of Wight. There is no danger to shipping, but it is possible that slight effects of the explosions will be felt. The explosion occurred three and a half miles astern of the *United States.*"

Another, much more pleasant event, occurred at this time. The 434-ton, three-masted schooner *Creole* passed the superliner in Cowes Roads. One of the world's most beautiful sailing ships, she was stretching a new set of sails prior to entering a race from Torbay to Lisbon. This race was the beginning of the Sail Training Association's series of every-two-year races along the coast of Europe which would blossom in 1964 into a trans-Atlantic tall ships race and the first Operation Sail. The *Creole* was owned by Greek shipowner Stavros Niarchos.

This was the period in which the *United States*, the Dutch liner *Nieuw Amsterdam*, and the Cunarder *Caronia* were all "gonged" for speeding by the Netley Parish Council. Their wash came "roaring ashore in large waves" as they passed Netley entering and leaving Southampton. Councillor Gilbert Ray, of the Parish Council, told reporters that the wash was a danger especially to visitors from outside the Parish. They allowed their children on the beach "when all of a sudden they would be frightened by the enormous wash as the vessels left Southampton at an estimated speed of 12 to 14 knots." Peter Ferguson, maritime historian who had a house on the sea front at Cowes also knew of the wash from the *United States*. While he admired her very much as a ship, he learned to be aware of the waves she created. Here are his memories:

"In front of our house was a public green and this extended down to the promenade and beach, which was steeply shelved so that what little beach was there became crowded with sunbathers and deck chairs in the summer. Now the Solent waters are sheltered and there are no customary breakers thundering in except man-made ones. The wash from a great liner took approximately 15 minutes to reach the shore, so that the vessel would be almost up to Calshot Spit Light Vessel by the time the first of about 6 to 12 miniature tidal waves hit the unsuspecting holiday makers and drenched them!

We locals knew all about it, but the visitors were always caught unawares as they sat or slept in their beach chairs and it caused us a lot of amusement. One of the worst offenders was the *United States* as she never could slow down and even at 12-16 knots she kicked up a bow wave that reached one-half way up her steeply raked stem. By the time this reached shore, and particularly if it was high water, the effect was devastating as the first wave still some 3 to 4 feet high would come in with a crash and send its gurgling, singing

President Truman, a passenger aboard the United States.
(Photo by Andrew Malmsea, Chief Steward, SS United States, *courtesy of Sven Olefeldt)*

mass right over the beach, across the promenade as far as the grassed edge of the green."

Mr. Ferguson continued: "Despite being 'held up for speeding,' the *United States* and her smaller sister *America* were great favorites with the locals. They formed part of the post war 'Big Six,' i.e. *Queen Elizabeth, Queen Mary, United States, America, Liberté,* and *Ile de France*. Our own national pride of course put the two *Queens* on the top, but the *United States* and the *America* always drew the crowds – the local boatmen who offered trips in the *Saucy Salt* out of the harbor to Cowes Roads to meet at close quarters these ocean giants inward or outward bound always got full loads for these liners and one of the most popular and eagerly anticipated local events was the regular, but rather rare, occasions when the *United States* would pass *America* off Cowes, one inward bound and the other outward."

Mr. Ferguson referred to the *United States* as "that amazing ship," and he also particularly remembered "the enormous girth of her funnels." Let him describe his impressions: "As she turned in front of our house by the Gurnard Ledge buoy to complete the Solent leg up to Calshot Spit one became aware of their colossal width compared with the relatively sleek breadth of the hull. The tops of the funnels were painted in a most unusual shade of blue that from a distance it was impossible to tell what colour it was – only when you came up really close to her could you realize that it was a rich steel blue and not black."

A major effort to build a sistership for the *United States* was launched in July, 1956. Clarence C. Morse, chairman of the Federal Maritime Board, headed a number of key witnesses heard by the House Merchant Marine & Fisheries Committee on the matter. He said the Maritime Administration planned to advertise for bids and would call for them to be opened in January, 1957. He assured the House that the bids would be kept open until August so that Congress would have a firm basis for appropriating the money to build the liner. He added that if Congress failed to provide the funds no contract would be awarded. Without elaborating he said that the proposed new ship would differ only in the matter of speed from the *United States*. He called the *United States* "the most advanced ship operating today." It was estimated that the new liner would cost from $90,000,000 to $100,000,000. It would take from three to five years to build her.

Several representatives of the Navy supported the plea for a second superliner. Captain William W. Outerbridge, speaking for the Chief of Naval Operations, called such a ship "essential to the national defense." Rear Admiral Albert G. Mumma, Defense Department coordinator of shipbuilding and chief of the Navy Bureau of Ships, said that "in time of war we would like dozens of such ships." He added: "We couldn't afford to build enough *United Stateses* to keep us happy." Like the *United States,* the new ship would be constructed in a private shipyard under government contract and then sold to the U.S. Lines for trans-Atlantic operation. In an emergency the government would use her as a troop carrier. General Franklin also testified: "Shipbuilding costs are not going down. The sooner another *United States is* built, the cheaper we will get it." The new ship would replace the *America* and that older ship would be sold to a friendly foreign nation for operation on a non-competing route, with the understanding that she could be taken back for troopship work in an emergency.

Ralph E. Casey, president of the American Merchant Marine Institute, also was at the hearing. He testified that the American passenger fleet had never recovered from the consequences of World War II. In September, 1939, there were 123 American passenger liners in commercial operation with a singletrip passenger lift of 38,000 travelers. The fleet had diminished, he noted, to only 39 ships with a lift of 11,170 passengers. Only four of these were capable of speeds of more than 20 knots. He concluded: "The American Merchant Marine Institute believes that this new superliner should, I might even say must, be built as a private enterprise. It will make a tremendous contribution not only to the American Merchant Marine, but to the prestige of our nation, as well as being a highly valuable national defense asset."

George Horne, of the *Times,* wrote a charming article about William Francis Gibbs entitled "His Fair Lady." It was carried in the Sunday magazine section on July 22 and began: "In the world of deep-sea ships, 'My Fair Lady' would be the story of William Francis Gibbs and his wonderful superliner *United States.* Pygmalion-like, he created her and he fell in love with her." His story noted that the ship had just had her fourth anniversary, adding that "for economy, and safety she has no peer." The article pointed out that "the tall, saturnine, dedicated genius" Gibbs had missed only one sailing since the ship made her maiden voyage.

"He can always be found prowling around, tapping here and there, listening deadpan in her great engine room, poring over dials, gazing silently at the massive drive shafts. He caresses the gleaming reaches of aluminum. He lopes through the public rooms, sniffing ozone from the air-conditioning ducts. He keeps encyclopedic notes on her performance and accumulates exhaustive data on the performance of every major liner on the Atlantic. He views it all against the shining record of the *United States.* He is jealous of the ship and delightedly frustrates foreign attempts to uncover her speed and economic secrets."

The article went on to explain the important part played by Gibbs in Navy work, and quoted Navy men as saying that no one had done as much as him to put more power into smaller space. "But, to Gibbs, what matters is the superliner. He's not worried. It's a fascination with perfection. Often, before the city stirs, the Gibbs chauffeur brings his car to a halt along Brooklyn's Shore Drive and the tall, gangling figure steps out. Through his metal-rimmed spectacles he watches for his ship standing in from sea."

"At precisely 8:15 a.m. on every one of the 773 days that the *United States* has been at sea on her trans-Atlantic route between Ambrose Light and Le Havre Light, Gibbs had telephoned Chief Engineer Kaiser to ask how things were going, what revolutions she was making, and the like. Bill Kaiser would respond, saying that she was doing very well, would talk a little about her speed, fuel consumption, and the wind. It was a routine that was never changed, a ritual. Men have loved ships before, but this kind of unflagging concern is rare. Ask him why, and he seems puzzled. 'I'm interested,' he retorts. 'My God, who wouldn't be?'"

The *Westsider,* magazine of the West Side Association, New York, had a cover picture showing the new Coliseum at 59th Street. The picture also showed six liners at their West Side piers: *Queen Mary, Mauretania, Liberté, United States, Andrea Doria,* and *Constitution.* Never again would all six be together. One was a doomed ship, the *Andrea Doria,* 30,000-ton Italian Line vessel which sank July 26, 1956 after colliding off Nantucket with the *Stockholm.* Fifty-two lives were lost in the tragedy. Had the Italian Line had a man like William Francis Gibbs to demand that stability standards be observed on their ships the *Doria* might not have sunk.

The loss of the *Andrea Doria* sent a shock wave around the world. The public could hardly imagine such a thing happening and the ship's name will go down in history along with that of the *Titanic* as one of the best known of all liners of the century. It was very much a topic of conversation aboard the *United States* when she sailed August 17, with 1,650 passengers aboard. Two nights out there was a storm and Anne Klein, rare-book dealer from Queens, became alarmed. The superliner was rolling and things began falling off her bureau. She became panicky and rang for her steward. He reassured her: "We are in a bit of a blow, Madam," he said as he picked things up. His British accent and his quiet manner calmed her. Later she would remember how proud she was to be one of the few people in the Dining Saloon for breakfast. Many others were sick. "I was treated like royalty because I was hungry," she remembered.

Prince Rainier and Princess Grace, of Monaco, were among the 1,722, people sailing back to the United States on that voyage. The Princess was expecting a child in February, and she had the horoscope of the expected infant already read, according to columnist E.V. Durling, who was also aboard. Later Durling devoted a whole column to riding in the boat train from Paris and boarding the *United States* for that trip. He wrote for the Hearst chain of newspapers. His column devoted considerable space to a harassed husband traveling with his wife, 19 pieces of luggage, and their Great Dane dog. His last paragraph was interesting: "The *United States* for this sailing was sold out weeks ago. And this is the off season. No question about, it. That beautiful ship is one of the most popular passenger vessels ever to travel the Atlantic."

Although travel was not quite up to the previous year, a record for the port of New York was set September 25, 1956, with the arrival of five liners bringing in more than 7,000 passengers. A photograph carried in many papers showed the lineup: *Cristoforo Colombo, America, United States, Queen Elizabeth,* and *Mauretania.* The Duke and Duchess of Windsor were on the *United States.* They had come for only a short visit and returned on the superliner's October 11 departure.

Prince Rainer and Princess Grace of Monaco. (Photo by Andrew Malmsea, Chief Steward, SS United States, *courtesy of Sven Olefeldt)*

The *United States* brought in a large number of passengers on November 27, 1,784 persons, including Salvador Dali, painter, and Merle Oberon, actress. Again the superliner was across the pier from her running mate, the *America*. Both the new American Export Lines' liners *Independence* and *Constitution* were also in port at the pier just to the south. For the first time and perhaps the only time, the four largest American liners were side by side in a row. The next arrival, December 13, marked the completion of the ship's 100th round trip. Her average speed in traveling a distance that was equal to about 25 times around the earth had been 30.64 knots. Again it was possible to make the claim that her propeller shafts had never been stopped or slowed at sea because of machinery trouble. In addition to her 312,878 passengers, she carried on these 100 round trips 2,815 pets in her air-conditioned kennels. The *Herald Tribune* asked for a breakdown of the pets and was told that there had been one hamster, one monkey, 271 cats, and 2,542 dogs. A total of 1,148,000 sacks of mail had been carried, in addition to 5,384 automobiles. Her December 13 passenger list included Rita Hayworth. Also aboard were Reginald Smith and Alan Battersby, with their wives. Smith and Battersby had sailed from Toronto to England in 67 days in their 26-foot home-made ketch, the *Orenda*. During the trip they had been given up for lost.

A longshore strike in the winter of 1956 was the beginning of real labor difficulties for the *United States*. Passengers using the new superliner and all liners at the port had to carry their own baggage, helped whenever possible by shoreside staff members from the companies involved. A blue-ditto warning was issued by the striking union, the International Longshoremen's Association, telling U.S. Lines personnel not to cross the picket lines. It was not cordial: "Your people have been crossing our lines in every strike. Have you no sense of fair play? We have families too. Their welfare depends upon the success of a good contract. We believe that our demands are necessary for the safety, health, and well being of our membership. The money that you take for the handling of lines, moving baggage, and helping to sail ships should make you feel self conscious, knowing that you are hurting working people like yourself. ... Perhaps some day you too may need our help."

The U.S. Lines annual report for 1956 blamed the Middle East "situation" for cutting slightly into the passenger business on the Atlantic, but cheerfully predicted that the Rotary International convention in May, 1957, the American Bar Association gathering in London in July, and the American Legion "pilgrimage" to France in September should stimulate travel in the new year.

The success of William Francis Gibbs and his experiment with aluminum on the *United States* was attested to in a full-page advertisement in the January, 1957, issue of *Marine Engineering Log* magazine. It was an Alcoa Aluminum ad and was headed: "Here's why Alcoa Aluminum is the shipbuilding metal of today and tomorrow." It went on: "After the 100 round-voyages, the service record of Alcoa Aluminum on the *United States* shows a rating of excellent. After four years of salt water service, the 2,000 tons of Alcoa aluminum is still as good as new." Two full-page U.S. Lines ads also put out in this same month hailed the superliner, the *America,* and the company's large freighter fleet, now grown to 53 vessels. Nine new high-speed Mariner-class cargo liners had been added to this fleet in the previous year.

Returning from her last round trip of 1956, the *United States* encountered severe weather and arrived one full day late. Commodore Anderson said he had been forced to reduce speed to 11 knots in the face of very rough seas combined with winds up to 50 miles an hour. The average speed was only 24.49 knots, he noted. Eight hours after her arrival she left on schedule for her annual winter overhaul at Newport News. During the brief time she was at Pier 86, seamen chipped the ice off her bow and gave it a fresh coat of paint, and photos of this effort were carried by the *United Press* nationwide.

On January 16 President Eisenhower's budget message included funds for a sistership to the *United States*. In addition to money for operating subsidies for fiscal 1957-58, the President proposed spending $120,000,000 for new ships. This plus an additional $157,000,000 carried over from the previous authorizations by the Mari-

Painting of the SS United States. (Photo by Andrew Malmsea, Chief Steward, SS United States, courtesy of Sven Olefeldt)

time Administration would fund some 21 vessels, including a new ship for American President Lines to be called *President Washington* and the sister for the *United States*. The President mentioned the sistership specifically in the budget message. Hope ran high that she might be built.

Commodore Anderson's favorite pet was a cocker spaniel named Chota Peg. The name meant small drink in Hindustani. On January 21 the U.S. Lines issued a press release about Chota Peg as he approached his 14th birthday. The docile-eyed little creature had joined the Commodore in 1943 when only four months old. The Commodore was then master of the transport *John Ericsson*. Since that time Chota had traveled well over 2,000,000 sea miles. The release noted that he was "now toothless and wobbly with middle aged spread," and added that his diet had been reduced to chopped meat and vegetables. He sailed January 23 with the Commodore when the *United States* began her 1957 schedule. On the return crossing, the big vessel brought home the ketch *Orenda*, which had been sailed from Canada to England by two Toronto men mentioned earlier. John L. Lewis, president of the United Mine Workers, was aboard, as were Mr. and Mrs. Yehudi Menuhin. The passenger list of 1,493 was not bad for mid-winter.

The next serious labor disturbance that hit the *United States*, a foretaste of the string of strikes and jurisdictional disputes which would finally lead to her lay up, came in February, 1957. When she reached New York on the morning of February 7 she found the port at a standstill. A tugmen's strike had been in progress for a week and there were no tugs to help her dock. Joseph J. Ryan, ship news reporter for the *New York Times*, summed up the situation beautifully: "For a tension-packed hour yesterday, Commodore John W. Anderson was the loneliest merchant mariner in the port." His feat of seamanship in bringing the liner in without tugs brought cheers from thousands of watchers on shore and the episode was front page news, The docking began at 9:25 a.m. It was timed by Commodore Anderson to coincide with the slack water period between tides. Dead slack was at 9:22 a.m. At one frightening moment the giant ship nearly touched Pier 88, her bulk completely spanning the end of the wide slip between her pier and the one just above it. She edged in toward the north side of Pier 86 with a port anchor out and dragging to hold her. Gently Commodore Anderson increased the turn to starboard. Alternately the four propellers were used to maneuver the 990-foot hull slowly around and into the slip between Piers 86 and 88. A heaving line with a monkey fist at its end snaked from the ship to Pier 86. Longshoremen caught the accurate toss and immediately began to haul in the lead line which was attached to a 10-inch hawser. This happened at 9:33. By 9:40 the hawser was made fast to a bollard and the ship began to winch her way in toward the reinforced northwest corner of the pier, the "knuckle" as it is known. By 9:46 she gently touched the knuckle and viewers breathed a sigh of relief. The worse seemed over. By 10:10 the huge ship was parallel to the pier and 18 minutes later she was tight up against the camels and made fast. Her 10 gangways were in place at 10:28 and the 58-year-old Commodore retired to his cabin to relax. He was promptly overwhelmed by friends eager to congratulate him and by reporters wanting to interview him. His picture was in all the papers the next day along with dramatic photos of the *United States* making her way unaided into the slip. The headlines: "Tugless Liner Docks," "Rope Trick Pulls Liner Into Dock," "Superliner Slips Unaided Into Dock," "Big Liner Inches to Berth Unaided," "Precision Maneuver Without Tugs." James Devlin's *Associated Press* story, which went throughout the nation, had the most humorous headline: "Look, Ma – No Tugs!"

The tug strike continued, dragged on, and when the superliner again arrived at New York, February 24, it was still going strong. Once again Commodore Anderson did it alone. As Joel Seldin of the *Herald Tribune* put it: "The liner *United States* put on one of the city's best attended dramatic performances yesterday when, for the second time in 16 days, the 53,300-ton flagship of the U.S. Lines docked without the aid of tugboats. The strike of tugboat crewmen went into its 25th day with no prospect of settlement in sight." Thousands were watching and again it was front page news. A five-column picture showed the ship, stem anchor dangling, on the knuckle, her bow just about touching the pier just to the north. The whole crossing had been filled with problems. At Le Havre high winds had prevented her from leaving her berth for seven hours. On the way over she encountered seas that were so high that Commodore Anderson was forced to slow down to 12 knots.

The ship in dry dock at Newport News, Virginia. (Photo by Andrew Malmsea, Chief Steward, SS United States, courtesy of Sven Olefeldt)

He reached New York in time for a late arrival Saturday night, but wisely chose not to attempt docking without tugs at night. The Duke and Duchess of Windsor were aboard, coming for a three-week vacation in Palm Beach. In his 20-odd trips across the Atlantic, the Duke said he had never seen such a rough sea. The ship brought in a total of 1,658 passengers.

Some time later the Duchess of Windsor would write William Francis Gibbs about this arrival, noting that "we saw you watching her come in without tugs." Her letter thanked Mr. Gibbs for the "beautiful roses," and joked about the Duke and herself becoming "almost commuters on the *United States.*" The Duchess praised the ship as "wonderful" and said that Mr. Gibbs should be "justly proud of her." An undated letter from Margaret Truman also preserved in the Gibbs archives thanked William Francis for "the lovely red roses." Miss Truman praised the *United States* as "defying description" and added that she only wished it would roll a little more "so I could feel I am on the ocean!"

The strike finally ended, but it was only a mild foretaste of what was to come.

District Attorney Frank S. Hogan, who had years before signed aboard the *Leviathan* under an assumed name as a steerage class steward, took on his staff a young Columbia Law School graduate named Thomas F. McBride who had served during his summer vacations as a deck yeoman on the *United States*. While on the ship he had seen how loan sharks worked and he reported his experiences to Mr. Hogan. He was promptly assigned to look into the matter and on March 13 made three arrests aboard the ship. If a seaman borrowed $100 in New York he was expected to pay $125 back when the ship reached Europe. If he could not pay it back, he would receive an extension which meant he owed $156.25 on the ship's return to New York. This amounted to interest at 25% a week.

Lord Beaverbrook, famed British newspaper chain owner, was a passenger on the *United States* and on March 19 he wrote a letter to Mr. Gibbs to thank him for the champagne sent to his cabin. "The ship is beautiful and every detail is worked out so splendidly. There is a sense of security all about on account of the fireproofing process. I am sure it is the strongest ship that sails the sea."

Bids for the construction of a sistership to the *United States* were opened on March 21, 1957. They varied between $109,436,289 and $117,730,000 for a ship without stabilizers. The low bid came from the New York Shipbuilding Company, Camden, NT, with Newport News bidding $112,200,000 and Bethlehem Steel Company's Quincy, Mass., yard being the high bidder. Bids with stabilizers were about $2,000,000 higher in each case. The new ship would have nickle-aluminum-bronze propellers instead of the manganese-bronze screws on the *United States.* Her passenger capacity would be 1,967 compared to the grand total of 2,000 berths on the *United States.* Her crew would be 1,006 instead of the 1,023 then serving on the existing superliner. The next step in the progress toward a second big ship was the drawing up of a contract between U.S. Lines and the Maritime Administration which would settle how much the company would pay.

The *United States* was the scene of a dramatic if totally unimportant peace pact when she sailed April 18. The battle had been of four years duration and was between society columnist Elsa Maxwell and the Duchess of Windsor. Both ladies had been involved in a charity ball at the Waldorf-Astoria. They had been close friends, but when the newspaper writer failed to recognize the help that had been given by the Duchess during the event the "velvet glove battle was on." The Duchess shunned parties where Elsa was expected and *vice versa.* "And if through some mixup they both came into the same room, caviar froze and souffles fell," wrote Cholly Gruenberg, of the *New York Post.* Then Miss Maxwell began making diplomatic peace overtures. She went so far as to publicly extend her thanks to the Duchess for her help in the charity ball in question in her column. Both of them sailed April 18 on the *United States,* Elsa told reporters that if the Duchess offered her hand she would take it. Aboard ship on Easter Sunday the Duchess sent a note to Elsa thanking her for her "personal thanks" and invited her to a cocktail party. She came and "the guests held their breaths." They shook hands. They smiled. And the rest of those on hand "exhaled." It was settled.

In May Congress eliminated $95,000,000 from the maritime construction funds proposed in the President's budget and hopes for the sistership to the *United States* took a nose dive. Representative Herbert C. Bonner, chairman of the House Merchant Marine & Fisheries Committee, and the committee's ranking minority member, Thor C. Tollefson, both denied that the cause was lost, however. There were still available $92,000,000 in uncommitted funds from the previous fiscal year, they said, and this would be enough to get underway any construction program that the Maritime Administration proposed.

Captain Leroy J. Alexanderson, replacing Captain Fender as the relief skipper of the *United States,* took the liner out June 28 with 1,750 passengers. It was an unfortunate coincidence that the Commodore should have chosen this crossing as his vacation. As the superliner was approaching Southampton on the morning of July 1 his pet cocker, the famous Chota Peg, died. Captain Alexanderson reported later that the ship's doctor had worked hard on him but to no avail. He radioed Commodore Anderson that "his little friend has passed on and then we buried Chota Peg at sea with full honors."

A feature article in the *World Telegram & Sun* for July 16 told of the joys of travel in Tourist Class on the *United States.* The reporter, Carol Taylor, went aboard at a July sailing and interviewed two working girls and others sailing in this class on the ship. "The *bon voyage* champagne is just as dry, passengers' spirits are just as high, and the Atlantic is just as wide and wet these summer days up the Tourist Class gangplank," her story began. The headline told the message: "Tourist Class is Classy – Thrifty Travelers Can Have Plenty of Fun."

Another of the more and more common magazine studies of William Francis Gibbs appeared in the August *Fortune*. It was entitled "The Love Affair of William Francis Gibbs," and was by Richard Austin Smith. Its opening sentence gave some indication of its content: "I think people thank God I'm no worse than I am," the subject was quoted as saying. Author Smith went on: "A terror to the shipyards, a genius to the Navy, this designer has raised more hell and had more fun than any man in his profession." Three photos above the magazine article's title showed the familiar figure watching his pride and joy. In the first he was seen at the Narrows, "where he could get a glimpse of her before anyone else." In the second he was shown looking out of his office window as she passed 21 West Street. The final view was of him, with his old felt hat on, watching her from the end of Pier 86 as she approached her slip. Author

Smith went with William Francis in his Cadillac down to Fort Hamilton and beyond to wait for her arrival early one morning. When the superliner came into view he took down notes as Mr. Gibbs talked: "'I know her fairly well by sight,' the old man remarked, his mouth resolutely turned down and the light in his taciturn brown eyes giving me indication that this ship was the embodiment of 30 years of dreaming." The story described once again how every single morning he telephoned both the captain and the chief engineer to learn how she was doing and only twice, on doctor's orders, had he missed an arrival or a sailing. A picture caption under a view of William Francis posing directly in front of the stem of the *United States* noted that "since her outlines first appeared on his drawing board in 1913 he never rested until she was built."

The *Fortune* piece highlighted the parallel between clipper ship designer John Willis Griffiths whose famous *Rainbow* of 1845 marked such a departure from conventional sailing ship design. It went on: "He keeps himself like a trainer would race a horse," Mrs. William Francis Gibbs told Dick Smith. "He's up regularly at 6:30, except the days when the *United States* comes in, then it's 4:45. He fixes his own breakfast of weak tea with lots of sugar and Uneeda biscuits. He really eats only one meal a day, dinner." Perfectly acclimated to living with a genius, Mrs. Gibbs (the former Vera Cravath) was not in the least abashed at one of the well-known Gibbs anecdotes quoted in the Smith article. It described the time a friend, in her presence, challenged Mr. Gibbs by saying: "I do believe that you love the *United States* more than your wife." The Gibbs reply: "You are 1,000% correct," and he said it with his usual deadpan expression.

Just as Mr. Gibbs was the *United States,* and the *United States* was Mr. Gibbs, so each fragment of information about William Francis is important to a book about the *United States.* For example it should be noted that he did not sit at a desk in his 21 West Street office; he always had a stool and drawing board. Three male secretaries headed by Nat Peavy watched over him, taking down in shorthand everything he said, even his frequent curses, loyally sticking with him for his 10-hour work day. A recording was made of every telephone conversation he had for many years as well as all his comments at planning and design sessions. The recordings were transcribed and kept. For many years after his death this record was retained in a company safe. It was my hope that they might be used for this book, but I learned early in the writing that the record had been destroyed.

The *Fortune* article had a good photograph of Frederic Gibbs, calling him the company's "anchor to windward," the "money man" of the pair. The last of many interviews I had with him began with a long discourse on the time the two brothers had met with J.P. Morgan in 1915. He then paused, leaned back in his chair and intoned in his friendly fashion: "Well – I want a book on 'the big ship.'" That is how this work began.

Another of the new series of U.S. Lines personality advertisements appeared in *Newsweek* in September, 1957. Mr. and Mrs. E.B. Chapin were shown being tucked into their deck chairs. "Our steward seemed to take a personal interest in making this one of the most wonderful times we've ever had," the caption said. Mr. Chapin was an attorney from Boston. The other two pictures featured two other couples. Lord and Lady Weeks were shown in the special *a la carte* private dining room. He was chairman of Vickers Nuclear Engineering, Ltd. Mr. and Mrs. Isaac B. Grainger were shown in their cabin. He was president of the Chemical Corn Exchange Bank. The ad's headline read: "You're a world away from worry – and less than 5 days from Europe."

A marvelous slice of life aboard the *United States* was offered the public by *Journal American* columnist Jim Bishop at this time. It was entitled: "Eating His Way Across the Ocean." It began 45 hours after the ship had left New York. Jim observed a Southern Congressman in the Navajo Room and took note of his bow tie and martini. He walked out on deck: "There is no sense of speed aboard this fastest of all ocean liners until passengers see a little speck far ahead. An hour later, we are abreast of the beautiful *Statendam.* An hour later, it is far astern." Jim told about how he phoned home and got his daughter on the wire. He heard his wife's voice saying: "It can't be your father, dear. He's out somewhere on the ocean." Trained to spot reader-interest items, Jim noted that "most of the women aboard belong to the Blue Hair Set. As they get older, they dress more daringly. At dinner, which is always formal, they arrive looking as though they're wearing half slips. A fat one had a concealed zipper in the back and, every time she laughed, it slid two notches. The younger ones are all in the Tourist Class and they wear horn-rimmed glasses and read books. Their young men play chess and push discs around the deck. The biggest thrill aboard ship is the next meal. ..." Food was always one of the most important things on American ships and one of the best. For the next six paragraphs Jim rolled in delicacies of the superliner's table. He undoubtedly was given his trip by the company, but this one column more than paid for it.

The work of Walter Jones and Dick Harris at the U.S. Lines public relations office was paying off well. The *Saturday Evening Post* was host to a long, well-illustrated piece entitled "Queen of the Seas" by Cornelius Ryan. Its subhead read: "A reporter takes us on a crossing with the master of the *United States.* His ship may be a queen, but when she's afloat Commodore Anderson is king."

The story began with Commodore Anderson arriving on the pier in civilian clothes, making his way to his two-room suite under the Bridge and calling Captain Leroy Alexanderson to say he was aboard. It detailed how in the next two hours he reviewed the status of things with his senior deck officers, the purser, and Chief Engineer Kaiser. The Chief had a sad duty to perform on that particular trip. He had the ashes of his dead brother with him to be buried at sea with the Commodore officiating. The brother had long served as a cargo ship master on U.S. Lines vessels. This was also the trip that Elsa Maxwell and the Duchess of Windsor had been on. Miss Maxwell had a staff of four not to mention three dogs and 126 pieces of luggage.

Loaded with human interest the article described the sailing in detail. When the ship was passing down the Hudson, the Commodore spotted a sheet waving from a skyscraper window. It was a signal from an old family friend, Dr. Edna Thompson. The Commodore pressed a button by his side and the ship's whistle blasted out a salute. Then he wrote a short note to his wife Mary to be taken ashore by the pilot. On the crossing they sighted the *Queen Elizabeth* up ahead and the *United States* moved off course as she had done so many times so that no one aboard either ship would see the passing. The Commodore always insisted that he was not racing, but not all his crew were "so modest," as the article explained: "As they passed the *Queen Mary* on another trip, the Big U's travel agent sent a message to his counterpart on the British liner. It read: 'Sorry, old girl.' Back came a message from the *Mary's* agent: 'Nice girls don't travel so fast.'"

Anderson had a most gentle manner belied by his six-foot frame and stern visage. The *Saturday Evening Post* writer reported a little vignette that illustrated this. A seven-year-old English boy had written to the Commodore asking him to find a job aboard for his kitten, Montague. The child's mother had decided that Montague must go, already having five other cats, two turtles, and 18 newts in the house. Without the mother's knowledge the boy managed to go the 250 miles from his home to Southampton with his beloved Montague. Commodore Anderson saw him and explained that cats could not be signed on. He gave the boy a tour of the ship, fed him ice cream and cookies, and found Montague a new home. The Commodore lived up to the highest traditions of the sea on September 21, 1957, two days out of New York. He answered a distress call from the Coast Guard cutter *Ingham,* aboard which a machinist named Stephen Long, of Selbyville, Del., was seriously ill. Despite bad weather the *United States* turned from her course, came up close to the cutter so she could take the man aboard from one of the cutter's lifeboats. Dr. John E. Sheedy, Chief Surgeon aboard the superliner, immediately performed an emergency operation. It was a case of ruptured appendix. Several distinguished surgeons who were aboard among the 1,625 passengers volunteered to help and stood by during the operation, as did several nurses. The man survived and was in good condition when he was brought home aboard the ship which arrived back at New York September 30.

A telegram received at the 945 Fifth Avenue home of William Francis Gibbs on October 14 must have been read with pleasure. "All superlatives fail to describe your magnificent ship. We are so happy we decided to return aboard her and greatly thank you for your attentions which surround us," It was signed by Alice and Lewis Strauss.

In late October several newspaper reporters in New York learned of the keen rivalry between American and British seamen at the game of darts. Across West Street (12th Ave.), within sight of the piers where the great liners docked, was the chromium-decorated Market Diner-Cafe. It was here that members of the crews of the *Queens* and the *United States* and *America* faced each other. Joseph Zelin, manager of the establishment, proudly told Jacques Nevard, of the *New York Times* (he had left the *Journal of Commerce,)* that he had donated more than 30 trophies since 1949 for various seamen's sports. The *United States* dart team was captained by Freddy Austin, a First Class Dining Saloon steward, who had left Cunard to join the superliner on her maiden voyage. A championship match was held on October 29 and the American team won five games to four. British seamen called the game "madhouse," but Americans preferred the name "Bellevue."

Another plum for the U.S. Lines public relations department appeared on November 16 in the form of a long piece in the *New Yorker* about William Francis Gibbs and his *United States.* Several lines from the story must suffice, although it was so entertaining that it would have been fun to quote the whole article.

"The thing that's so interesting about the *United States is* that it's so different from every other ship from start to finish," Brendon Gill quoted William Francis as saying. "The performance of the *United States is* even better than any of us thought it might be. For the last five years, the ship has been almost 95% occupied, on the average," was another Gibbs quote. Gibbs explained how he remembered General Franklin outlining what he wanted in the new ship: "We must have an outstanding ship that the public can get behind, like a cup defender, a sort of mythical flagship of our fleet." Finally, the *New Yorker* speaking: "Is it possible for a mature man, a member of the University, Century, Broad Street, India House, Piping Rock, and New York Yacht Clubs, to fall in love with a ship?" The answer was obvious: Yes!

Hopes for a sistership remained alive as the year 1957 passed into history. Bills to this end were before Congress and hearings were expected to begin early in the new year.

On December 5, 1957, the ornate Robert L. Hague Trophy was presented to Commodore Anderson at ceremonies aboard the *United States.* Given by the American Legion Post named after a famed New York port maritime executive, the trophy was handed over to the Commodore by William B. Franke, Under Secretary of the Navy. The Commodore was hailed for bringing new glory to the American Merchant Marine, for his superb seamanship and for his character.

The U.S. Lines annual report for 1957 hailed the completion of the superliner's fifth year of operation in July and noted that up to that time she had carried 348,754 passengers. In 1957, on her 23 round trips, she carried 33,032 eastbound and 36,660 westbound for an average of 3,030 per round trip. The report noted that the fall-off was due to the Suez situation. It pointed out that the Brussels World's Fair and the Centennial Celebration at Lourdes in 1958 were expected to stimulate interest in trans-Atlantic travel the next year. No mention was made of the airplane, which in 1957 surpassed the Atlantic liner in the number of passengers carried across the Western ocean.

The year 1958 would not be as good as the previous six years had been. In June the *United States* would be held up by an engineer's strike for eight hours. In October she would lose an entire round trip, cancelled because of more labor trouble. Because of this she would carry about 4,000 fewer passengers than in 1957, but her average per round trip would rise slightly, to 3,106 passengers per voyage. Since the high point of her passenger business in 1955, the average had declined slightly in the next two years, so the turnaround in 1958 was viewed as a favorable sign.

Hope was high again during 1958 for a sistership to the *United States.* The legislation introduced to this end in 1957 was actually enacted as Public Law 85-521, and signed by President Eisenhower on July 15,1958. The bill authorized the U.S. Lines to buy the vessel from the Government for a fixed price of $47,000,000 subject to increase only if changes were made in the bid specifications. The bill provided that the company could borrow 75% of the purchase price from the Government under the provisions of the 1936 Merchant Marine Act. This meant a most favorable interest rate of only 3 1/2%. As the year went on, however, it looked less and less likely that the funds to implement the legislation would be provided by Congress.

John Kane, who was as close to the projected new superliner as anyone in the Newport News shipyard, wrote a 96-page letter listing all the changes in specifications in comparison to the *United States.* William Francis Gibbs, as always, seeking perfection, had made most of the changes, updating the materials called for and otherwise adding substantially to the cost estimates during the period when the plans for the second ship were being completed. Mr. Kane believed that these cost increases were a major factor in killing the project. It was also unfortunately true that not everyone was pushing for the second superliner. The Seafarers International Union, rival to the National Maritime Union, actually opposed the spending of so much money on one ship. They preferred, since none of their members worked on the *United States,* that building subsidies be paid to help construct small cargo ships for the companies with which they had contracts.

Except for the discouraging labor picture and the equally depressing lack of unanimity about a second superliner the year 1958 would be a good one. The passenger lists continued large and were just as studded with famous names as ever. On the February 19 arrival there was a slight delay in docking because of masses of ice in the slip between Piers 86 and 88. Commodore Anderson said it was the worst ice he had seen in four seasons. It took the tug *Carol Moran* more than an hour to clear the way for the big liner. On her March 27 sailing out of New York she docked at Southampton 24 hours late after fighting 40-foot seas. Again Commodore Anderson was quoted. He called the gales the worst he had ever seen. Fortunately there were no injuries apart from a few bruises, and no damage to the ship. The Duke and Duchess of Windsor made two more crossings during the year, always using U-87-89 which had just about become their cabin.

Three mid-summer crossings saw an average of 1,751 passengers choose the *United States,* encouraging to 1 Broadway. The arrival on September 2 witnessed perhaps the closest shave many New York tugmen had experienced with big liner docking for a good time. The port was at its busiest, with six liners bringing in 7,144 persons. The *Independence* docked first, followed by the *United States* and the *Queen Mary.* The U.S. Lines superliner was "on the knuckle" of Pier 86 and slowly moving in when the Cunarder came past her, very close. The two ships were in the hands of five Moran tugs each, but either the *Mary* came up from behind just a little too fast or the *United States* took longer to get into her slip than expected. It was a decidedly close call. The 1,018-foot hull of the *Mary* slipped by the 990-foot *United States* with not much more than one tug's length separating them. Everything went calmly, however. Neither of the docking pilots lost their composure. A five-column picture of the passing was published that evening in the *World-Telegram and Sun.* The caption made no mention of the dangerous situation, casually telling the story of the arrival of the six ships. Following the *Mary* came the *Kungsholm, Ryndam,* and *Mauretania.*

The *United States* logged her millionth mile as she passed the Statue of Liberty inbound on September 30, 1958. She was due to sail October 2 with 1,100 passengers, including Clarence C. Morse, Chairman of the Federal Maritime Board, and Harold Lloyd, famed motion picture star. She did not sail. A strike of Masters, Mates and Pilots forced the company to cancel her voyage. It was the first of many such cancellations, and, although no one realized it at the time, it was the handwriting on the wall that spelled the end of the ship's trans-Atlantic career long before it should have ended. She had made 140 round trips in her first six years of service. Over the next 11 years she would make 260 more, with frequent interruptions because of strikes.

The officers' strike lasted six days and was finally settled when the American Merchant Marine Institute called upon George Meany, president of the recently merged AFL and CIO, to mediate. It was a strike that had been vehemently opposed by the National Maritime Union, which called it a fiasco. The NMU, however, had honored the picket lines. There were jurisdictional overtones, with the NMU threatening to call a conference with the Teamsters union and the International Longshoremen's Association, two independent labor groups outside the AFL-CIO. The surprise management move in calling on the nation's top labor leader to arbitrate succeeded because Mr. Meany was fearful of a link up between one of his main unions, the NMU, and two unions outside his control. As press representative for the AMMI, I was deeply involved in the strike.

The officers' strike was a disaster, but something happened during the strike that was to have even more disastrous eventual effects in the future of the *United States* and all Atlantic liners. On October 4, 1958, the first trans-Atlantic jet aircraft passenger service was established by British Overseas Airways. The coming of the jet, cutting the trans-Atlantic time by half, spelled the final doom of all point to point ocean liner services. Up to the jet the air trip across the Atlantic had been a very long, very tiresome thing – 16 hours or more. With the jet it was an entirely different story. There remained many who disliked flying and would not take a plane, but more and more people, especially businessmen, now simply had to fly; their time was too valuable. The famous Cunard motto, "Getting There is Half the Fun," finally became academic. True as it was, it was no longer an argument for those who were seeking just transportation.

The *Boston Sunday Globe* had an unusual feature article on seaman Nicholas Landiak, of the *United States.* He served on the side as a washing machine attendant and was charged with keeping the white overalls of the engineering department spotless. His work was unique in that the washing machine was installed in the forward smokestack. He enjoyed the extra duty because he liked working in the funnel, he said. One of the pictures with the article showed his head and shoulders poking out from an opening 175 feet above the waterline at the top of the stack, just under the sampan. Passengers got bewildered when they spotted him. In stormy weather he had to hang on because of the exaggerated effect of the ship's roll at such a height.

Greer Garson and Merle Oberon headed the list of VIPs arriving on the *United States* on November 15. One of the ship's 1,689 passengers never landed. He was a 78-year-old man named David Benzaria, and he committed suicide two days before the ship reached port, leaping 50 feet into the North Atlantic.

The company's annual report for 1958 was optimistic about the prospects for the following year. Commenting on the probable lack of funds to build a sistership, the report noted that while the *America* would be 20 years old in mid 1960 she was "in good operating condition and can be efficiently operated for several more years." The company stated that it would request the Maritime Administration to extend the termination date of the ship's subsidy contract "for a suitable period to make it possible to schedule her after the end of 1959." Little did anyone surmise that the *America,* under another name, would continue operating for more than a decade after the layup of the *United States,* in fact would still be in service at this writing.

10

More Labor Troubles

President Eisenhower's new budget for the fiscal year ending June 30, 1960, failed to include funds for a sistership to the *United States,* but efforts continued to convince Washington that one was needed. The French had laid the keel for a new superliner and Britain was in the last stages of designing their new big ship for the Atlantic. Although airplanes were now carrying more passengers across the world's premier steamship route than liners, the talk of superliners was far from dead. And liners in general were still doing very well. Cunard had a fleet of eleven serving the Atlantic.

The *United States* began her year on January 16, 1959, sailing with only 925 aboard. Her passenger lists ranged around the 1,100 mark for the next few departures, rising to 1,313 for the March 4 arrival westbound. The early Spring storms on the Atlantic were at their worst at this point. The *Queen Elizabeth* reached Cherbourg on March 6 after having passed through the worst gales those aboard could remember. She was 14 hours late. The projected *United States* sistership received some rough buffeting. Senator Henry Dworshak, Republican of Idaho, spoke out against the project on March 11. He was blunt: "Rather than camouflage it under the military budget the government should admit the payment is a direct grant to the shipping interests to compensate them for their inability to compete with foreign shipbuilders." He said the proposed new liner and her trans-Pacific counterpart for American President Line would be "sitting ducks in today's warfare."

Samuel Barber, Pulitzer winning American composer, and Gian-Carlo Menotti, operatic composer, were among the 1,350 passengers on the *United States* March 24. Also aboard was AMMI President Ralph Casey, en route to London to attend a meeting of the International Chamber of Shipping. The season's first large passenger list came with the next sailing, April 9, when there were 1,600 aboard.

The talk of superliners was not restricted to shipping people. Well known New York hotel owner H.B. Cantor, on May 26, 1959, unveiled a model of a 90,000 ton passenger liner designed to carry 6,000 voyagers across the Atlantic. With cafeteria-style meal service the ship would charge fares ranging from $50 to $125. Although he created considerable interest, his project never got very far. The model was still on display in his Hotel Empire at this writing. A number of close-to-capacity lists followed for the *United States* as 1959 progressed with the June 19 departure seeing 1,755 passengers embark for Europe. Three pages were needed by U.S. Lines to list the VIP passengers for this sailing. The return crossing marked the completion of the ship's seventh year of service. The U.S. Lines announced that during this period she had carried 467,984 passengers and had operated at 93.3% of her normal capacity (of 1,650). An all-time record for one crossing was set on the next sailing, when 1,790 passengers crowded aboard. Kenneth F. Gautier, Vice President for Passenger Traffic, predicted on July 20 that 1960 would be an outstanding year for

the superliner. He released the extended sailing schedule for her and the *America* through May, 1960.

The new *Savannah,* world's first nuclear passenger cargo liner, was launched with much pomp and ceremony on July 21, 1959, at Camden, N.J. She was christened by Mrs. Dwight D. Eisenhower amid many predictions that atomic power was the way of the future in shipping.

The regular mid-summer drydocking for the *United States* took place in late July and produced the usual splash of fine newspaper photographs. Two packed crossings followed, with the ship taking Out 1,770 passengers and returning with 1,748. Another strong push for the second superliner came in August, 1959, with a cover story in *Newsweek.* The cover showed a rendering of what the second big ship would look like. Other drawings inside depicted the proposed *President Washington* for APL and other projected new American liners. The hopes of many rose again, but to others who were on the inside the chances of finding money from Washington seemed small indeed.

The French Line's superliner was well along at this point. Her keel had been laid in October, 1957, and she would be launched in May, 1960. Building at the famed Chantiers de L'Atlantique, St. Nazaire, she was listed in first reports as being 985 feet in length, although in due course it would be announced that overall she would be 1,035 – making her the longest liner ever built. Her beam was given as 109 feet, but eventually would be established as 110. The first artist's conceptions came out in the Fall of 1959 and showed a ship reminiscent of the *Normandie,* but with two concave stacks instead of three oval ones. The stacks were very far apart, a most distinguishing feature. Later their remarkable sampan or toreador tops, an outgrowth of the style first introduced in 1932 by William Francis Gibbs on the four Grace Line ships, would be added to give them a special flare.

One of the top officials of the famed French shipyard Chantiers de L'Atlantique, J. Coune, made a channel crossing on the *United States.* Unable to find out anything about some of the Gibbs techniques, he was determined to see for himself. He crossed from LeHavre to Southampton specifically to find out what he could learn about the construction methods of the American superliner. He was helping to design the *France* at the time. Once aboard he locked himself into his Suite and proceeded to take the place apart, measuring ducts, examining fastening devices and checking each and every detail.

William Francis Gibbs continued to be on hand for every arrival and sailing. He used these occasions to welcome well-known passengers and a steady stream of thank you notes came into 21 West Street. One dated September 2, 1959, was from George Anderson, Admiral of the U.S. Mediterranean fleet. "I share your pride in this wonderful ship," he wrote. "This passage has been an inspiration to us in every way, but particularly so because we have seen such continuing tangible evidence that the ship herself deserves her great name. It was indeed kind of you to send us the champagne, the beautiful flowers, the story of the *Bismarck* episode, but especially to drop in yourself and to take the time from your busy schedule to see us. Perhaps some time during the next year you will be in the Mediterranean. If you are I plea that you let me know so that I may have the pleasure of your company in my flagship."

In mid September U.S. Lines announced that the *United States* would make 48 crossings during 1960, two more than ever before. The additional trips were to be made possible by reducing slightly the ship's turnaround time at New York.

In mid-October, Jean Marie, chairman of the French Line, stated for the record that the *France* would be equal to the *United States* in speed, but would not compete for the Blue Ribbon. "Flying has cut down trans-Atlantic travel time so that there is no meaning to surface speed records," he added. With the completion of the October 19 crossing the U.S. Lines made known that the *United States* had carried her half-millionth passenger. "This is by far the largest number of passengers carried in such a short period by any American flag ship," the company noted.

Despite the steady advances of air travel, many ship lines were building new ships. Two great British companies' had under construction ships that should be called superliners. The Orient Line's 42,000-ton *Oriana* was launched on November 3, 1959. Costing $40,000,000 she would have a speed of 27 1/2 knots, reducing the trip from London to Sydney from four to three weeks. Their companion company, the famous P & O Line (Peninsular & Oriental) was building an even larger ship (45,000 tons) to be called *Canberra.* She would bring to the largest of ships the new engines and smokestack aft style.

The December 9 sailing was widely advertised by U.S. Lines as the start of a Christmas homecoming cruise. Brochures explained that special trains would meet the *United States* and take passengers directly to most major cities in Europe. Minimum fares to Bremerhaven were $201 for Tourist, $252 in Cabin and $392 in First Class, with corresponding but slightly lower rates for passengers to Le Havre or Southampton. "This Christmas give yourself and your family the most wonderful Christmas present of all ... the Christmas you have dreamed about for so long ... a trip to Europe to celebrate the Yuletide Season with your family and friends. Christmas is a family holiday and that is just the way these trips are planned-for the whole family together. ... "

Another Christmas oriented effort was announced by U.S. Lines. It resulted from impromptu affairs held on cargo ships the previous season. The plan was to have a party for orphans on every U.S. Lines ship that would be in port for the 15-day period before December 25. Called "Project Santa Claus" the campaign had started with the freighter *American Traveler.* On the *United States* it was hoped that as many as 75 orphans could be given a good time. Crew members joined in the fun and contributed money towards presents.

The 1959 annual report was pessimistic about the possibilities of a replacement for the *America.* The 1961 fiscal year budget had provided no funds for a sistership to the *United States* and Public Law 85-521 authorizing her construction was becoming something of a dead letter. The report also noted that passenger totals for the year were down. It was hoped that by speeding up the ship's schedule this could be kept from getting any worse.

The year 1960 was a turning point in the history of the *United States.* It was the year in which competition from the air really began to hurt. In one particular way this competition would strike where it could be felt the mostin the Fall of the year. The transportation of dependents of the Armed Forces stationed overseas had been one of the key factors seen as sustaining sea travel

Promotional Advertisements for the SS United States. *(Courtesy of Bill McBride with McBride Publishing)*

116

Promotional Advertisements for the SS United States. (Courtesy of Bill McBride with McBride Publishing)

when the superliner was planned. William Francis Gibbs knew that the Military Sea Transport Service would not be able to continue its large fleet of troopships on the Atlantic run and anticipated a continuing long range source of voyagers in both directions, particularly from and to Germany. The decision to have three classes on the *United States* was made with this source of business in mind. No one dreamed in the late 1940S that air travel would advance so rapidly that all military dependents would be transported over and back by air. And yet this was what was to happen in 1960. New sources of business had to be sought out and the company worked hard all through the year to develop new ways of getting passengers. The possibility of rebuilding the *United States* as a cruise liner was reviewed. It would be a year of new thinking and greater striving. Meanwhile the mechanical perfection of the *United States* continued to amaze. The initial bad publicity about her being more a troopship than a luxury liner had been largely overcome and her passenger lists continued both large and elegant.

A few of the year's highlights might be mentioned. When she was at Newport News for her annual overhaul she was docked next to the rising hull of the world's first nuclear- powered aircraft carrier, the the 1,100-foot carrier *Enterprise*. As an illustration of how William Francis Gibbs maintained his control over news about the speed and other secrets of the *United States,* there is a true story about the trial trip of this huge carrier. Vice Admiral Hyman G. Rickover was aboard with W.E. Blewett, Jr., then the yard president. The Admiral had never been able to find out what was the top speed of the *United States* and he was most interested in comparing the Rank speed of the new carrier with that of the liner. He asked Mr. Blewett point blank. Believe it or not Mr. Blewett had never been told either, according to John Kane, the Newport News man who had worked most closely with Gibbs on the superliner project. So aboard the *Enterprise* Mr. Blewett went to Mr. Kane and repeated the question. Although he knew he was talking to his own boss, the power of the Gibbs lip-sealing orders was still so strong that Mr. Kane replied: "Does Admiral Rickover have a need to know?" The resulting ruckus almost cost John Kane his job, but he survived. And he did not reveal his secret!

The SS United States *alongside the aircraft carrier* USS Enterprise. *(Courtesy of Bill DiBenedetto)*

In order to get two extra crossings into her schedule it was necessary to reduce her time in port substantially. Her first sailing in 1960 was on January 12, a Tuesday. The press release of this departure did not mention how many she was carrying, hinting at company embarrassment at how few were sailing. She brought back 1,146, arriving on a Monday. Her next sailing was on the following Wednesday, and again the press release did not show how many were aboard. She returned with 1,040 docking Tuesday. She sailed on Thursday, again with the number not mentioned. Her regular sailing time was noon. The time in port was kept to 48 hours instead of the old 72 hours, quite remarkable for that day and age, but far from fast in contrast to the eight-hour turnarounds regularly achieved by cruise liners at this writing.

The squeeze from air competition was not only being felt by the U.S. Lines. A report in March from England noted that there was concern in Parliament over the acquisition by Cunard of Eagle Airways. Fear was expressed that shipbuilding would be sacrificed in favor of subsidized aircraft construction. United Kingdom shipbuilders were reported worried that too much money was being spent on aircraft research at the expense of shipbuilding and ship operation. At the heart of the issue was the fear that plans to replace the *Queen Mary* and the *Queen Elizabeth* with two new superliners might be abandoned.

Through the Spring and early Summer passenger lists gradually rose until by late May they were up to the old 1,700 level. In June General Franklin was made Chairman of the Board of U.S. Lines and C.D. Gibbons, formerly treasurer, became President. William B. Rand was named Executive Vice President. One of Bill Rand's first acts was to ask Gibbs & Cox to submit a design for rebuilding the *United States* as a cruise liner. By then most people were fully aware of the writing on the wall as far as air competition was concerned. The importance of finding other uses for the superliner during the winter months was obvious. Cruising was the coming thing. A set of plans was prepared with a number of radical changes. The Cabin Class Lounge aft on the Upper Deck would become an open air swimming pool. The Tourist Class Dining Saloon forward on A Deck would be eliminated and the space used for enlarging cabins, all of which would have facilities. But the making of plans was one thing and the doing of them was another. Company earnings were down, the possibility of a second superliner was virtually nil; what to do with the *America* was a problem. Shipyard prices were going up and the idea of spending up to $15,000,000 to rebuild the *United States* was not in the cards.

The tightened schedule proved completely feasible and rapidly became the order of the day. As school closed more very large passenger lists boosted company morale. On June 24, a total of 1,809 sailed, the second largest list the ship had ever had. Sol Hurok, impresario, was among the 1,750 who sailed on the next departure, July 8. A feature article by John P. Callahan of the *New York Times* proclaimed the end of speed competition on the Atlantic for all time. Printed July 13, 1960, it was based on the French Line's announcement that it would not even try for the Blue Ribbon when their new *France* came out. The Hales Trophy was described as "a symbol of the end of an era in ocean travel." Unless some new hydrofoil-type liner was built which could cross the Atlantic at 100 knots, the story asserted, there would be no more competition for the speed crown. "Gone are the days when the luxury liners competed in crossing the Atlantic at record speed to win the Hales Trophy-and the resulting prestige that often gave the winning liner a competitive edge on attracting passengers."

In August the entrance into Atlantic service of the 33,340 ton Italian liner *Leonardo Da Vinci*, replacement for the *Andrea Doria*, caused much comment. An editorial in the *Maritime Reporter* hailed the event as one in which the shipping industry could take much pride: "In building this lovely ship the Italian Line demonstrated a faith in the future of steamship travel which even the tragic loss of the *Doria* had not shaken." Noting that Holland had recently introduced the slightly larger *Rotterdam* and that Canadian Pacific would shortly enter their new *Empress of Canada* into the trans-Atlantic scene, the editorial contrasted the foreign passenger ship initiative with the lack of activity on the part of America. "The British are planning two new 75,000 ton liners to replace the two *Queens,*" the editorial concluded. "The U.S. Lines, American President, and American Export have been eager for some time to get new ships under construction but the Administration has consistently bypassed their proposals for almost five years."

As of September 1, 1960, the Department of Defense ended the use of the *United States* and the *America* to transport dependents to and from Europe. The U.S. Lines and other American carriers began a most intensive effort to convince the government that this was a mistake. The coming of the jet two years before had been the deciding factor. For an eight hour flight almost anyone could put up with the inconvenience of being packed into a tight and uncomfortable seat. The passion for speed overcame even fear for most people. The days of the trans-Atlantic liner were numbered. Despite all this the Italian government on September 9 laid the keels for two new superliners for transAtlantic service. To be over 40,000 tons, the new ships would each carry 1,800 passengers. They would have a speed of 27 knots. In due course they would be named *Michelangelo* and *Raffaello*. They would have the sad distinction of being the shortest-lived Atlantic superliners ever to serve and would be taken out of operation when they were only eleven years old. The British Government announced on November 3 that it would provide a large direct grant to Cunard Line and an additional large loan toward construction of a replacement for the *Queen Mary,* already well past the 20-year average ship's life. The new Cunarder would be built for cruising in the winter and trans-Atlantic service during the summer. The *America,* during her winter overhaul at Newport News, was converted from a three-class to a two-class liner, in line with the trend of the times. Her Tourist Class was increased from 165 to 530 berths.

An excellent article on the problems of a quick turnaround was carried in the November 27, 1960 *Herald Tribune.* Written by Creighton Peet it outlined all the types of damage that might happen to rugs, furniture, cabin walls, and the like during a typical voyage and detailed how repairs were made in the 48-hour layover. A few sentences show the vivid reporting of this piece: "Now it's 7:30 a.m. of arrival day and the tremendous bulk of the *United States* is beginning to darken the pier, while shrill whistles scream and half a dozen frantic tugs scuffle about, pushing and puffing and churning the water. In a few minutes big hawsers are holding her fast against the pier. And then, suddenly, everything happens at once. Eleven gangplanks and 10 conveyor belts, poised in mid-air, are lowered and made fast to the ship. Even before the first passengers start toward the pier, com-

Passengers at various locations throughout the ship. (Courtesy of Bill DiBenedetto)

pany officials, followed by newspapermen in search of cheesecake, cute children, and quotable celebrities, are crowding onto the ship. They're followed at close range by chemists going on board to check the water in the ship's boilers, elevator maintenance men, upholsterers, painters, and a man who'll replace all the ship's 1,200 air-conditioning filters before the next voyage."

The article was describing an ordinary 48-hour turnaround, never anticipating that on the ship's next visit she would have to do it all in only 28 hours. She had been held up at Le Havre for 16 hours because of storm conditions and did not reach New York until Friday, December 9, 24 hours behind schedule. But she sailed on schedule at noon the next day, having discharged and embarked 1,600 passengers, unloaded 5,304 sacks of mail and 8,000 pieces of baggage, automobiles, being stored with food, taking on another 15,000 sacks of mail, and filling the fuel tanks. To make matters worse the *America* was at the same pier loading 575 passengers for her next departure. With the increased traffic generated by the simultaneous handling of the two vessels, it was necessary to draw up a special arrival and departure schedule for trucks. Both ships sailed on time.

A new set of inspection rules for the public was drawn up as 1960 came to a close. Six days were set aside in 1961 for public inspection of the *United States*. Admission was without charge and no official passes were required. Cameras were encouraged. Children in groups had to be 10 years of age or older and each six had to be accompanied by an adult.

The December issue of *Via Port of New York,* publication of the Port of New York Authority, featured a night color shot of a brightly illuminated Christmas tree on the foredeck of the superliner. Her lit-up pilot house and illuminated forward stack made a bright background for the picture. "Project Santa Claus" was again celebrated on all the company's ships with parties for orphans. In late December the American Export and U.S. Lines announced seven jointly-sponsored cruises, with eastbound sailings on the *Independence* or the *Constitution* and return crossings on the *United States* or the *America*. A travel promotion scheme, the cruises included land arrangements and shore excursions directed by American Express and Thos. Cook & Sons. A special folder was put out listing the cruises and having photos of all four liners.

Even with the two extra crossings, the 1960 passenger totals were below those for 1959, continuing the steady decline since the high of 1955. On her 24 round trips the *United States* carried 30,228 eastbound and 32,153 westbound, for an average of 2,599 passengers per round trip.

As the new year came, Ralph E. Casey, AMMI President, criticized the last Eisenhower budget for not including funds for the sistership. He was hitting a dead horse, for with the departure of President Eisenhower and the arrival of young President Kennedy there was less chance than ever of getting the government to subsidize the building of a second big ship. There was, however, a feeling of real urgency in 1 Broadway, and 1961 saw a number of new projects initiated to try to bolster business for the *United States*. An arrangement was made with Autourist Cars in Europe, Inc., to provide rented cars, with chauffeur-guides if required, for passengers. The cars would be available for sale as well and could then be brought home under the "Sail 'n Drive" program. A full-page ad in color was taken in many newspapers on January 8 to push this concept. It included a half-page color photo of the *United States* in mid-Atlantic. Another money saving device adopted at this time came as a shocker to the many who loved the superliner. The U.S. Lines, in order to save port fees, had her remeasured by Customs officials. Her new gross was 51,988 tons. New sailing lists and brochures dropped the old 53,329-ton figure.

Still another promotion device was an arrangement with Pan American Airways announced February 1. It offered "Sea-Air Holidays" for all season voyages. As an inducement a 10% reduction on the steamer portion of the round-trip combination was offered. The reduced fare by the *United States* to Southampton began at $356.85 in First Class. A return flight cost $243 from London. The U.S. Lines put out a brochure showing a Pan American clipper and the *United States* on the cover. It must have been very hard for a U.S. Lines publicity man to write copy praising the "amenities and comforts" of service on the plane, but it was done. A series of all-expense tours were offered. A seven-day tour of Ireland cost $109 and a 21-day tour of Rome, Florence, Venice, Innsbruck, Lucerne, Interlaken, Geneva, Paris, and London cost $475. Ship and air fares were in addition, but all were available in one package. A summary paragraph in this first sea-air folder went like this: "Extend Your Holiday! This year get more out of your travels by taking a Sea-Air Holiday. You'll enjoy the thrill and fun of traveling aboard a luxury liner and flying high in a modern jet aircraft. You'll see all your favorite places in Europe too."

The seriousness of the financial situation for the company was highlighted early in February when U.S. Lines cancelled the February 11 sailing of the *America* as an economy measure. The 350 passengers who had booked were offered space on the February 10 sailing of the *United States*. The problem of U.S. Lines and other American subsidized lines was complicated by rigid government rules. In order to get an operating subsidy, American ships could not deviate from their scheduled service route one iota. While foreign lines enjoyed the freedom to send their ships on cruises during the winter months, American ships had to continue their regular route. Over 80 cruises were offered during January and February 1961 by foreign ships out of New York while the *America* had to be idled for one round trip and the *United States* ploughed back and forth with small lists. To make matters worse only limited reductions in Dining Saloon and Bed Room Stewards were permitted on slack sailings because of tight union contracts. An amendment of the 1936 Merchant Act was introduced to permit American ships to make cruises in off-season and still get subsidies. It was passed by Congress and signed by the President but not in time to permit any cruises by the *United States* in 1961. The *America* made a five-day cruise to Bermuda.

As Spring blossomed passenger lists became more respectable. The Duke and Duchess of Windsor were passengers in May. William Francis Gibbs continued his visits to the ship every arrival and every sailing day. He made the most of these, continuing to bring flowers and presents to important passengers and getting more glowing letters. One letter spoke particularly of the contribution the *United States* had made to the U.S. Navy. "The engineering plant is beautifully maintained and much quieter than I expected for a high speed installation. I marvel at the low vibration of the ship. I wonder why we can't put the speed and smoothness of operation into our new carriers. I understand our Navy engineers have learned quite a bit about evaporator operations and boiler upkeep techniques from the life-long practice in the *United States*. A good and correct start means so much to the success of a ship and it's a pleasure to observe." The letter was from Rear Admiral G.S. Patrick, Chief of Military Assistance Group. Another nice note came from W.B. Franke, former Secretary of the Navy. He thanked Mr. Gibbs for the champagne: "It was my favorite brand and year and we both thoroughly enjoyed it. We also enjoyed our trip on the *United States*. Of course we had an unusually smooth crossing but I was still impressed with the stability of the ship and with everything else about her. We liked her so much better than we did the *Liberté*."

Just as the ship was beginning to carry large passenger lists, the blow fell. Another strike. The *United States* arrived June 21, 1961, with 1,595 aboard only to find that all American ships were idled because of a work stoppage by the National Maritime Union, the Masters, Mates & Pilots and the Marine Engineers Beneficial Association. The strike had nothing to do with U.S. Lines, because it was aimed at companies that operated ships flying the flags of Panama, Honduras, and Liberia. The unions were demanding that they be permitted to organize officers and seamen on American-owned ships under these "flags of convenience," as the unions called them, or "flags of necessity" as the shipowners described them. The U.S. Lines had no ships under such flags but they were not exempted from the strike. The *United States* was to have sailed June 24 with more than 1,700 persons, her largest passenger total of the year. Another 1,325 had booked to return from Europe on her July 1 departure from abroad. Both sailings were cancelled "with great reluctance," General Franklin announced. Many passengers were transferred to foreign flag ships or got refunds and went by air. It was another disaster, another nail in the coffin, as people were beginning to say.

While the strike dragged on, a skeleton crew of engineers and fire wardens were "Permitted" by the unions to remain aboard the superliner. Officials of the MEBA gave the company a 48-hour deadline to shut down the huge power plant and secure the ship. It normally took about 16 hours to cool the boilers. Robert S. Burns, ship news reporter from the *Herald Tribune*, who had previously served as an engineer aboard U.S. Lines ships,

Passengers at various locations throughout the ship. (Courtesy of Bill DiBenedetto)

121

interviewed a number of men involved. They said this was the first time the *United States* had been "completely dead" since she had left the builders yard in 1952. Because the strike continued, the June 30 sailing of the *America* was also cancelled. It finally came to an end permitting the *America* to sail July 6, but her voyage had to be terminated at Southampton so that she could get back on her remaining schedule. The *United States* sailed on July 8 having missed one complete round trip. The repercussions of this and the earlier strikes against the *United States* did her grave harm long after the various settlements. Passengers came to doubt the regularity of the ship's schedule. Many who turned to foreign ships did so never to return to U.S. Lines ships. Others who were forced to take airplanes were also lost. The spirit of the company itself was damaged. There came to be many at 1 Broadway who leaned toward the idea of getting rid of the company's passenger service entirely. The unions were killing their golden goose.

The strike ended only after President Kennedy had intervened under the provisions of the Taft-Hartley Act, having decided that the continuance of the dispute would "imperil the national health and safety." The Department of Justice on July 3 issued a restraining order effective for 80 days. Negotiations reached a settlement just before this time limit expired and a new three to four year contract was signed by all parties. While the strike was in progress Bill Rand was named President of U.S. Lines.

The *United States* and the *America* would make special cruises in the winter of 1961-62 to the Caribbean and South America. The company had wasted no time to get into this lucrative field after the passage and signing of the operating subsidy extension bill. On July 31 Ken Gautier announced that the *America* would make her first cruise – a five day trip to Bermuda over the Thanksgiving weekend. Two cruises in January and February, 1962, were scheduled for the *United States*.

Four days before the August 17 sailing there was great excitement and activity around the entrance to Pier 86. Walt Disney was shooting a new movie to be called "Bon Voyage" and a third of it would be done aboard the *United States*. For the scenes showing the sailing a major Hollywood production took place on 12th Avenue. Over 200 extras were used to portray passengers, wellwishers, porters, and dock workers. Some 500 pieces of luggage were brought to the pier for background shots. Seventy-five taxis, limousines, and cars were rented to create a traffic jam around the pier head. Some 100 cameras were placed here and there to film every nuance. Stars Fred MacMurray, Jane Wyman, Michael Callan, Deborah Wally, Tommy Kirk, Kevin Corcoran, and Anna Maria Majalca went through their paces, getting out of taxis, lugging suitcases, taking snapshots and all. It took four full days and then the real sailing came and the cameras continued to roll aboard ship as the liner departed. The passenger list included Walt Disney himself and producer William Walsh and their families. All the color of the actual departure was captured, with people hurling confetti over the side and Tommy Kirk and Jane Wyman and others waving goodby to friends on the pier, and the great liner being backed into the stream.

Three camera crews worked to film the actual sailing for there were no re-takes with this one. One camera crew was on the pier shooting up. A second shot across the actors from the ship down toward the pier. The third filmed from a helicopter overhead. This last unit later boarded a Coast Guard cutter and raced alongside, trying to keep up. Commodore Anderson made sure he did not out-speed the little craft alongside, allowing them to go as far as 75 miles out of the port to get good shots of the vessel with no sign of land around her. For the next four and a half days the Disney production unit aboard was busy filming deck scenes and other shots on the liner. Many regular passengers participated as extras. It was said to be the first time a full film company had actually made a regular motion picture aboard a ship during a scheduled crossing. There was perfect weather and smooth sailing all the way, permitting the filming to continue right up to the debarkation at Le Havre. One of the other passengers aboard was Captain Walter F. Schlecht, Jr., USN, commander squadron of 14 Polaris submarines. Later he would be made an Admiral and would eventually become chairman of the board of the National Maritime Historical Society.

The dates of the two *United States* cruises were finally announced in the early Fall. They were to be 14-day trips to Nassau, St. Thomas, Trinidad, Curacao, and Cristobal. Fares were from $520 up. Departures were set for January 30 and February 16. No Tourist Class cabins were used and the advertisement stated: "Every stateroom on the *United States* has a private bath, shower, or both." The high speed of the superliner was mentioned as making it possible for passengers to enjoy not only the daylight hours at each stop "but a full evening in every port." An outdoor swimming pool was mentioned.

The effort to persuade the Defense Department to change its policy on flying home all dependents succeeded. Early in 1962 this traffic would be resumed.

Edward A. Garmatz, member of the House Merchant Marine Committee, was a passenger on the September 28 sailing. There were only 825 passengers aboard. He was visited by William Francis and later wrote a warm letter about the "magnificent ship" and gifts Mr. Gibbs had given him.

On November 23 many newspapers had stories about the successful trials of the new liner *France*. She had maintained an average trial speed of 34-13 knots. The year closed with the most depressing passenger totals for the *United States*. She carried 25,694 eastbound and 26,749 westbound, for an average 2,280 passengers per round trip. On the encouraging side the *America* sailed on her first cruise since before World War II with 737 passengers, a capacity load.

Despite more voyage cancellations due to labor strikes during 1962, the new year would show a remarkable improvement due to the resumption of military dependent travel by ship and other energetic sales promotion devices. For one thing a discount was offered for sailings in the off-season periods. The sea-air idea helped, as did the cooperative cruise program with American Export Lines. A total of 1,593 passengers went on the *United States* for these two first cruises of her career.

A quaint little sidelight of the first cruise saw the superliner diverted so that she could be seen when she passed the tiny island of Dominica, between St. Thomas and Trinidad. A Dominican businessman had asked for a passing as close to shore as possible, noting that he and his fellow islanders had never seen a big passenger liner. He recalled that prior to World War II the *Normandie* twice came close to the islands but on both occasions had been obscured by heavy rain squalls. Islanders traveled from all parts of the 29-mile long island to be on the western shore just to catch a glimpse of the *United States* when it was made known that she would make this special maneuver on her first cruise.

Walt Disney

Kim Novak

Charlton Heston

Mahalia Jackson

Jane Wyman and Walt Disney

Glenn Ford

(Photo by Andrew Malmsea, Chief Steward, SS United States, courtesy of Sven Olefeldt)

And passengers aboard were told to pay special note to the rugged beauty of the rarely-visited island.

Elaborate receptions were given to the American superliner at each of the five ports she visited and a gold plaque was presented to Commodore Anderson by the government of the Virgin Islands when she stopped at St. Thomas. A specially-trained staff of cruise directors and professional entertainers worked under the leadership of Fred Sperie and Agnes Woodrum for the cruises. Bingo, midnight buffets, and after-hours club activities for night owls were offered along with two complete floor shows during each cruise. Dance classes featured the new dance craze known as "The Twist."

While the *United States* was on her first cruise she dropped from the world's third largest ship to the world's fourth largest with the entry into service of the new liner *France*. This beautiful French ship arrived at New York February 8, 1962, receiving a warm welcome despite it being a very cold day. One French passenger died of excitement when the liner passed the Statue of Liberty. It was just too much for him. I was aboard one of the welcoming Moran tugs and remember being soaked with freezing water when the tug passed too close to one of the fireboats which was spraying her salute. Only two weeks before the same fireboats had honored the departing French *Liberté,* leaving on her last voyage after having been sold for scrap. When the *United States* returned from her first cruise she tied up across the way from the *France*. By special arrangement with the Maritime Administration, the French Line and U.S. Lines had agreed to operate their respective superliners as a team. The *France* was scheduled to sail from Le Havre when the *United States* sailed from *New York,* so that while competing for business, they would complement each other in serving the route.

On March 6 the *United States* had an unexpected passenger. He was Captain Harold Kaiser, Sandy Hook pilot, and he had to remain aboard because the seas were too high to permit him to transfer from the liner to the pilot boat off Ambrose Lightship. His surprise trip stimulated an article on piloting by Walter Hamshar in the *Herald Tribune.* Captain William Sherwood, president of the New York Sandy Hook Pilots Association, was quoted as saying that on the average two pilots made unanticipated sailings to foreign ports each year because of weather. It had happened only once in 1961, he added, a year that saw some 12,600 ships sail from New York. Captain Charles Reid, of the New Jersey Sandy Hook Pilots Association, said that being forced to take a long trip involuntarily was often quite a hardship for the pilot, but it wasn't that way on the *United States* he added.

An editorial in the *Maritime Reporter* commented on the new $80,000,000 *France* and the two new Italian superliners and criticized the U.S. Government for its failure in this area. "Surely this great country can afford funds for building ships that would help to weld us closer to our friends abroad in peacetime and, in a possible war, be on hand to carry the men who still will have to fight for victory despite the space age. To the *France* we say: 'Bon Voyage,' to our Government we add: 'Get Going!'" On the same day it was reported that Cunard had abandoned the idea of replacing the aging *Queen Mary* with a super class liner and was looking forward instead to construction of two cafeteria type self-service ships.

On April 3 the nuclear *Savannah* sailed on a four-day sea test trial and reached full power operation for the first time. She had finally been put into service after a full year's delay due to a jurisdictional labor strike. The strike proved impossible to solve and it was necessary to let all her highly-trained officers and seamen go and to sign on a new set provided by a different union. Instead of being operated by States Marine Lines, she was turned over to American Export for operation.

The success of the professional entertainment on the cruises convinced U.S. Lines that similar entertainment should be added to the regular trans-Atlantic crossings. The Bramson Entertainment Bureau was appointed for this purpose. A dance team, a master of ceremonies-comedian, and a social directress were added to the ship's staff to give cruise atmosphere to the North Atlantic voyages.

On April 24 the *Queen Mary* made headlines. She arrived at Southampton after the fastest crossing since she won the Blue Ribbon in 1938. She steamed the 3,194 miles from New York in 4 days, 9 hours and 51 minutes for an average of 30.18 knots.

In May the movie "Bon Voyage" opened in New York at the Radio City Music Hall with many *United States* officers and U.S. Lines people in the audience. The June issue of *Readers Digest* had a good article about the superliner entitled "Grand Hotel at 30 Knots." Written by James Nathan Miller it was digested from a piece

Looking down into the First Class Dining Salon from the main deck. (Photo by Andrew Malmsea, Chief Steward, SS United States, *courtesy of Sven Olefeldt)*

in *The Diplomat* magazine. It began with a description of the work of the painters, who "hang like ants from her superstructure, for, while an ordinary ship will tolerate a patch of rust here and there, this lady's makeup must always be impeccable." And it describes the 33 men who on each turnaround paint a pre-arranged block of staterooms. And it told of the two dozen passengers under consideration, as each crossing began for seats at the captain's table, and how that number always had to be cut down to only nine. "And so life goes on as we rush toward the coast of France. First Class is atinkle with gaiety, a blaze of Dior and Givenchy gowns, and white shirt fronts. It is self-satisfied, opulent, decorous-some would say stuffy. Cabin is a little younger, not quite so rich and considerably less formal. Tourist is far out in Happyville with little cliques forming, disbanding, and exchanging members."

On June 7, 1962 it was announced that the *United States* would make one 15-day and one 16-day cruise to the Caribbean in the Fall. The *America* would do eight cruises of from 5 to 11 days. New wage scales won by the NMU were heralded in a four-page supplement to the union's newspaper, *The Pilot,* at this time. They ranged from $1,103-25 a month for the Chief Steward to $302-56 for the bootblack.

My wife Doris, son David, and daughter Noelle joined me in a round trip in the summer of 1962. We loved the *United States* and will never forget the experience. I was going over to push the 1964 Operation Sail, and we made a vacation out of the trip. Since Operation Sail had no travel funds we paid our own way in Tourist Class. Our room, with four berths, was packed with 33 friends before sailing, including Dick Shepard, of the *Times,* and Alexander Purdon, Executive Vice President of U.S. Lines. On the trip we were particularly impressed with our dining saloon steward Ramon Cruz. After the crossing was over and we were heading across the pier for the train to London we spotted him jogging after us waving. He had two tins of sardines. They were for Dave, he said. He remembered how much David liked sardines. Who said U.S. service was not as good as that on foreign liners? On the way home we were "elevated" to First Class, much to the displeasure of the two children, who preferred our Tourist cabin far forward with two portholes to the inside cabin we were given. Noelle literally crashed into actor Glenn Ford one time. David has always maintained ever since that the *United States* was his favorite of all liners.

Over the July 6-8 weekend both the *United States* and the *Queen Mary* made rescues. The *United States* was diverted 150 miles off course to pick up Captain

Richard Hughes from the British schooner yacht *Ramona C.*, after he was injured by a swinging boom. The *Mary* steamed eight hours off course to pick up William B. Day, an American seaman on the freighter *Lena Luckenbach*. Mr. Day required hospitalization, which the *Mary* provided. Both superliners arrived late in port after having reciprocally rescued seamen of rival nationalities in the highest traditions of the sea.

My family's return crossing marked the completion of the tenth anniversary of the *United States*. As Werner Bamberger put it in an article in the *New York Times*: "The vessel is credited with having done more than any other ship in recent maritime history to restore this country's shipping prestige." In the decade she averaged 1,460 passengers per round trip or 88.5% of her normal capacity. A measure of her popularity was seen in the sale of more than 500,000 plastic self-assembly models by Revell, Inc., of Venice, Calif., and the distribution of over 1,000,000 descriptive folders about the superliner. In steaming 1,621,165 nautical miles she had never been forced to stop her four massive propellers from turning due to mechanical breakdown. U.S. Lines issued a few figures explaining how it cost $20,000,000 a year to operate the big ship: $7,000,000 went for crew expenses; fuel cost $3,500,000; subsistence, stores, and supplies accounted for $3,300,000; brokerage commissions and union welfare contributions cost $1,000,000 each; and port expenses and such miscellaneous items as handling mail cost another $2,400,000.

Perhaps the most satisfied of all passengers ever to sail on the *United States* was described in the Lou Walters newspaper column. His name was Jorge Sanchez and he lived in Miami Beach. He sailed with Lou on the superliner, although he had wanted to fly. On the arrival at Le Havre, Mr. Sanchez was having so much fun that he decided not to go on to Paris, but to continue on the superliner to Southampton. At Southampton he again stayed on to Bremerhaven, and then back to Southampton and to Le Havre and to New York. And even then he did not want to leave, he just stayed aboard for the next crossing and finally three weeks after he had planned he arrived in Paris. "I have never," he told Lou Walter, "had such a wonderful time." From then on he would refer to the *United States* as "my idea of paradise."

Summer passed and Fall came and the *United States* continued with large lists and trouble-free operation. Shortly before the December 10 sailing a special dinner aboard honored William Francis Gibbs. The dinner was sponsored by the United Seamen's Service, and it was held to mark its 20th anniversary. The United Seamen's Service was founded during World War II to offer services to merchant seamen similar to those provided members of the armed forces by the USO. Mr. Gibbs had been a director from the start. NMU President Curran, out of the city on union business, sent a message describing William Francis as "a genius, a giant of the maritime industry, and a great humanitarian."

And then more labor difficulties brought one of the ship's best years to a grinding halt. The longshoremen's contract had expired on September 30 and a strike was called on October 1. The *United States* was scheduled to sail on October 4 but did not get away until the Taft-Hartley Act was invoked and the longshoremen went back to work two days later. After the 80-day cooling off period the strike was resumed and U.S. Lines was forced to cancel two cruises with the *America* and the last round trip of the year for the *United States*. The trans-Atlantic sailing cancellation was made "with the greatest reluctance," General Franklin said, because it seriously inconvenienced the travel plans of several thousand passengers. For the duration of the strike the two U.S. Lines passenger ships were laid up at the Newport News shipyard. Despite this the 1962 passenger results were described in the U.S. Lines' annual report as being "most satisfactory." The *United States* carried 59,952 passengers trans-Atlantic, not to mention the 1,593 on her cruises. The longshore strike would last well into 1963, however, and was another in the long string of labor disasters that would shorten the life of the magnificent *United States*. The writing was on the wall.

A travel agent's promotional brochure featuring all the comforts and pleasures of the ship.

11

More Passengers Than Any Other Liner

In 1963, the U.S. Lines was harassed by more labor problems. One European voyage and one cruise had to be cancelled because of the continuing longshoremen's strike. Six European voyages and three cruises of the *America* were cancelled. The flow of military dependents was reduced and the year was a most discouraging one. In a statement released January 10, General Franklin noted that the "strike situation had created so much uncertainty and doubt in the minds of the traveling public that the demand for accommodations had virtually ceased." A pattern of labor problems that seemed to have no solution was emerging. The engineers, deck officers, and unlicensed seamen all had separate unions, to name only the major ones. Jurisdictional battles between them were common. One would make peace and the other would go out on strike. The longshore strike which had begun October 1, 1962, had gone through one Taft-Hartley cooling off period and was finally settled on January 26 after a special Presidential committee had offered new concessions.

The *United States* was tied up by the ILA strike all through January and until February 16, when she began what was to have been her second Caribbean cruise. The *America* was rescheduled after her long strike idleness to make three cruises in March and April, getting back into trans-Atlantic service on April 30. Of the eight cruises so hopefully announced for the two ships back in mid-1962 only four were made.

The new joint service between the *United States* and the *France* produced new folders in which both superliners were pictured and their combined sailing schedule for 1963 announced. The rates on the *France*, as set forth by the Atlantic Passenger Conference, were slightly higher than those on the *United States*, as she was the newer ship. First Class on the French liner in the thrift season was $427.50 minimum, compared with $411.50 on the *United States*. The *France* had only two classes. Her Tourist Class rate was $225.00 compared with $200.50 on the American ship.

Returning from her one cruise of the season the *United States* sailed March 7 on her first trans-Atlantic crossing of 1963. In addition to 1,400 passengers she carried the famous painting "Mona Lisa," being returned to the Louvre in Paris after exhibitions in Washington and New York. The 460-year old masterpiece by Leonardo da Vinci had made an 11-week visit to America during which time it had been seen by 1,500,000 persons. Remembering the 1911 theft of this same painting, the U.S. Secret Service set up one of the most elaborate plans for its protection, while it was being moved from the United States back to France. Two carloads of secret servicemen and two carloads of French officials and museum representatives were part of the caravan that brought it to Pier 86. The route was not divulged beforehand. It was not put in a cargo hold, but instead was given a three-room suite which was guarded day and night by special men provided by the Louvre and by the Pinkerton National Detective Agency. Both the temperature and the humidity of the suite were carefully planned by Louvre and French Government authorities. A four-page U.S. Lines press release announced these and other details of the painting's voyage. In the First Class passenger list under "L" was listed the painting by its familiar name: "Mona Lisa."

Passenger lists for the *United States* were fair in the first half of 1963, with an occasional capacity load. On July 5 as the second half of the year began the ship sailed with 1,750 passengers, including the Duke and Duchess of Windsor. The schedule to November of 1964 for both the *United States* and the *America* was announced, with the superliner to make 19 trans-Atlantic crossings and two cruises.

Once again the frantic effort toward economy of operation brought a tonnage reduction. A new measurement was requested of Customs and the *United States* came out of it a ship of only 44,893 gross tons, by American rules. The company's publicity department was well aware of the importance of the British tonnage figure of about 52,000 tons and continued to use this in all literature. However, the new tonnage brought a tongue-in-cheek article by Werner Bamberger of the *New York Times* about how shipping men were wondering whether the new measurement would put the *United States* behind the new *Canberra* in comparative size tables. The new P & O liner was 45,270 gross tons. It was obvious to anyone who knew the comparative lengths of the two ships, 818 feet for *Canberra* and 990 for *United States,* that the two ships had to be measured by different yardsticks if the Britisher were put ahead of the American liner. The change reduced American tonnage dues slightly, but the *United States* still had to pay on the basis of her British tonnage when visiting foreign ports.

In my capacity at this time as public relations director for the Moran Towing Company, it was my pleasure to take out distinguished visitors on tugs to observe arrivals or departures of great liners. On the August 28, 1963, sailing of the *United States* I had as my guest aboard the steam tug *Alice M. Moran* Alexander Crosby Brown, noted maritime author and newspaper man from Newport News, Virginia. He later wrote about his experiences in a delightful essay. He introduced his story by hailing the *United States* as "the swiftest and most beautiful ship of them all, the proud behemoth." His writing was poetical: "Morning mists still lay close to the surface of the water while horizontal fingers of sunlight probed their ways through the labrynth of skyscrapers to pick up, bathing them in a rosy glow, ships in the harbor and structures over on the Jersey shore beyond. Then abruptly the giant liner materialized out of the haze down the bay, heading straight up the Hudson River steaming on a mid-channel course. Patterns of light and shade played over her nearly thousand-foot hull surmounted by its gleaming white superstructure and crowned by the pair of lofty red, white, and blue funnels." It was a splendid piece of writing, and its last line showed what a professional Alec Brown was: "Chalk up a routine crossing for Commodore Anderson; a routine docking for Captain Johansen of the *Alice M. Moran.* But a memorable experience for this correspondent."

The ship gets some help from a few tugs while she was in port in New York City. (Courtesy of Bill DiBenedetto)

It was on this trip that sharp-eyed Brown spotted a piece of redundancy: "Poking around under the stern I saw outlined in beaded welds these words: 'No Tugs Abaft (of) This Line.' The 'of' had been painted out by a seaman whose sense of niceties about the English language and its use at sea must have been offended. No self-respecting deck-hand would ever say 'abaft of.'" Fifteen years later Alec and I were visiting the laid-up superliner. We walked along the pier where she lay toward her stern and saw the same sign, painted the same way.

Good summer passenger lists continued into the Fall of 1963. On September 27 the liner sailed with Rita Hayworth among those aboard. It was on this trip that the toilet seat from her cabin (M-69) was missing after the crossing, a souvenir for some moon-struck crew member.

On the subject of toilets the U.S. Lines had asked a special subsidy to help install private facilities and showers in all Tourist Class cabins so the *United States* would be able to compete better with the new *France*, all of whose cabins had such features. The cost was estimated at $1,270,000 and the request was denied by the Maritime Administration. In saying "no" the shipping agency noted that the *United States* had carried more passengers in Tourist Class than the new French ship in 1962 and that the percentage of Tourist Class occupancy of the American liner was "substantially greater than was the percentage of Tourist Class occupancy on the *France.*" The change would have eliminated 40 Tourist Class berths and made it necessary for an increased subsidy, Maritime noted. The U.S. Lines contended that without these facilities they would not be able to meet

Companies using the SS United States in their Advertisements. (Courtesy of Bill McBride with McBride Publishing)

128

foreign competition and hold their position of "prestige and passenger acceptability," but the Maritime Administration said this was "conjectural." The improvement would have meant much to the *United States*. The turn down by Maritime was bad judgement.

The cold war was at its hottest. The Berlin Wall had been erected by East Germany and the threat of stopping Western access into Berlin was more and more serious. In mid-1963 the East Germans made several attempts to stop all land links with the old German capital city. An airlift by western powers supplied West Berlin with food and supplies. A dramatic move by the United States saw a trans-Atlantic airlift of 15,000 troops to Germany. It took three days and cost an estimated $20,000,000. Shipping men pointed out that the *United States* could have done the same thing in five days at a cost of only $420,000.

The Fall of 1963 was very bad for U.S. Lines from the labor standpoint. On September 14 the *America* was forced to cancel her scheduled trans-Atlantic voyage because of a jurisdictional labor dispute. Only six weeks earlier the NMU had signed a six-year no strike pledge. The dispute was entirely jurisdictional in nature. U.S. Lines was told by NMU to remove an engineering officer or the ship would not be sailed. The Marine Engineers Beneficial Assoc. said if the officer was removed the liner would not be allowed to depart. U.S. Lines tactfully described the matter as a case of "alleged racial and religious discrimination." As one who was right in the middle of it I know it involved a dispute over the use of a bathroom with resulting heated remarks involving race and color. An aribtrator eventually supported the NMU's contention and then a judge supported the MEBA side. The U.S. Lines was in the middle and the *America* lay idle until February 7, 1962, almost half a year. The NMU eventually backed down and the ship finally was permitted to sail. A book could and should be written on this classic intra-union dispute which did so much to destroy American-flag passenger services on the seven seas. And one of the victims would eventually be the *United States* herself.

A U.S. Lines press release in December, 1963, touted the "unbelievable wine list of the *United States*." It began with a question: "Can you imagine inviting eight people to a pre-dinner cocktail party, replete with delicious canapes and at least four invigorating drinks per person, served in super-smart surroundings at a total cost of less than $20?" The answer, of course, was that it could be done on the American superliner. A red, white, and blue, 24-page wine list had just been issued. "This attractively-bound booklet offers the finest selections of wines, whiskies, brandies, and other beverages available most anywhere at prices so low it takes the first-time passenger half the ocean to get over the surprise," the release chortled. There were 46 varieties of Scotch whiskey aboard. The cost for 31 of them was 40¢ a glass, while others cost 50¢ a glass. Hard liquor was served in 1 3/4th ounce glasses. American Bourbons ranged from 35¢ to 45¢ a glass. Vodka was 25¢. All but one kind of cocktail was either 40¢ or 45¢ "per copious drink." Fifteen varieties of imported beers aboard were offered at 30¢ a bottle, while 11 types of American beer could be had for 25¢.

Preparations for the December 27 cruise of the *United States* were elaborate. The company decided to have a professionally staged show aboard every evening that the ship would be at sea, in addition to the usual costume balls, novelty dances, and special late night parties. Nine "internationally known acts" were retained to perform for the 990 passengers booked. On four of the six nights there would be two night club shows running simultaneously in the Grand Ballroom and the Showboat Room, as the Cabin Class Lounge was called at that time. Each evening the shows would be alternated in the two rooms. On the other two evenings at sea "a large five-act revue would be presented in the theatre twice nightly." Prices for the cruise ranged from $1,100 for U-87-89 to $315 for an inside room with one lower bed and one upper.

How successful the *United States* had been in overcoming the "troopship" image foisted upon her because of the dispute over her construction costs was shown in an article in the *Times* on December 15. Paul J.C. Friedlander, who had been somewhat critical of her in 1952, sailed from Newport News to New York on her again eleven years later, and wrote his Sunday column on the trip. He began: "When the *United States* came out it was chic to describe her as the most luxurious troopship afloat. Thus, almost every account of the delivery run of the new flagship used that or a similar phrase. This reporter also succumbed to that old-time temptation, and so it was with considerable anticipation that he seized the opportunity to repeat the 1952 delivery last weekend. The *United States* had spent two weeks in the Newport News yard being repainted, refurbished, and repaired. It is reassuring, since all those who were aboard the ship in 1952 also have weathered considerably since then, to be able to report that the *United States* has aged gracefully, as a lady should, and that much of the starkness verging on austerity, something that was so evident in her youth, has been softened and mellowed by use. And she also has had time to develop her own character, one of the distinctive qualities of ships shared by almost no other commercial conveyance. The *United States* gives the impression of flexing powerful muscles even when she is idling along. . . ."

On her last Atlantic round trip of 1963 the *United States* was delayed 21 hours by bad storms. She made a remarkable quick turnaround in only six hours at Southampton to enable her to get her 1,150 returning passengers back to New York in time for Christmas. Her normal turnaround time at the British port was 22 hours. U.S. Lines put out a special release about the quick turnaround noting that the best turnaround time of a foreign liner at New York was 16 hours and 35 minutes. The ship got back to New York early on December 23. A 40-foot Christmas tree was hoisted atop her radar mast that afternoon, 153 feet above the Hudson. It was illuminated with colored lights and remained up until minutes before she departed on her "Gala New Year's Cruise" on December 27.

During her annual overhaul at Newport News the *United States* lay alongside the 1,052-foot long carrier *America,* due to be launched February 1. The new war vessel was 252 feet wide, extreme beam, and could have, theoretically, accommodated both the *Queen Mary* and the *Queen Elizabeth* side by side on her flight deck.

Back in trans-Atlantic service, the *United States* completed her first round trip of 1964 on January 21. Among her 1,243 passengers arriving that day was Queen Frederika, of Greece. More labor problems were in the wind. A tug strike began while the *United States* was on her second voyage of the year. The *Queen Elizabeth* grazed a pier while coming in, bending her jackstaff and causing slight damage to the dock. When the *United*

States arrived February 5 she, too, had to come in without tugs, the third time in her career. Aside from one hawser that snapped and a five-hour delay for passengers because the ship had to wait for exactly the right tide situation, the maneuver was carried out by Commodore Anderson with his usual finesse. He was on his next to last trip. When he returned again on the big liner two weeks later he retired, with suitable ceremony. Before retiring, however, he had to once again bring the ship in without tugs.

An official New York harbor welcome was arranged for Commodore Anderson's last arrival. Fireboats, helicopters, and surface craft joined in greeting the *United States* off the Statue of Liberty. A flag-bedecked Pier 86 greeted him. The New York State Maritime Academy band played while the ship came in. Later there were speeches and a citation from New York's Mayor Robert Wagner. The Commodore was presented with an original painting of the *United States*. Captain Leroy J. Alexanderson, it was announced, would succeed Commodore Anderson on the bridge. He had served aboard her for nine years and his sea career had stretched back for 34 years. Like Commodore Anderson he was a graduate of the New York State Maritime Academy. He had joined U.S. Lines in 1936 as Senior Third Officer on the *California,* of the Panama Pacific Line. His first command had come in 1950 and was the cargo ship *American Forwarder*. He was named Executive Officer on the *America* in 1953 and in 1955 took up his post on the *United States*. Captain Richard W. Ridington was elevated from Chief Officer to Executive Officer and relieving master of the *United States*. Captain John S. Tucker went up from First Officer to Chief Officer. Captain Thomas Hannigan was elevated from Second to First Officer.

The U.S. Public Health Service Special Citation for excellent sanitation was awarded to the *United States* in March for the eighth successive year. On March 26 the superliner sailed on her second cruise, taking out a capacity list of passengers. Captain Richard Ridington took her out on his first crossing as master on April 23.

Another splendid piece on William Francis Gibbs and his *United States* was carried June 6, 1964, in the *New Yorker*. Still proud of how the ship's top speed had been kept a secret, he was quoted as saying: "The reason we managed to construct that ship was that the government left us to ourselves, putting no regulations in the way. So we designed the ideal ship. Nobody knows how fast it can go. Nobody is allowed below decks without a special permit. I've asked them in Washington to put a Russian on board – he'd be more impressed than by any speeches you could think up. Lots of people would like to see that engine room. It's clean as a whistle. There's a big roar of air but not a bit of vibration. The crew is absolutely trustworthy. Even in an English pub on the other side, with the British trying to find out, they don't open their mouths. There's no love lost between us and the British designers, you know. They're condescending, supercilious bastards."

Rumors were everywhere that the *America* was to be sold and on August 1, 1964, when the new sailing schedule came out, it was obvious that something big was happening. This was to be the last sailing list with both the *United States* and the *America* listed. The latter was shown as making seven more crossings and then she was not mentioned again. The *United States* was scheduled to make 23 round trips in the upcoming year of 1965. The marine community knew that Greek shipping interests were seeking to buy the *America* and although it was never officially announced by U.S. Lines her last voyage for them was to begin October 9. Joseph Curran, president of the NMU, complained bitterly: "This is a grave mistake. It will cost us dearly in international prestige, which is a crucial factor in today's world situation." He denounced both U.S. Lines and the Maritime Administration for not having plans to replace the *America*.

Wishing to come into the harbor of New York aboard the *America* on her last trip, I asked permission of the Sandy Hook Pilots Association to spend the night on a pilot boat and board the famous liner when she reached the pilot station area. It was pitch black when I swung out on a rope from the pilot mother ship and dropped into a tiny bobbing pilot launch. The trip in on the *America* with Captain Fender was a sad one. He had just lost his son in a tragic accident at home. It was still partly dark as we passed the Statue of Liberty and Captain Fender turned to me to complain sharply about the fact that the Statue was not illuminated. He said he had tried repeatedly to convince the government that it should be lit 24 hours a day, but had gotten nowhere. Later I reported the situation to columnist Allan Keller of the *World Telegram & Sun*. On October 20 Mr. Keller published a strongly-worded piece on the matter. Thereafter the Statue of Liberty has been kept illuminated all day and all night. It was Captain Fender's last voyage as well as the *America*'s but at least something good came out of it.

On November 2 the *United States* arrived bringing the Duke and Duchess of Windsor for their third crossing of the year aboard the American superliner. The new sailing schedule just released had no reference to the *America*. On November 5, 1964, her sale to the Chandris Line for $4,250,000 was announced.

The *United States* went to Newport News early in November for her winter checkup. The *America* was there, being readied for turnover to the Greeks. When the *United States* returned on November 21, she sailed under the new Verrazano Bridge, on which opening day ceremonies were being held. Many reporters went out on a Moran tug to board the ship and come up under the beautiful new span, painted a bright red. A special stamp honored the new structure, longest suspension bridge in the world. And a special-first-day-of-issue cachet picturing the *United States* passing under the bridge was bought by thousands of stamp collectors on that day.

The 1964-1965 cruise schedule included four *United States* cruises. One was for five days with a minimum rate of $185. It went to Bermuda and was advertised as a Thanksgiving Holiday Cruise. The next was for nine days and the minimum was $315. The ship sailed December 18 and visited Curacao, Martinique, and St. Thomas. The two other cruises were scheduled for the early part of 1965. Both would be of nine day's duration. One was listed as a Tropical Winter Cruise and the other was called the Festive Spring Cruise. Each had calls at Nassau, Curacao, and St. Thomas.

The America had suffered particularly in 1963-1964 from labor difficulties, but as 1965 began it was to be the *United States*' turn to be hurt again and again. When she made her first landfall in New York on January 11 she arrived to find the port shut down by another strike of longshoremen. Under the direction of Francis Grant, U.S. Lines vice president, 120 shoreside supervisory

The United States *as seen at night with lights on. (Photo by Andrew Malmsea, Chief Steward,* SS United States, *courtesy of Sven Olefeldt)*

personnel were rallied to help the 1,000 passengers with their mountains of baggage. The January 14 sailing had to be cancelled and President Rand published an agonizing notice calling the strike "an extremely damaging blow to the American Merchant Marine and the entire shipping industry." He charged that the walkout was taken without regard to the welfare of the public, the nation, and the longshoremen themselves, and noted that the union had just been offered a four-year contract which even union leadership had described as "the best we ever had." It was another nail in the coffin of the American passenger ship fleet. American ships were unable to sail because the seagoing unions refused to pass through the picket lines set up by the longshoremen. Foreign liners continued to sail, with shore staffs helping with their baggage.

A strike settlement was reached on January 21, but the longshoremen refused to go back to work until February 13, awaiting similar agreements in other ports up and down the coast. Although there were no longshoremen to handle the lines or baggage the *United States* sailed on January 29 because picket lines had been suspended with the settlement in New York. The Duke and Duchess of Windsor were aboard as well as Princess Elisabeth de Faucigny-Lucinge, of Paris. It would be the last voyage for Chief Purser Clarence P. Gehrig, who was retiring after 44 years at sea. Widely known as a man with an uncanny memory for names, "Bob" Gehrig had joined U.S. Lines in 1922 as a deck yeoman aboard the *Old North State*.

The sailing attracted considerable press interest because of the longshoremen problem. McCandish Phillips of the *New York Times* had a feature about how landbound personnel "from office boys to chief executives bent their backs" to carry the baggage. "Palms used to paper work blossomed with blisters," he wrote, as the task of loading 490 pieces of heavy luggage, 3 tons of ice cream, 19 tons of vegetables, 13 tons of beer, and 32 automobiles was accomplished. The Duke and Duchess alone had 83 items of luggage and the rest of the voyagers had about 3,500 pieces of hand baggage. But the 125 volunteers from the office did the work that normally took 250 longshoremen. Company officials, however, hastened to point out that that was "no reflection on longshoremen as they would have done it faster."

One of those drafted office workers was "a sharp-nosed man with cheeks as red as a Macintosh apple." He was Captain Donald McKay, former master of the U.S. Lines *American Planter* and then assistant terminal manager. Andrew Warwick, president of T. Hogan and Sons, Inc., stevedores, was helping to handle the chain that opened and closed the huge cargo doors on the pier. Raymond Weigele, general operating manager for U.S. Lines, made no secret of his long thermal underwear as he worked. The temperature was 20 degrees when he arrived at 6:40 a.m. on sailing day. The work stoppage was still in effect on February 11 when the superliner returned and all the tremendous effort had to be repeated. Finally, on February 13 the longshoremen in New York went back to work. Once again the dispute had involved the Secretary of Labor and the President of the United States.

On the day the strike finally ended the *United States* set off on her 9-day Tropical Winter Cruise to Nassau, Curacao, and St. Thomas. Lindsey Nelson, sportscaster for the New York "Mets," was aboard with his wife and a nearly capacity list. After two more trans-Atlantic sailings, the big liner made her second Caribbean cruise of 1965 and then settled down to regular service between New York and Europe. With the *America* gone, she was scheduled to go all the way to Bremerhaven for more than half her crossings.

A note from Captain Alexanderson written to me on April 4 at sea summed up his feelings about the maritime scene at that time: "It is really shortsightedness that a great nation like ours cannot have a sistership to the *United States* and additional passenger ships in our merchant marine, especially when you see the new passenger ships that all of the foreign nations are coming out with. It is discouraging to realize that we, the greatest and richest nation in the world, are becoming a second-rate seagoing power." Little did Captain Alexanderson realize that in less than five years he would no longer be on the bridge of the *United States* but would instead be serving on a cargo ship.

A new U.S. Lines publication appeared at this time. It was called *Sales News* and was edited by Clifford S. Morgan. The 10-page, slick-paper offering was packed with short articles and photos, with drawings, diagrams, and helpful hints to assist company agents to promote the *United States*. Very well prepared, it must have done much to encourage tourist agents to book passengers on the American superliner. With the continuous interruption of service by labor difficulties, every kind of effort was needed to keep the passenger lists respectable. And the worst was yet to come.

The *United States* returned to New York June 25 with a large passenger list, and bookings for the rest of the season were excellent. She was to sail on July 1 with 1,700 passengers, including Joseph Curran and his wife. But she did not sail. This time it was three unions that were striking, the American Radio Association, representing the radio operators, the Masters, Mates and Pilots, and the Marine Engineers Beneficial Association. At issue were various pension and manning problems. The American Merchant Marine Institute was handling the collective bargaining for the ship lines, as usual. Ships of eight major lines operating 120 vessels were held up. The nation's leading passenger liners owned by American Export Lines, Moore-McCormack Lines, and Grace Lines were involved. At first sailings were postponed day by day in hope that some sort of agreement could be reached. With her largest passenger list of the year the *United States* was rescheduled to leave July 2. Even Joseph Curran warned that the merchant marine was at its last crossroad. He attacked what he called the "arrogant refusal" of leaders of the engineers union to exempt passenger liners as had been proposed by the mates and the radio unions. Jesse M. Calhoon, president of the MEBA, would not compromise. He said the main issue was extra compensation for especially trained crews on automated ships. The container ship was coming into the picture, and Mr. Calhoon was determined to have his share of any benefits its economy of operation would produce.

Finally, it had to be announced that the sailing of the *United States* was cancelled. Kenneth Gautier called it a "shattering blow" and the company did everything it could to find transportation for those who had chosen to sail on the *United States*. Unfortunately, it was the peak of the season and most other ships were booked to capacity. It was, of course, the worst time of the year for a strike from management's standpoint. And it would be the worst strike the *United States* had ever experienced. Three more trans-Atlantic sailings would have to be cancelled. I sailed that year for France with my wife and two children on the liner *France.* When we went out the *United States* was a sad sight, idle at her pier. When we came back, also on the *France,* she was still there, deserted and lonely looking.

From time to time as each sailing was cancelled the U.S. Lines and other struck American passenger ship lines issued statements of regret. The companies repeatedly agreed to submit the issues to impartial arbitration and to be bound by the results, but the engineers' union refused. The strike dragged on. Foreign ships came and went loaded with happy passengers. More and more people turned to airplanes. The message to shipowners was loud and clear. Get out of the passenger ship business. A total of 9,000 passengers were stranded as the result of the cancellation of the first three trips of the *United States,* the company announced on August 10, when it called off the fourth round trip. Gross revenue losses to the company on the first three voyages came to about $3,000,000. The fourth voyage would have earned $900,000 which was also lost.

On August 19, 1965, a special stamp was issued honoring Robert Fulton and his first steamboat. First day covers were sent out with a cachet showing the *Clermont* of 1807 and having the *United States* in the background. The day marked the 200th anniversary of the birth of Fulton. It was ironic that the superliner lay strikebound.

Finally, the MEBA agreed to permit passenger liners to sail and on August 24, with the strike 70 days old and still unsettled, it was announced by U.S. Lines that the *United States* would sail on August 26. Preparations to get her ready in just two days made news. Bedroom stewards swarmed through the 672 passenger staterooms to set the climate controls. They cleaned and polished. The 26 public rooms were restored to life after their long summer stretch of idleness. The huge hull was repainted and the miles of corridors on the 12 decks were washed and waxed. Joseph Muchulsky, Chief Steward for Cabin Class, said that his Gay 90s lounge was being repainted a cream color. He told one reporter that wrought iron work had been built into its decoration to make it look like New Orleans. Captain Alexanderson said: "I think all the crew are glad to be back." The strike, he added, had damaged relations with passengers. He had changed his own vacation to be aboard the ship when close friends were supposed to sail the previous July 1. "They both had to go by airplane," he said. He had come in several times from his summer home in Brookhaven, Long Island, to visit the ship during the strike. "You just don't leave a ship idle." He said he hoped everything would go smoothly "from now on." He would be sadly disappointed.

Sailing day saw a bare 809 passengers aboard, although the full complement of 1,018 crew members had to be on hand to take care of the 1,650 due to return home aboard the big ship. She was the first of the five major strike-bound ships tied up in New York to sail. "The strike has hurt a lot of people, not only seamen, but also ashore," one lounge steward said just before the departure. "I wasn't hurt too badly since I am single, but lots of fellows with families were." No settlement was in sight for the 110 American freighters still idled.

The Summer passed and the Fall of 1965 came, with the *United States* sailing regularly. A promotional folder issued by seven American liner companies showed pictures of the *United States* with the liners of the six other companies. "Sail on an American ship," was the theme. It was hoped that this and a more active advertising campaign would help overcome some of the disastrous anti-American ship publicity of the long summer strike. The superliner's 1966 schedule of 20 North Atlantic voyages and two Caribbean cruises was announced. Because of the cruises the ship had changed her annual overhaul time from December to November. She went to Newport News on November 19. Machinery repairs were made and her hull cleaned and repainted. The crew painted her twin smokestacks and completed many other fix-up assignments. She sailed back to New York on December 4 ready for her December 9 departure. Passenger totals were rarely if ever given in company press releases at this point.

A news story by George Horne of the *New York Times* revealed for the first time one of the secrets of the William Francis Gibbs design. It was a story noting that all American passenger ships would have to spend money to equip themselves with inflatable rafts, all, that is, except the *United States.* Mr. Horne pointed out that the superliner was a four- compartment ship, explaining that even if four of her watertight compartments were flooded she would float.

The liner's Christmas 1965 cruise to the West Indies commenced December 23, and two days later one of the most unusual of ship news stories broke. Two college girls had applied for permission to travel on the *United States* in the doghouse, and had sent $50 each to cover the ticket cost. That was the price listed in the company's rate schedule for dogs ("any size"). The girls were Suzanne L. Pineau and Hilde M. Lehmann, seniors at Middlebury College, Middlebury, Vt. In their application they had volunteered to don dog disguises, with Miss Pineau offering to be a St. Bernard and Miss Lehmann a collie. U.S. Lines turned them down, but did it in a humorous way. Were they to be accepted as dogs "a dreadful chain of events would follow, with others traveling as cats, birds, excess baggage, and even tangerines." The company added: "In the end the confusion would become so great that we might be hounded into thinking we were an airline and by then our collapse would be complete."

While the *United States* was being built, Cliff E. Parkhurst, talented employee of Gibbs & Cox, did a series of 13 superior sketches of her hull rising in various stages of completion. Eight of them were used as covers for the Gibbs & Cox house organ *Compass Points,* and an article in that magazine in late 1965 noted that the set had been turned over to The Mariners' Museum as a gift from William Francis Gibbs.

The U.S. Lines 1965 annual report was dour: "The maritime labor difficulties which plagued the American economy in 1965, were the most severe and by far the most costly in history. During the two prolonged strike periods lasting a total of 110 days, many cargo and several passenger voyages scheduled by your company were cancelled. Nevertheless, we operated profitably in 1965." The report noted that even after the summer strike the *United States* lost revenue due to "the reluctance of travelers to book passage on our vessel while it was strikebound." A total of 33,095 passengers were carried trans-Atlantic and 1,988 on cruises.

The year 1966 would prove to be remarkable for the *United States.* There would be some labor problems, but the liner would make all her scheduled voyages and carry more passengers than any other ship on the Atlantic. It would be one of the best years of her life. One reason for the return to better days was the lively publication *Sales News,* which was reaching and being read by many travel agents. A typical article debunked the myth of ship dress. It began:

"Come sail as you are. Dress aboard the *United States* regardless of Class, is just as uncomplicated as dress at home; the sports, social, and business apparel normally worn is basically perfect for shipboard life. Beyond that it's purely a matter of taste. There is a misconception, perhaps a by-product of posh ship advertising, that packing a wardrobe for a sea trip is a mysterious problem familiar only to the 'in' traveler. Not so! Actually, part of the special thrill of preparing to sail aboard the *United States is* the fun of planning and putting together a travel wardrobe." The article spelled out a few don' ts and a few musts such as no shorts in the dining saloons and formal dress on two evenings in First Class.

It concluded: "There is a unique party atmosphere aboard ship and in such a glamorous setting the average person seems to revel in the luxury of 'dressing up' a bit more than usual."

After two January round trips to Europe, the *United States* made a 12-day "Mid-Winter Cruise" to the Caribbean. The *France,* whose sailings were still coordinated with the *United States,* made no trans-Atlantic trips until April 14, being employed early in 1966 making three Caribbean cruises and one to the Mediterranean.

The bulk of the crew members of the *United States* belonged to the NMU and frequent meetings were held aboard ship to discuss "gripes." The union's newspaper often carried reports of these meetings. One that was held on March 17 was typical: "The ship's chairman led a discussion on the duties of the messmen and the fact that they have to make Fire and Boat drills in Germany which gives them very little time to set up the mess halls for meals. It was requested that because of this they be excused from Fire and Boat Drill. The crew requested that the union negotiate a substantial pay raise when the contract is reopened. A motion was passed that the Customs in New York be contacted and a complaint be made about the poor handling of the crew on arrival day. There were not enough inspectors on hand which caused delays for the members. Adequate space could be furnished on the ship and the inspectors could begin processing earlier if they are short of help. Brothers McFadden and Taylor were elected steward delegates."

The NMU was beginning to be aware of the dangers ahead for crews employed on American passenger ships. The Alcoa Steamship Company had sold its three little liners in 1960. The United Fruit Company had given up its large liner business. There were fewer and fewer liners flying the American flag. A photo in *The Pilot* for April, 1966, showed the four largest American liners together: the *United States*, *America*, *Independence*, and *Constitution.* Its caption read: "Happier days. Back in 1956, acres of American-flag passenger ships, nudged each other at their docks in the port of New York. ... Today the *America is* under Panamanian flag; the fight is on to save the others."

The Duke and Duchess of Windsor were among the passengers arriving March 21 for their annual trip. Another personal letter to William Francis Gibbs written at sea March 28 was interesting. "Day before yesterday with the wind and sea slightly off the port bow, I expected to see some green water over the bow, but we knifed through beautifully. I'm sure we could not have done 30 knots in any of our carriers without water on the flight deck and probably structural damage. But then that's what you have been saying for some time." The letter was written by Rear Admiral E.R. Eastwold.

One of the most colorful accounts of life on the *United States* was written by Denny B. Beattie, a passenger on the April 8 cruise to Jamaica, St. Thomas, and Bermuda. Some of his comments follow: "The *United States* was a contradiction. On the one hand, she was the world's most sophisticated expression of marine architecture and engineering. On the other, her lifestyle was closer in time to the Twenties and Thirties than to the Fifties and Sixties. Despite the technological advances secreted within her engineering spaces, the 'Big U' carried forward the legendary passenger services of the North Atlantic's age of magnificence. In First Class not dressing for dinner on nights when the *United States* was at sea was unthinkable. From cocktail time on, young stewards manned the elevators and snapped open the glass doors as diners approached the liner's red-white-and-gold dining room. Low rose-shaded lamps cast a soft glow over white linen, china, silver, and crystal. And from the musicians' gallery, the orchestra filled the room with the strains of Strauss, Lehar, and Friml. Passengers preferring more privacy when dining found it in the intimate Grill on the Promenade Deck. Service on board the 'Big U' was in the traditional mold, as well, contradicting the popular belief that service on U.S. flag passenger ships was, at best, tolerable. Whether in your cabin, the public rooms or on deck, service was polished, polite and prompt ... provided by disciplined professionals who were obviously proud of their ship. And showed it in their dress, manners, and eagerness to fulfill your requests."

The drydocking for winter overhaul was advanced from November to December and announcement of the schedule change was made in early May, 1966. Joan Crawford and many other famous names were on the passenger lists in the Spring, but the story that got the most publicity was about a 21-inch silver oar carried aboard the *United States* when she sailed May 20. The oar was valued at $25,000 and was to be a part of an exhibition of Admiralty Silver Oar Maces at the National Maritime Museum in Greenwich, England. It was loaned by the U.S. District Court for the Southern District of New York, out of whose "museum" of court case exhibitions and other trophies it was taken. The oar had been made around 1725 by Charles Le Roux, a noted Colonial silversmith.

The June 28th arrival was notable as the completion of the most successful round trip to Europe since the ship began service in 1952. More passengers were carried than on any previous voyage. The 'Big Ship' took 1,789 over and returned with 1,784, a total of 3,573, topping her previous record made in late 1958 when she carried 3,513 on one round trip. The press release announcing this new record added: "The *United States* has an actual capacity of 1,930 passengers, but many sofa beds must necessarily go unused in First Class staterooms occupied by couples." (Every time the "real" passenger total was mentioned somewhere it was different.) It was undoubtedly a three-crossing record, for the liner sailed again June 30 with 1,750 passengers.

The Commodore's flag and rank were officially presented on the bridge of the *United States* to Captain Leroy J. Alexanderson on July 29, 1966. The U.S. Lines president William B. Rand made the presentation. The flag was a blue eagle superimposed on a white field with a deep red border. It had originally been the old American Line houseflag. It was to be flown when the superliner entered or left port and while the Commodore was aboard at the pier. A few days later the company's 1967 sailing schedule was announced. There would be 18 North Atlantic voyages and four cruises. The swing to cruises was taking place. Another new passenger record was set on the return crossing arriving at New York August 11. The ship brought in 1,844 passengers. A British seamens' strike helped, and, for a change, the American superliner received passengers who had booked on British ships.

And then another strike! The *United States* was due to sail at noon on Friday, August 26, but a dispute with the Masters, Mates and Pilots held up her departure. Her passengers were already aboard and they were entertained royally while company officials tried to iron out the difficulties. The afternoon went by, and the evening, and still the deck officers would not permit the ship to sail. Finally, at 2 a.m. things were settled and she got underway, with the terms of the agreement not announced. She was 14 hours behind schedule, but a very large homeward-bound list awaited in Southampton and Le Havre and so Commodore Alexanderson was told to let her out. She made the crossing in 3 days, 17 hours and 11 minutes, her second fastest eastbound trip ever, averaging 33.06 knots. On one day during the passage she averaged 33.63 knots, almost 40 miles an hour. She reached Le Havre only five hours behind schedule and was able to sail for home back on her original schedule. A U.S. Lines press release hailed the "amazing record" as "one that no other ship could attain."

Heinz Arntz, holder of the world endurance record for sustained piano playing, played his way across the Atlantic on the crossing that reached New York on September 21, 1966. His own mark was 1,003 hours and he was going to a fair on Long Island to play through the exhibit's 10-day duration. On the ship he played daily in various public rooms. The 66-year old pianist was in his 34th day of the marathon (816 hours) playing when the ship docked. After a brief interruption to go through Customs, he and his piano were put aboard a baggage vehicle and, still playing, he was wheeled to an elevator, taken to the lower level and placed on a truck to go to the fair. He succeeded in breaking the record, performing for 1,054 consecutive hours, returning home aboard the *United States* on her October 22 sailing for Bremerhaven.

The U.S. Lines put out late in 1966 an attractive little flyer, reading time two minutes, aimed at proving to the businessman that crossing on the *United States* was "good business." It pointed out how important a brief period of relaxation was to the executive, how after such relaxation he would be at a peak of efficiency, how the on-time arrival record of the *United States* was unsurpassed and how bad "time-zone fatigue" was for the businessman. It quoted a survey that showed air travelers going from one to another time zone to be "below normal efficiency for two or more days after their experience." It agreed that a businessman must travel quickly, "but not at the price of sharply diminished capabilities."

Hermann Mueller, Chief Steward of the *United States* since her first crossing, retired after the voyage ending November 4, 1966. His career had spanned 43 years. On the "big ship" alone he had served over 900,000 passengers. He was known by his first name to such luminaries as Margaret Truman, the Duke and Duchess of Windsor, Haile Selassie, Queen Frederika, and former presidents Kennedy and Eisenhower. Well loved by fellow crew members he retired to a farm in Copley, Pennsylvania Dutch country.

The five-day Thanksgiving Day cruise to Nassau was notable because the ship never got to Nassau. Commodore Alexanderson was advised by radio that weather conditions were so poor that tender service to shore would be unsafe. The ship headed back for Bermuda, where because of her speed capacity she arrived in time to permit an afternoon and full evening of sightseeing. Aboard were Mr. and Mrs. Michael Shindler. Michael had sailed as a lad with his parents early in the ship's career and had developed a passion for the liner that would endure for many years. Other cruise ships which lacked the speed of the *United States* could not make the alternate visit to Bermuda and had to return to New York with disgruntled passengers.

When the liner returned from this cruise she was sent to Newport News for routine repairs. The gold leaf decorations in several lounges and foyers were retouched and the First Class Theatre and Cabin Class Dining Saloon received a new coat of paint.

Andrew B. Malmsea, from Landskrona, Sweden, was named Chief Steward. At sea for 45 years, he had jumped ship in New Orleans in 1921 and became a naturalized United States citizen in 1937. When the *United States* was about ready to enter service he had been put in charge of the training school for stewards at Sheepshead Bay and had sailed with her as Assistant Chief Steward. It was a natural promotion for him to the top steward's spot.

Returning to New York the superliner sailed December 22 for her 11-day Christmas-New Year's Cruise. The minimum fare was $425 and the cruise saw stops made at St. Thomas, Curacao, Cristobal, and Nassau. The four cruises for 1967 were widely advertised and, happily, all would actually take place. Passenger business in 1966 had been excellent, with 52,109 carried trans-Atlantic and 4,043 on cruises. Compared to the 35,083 passengers carried in 1965 this was a remarkable comeback, and it was made even more significant in that the company was able to state that the *United States* had carried more passengers than any other liner on the Atlantic.

Promotional Advertisements.
(Courtesy of Bill McBride with McBride Publishing)

12

The End

The *United States* had just three years left, 1967, 1968 and 1969, although those who served aboard her had no way of knowing this. She was still America's greatest ship and was maintained in the finest condition. The traditions of care and superior upkeep instilled in everyone who came in contact with her by William Francis Gibbs were still very much alive and well. Despite all the labor difficulties the U.S. Lines passenger department continued to apply new and fresh thinking to their sales and promotion efforts. A special booklet about discount fares was put out with a wide variety of inducements to sail on the superliner. Discounts ranged from 5% off for what was called "summer fringe" round trips to 25% off for groups of 25 in the off season. Special "emigrant fares" were offered with 10% off for any time except the peak season from Europe. The folder pictured three typical minimum staterooms in the three different classes. The copy was enticing:

"The ocean seems smaller and the vacation 'is' longer aboard the *United States*. Live like royalty for several luxurious sun-and-fun filled days and nights at sea aboard the superliner. Delectable meals prepared to your taste, spacious staterooms, all kinds of choose-your-own entertainment; movies, games, professional shows, deck sports, all included in the cost of your ticket. A huge city afloat ... 5 city blocks long."

The 1967 sailing schedule included a new qualification, undoubtedly provoked by the perpetual labor difficulties endured by passengers and company. The information provided was "subject to change, individual cancellation, or postponement without notice. The dates of arrival shown, while fully anticipated, cannot be guaranteed." It had to be spelled out, a sad commentary on the disjointed situation.

A run down of the principal officers aboard as the year 1967 began showed Commodore Alexanderson as master, with Captain Richard W. Ridington as his Executive Officer. Bill Kaiser was Chief and John M. Logue was Executive Engineer. The Chief Purser was Edward C. Laflen and his top assistant was David T. FitzGerald. Robert L. Theander was Chief Radio Officer. Dr. Sheedy remained as Chief Surgeon and his deputy was Dr. Arnulf R. VanDyk. The Chief Steward was Gustave Kunze.

The first voyage, sailing on January 4, was all the way to Bremerhaven. A run down of the return crossing with times and distances might be interesting to show here. The liner sailed at noon from the German seaport. She left Weser Light Vessel astern at 2:51 p.m. on January 11. It was 474 nautical miles from there to Nab Tower off Southampton, and she did this reach in 16 hours and 51 minutes at an average speed of 28.13 knots. She passed Nab Tower at precisely 7:42 a.m. on the 12th, spent about five hours in Southampton and sped past the same point outward bound at 3:47 p.m. for Le Havre. It was 75 miles between there and the Le Havre Light Vessel and she did this short distance in 2 hours and 40 minutes, averaging 28.13 knots. After a three hour breather at Le Havre she was off again, passing the French Light Vessel en route to America at 11:57 p.m. With a northwest wind and slight seas she averaged 31.12 knots on the first day out. The next day, despite "very rough seas," she continued her high speed, averaging 31.06 knots and making a most respectable 792 miles. For the next two days the speed continued above 30 knots, but on the final day her average dropped to 24-32 knots. The crossing from France to America took 4 days, 10 hours, and 51 minutes at an average of 29.55 knots.

The year's first cruise took place in February with a capacity list. A goodlooking brochure for this and the three other Caribbean cruises planned for this season was issued in yellow, red, and pink-well illustrated with color photographs. A central picture showed the *United States,* looking serene and magnificent, at anchor in the light blue waters off St. Thomas. Famed British actress Hermione Gingold sailed February 16 on the next trans-Atlantic crossing and the superliner returned with the Duke and Duchess of Windsor in Cabin U-87. Then two short cruises. Commodore John S. Baylis, former Coast Guard Captain of the Port of New York, took both of them, back to back. Then one more trans-Atlantic voyage and a nine-day Caribbean cruise. After that the year's trans-Atlantic service began in earnest. There were fewer military dependents because the major portion of the budget voted to transport them had been used up in 1968. Nor was there a British seamen's strike to help swell

137

passenger lists, but the business was good and the press releases issued for each sailing and arrival continued to read like an international Who's Who.

A major departure in the voyage itinerary was announced in June, 1967, heralding a whole new cruise pattern for the *United States*. It was a 13,500-mile cruise to the Caribbean, South America, Africa, and Europe. Scheduled to start February 3, 1968, it would last one month. The ship would cover 13,540 nautical miles. After a first stop at Curacao, she would sail to Rio de Janeiro, crossing the Equator in the process for the first time. While there her people would visit Brasilia and Sao Paulo. Crossing the South Atlantic the cruise would take the superliner to Dakar in Senegal. Day long visits would follow at Tenerife, Gibraltar, and Lisbon and then the return. A minimum fare of $1,225 for cabins with conveniences and $1,025 for those without was set.

The Vietnam war was at its worst and *The Ocean Press* carried horrible stories of the wasting of American lives. One led off with the fact that American casualties had reached 11,325 and that the 590th American plane had been lost with its two-man crew "listed as missing." The Pentagon proudly boasted in another that 1,900 "Communists were killed in action last week, while 274 Americans died." The body-count mentality was in full fettle.

As the summer went on, another cruise was announced. It was called the "Gala Christmas-New Year's Cruise" and would begin December 22. Of eleven days duration, it would call at Cristobal, Curacao, St. Thomas, and Nassau. A minimum fare of $425 was set for the trip. A number of new folders were issued promoting this trip and the "Three Continent Seafari," as the February 3, 1968, cruise

Festivities on the Promenade Deck celebrating the crossing of the Equator.
(Courtesy of Bill DiBenedetto)

was dubbed. Special emphasis in these brochures was placed on the fact that the *United States* exceeded the 1960 international safety standards for new ships. "Cruise passengers travel 'worry free,'" it was said under the section marked safety information.

"Fifteen years in a ship's life means a vessel had completed three-quarters of her commercial usefulness," wrote Werner Bamberger in the *New York Times* on July 2, 1967. The headline of his story was: "The *United States* Still Young at 15." Its subtitle ran: "Old by Ordinary Standards, Liner Is In Good Condition." The article quoted Chief Kaiser as saying: "She is in better shape now, because we've been taking care of her, and whenever something in her 150,000-horsepower engines or her auxiliaries breaks down, we renew it." He revealed that the liner could make 22.7 knots going astern. Asked whether the ship had been profitable, Kenneth Gautier observed in the same news story: "On an individual accounting basis, not within the over-all financial picture of our shipping operation, she's supported herself over an average year." He added that in the 15 years she had steamed 2,381,572 miles and carried 907,999 passengers. Harry Manning, who had just been named an Admiral in the U.S. Maritime Service, sent the ship his best wishes. "She should have a sistership, or better yet there should be two vessels of her class in service each on the North Atlantic, the Pacific, and on the Mediterranean run. This business of putting it all in airplanes is nonsense."

The *United States* completed her voyage No. 352 on September 5. William Francis Gibbs died the following morning. At noon on September 7 the liner sailed and Commodore Alexanderson was on the port wing of the bridge as she passed 21

West Street. The ship's ensign fluttered at half mast. As the superliner slowly passed the office where Mr. Gibbs had so staunchly watched each arrival and departure, the Commodore raised his arm in salute. He dropped it and the ship's horn bellowed three blasts.

By coincidence the *Queen Frederica*, ex *Malolo*, the first great ship designed from the keel up by Gibbs, sailed from New York on her last departure from that port that same evening. I was aboard an escorting Moran tug with John McFarland, Gibbs & Cox editor. As we reached a point opposite 21 West Street I turned to John and said it was too bad that in all likelihood no one on board the passing liner knew of Mr. Gibbs passing. Barely had the words been uttered than three hoarse bellows came one after the other from the forward stack of the Greek liner. Someone aboard did know and did remember and did salute.

A moment by moment description of how the *United States* was brought into Shipway 10 at the Newport News yard was carried in the November, 1967, *Shipyard Bulletin*. Shipyard tugmaster M.L. Ambrose was in charge, as he had been on each of the 14 other occasions that the same thing had happened. There were 187 keel blocks on which the 990-foot hull would rest. The dock was only 960 feet long and the liner would overhang at both ends. To get her in, the floating entrance gate had to be removed and moored nearby. Careful sightings at the bow and at frame 200 were made as the ship approached her final location to make sure she was properly aligned. It took nearly an hour to get the gate back into the closed position and then pumping was begun until the water had gone down to the ship's 23-foot mark. At this point the pumping was stopped for the next eight and one-half hours while the liner's turbines cooled. At 10:30 p.m. it was resumed and by one the next morning the *United States* was high and dry and ready for work on her hull. Returning to New York after the drydocking she made one more round trip to Bremerhaven and then set out on her 11-day Caribbean cruise to end the year's service.

In the last week of December the firm of Walter Kidde & Co., a huge conglomerate, offered to buy what amounted to a controlling share of U.S. Lines. Kidde was attracted to the steamship company because of its large tax-exempt cash construction reserve. The offer to purchase was made on December 26 and three days later the company announced to its stockholders that the proposal had come "without prior communication with management and we have therefore had less time than we would like to prepare informative material for you." I was one to whom the stockholders' information letter went; having owned several shares of so-called "preferred stock" since 1929. The stock had been bought at $21 a share, but in 1967 was worth about 300 due to various forms of manipulation understood only by those who gained from it. For the record 45,022 passengers were carried trans-Atlantic in 1967 and 4,205 more on cruises.

The year 1968 would be the last full year of operation for the *United States*. Rumors were continuous about her sale and/or lay up. She would turn to cruising more, substituting long trans-Atlantic cruises to Africa and Europe for her previous short Caribbean trips. The year would see the company sold and many changes in top management including a new president once again.

Just how far out of the Administration's eye the *United States* and the merchant marine as a whole had gone was illustrated when President Johnson called upon Americans to curtail travel to Europe as a means of saving dollars. A pathetic comment in the 1967 Annual Report of U.S. Lines noted: "As a U.S. flag carrier we are striving to stimulate 1968 carrying by pointing out that by traveling on the *United States*, virtually all of the dollars received in passenger revenue remain in the United States and help to improve our country's balance of payments." The White House, completely ignoring the needs of the company, was floundering frantically because the bottomless pit of Vietnam was taking so many millions out of normal circulation.

Alexander Purdon, who had replaced Bill Rand as president, made known on January 3 that a second large corporate combine was seeking to buy the company. An offer of $50 a share from a group made up of U.S. Freight Co., Matson Navigation Co., and Waterman Industries Corp. had been received. The Kidde offer had been $47.50 per share. Two weeks later the Kidde offer was increased to $51 per share and was accepted.

After two trans-Atlantic voyages in January, the *United States* set out on February 3 on her longest cruise ever, a month-long trip with 800 passengers aboard. Among them was Mrs. Wendell L. Wilkie, widow of the former Republican nominee for the Presidency. Some cabins were priced as high as $4,425 and the trip would prove a money-maker worthy of special note in the annual report. Two more similar trans-Atlantic cruises were in the planning stages for late 1968 and an even longer one for early 1969.

Another strike of New York longshoremen in March caused inconvenience to departing and arriving passengers all through that month. It was a protest by the ILA of a decision by the Waterfront Commission to open the longshoremen registers to new applicants. Fortunately, no sailings had to be cancelled. What was to prove the ship's next to last Caribbean cruise was made in April, after which the superliner began eight months of steady trans-Atlantic voyages.

Chief Engineer Bill Kaiser retired in May. On the occasion of his last departure he was visited in his cabin by former Commodore Anderson and other old sailing companions: "I know I will miss it, but the time has come. My wife deserves some of my attention; she says she doesn't care if I get drunk every night, she just wants me home in Peter Cooper Village. You can see how it is. We got in here two days ago and here we are off again." Conversation turned to the late William Francis Gibbs, who had called the chief every day the ship was at sea. "I miss the old so-and-so, asking every morning how things were going and how many revolutions are we making," the Chief said. "He would never let me discuss the rate of oil consumption over the air," Chief Kaiser added. "I was reading about the new liner *Queen Elizabeth 2*. She will have two power plants, and they will be very economical. In fact, they are getting close to the rate our four are burning. But they are not up to us yet," he remarked. When his final day of retirement came on May 28, 1968, Chief Kaiser took ashore with him his pet souvenir of the ship, a small block of wood, which he kept handy for "knocking on," in as much as the only other wood on the superliner was in the butcher's blocks and the pianos.

An hour-long TV show was filmed aboard the United States on her July 11 departure, with Merv Griffin as the star. Dockside interviews were conducted and shots of the departure and the passing down the Hudson were made and then the whole crew departed via a Moran tug, waving good-bye to the great liner as she picked up speed and headed for the open seas. I remember noting how well kept-up she looked, how her hull was not dented and bent in here and there as other hulls so often were. It was my last time aboard her at a sailing.

On July 22 I received a letter from L. Porter Moore, Secretary of the New York City National Shrines Association. He described a recent conversation with Chief Kaiser: "I took up with him the practicability of and his possible interest in a hopeful effort to ultimately secure the *SS United States* for use as a historic museum piece along the shoreline of Manhattan. He is certainly most enthusiastic, agreeing that it should not likely be long before that great vessel will be up for sale." We held a number of meetings on the subject.

The August issue of the NMU *Pilot* had a full page of wages for the *United States,* pointing out with pride how much more each rating was receiving than it had been getting under the previous wage scale.

In early August, 1968, Admiral T.H. Moorer, Chief of Naval Operations, lifted the classified status on the secrets of the *United States.* As *New York Times* maritime editor George Horne put it, the word from Washington left most U.S. Lines officials "slightly stunned." They were uncertain just what to announce, but the engine rooms details came out first, The company made known that from then on passengers would be permitted to make tours of the engine rooms. The Horne article began: "A Brass curtain that high-Navy officials secured 16 years ago to hide design secrets of the superliner *United States* was quietly rolled back yesterday." He then proceeded to state, without any particular attribution, that the ship "could make 42 knots, or better than 48 land-miles an hour." The ship's 240,000 horsepower was also revealed in his story. In a few days the company released photos of the 200-foot side bilge keels, the four and five-bladed propellers, the underwater bow and stern, and the engine rooms. It was a field day for the maritime magazines. Most of the stories mentioned the 42-knot top speed having picked it up without attribution from the *Times* piece.

A follow-up story published in the *Times* again made the 42-knot statement and quoted "an earlier announcement." The whole world accepted these statements and the 42-knot speed was repeated in other places and even in books about the sea. It would come as quite a shock ten years later when John Kane's technical paper on the speed and power of the superliner, mentioned earlier, disclosed that her best speed had been 38.32 knots.

Nicholas Bachko, U.S. Lines executive, contributed two anecdotes about the early life of the *United States* for the second *Times* story. On an early voyage he was summoned to the stateroom of a top company executive who had heard a disturbing sound. "Sit over there. Hear that," the official said. "I hear some coat hangers rattling in the next cabin," Mr. Bachko said. "No. This is something coming apart," the concerned executive said. Together they went into the next cabin and took the hangers out of the closet. The noise stopped. One night during a gala party on the same trip a water leak was discovered in a Tourist public room. Mr. Bachko was called from dinner. He and some others got a ladder, removed some ceiling panels and crawled into the space above to fix the situation. The Tourist passengers stood around, marveling that the plumbers on their ship wore tuxedos and black tie!

The *Marine Engineering* in its story entitled: "Now It Can Be Told," pointed out that in the past 15 years the superliner had only used six out of her eight boilers and even those had been run at only 60% of capacity on the average. Of course, it was noted, the boilers were rotated. The article went into great detail about the four-bladed propellers on the forward shafts and the fivebladed screws on the after shafts. The piece concluded that if the ship were to be refitted "It is not likely that any of her machinery would be changed." The only updating that might be done would be in plant automation, more modern combustion controls, wider-range burners, and feedback between the turbines and boiler outlets. The technical journal concluded that there were rumors that U.S. Lines was "in hopes of selling the vessel."

Long cruises were the coming thing and the winter 1968-1969 would have four such trans-Atlantic cruise voyages scheduled for the *United States,* a substantial departure from the short Caribbean trips she had been making. The longest of these would take 39 days and would cover 19,000 miles, calling at ten ports in three continents. It was announced in late August, 1968. Called the "Great Adventure Cruise" it would see the superliner going into seas she had never sailed before. After calls at Curacao and Rio the liner would cross the South Atlantic to Cape Town and Port Elizabeth. Then up the western coast of Africa to Luanda, capital of Angola, and to Dakar. Calls at Tenerife, Gibraltar, Lisbon, and Funchal would be made and then home to New York. The company was breaking fresh ground with all these long cruises, and they were to prove highly successful.

Another pioneering cruise was announced on October 3, 1968. It would visit Gibraltar, Cannes, Palma, Madeira, and Bermuda. Scheduled to leave New York on March 28, 1969, the 15 1/2 day trip was dubbed the "Easter Cruise."

John J. McMullen was elected President of U.S. Lines and on October 17 he announced that the company had operated on a profitable basis for the third quarter of the year after having lost $12,450,000 during the first two quarters.

The November cruise to Bermuda, Lisbon, Madeira, Tenerife, Dakar, and St. Thomas was one of the most successful in the ship's career. She carried 895 passengers. Returning to New York on November 25, she immediately set sail for Newport News for what the company described as "the biggest refurbishing, repairing, and rejuvenating job in the American Merchant Marine." The 20-day overhaul was designed "to maintain the tip-top mechanical perfection and luxury of the largest ship under the American flag and prepare her for another year of trans-Atlantic voyages and special, warm-water cruises." The job was done on schedule and the famous liner left the yard on December 17 for New York. Three days later she embarked 1,000 cruise passengers for her 16-day "Christmas-New Year's Cruise" to St. Thomas, Dakar, Funchal, and Tenerife. The long cruise concept was paying off, and everyone hoped that somehow it would prolong the ship's life.

The last year for the *United States* began with a strike, symbolic of the labor difficulties that had dogged her career. The strike had actually begun on October 1, 1968. It was another longshore strike and it went through the 80-day Taft-Hartley cooling off period. On December 20 it flared up again with picket lines around all New York piers. The *United States* was on her Christmas-New Year's cruise. Realizing how disastrous the longshore picket lines would be for their own jobs on the superliner, the NMU appealed to the longshore union to permit the big liner to sail on her January 7 trans-Atlantic crossing. But, just as the NMU had refused to compromise when the shoe was on the other foot, so the ILA would not relent in this case. "We couldn't do it. The next thing we would be asked to release freighter cargo that is perishable, and our strike would be broken." So spoke John Bowers, Executive Vice President of the longshore union. A dramatic last minute plea to the ILA was made by William Perry, special assistant to NMU President Curran. He asked the ILA to consider the 650 NMU jobs aboard the superliner, but Bowers was adamant. The NMU was in a tough spot, with a dissident group fighting the age-old Curran domination. When all efforts had obviously failed the voyage was cancelled. A U.S. Lines announcement to this effect noted that it was "impossible to expect that the stores, supplies, mail etc. could be transported through picket lines to the ship." The cancellation was made "with great reluctance because the offshore unions had indicated they would operate the ship and the Company had been prepared to use its office personnel to handle the functions normally carried out by the longshoremen." The company added that it "fully expects that the *United States* will sail on its 39-day Great Adventure Cruise on January 23. A number of passengers, on this, the longest and most glamorous cruise ever attempted by the superliner, had already cancelled their bookings because of the uncertain situation.

As the strike continued, all but a skeleton crew were dismissed and the liner lay idle at her pier. Talks with the ILA continued, and on Monday, January 6, the U.S. Lines announced an agreement that would permit the long cruise. The next day Anthony Scotto, leader of the ILA Brooklyn unit, cast doubts on the exemption from picket action. At issue was whether all the stores needed for the 39-day voyage could physically be loaded without help from the longshoremen. But the U.S. Lines was desperate. It had already lost $1,000,000 on the cancellation of the January 6 round trip to Bremerhaven. To have to call off the "Great Adventure" cruise would have been catastrophic.

The cruise took place, although only 750 passengers were aboard. Longshoremen looked the other way while 50 department supervisors spent a whole week putting aboard such stores as 230,000 pieces of fresh linen, five tons of sugar, 12,000 dozen eggs, 28,000 quarts of milk, 1,000 pounds of caviar, and 35 tons of filet mignon, prime ribs of beef, and steak. The strike continued with mounting economic losses and 408 immobilized American cargo ships from Maine to Texas representing only the visible evidences of the work stoppage. "You cannot see what's happening to our industry, but we are facing a disaster, 11 a trucking operator said. Admiral John M. Will, president of the New York Shipping Association, appealed to Washington for help. He noted that the employer group had reached an agreement with the ILA only 10 days before but that the longshoremen refused to call for a ratification vote until all ports had worked out settlements. Foreign liners were coming and going with no interruption.

When the *United States* returned from her African cruise the longshoremen were back to work. Her long battle with labor was over. She would have seven months of relative peace to last out her active career, but the damage had been done. The new management had made up their minds to lay the superliner up as soon as they could. There would be one last ditch effort to get more help from the government, but the end was clearly in sight.

Nevertheless the same bright cruise announcements and colorful folders were being issued. The art work on the literature about the Early Spring Cruise to the Caribbean was fresh and appealing. The liner sailed March 5. Rates for the seven-day trip began at $235. "Trade in the bleakness of winter for seven golden days of Caribbean cruising," the folders urged. Equally attractive brochures proclaimed the March 28 Easter Cruise. A white bunny rabbit, with a garland of green, pink, and red posies around his head, held up a round shield on which was a fine colored photo of the *United States*. "On our gala Easter Cruise, you'll be whisked off on a magical Mediterranean holiday, visiting Funchal on picturesque Madeira, the seaport of Palma, on the island of Majorca, glamorous Cannes – jewel of the French Riviera and Gibraltar. ... then homeward bound we'll stop off at the British Crown Colony of Bermuda. ... Make your reservations now for more than two marvelous weeks at sea enjoy the superb services of our courteous, well-trained staff, savor the culinary creations of our world-famous chefs, play, dance, unwind, relax!"

As its final effort to keep the *United States* going, the U.S. Lines on June 10 asked an additional subsidy grant from the government. In a letter to the Maritime Administration the company hinted that if the "contervailing subsidy" was not forthcoming it might have to take the liner out of service. "As you know continued operation of passenger ships, and of the *United States* in particular, is a matter of deep concern to government; to responsible labor unions and to the owners. The planning of all concerned is dependent upon a solution to the passenger ship problem," the letter said. The communication noted the direct competition of the France, which it added was heavily subsidized by the French government. It asked for additional Federal aid "in sufficient amount to make our North Atlantic passenger trade a viable operation."

The *United States,* at this point was the last American-flag ship on the Atlantic, since the *Constitution* and the *Independence* had been laid up the year before. Moore-McCormack Lines was seen on the verge of laying up their even newer pair, the *Argentina* and the *Brasil,* and the word was the Grace Line's two largest ships would also be idled soon. To reenforce their plea for more subsidy the U.S. Lines put out a six page study of the economic impact of the superliner. Each voyage 200 blankets, 300 deck robes, 150 bed spreads, and uniforms for 35 bellboys were sent ashore for dry cleaning. Of the 3,700 pieces of portable furniture aboard, an average of 125 were cleaned and 25 re-upholstered each voyage. The ship cost well over $20,000,000 a year to operate, of which $7,500,000 was paid to the crew, "virtually all of whom live and wield their purchasing power in New York metropolitan area." Each of the ship's arrivals and departures required the hiring of a staff of 400 porters and 500 longshoremen.

Three new and appealing cruises were announced in mid 1969. The first, to Bermuda, Lisbon, Madeira, Tenerife, Dakar, St. Thomas, and Nassau was scheduled for November 9. It would last 21 days. The second would depart December 19 and last 16 days. It would visit Madeira, Tenerife, Dakar, and St. Thomas. The third, more elaborate and ambitious than anything ever attempted, was called the "Grand Pacific Cruise" and would take 55 days. The ground work to make this two-month trip possible had taken a year and involved the work of several hundred people. It would see the *United States* pass through the Panama Canal for the first time. The minimum rate with facilities would be $2,350 and there were high hopes in the passenger department for the success of the epoch-making cruise. None of these three glamorous voyages would take place, although many passengers would hopefully sign up for them.

The new subsidy was not forthcoming. The ship's days were numbered. Her last nine trips were all trans-Atlantic. There were two in July, three in August, two in September, and two in October. The well established routine was maintained. Beautiful menus were printed for each meal, glistening red, white, and blue passenger lists were issued, the daily newspaper continued as if nothing was about to happen. On September 4 the Maritime Administration, doing too little too late, agreed to a moratorium on amortization payments required by U.S. Lines. This meant a saving of $850,000 a year for the next nine years if the ship were kept in service. The operating subsidy was due to come up for renewal at the end of 1969 and there was some question whether the government could justify continuing it. just as those Frenchmen who opposed the subsidy paid to the *France* would say some years later, the subsidy paid to U.S. Lines for the *United States* was in effect a subsidy of some $400 per passenger ticket sold. Or as the company liked to point out, the operating subsidy was in reality a subsidy paid to American labor. There were those who proposed that all American passenger ships should be put under one management to save overhead costs, but company rivalry and battles for a most favored position killed the idea. The NMU, now really worried, said that a conference on alternative ideas should be held in Washington. The Union strongly supported the idea of one company running all the liners. "It would not only save money, but it would remove the sword, the threat hanging over the heads of industry and of the seamen on the ships, who do not know what their future is," one union spokesman said.

Although it was much too late, both the NMU and the MEBA had gone on record as stating they would sit down with management to consider eliminating some jobs. The NMU stated point blank: "We have agreed to a fluctuating manning scale to meet the rise and fall of passenger volume. But we cannot cut so far as to affect the health and safety, and the seamen cannot be expected to carry the ship on their backs."

A six-column story under the byline of George Horne appeared in the *New York Times* for September 21, 1969. The headline went: "LINER *UNITED STATES* IS BEAUTIFUL, FAST, POWERFUL, AND BROKE." The subhead: "Pride of Fleet Is Threatened by Finances." The story explained that the ship was losing money "on an Olympian scale." Despite a government subsidy of $12,000,000 a year, the story said that the ship was in the red to the tune of $4,800,000 each year.

"On every voyage, through the long corridors and in the air-conditioned crew quarters, the scuttlebutt is that she is about to be laid up. Seamen ask: Will she come back after her annual drydocking in November? Will she make the long cruise through the Panama Canal and to the Pacific, scheduled for January? It is the big unknown in the nation's hard-pressed merchant marine."

John J. McMullen said: "I am as much a romantic as the next fellow, as an admirer of a truly great ship. But I am also a practical shipping man."

Andrew E. Gibson, head of the Maritime Administration, stated: "The *United States* must be considered one of the finest vessels ever built in this or any other country. She is a symbol, and how do you lay up a national symbol?"

On October 23 it became known that the November 9 cruise was cancelled and rumors of imminent layup were on every tongue. There was no official announcement from the company, but instead the U.S. Lines notified travel agents not to book for the cruise. The word quickly got around. The Christmas voyage of 16 days and the 55-day Pacific cruise were still being promoted and many passengers were booked.

By this time the *Brasil* and *Argentina* had joined the *Independence* and the *Constitution* in lay-up and industry and labor leaders were frantic. Appeals from many different sources were sent to the White House and to Congress to keep the *United States* sailing as a matter of national prestige. A two-column story dated October 24 appeared in *Time*. It compared the fate of the superliner to that of the USS *Constitution* which was saved in 1830 from the wreckers by the famous Oliver Wendell Holmes poem which began: "Ay, tear her tattered ensign down!" The report went on: "Poetry may have been enough to save a ship from the scrap heap then, but in an age more closely attuned to the demands of economics the sight of the Stars and Stripes fluttering from the flagstaff of a liner appears to be a luxury that is excessively costly to support." A photo of the *United States* carried with the story had the ominous caption: "Voyage to Oblivion?"

With the November 9 cruise cancelled it became obvious that the October 25 departure from Bremerhaven would be the ship's last voyage. An ancedote about this sailing from one of the thousands for whom the *United States* was a passion can help to illustrate the force of realization that the end was near for "the Big Ship." As a boy of 12, Howard W. Serig, Jr., had fallen in love with the superliner when the father of a school classmate, Captain Archie Horka, master of the *American Scout,* had arranged for the entire school to visit the ship. Fifteen years later when he was living in Baltimore he heard that the October 25 sailing would be the last. Let him tell it in his words:

"I decided to get up early and drive to New York to photograph this ship which I had taken for granted for so long. I'd have to drive faster than normal to arrive before the noon departure. Outside of Harrisburg, mostly for company, I picked up a hitchhiker who was going to New York – 'The Village' he said. He was appropriately dressed – complete with bedroll and knapsack. Faster and faster I drove until the outline of New York appeared ahead. We zoomed up the Pulaski Skyway past the blinking construction signs which warn of a 35 MPH speed limit. I was going 75 when I heard the sirens and looked into the mirror, which had suddenly become alive with flashing red lights. Last sailing or not there was but one thing to do and as I slowed down my hitchhiker companion abruptly confided that his knapsack contained a sizeable amount of marijuana. Before I could assimilate this or protest he had stuffed a bundle under the front seat. God! The car came to a stop and I heard a door slam behind me. A loud voice commanded us to get out with our hands up.

"I looked around. Two police officers, guns drawn, motioned us over to the bridge railing where, spread eagle, one began to search us. I tried to explain about why I had been speeding – 'the last run of the *United*

States; the most beautiful ship in the world.' He yelled in my ear that we would go to jail. My mind went numb. I was trying to figure out how I would get an attorney when the police radio nearest us began squelching and squawking orders. For a moment all stopped. A hasty discussion ensued between the two officers and suddenly one of the patrol cars sped away. My companion and I cautiously looked around. The other officer was talking on his radio. A few words became intelligible: 'bank robbery suspects' ... 'red '69 Mustang' ... 'now proceeding north on such-and-such an avenue.' 'Ten four,' the officer snapped into the mike and squealed away, siren wailing. The flashing red lights disappeared toward Jersey City and we were alone over the meadows. My long-haired friend and I walked back to my red '69 Mustang with the dope under the front seat. 'Come on,' I said, 'let's get the hell out of here.' There was still time to make Pier 86 – if I hurried."

The final voyage was No. 400. The eastbound crossing to Le Havre was made in 4 days, 8 hours and 6 minutes at an average speed of 30.79 knots. The return took 4 days, 10 hours, and 51 minutes at an average of 29.64 knots. The liner passed Ambrose Light Ship at 4:48 a.m. on November 7. Commodore L.J. Alexanderson rang "Finished With Engines" for the last time.

A final editorial salute in the *New York Times* appeared November 16, 1969: "Goodbye to the 'Big U'" was its title. It called the ending of trans-Atlantic service by the *United States* "a tombstone for the once proud fleet of American-flag passenger ships." A recent decision by the trans-Atlantic airlines to sharply reduce round-trip fares making it possible for travelers to go back and forth at less than half the cost of sea passage was blamed as the "immediate cause of the lay up." The editorial concluded: "But the doom of the *United States* had been sealed long ago. Its operating costs were too high and too frozen by the rigidities of union contract to enable it to compete on the high seas, even with the sizable subsidies it got. The sun has set for glamour on the sea lanes."

The Atlantic was left to the *QE2* and the *France*, both of which were doing very well. The new British superliner was slightly ahead from the load factor standpoint. She had carried 84.2% of capacity in First Class, 82.2% in Tourist compared with the *France's* 84.5% in First Class and 74.3% in Tourist. Despite the New York dock strike and the *QE2*s teething troubles, Cunard was expecting to earn more than $4,800,000 profit from her first year of operation.

Reaction to the ending of the *United States*' career was loud and widespread. John Bowers, president of the ILA local whose strikes had so hampered her, was vehement in his denunciation of the government for permitting the layup. It is a "disgrace" he charged in the December, 1969, issue of *The Longshore News,* his local's publication.

Commodore Alexanderson took his beautiful ship to the Newport News shipyard and then sat down to write a letter to the high school class which had "adopted" her as a social studies project. His letter began: "Dear Children: It is with heavy heart and deep regret that I must inform you that the Management of U.S. Lines has issued orders to deactivate your adopted ship. We cannot tell you at this time whether this will be a temporary or permanent lay-up of this great ship. Most of our crew have been dismissed and almost all will be gone by November 21. A few of us will compose the standby crew. Needless to say this is a very sad and uncertain time for all of the crew and officers of this famous ship and we hope and pray that we will be sailing again before too many weeks pass." The eternal optimist, he was writing to the sixth grade class in Ocean City, Md.

The deactivation was a lengthy thing. Much of the ship's food was taken off and carried to the cargo ship *American Legion,* which happened to be docked nearby. Commodore Alexanderson talked to Reporter Barbara Spector of the *Newark News.* He told her that the ship had already been stripped of her sophisticated Omega navigator and other accessories. He gave her some marvelous quotes: "She's a big beauty. The last of the floating Waldorf-Astorias. I was looking forward to the world cruise. It would have been the first time through the Panama Canal. It's a tight squeeze, but it would have been nice doing it." He said he had not known of the lay-up order until after he had reached the shipyard. The news came via a telephone call to the ship at the yard, just a few hours before it was released to the rest of the world. "There had been rumors, but none of us on the ship believed them. We always felt there was hope. I'm a born optimist. I think we'll return to the seas someday. How did I feel? Well, my wife, Dorothea, broke down. I didn't feel so good myself.

The ship had logged 2,772,840 miles. In her 17 years of service she had carried 1,002,936 passengers across the Atlantic and 22,755 on cruises. Many of the passengers were frequent repeaters.

Chief Steward William McCrann on his last day aboard wandered the miles of wide corridors checking the staterooms which had been stripped and left with their mattresses turned up and chairs piled on one another. He showed Ms. Spector a three-room suite that had been occupied only the past summer by Mrs. Eisenhower. She had one bedroom herself and her maid and butler the others. The walls of the suite were decorated with ivory shell figurines and painted in soft pastels. He showed her the First Class Ballroom, whose dance floor was covered with paper. "We planned to have this room redonepainted and re-upholstery. I intended to have this ship spick and span after the overhauling and now it will be left as is. I hope it won't become a junkhouse. It was never known for that." The deathlike silence aboard was shattering.

Dr. Sheedy talked about the nine children born aboard the ship and the thousands of patients he had treated. "It was like being a doctor in a city when you think of having more than a million people here." With Dr. Sheedy was Miss Helen Brougham, chief nurse. She was packing the belongings of the three other nurses. "We usually leave our things on board during an annual overhaul. Then they called and said there would be no more trips, so I'm getting their stuff together." Miss Brougham was making a "care package" of medications for colds and the like. The Commodore and a few crew members would stay aboard until further notice.

"There is some contempt felt for the crew whose work rules and pay demands were said to have made operating the ship unprofitable." the reporter wrote. "The rules might mean that with overtime obligations a passenger ordering a hamburger at 3 a.m. might cost the company more than $30 because of the rule which says a minimum of four hours of overtime must be guaranteed. A waiter carrying a drink from bar to deck might get an extra $10 for walking a few feet out of his jurisdiction."

The laying up of the *United States* and the other New York based American liners meant a loss of $25,000,000 a year in supplies and services to the City of New York, Mayor John Lindsay said in a letter to the White House. He wrote that the 6,000 crewmen who were idled lost a total of $37,500,000 a year in salaries. He asked that the President bend every effort to see that the ships were returned to service.

Joseph Curran, speaking for the union which was hit the hardest by all the layups, told his members that in order to get the ships to return to service "we are going to have to make some sacrifices." He was much too late.

As the year ended, the crew of the *United States* was reduced to two men: Staff Captain John S. Tucker and Chief Engineer John Logue. There was heat and electricity aboard the liner, but no water, and so both men had to live ashore. They came to work each day at 8 a.m., carrying a sandwich and bottle of drinking water. Among other chores they had to replace as many as 50 light bulbs each day. "I get stuck with reaching up there and changing them all the time," said six-foot tall Tucker, grinning. "All he does is carry his shopping basket and hand them up to me," he added, referring to Logue who was five feet, 3 inches tall. The ship's air-conditioning system was still working, tied to a power source on shore. It was important as a means of keeping the ship free of dust. When moisture and dust combine, Captain Tucker noted, they develop corrosive acids that damage the paint, woodwork, and metal surfaces. This must be prevented, he added.

Although there were only two of them, the spirit of William Francis Gibbs was still there within them both. Captain Tucker and Chief Logue loved their charge.

From 1970 to this writing the *United States* has been idle. Her decade of layup is worth a book in itself, but the story of the countless plans for her reactivation will not be described here, except to say that they run the gamut from insane and even humorous to serious and quite possible. I visited her three times and was impressed more with her remarkably good condition than with the numerous specific illustrations of neglect. Compared to any other ship idled so long she was in superb condition in mid-1980 when this was written, a tribute to the Maritime Administration under whose care she had been for the previous half decade.

The most promising effort to bring the *United States* back into commercial service to date was initiated in early 1979. Richard Hadley, of Seattle, created a company called United States Cruises, Inc., to restore and operate the superliner. A special bill was introduced in the Senate to permit her to operate between the West Coast and Hawaii. It was passed. Offices were opened and brochures published. The great liner was given a bottom survey and inspection in May, 1980, and found to be in excellent condition. At this writing, funds are being raised to complete an extensive reconstruction of the liner. The cost of the rebuilding would far exceed the original cost of the ship. While United States Cruises was working very hard to acquire and rebuild the great liner, another proposal also made news. It was to rebuild her to serve as a hospital ship. She would be used to support the new Rapid Deployment Force. The government has the right to take over the *United States* at any time for national security purposes. We can hope that she will serve again and that her use will be for happy passengers under the American flag.

SS United States *leaving yard "cropped" June 19, 1970. (Courtesy of Robert Hudson Westover)*

13

Adrift: 1982 through 1996
Written by Robert Hudson Westover

Richard Hadley's ownership of the *SS United States*—in historic preservation terms—was disastrous. A vessel handed over to him in near perfect condition was brought up for auction in 1992 a pillaged mess. When Hadley took possession of the *United States*, the ship had been meticulously cared for by the Navy – even newspapers from the last voyage in 1969 were preserved in near first day condition. This would have been a preservationist's dream come true. A more visionary entrepreneur would have recognized the value of the ship in nostalgia alone.

At the time Hadley purchased the *United States*, had the vessel been opened for tours, the revenue alone could have helped offset the cost of the pier fees while a more conscientious business plan was devised, taking in the vessel's historic value. Alas, this was not to be the fate of the great ship. There were none in Hadley's team who were aware of the huge revenue potential in an industry known as Preservation Tourism. This is unfortunate, because Preservation Tourism accounts for $400 billion annually (Preservation Tourism is described as money generated from tourist planning vacations around certain historic sites – i.e. visiting the RMS *Queen Mary*, because it so close to Disneyland or visiting the *SS United States* in Newport News Virginia because it is [was] so close to Williamsburg) and had any of those who worked for Hadley been aware of this potential, what happened later to the ship, would have never happened; because had they, they would have seen how stupid and short-sighted such a plunder of an irreplaceable engineering marvel and architectural masterpiece would be and how such irresponsible stewardship of a national treasure would never be forgotten.

But, they didn't and in October of 1984, the largest auction (in terms of numbers of items) ever held took place dockside of the *United States* in Newport News. Over 12,000 attended the massive auction to purchase something from the fastest ship in the world—over 3000 persons bid for everything from ashtrays to the entire First Class Dinning Room suite!

By day's end, the interior of the *United States*, an interior of such sleek and all custom made design that it helped to usher in what is now known as the mid-twentieth century look, was completely decimated. Anything that wasn't welded into place – and some things that were – was sold.

In the elegant staterooms where once the Mona Lisa was guarded on it way to America; where Elisabeth Taylor, President Truman and Princess Grace slept, now nothing remained. Once dramatic great spaces where Ginger Rogers danced under a gleaming dome and Duke Ellington's orchestra accompanied Judy Garland—now nothing remained. That October, the *United States* took its place in history as one of the great pillaged marvels of antiquity.

For years after "the auction" the *United States* remained in this state – like a forgotten plundered tomb of a Pharaoh – until Hadley's bizarre vision of a timeshare condo collapsed and the ship was once again on the auction block.

The year was 1992 and finally a concerned group of citizens – disgusted by the Hadley debacle – started the first preservation rescue attempt. Headed by Bill DiBenedetto, the *SS United States* Preservation Society (SSUSPS) went to work immediately to save the ship from a now even greater threat than Hadley. The new business consortium wanted not only to have the vessel completely altered in appearance, but to have her converted into a cruise ship design that would emulate the look of a modern wedding cake cruise ship. To make things worse, the only remaining historic integrity of the ship that remained – her architecture and her engine rooms – were to be done away with. And all of this was to take place in Turkey!

The SSUSPS went into full gear. DiBenedetto launched a Congressional initiative to bring legislation to the floor of the House of Representatives. He was initially successful and a bill was drawn up. The rational for the bill—preventing a sale of the ocean liner—was to cite a 1974 law that actually forbade the sale of the *United States* to overseas interests. However, this law was written when much – it not all – of the *United States*' engineering designs remained top secret.

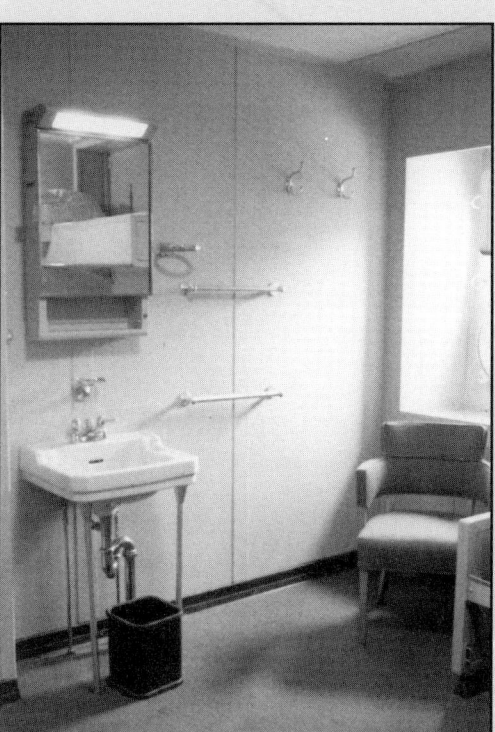

The interior of the United States *as seen in July 1981. (Courtesy of Bill DiBenedetto)*

146

However, during the late 1970s and early 1980s all of the *United States'* top-secret classified materials were declassified. The law therefore was deemed null and void and the bill never made it to the floor of the House of Representatives for a vote. The ship was then sold for $2 million dollars to a business consortium involving the Turkish government (with interest from the President of that nation), Edward A. Cantor and several other smaller interests.

Much fan fair followed the great ship's departure from the home of its construction, Newport News Shipbuilding (an interesting phenomenon which suggests that had any of her owners realized the fascination the ship had locally, that this could be replicated nationally, bringing in millions more in revenue for a longer period of time than just leaving her as is) and her lay-up for over 22 years.

As the two sea-going tugs began to tow her out to sea, something interesting happened. Instead of the two tugs that were thought to be needed, the ship glided so easily in the water, that only one was needed. Again, another testament to the incredible design of this magnificent vessel.

It was in foreign waters that the *United States* was nearly lost forever. The Turkish based business consortium collapsed and four years later the ship returned to American waters. When she did return, though, she was now even more unrecognizable than before. Somewhere along the way, the lifeboats and davits were removed and forever gone. All of the plumbing was removed as well.

All toll, the scrap value must have been in the millions for these lost items. It is a tragic loss because no other ship ever constructed had such unique lifeboats – they were each one made from hand, slender, light looking but very safe. The all aluminum lifeboats alone would have fetched a couple of million dollars on the scrape market.

There have been few straight answers as to why these items were removed. One story is that once the Turkish based consortium lost interest in the original project, dockworkers in Istanbul began striping the vessel. The other is that while in Sevastole, in the Ukraine, to pay for the removal of tons of asbestos, the workers were paid by being allowed to take the lifeboats and plumbing to sell for scrap. Whatever the excuse, the items are missing and will never be returned in their entirety.

In 1996, the *United States* sailed into Philadelphia up the Delaware River. She made headlines because the profile of the ship was so high that she could not make it under the Walt Whitman Bridge! Eventually her radar was taken down and the *United States* was brought to pier 82 where she remains until this day.

Several other ill-conceived ventures have materialized since her lay-up began in Philadelphia. Most were hatched from mind's of greedy "get rich quick" schemers who lathered at the mouth over the thought of claiming a large commission from the sale of the ship. At publication of this book, her asking price is believed to be $18 million. She is now owned by one owner – the surviving member of the Turkish consortium: Cantor Affiliated Interests.

The current owner has expressed no interest whatsoever in having the *SS United States* restored and opened as a museum or in helping in anyway to have the irreplaceable American icon turned into a national monument. Perhaps the owner should learn a lesson from those who have in past been on the wrong side of history.

A skeleton of her former self, the SS United States sits waiting for her future. (Courtesy of J. Fred Rodriguez, Jr.)

14

Save the *United States*
The Story of the SS United States Foundation
Written by Robert Hudson Westover

It was December of 1997 and I, like millions of other Americans, had recently seen James Cameron's *Titanic*. And, like so many others, I was moved by this adaptation of the horrific night of April 15-16 when the mighty ship sank beneath the North Atlantic. But unlike those in my generation – born after the Kennedy assassination – I had studied and been long familiar with the story of *Titanic*. In fact, the first book I ever read was *A Night to Remember* while in the second grade.

One of the reasons *Titanic* was such an enormous success at the box office was due in part to director James Cameron's realization that the real story of that film was the almost mythological Greek like tragedy of the greatest ship built in that era. Had a novelist invented the story, it would have been hard to believe. And, perhaps he realized that the real star of the film was the vessel itself. It is interesting to note that five years after *Titanic* disappeared from the movie screens of the world, the legend of the ship, not the star worship of its human actors, remains stronger than ever. It was this very movie that once again inspired the unsuspecting founder of the SS United States Foundation to launch an organization to save our national flagship – *SS United States*.

I had grown up with an appreciation for great naval ships.

As the son of a second generation sea going Marine, I was never to forget the impressions made by my father as he told his sea stories as a Marine Corporal on board the aircraft carrier *Ticonderoga*.

I was hooked on the legends and drawn into the cult of great ships like so many millions of others. There were the books and ships. National Geographic's *Men, Ships and the Sea*, and a plethora of other books from renowned maritime historians Bill Miller and Frank Braynard.

From the early age of six, I was building models of all types of ships from destroyers to ocean liners. However, of all the models I built the one that stood out most in his mind was the *SS United States*. The 18-inch all plastic model from the Revel Model company was the only one without a hull. Cut off at the waterline, the model of the *United States* revealed no hull because it was a top-secret design, that was not made public until over twenty years after the great ship was launched. That and other "top-secret" facts about the Big U would intrigue me for the rest of my life.

Years went by before I too took the title of United States Marine to carry on the family tradition to the third generation. My grandfather, who had been in the crows nest of the battleship *Tennessee* when it was bombed at Pearl Harbor and my own father (who had never seen combat while in the Corps) were both present at my graduation from boot camp at Marine Corp Recruit Depot San Diego. Ironically, I would never go to sea.

After receiving my honorable discharge from the Marines, I became heavily involved in a media relations career and let my passion for ships fade away and mothballed, as it were, my artifacts and memorabilia. But, *Titanic* brought it all back. I once again began thinking about what had happened to the once great *SS United States*. The last I heard, it had been sold to a business consortium and towed away to Turkey. So, that night after the movie, I went online and began a search. The website that came up was the now world famous ss-united states.com. The site, a personal tribute by Mike Alexander for the ship he loved so much, was many pages in length and had dozens of photographs. Photographs that showed her in her present home, the home that at this writing is where she is still moored: Pier 82 in Philadelphia.

Philadelphia, I thought, is just up the road from Washington D.C. (my home at the time) so I went to see the great lady.

It was the first time I had ever seen the once pride of the American Merchant Fleet, the still undisputed speed champion and unforgettable icon of our maritime prowess. Despite her aging condition, the faded red, white and blue funnels, the near thousand-foot wall of black peeling paint that her once gleaming hull had become, despite the ravages of time, I saw perfection. I saw a perfect masterpiece faded like an old oil painting, but a masterpiece. It was at that point that I heard her. I know it sounds ludicrous, but it was as if she was crying out to me for help – as if the millions who once crossed the Atlantic Ocean on board her sturdy decks; the tens of thousands who built and worked on her were saying in one omnipresent voice: Help her!

Looking at the great *SS United States*, I knew, she could be saved. It would take dedication, but it had to happen. She was too much a symbol of what we are as Americans, of our dreams, of what could be imagined and achieved. Despite the odds, I committed that day to begin a foundation to rescue the ship. A fellow admirer was standing next to me as we peered through the chain link fence at the knife like prow of the ship. She looked at me and said, "What's your interest in the *United States*?" I looked at her and said, "I'm going to save her."

The start of the foundation was shaky at best. At the time, I worked as a staffer for the National Endowment for the Arts in Washington D.C. and had had experience working with other non-profit organizations attempting to restore localized historical properties. The attempt to launch a national movement, without any sort of Federal or local government assistance was without precedence in American history. Consequently, I would have no prototype to emulate and certainly no monetary assistance to launch such an undertaking.

At first, I tried the route I was most familiar with — applying for grants. That meant, if my foundation were ever to receive assistance through grants, I would have to create a 501c3 corporation, without the assistance of legal council!

It was at this point as well that I had to devise a communication campaign strategy for the direction my fledgling organization was to take. As a journalism student, I did have an advantage in this aspect of the strategy.

I quickly realized that asking for donations to buy a ship, which at the time was listed for sale at $18 million, with no guarantees from the owner, would be impossible. But creating awareness was certainly a possibility. So that became, and still is, the main objective of the SS United States Foundation. And it has been an unparallel success. In 1999 alone, the Foundation's efforts to bring awareness to the plight of the *United States* was covered three times in *The New York Times*. CNN, *The Associated Press* and *The World News Service* of the BBC all ran stories about the rescue effort I had launched. All in all, the media impressions, to use a public relations term for the audience reached, in 1999 were international and numbered well over two billion! To give a comparison, all the coverage for the 11 million member National Trust for Historic Preservation was a fraction of the 2 billion the SS United States Foundation had received!

However, the first year of the effort seemed to indicate that this was not inevitable. In fact, three months into the official launch of the foundation in March of 1998, I almost shut down operations after a controversy with a board member threatened to dissolve the existing board. As with all organizations, controversies arise and it is important sometimes to remove a body part to save the whole body. The controversy involved the standards of ethics which would be employed with the Foundation.

Some early board members felt that they could use their positions to effect a sale of the vessel and collect on a 10 percent commission that was to be supposedly paid to whomever brokered this deal. From my workings at the NEA, and with non-profit historic preservation organizations, I knew immediately that this was a conflict of interest and created a new standard for the Foundation which has been emulated in other organizations. From that point forward, no board member of this organization would seek to broker a deal for the sale of this ship. In fact, the organization existed to save a relic of our history. But until that point, the ship had never been officially recognized as a great symbol of our nation.

National Register Designation

This presented the next and crucial phase of the Foundation. We would have to get the *SS United States* placed on the National Register of Historic Places. The problem was, she was under 50 years of age. The Register will not list a site less than 50 years of age unless it can be proved to have had "compelling national significance". Of the 70,000 plus sites listed on the register, less than 1 percent have ever obtained this significance. It was a criterion that would be difficult to achieve. Not only would the ship have to meet our nation's highest test for listing, I would have to convince both the Philadelphia Historic Commission as well as the Pennsylvania Historic Commission, that a ship, never having seen Philadelphia before being towed there in 1996, was not only important to the nation, but important to them. On top of it all, it could be moved in hours out of their historic jurisdiction, with no warning, thus thwarting hundreds of man-hours in research and Commission hearings on the subject.

Still, I went ahead with the campaign to get the Big U listed on the Register anyway.

This campaign, which was simply titled, "The Awareness Campaign," would soon get help from an unlikely source that would alter its image for years to come.

A process that had begun shortly after the launching of the Foundation soon had dragged on for months. During this uncertain period of direction and awareness creation the Foundation began to form alliances with other organizations that had the ship and her history close at heart. The first was the SS United State Preservation Society, founded by, William DiBenedetto. The Society was just about to give up hope when Bill saw a letter I wrote which appeared in *Nautical World Magazine*. Within a month the two organizations were working in concert to spread awareness across the nation. Letters to the editor began springing up in newspapers throughout the country, but still, the momentum to have the ship nominated to the National Register, was stalled in Philadelphia. Things began to move when I discovered the fact that William Francis Gibbs was from Philadelphia and not only that, had envisioned the great ship he would someday build on the wharfs of Penns Landing within site of where she was moored.

Armed with this information, I contacted the Philadelphia Historic Commission and a unanimous vote followed on the recommendation by the venerated historic board that the *United States* should be placed on the National Register under the Compelling National Significance criterion. We had won an important victory but were delivered an equally disastrous defeat that same year when the National Trust for Historic Preservation refused to place the ship among its 11 Most Endangered Historic Sites List—a recognition that would have ensured listing on the National Register.

Then the Harrisburg Historic Commission (aka the Pennsylvania Historic Commission) was in great doubt as to whether it would concur with the findings of the Philadelphia Commission. Added to this was the fact that no money was in the coffers of the Foundation and the current owner was delaying the hearing date in Harrisburg. It now seemed evident that a supply of money had to come in to cover basic costs of running the organization. It was at this point that a Foundation board meeting at the Old Post Office Pavilion's National Endowment for the Arts and Humanities Room voted to accept members. Immediately, a small supply of money through membership dues and contributions began to trickle in. It wasn't much, but it was enough to pay the basic operating expenses. I then began to solicit high profile board members and secured legal council through the Washington Area Lawyers for the Arts. The bringing on board of our legal council also signaled a new seriousness for the effort. By December of 1998, we had a former Presidential sub-cabinet official, The Honorable Bill Lehman, an attorney and Bill Miller on the advisory board of the foundation. We would need it.

The SS United States *as she looks today. (Courtesy of Robert Hudson Westover)*

Another blow was delivered when the Maritime Commission rejected the foundation's application for a grant to fund the awareness campaign. By January of 1999, I was seriously beginning to doubt the listing would ever happen. There had been some great media coverage: *The Chicago Tribune*, the *Associated Press* and even a radio talk show host interviewed me from Johannesburg, South Africa.

But all this wasn't bringing in enough new members to cover expenses and more and more money was coming out of my checking account. It was in this low ebb that Matt Smith, now president of the Foundation called me with news that would establish this organization as a serious effort and ultimately turn it into the largest non-government historic preservation effort ever undertaken in American history.

Matt was the creative director for a large advertising agency and had sailed on board the *United States* with his family when he was a child in the 1960s. He had heard about the effort to save the ship and wanted to help. Here was the deal: He would design an ad campaign, including brochures and posters, promote the campaign through his agency's PR department, and design a logo for the organization. All we had to do was supply artwork and let the agency do its work.

O.K.

Needless to say, Matt and I would spend a great deal of time together on this project that ultimately would win two Addy Awards for its originality. The campaign would be called *Save the United States* and would become the singular focus of the organization. It was brilliant.

That April *The New York Times'* Iver Peterson took a tour of the ship and wrote an emotionally stirring article that ran front page on the Easter Sunday National Page of that venerable publication. It also catapulted me into a celebrity of sorts for historic preservation. The *Times* chose to run my picture next to the *SS United States* and from that point on the name Robert Hudson Westover and *SS United States* would be forever linked.

The requests for interviews never seemed to stop. First it was the BBC World News from London calling, then CNN, then radio stations and newspapers from all over the world. The power of the press worked. The Harrisburg Commission unanimously voted to nominate the *United States* to the National Register and that June, on Flag Day, the *SS United States* took its place on the National Register of Historic Places as the only flagship to have ever been placed on the Register under 50 years of age. The ship had indeed passed the test as having national compelling interest.

SS United States.Org

But our greatest victory was to follow. It was shortly after the listing on the Register that I asked a web designer in Madison Wisconsin to please help us with our *Save the United States* campaign. Paul Robinson agreed and a month later, the single greatest tool in our arsenal was launched. The now internationally known www.ssunitedstates.org has been written about in countries as far away as Japan and Saudi Arabia. It has become – next to the National Trust for Historic Preservation – one of the most visited sites in historic preservation. It is through this Website that the Foundation has grown from just me in March of 1998, to over 1000 members today—members from all walks of life; from engineers to schoolchildren from housewives to CEOs.

I knew this organization and our efforts to *Save the United States* had a timeless appeal when a schoolteacher from upstate New York e-mailed me and told me that her 5th grade class had voted to come to Philadelphia to see the *United States*.

The Power of Dedication

When I said our greatest victory was to follow, I was also referring to what transpired in February 2000. I had just finished writing a report for a historic organization about the success of the Foundation's *Save the United States* campaign. I had written, and with much satisfaction, how just before the founding of the SS United States Foundation a headline in *The Philadelphia Inquirer* referring to the Big U had read "Hunk of Junk should be Sunk." And how just two years later, no one with a rational awareness of history would dare say such a thing.

The next day I received a frantic volley of e-mails saying: "Did you read the editorial in *The Philadelphia Daily News?*" It could not have been worse. The edito-

Reprinted from
The New York Times

Group Battles to Save Luxury Liner 'Big U,' and Glory of Its Day

By IVER PETERSON

PHILADELPHIA, April 2 — An enormous luxury liner lies empty and dark at the municipal pier here, pulling against its shore lines and straining, people who are fighting to save it say, for open water.

But seafaring is a distant past and unlikely future for the ship, the United States. The ship's paint is chipped and flaking, the lifeboats long gone, and even the reds, whites and blues of its raked funnels have faded into pastels.

The task facing the ship's owner and an avid band of preservationists is not focused on ocean voyages but simply on gaining a secure future for a behemoth that is 17 stories high, weighs 59,000 tons and stretches nearly 1,000 feet — or "110 feet longer than Titanic and she's still floating," as one slogans says.

"This ship is just too beautiful and too important to let slip through our fingers," said Robert Hudson Westover, who has formed the S.S. United States Foundation and a Web site, SS-United-States.com, to raise money for the ship's preservation.

"She represents the finest American engineering and the fastest ocean travel of her day," Mr. Westover said. "I can't imagine people wouldn't care about that."

"Big U," as the ship came to be known to sailors, steamed out of New York on its first voyage on July 3, 1952, and passed Bishop's Rock off the coast of England 3 days, 10 hours and 40 minutes later, shaving 10 hours from the record the Queen Mary had held since 1938.

The ship's average speed was 35 knots, or 40 miles an hour, and its top speed was a national security secret in a day when passenger liners were still on reserve as troop carriers.

When the United States passed the Queen Mary on a later voyage, it radioed, "Sorry, old girl." The Queen Mary radioed back, "Your girls are faster than our girls."

The United States made 400 crossings before being pushed aside by jet travel in 1969, and its backers hope that fond memories among its one million passengers still living will help preserve the liner.

With the drama of the Titanic still in the air, and the fashion-conscious in love with retro style, the ship's owner and the preservationists are following a two-pronged campaign to give the ship a new life. While the owner looks for deals, Mr. Westover and a loose alliance of other fans of the ship are raising money to build a safety net under it.

Edward A. Cantor, a major developer of commercial real estate in northern New Jersey, bought the United States in 1997 for $6 million from one of several failed ventures that have tried to turn the ship into a commercial success.

Robert D. Fair, an engineer who supervises Mr. Cantor's interest in the ship, said several groups had presented different options, most of them with the goal of duplicating the role of the Queen Mary, now a successful hotel and convention center at Long Beach, Calif.

The United States was stripped of its fittings after the final voyage, in 1969, and Mr. Fair estimated that it would cost at least $250 million to make the ship habitable. So, he was asked, was it profit or romance that lured Mr. Cantor to buy the ship and spend $100,000 a month in wharfage, security, insurance and upkeep ever since?

"Romance is part of it," Mr. Fair replied. "If it was just about money, he could have scrapped it when he didn't have so much invested and still taken a profit."

A possible solution was offered by Frank O. Braynard, a maritime museum curator at the United States Merchant Marine Academy, in Kings Point, N.Y., and the author of "The Big Ship," about the United States.

"The one hope is that New York City may do what California did with the Queen Mary and put her next to the carrier" Intrepid, a World War II ship that is a museum on a Hudson River pier in Manhattan, Mr. Braynard said. "But it would be a headache," he added, "because it's very, very expensive to keep a ship up." Mr. Cantor is looking for buyers — the price is $30 million, firm — but says he will listen to proposals for joint ventures.

Late last month, the Arnold Agency, a Richmond advertising firm, began creating material for a nationwide publicity campaign built around the theme "Save the United States."

But saving large artifacts from the age of steam is one of the most difficult tasks for preservationists these days, said Emory L. Kemp, a professor of history and civil engineering at West Virginia University, where he heads the Institute for the History of Technology and Industrial Archeology.

"There are a number of surviving battleships that are preserved by various states — the Texas, the North Carolina and the Massachusetts — but they are strictly tourist sites," Professor Kemp said.

At 990 feet, the United States is bigger than any American battleship; and to visitors who delve like spelunkers into the silent, cave-black lower decks, the ship presents an eerie and seemingly endless maze of heavy machinery, ladders, pipes and motors.

The reduction gears that drove the ship's four propeller shafts still glisten under bolted hatches. Engineers' reports, in pencil and fountain pen, still rest in filing cabinets next to the enormous boilers, and 30-year-old metal shavings are scattered around an industrial-sized lathe in the repair shop.

"Imagine how many people would love to see this," Mr. Westover said on a recent exploration. "It's like being underwater."

Robert Hudson Westover is leading an effort to preserve the liner United States, which is 17 stories high, weighs 59,000 tons and is 990 feet long. The ship, which made its first voyage in 1952, made its last in 1969.

An S.O.S. to the fond memories of a million passengers of a special ship.

151

rial likened the great *United States*, the ship that had been recently placed on the National Register of Historic places, as the biggest abandoned vehicle in the world and that the ship should have all the rusting old cars in and around the Philadelphia area placed on her decks and hopefully sink from the weight.

That this was a large metropolitan daily with half a million readers didn't help either.

I was mortified. How could they be so horrible? How could they lampoon such a noble effort to save an American Icon on par with the Statue of Liberty? Didn't they know that she was the fastest moving object of her size ever built – still a record holder for speed on the Atlantic? Didn't they know that thousands immigrated to this country on this mighty symbol of our national pride?

Well, they would.

That night, I sent a message out to the membership to write the newspaper – not to rant – but to kindly explain to the editors their mistake.

No less then 27 letters to the editor appeared in the following days. In fact, the chief editor called me directly and wanted an interview. It seems that in the newspaper's nearly 75 years of coverage they had never received so much mail on any one story.

By March the editorial board of *The Philadelphia Daily News* made an about face and wrote an editorial apologizing for its previous stance in regards to the *SS United States*. And, in their 75th Anniversary edition they ran a two-page article on the history of the *SS United States*.

I would like to end this by stating that we have rescued the *SS United States*, but the battle, as I write this, is still waging. From *The Philadelphia Daily News* victory, I have learned the strongest tool in our arsenal is the dedication of the thousands of supporters who are helping out everyday; by writing letters to their elected officials, contacting their local news media to tell them they want to hear about the effort. It is because of this that we have a chance to *Save the United States*. As Margaret Mead once wrote: "Never think that a band of thoughtful committed citizens can't change the world. Indeed, it is the only thing that ever has."

Literature promoting the saving of the SS United States.

15

Stories From Passengers & Crew

The Big "U" Conception and Construction

by D. Scott Hicks

My father was Col. Raymond M. Hicks, Executive Vice President of The United States Lines Company located at One Broadway New York City. Leading the company at the time was Gen. John M. Franklin, son of the founder of U.S. Lines. Their respective officer titles resulted from both men being asked to join the Water Division of the Transportation Corpse of the U.S Army. They were stationed in the Pentagon. This assignment of course was during World War II. Both men served with distinction and were so honored by Gen. Dwight D. Eisenhower.

It was during that period of time that they conceived the idea of building a ship that would be the pride of the U. S. Lines and the Nation: and be able to respond to military needs of our country. Dad was the financial side and the General the Company authorization.

In addition, the need to prepare for the eventual retirement of the *SS America*, which was used during the war as a troop ship. Naturally, William Francis Gibbs, designer of the *SS America*, was included in their plans. He had been preparing for such a ship as the Big "U" when contacted by U.S Lines. It was a dream come true as far as Mr. Gibbs and his firm Gibbs & Cox were concerned. And as long as Mr. Gibbs was involved with Gibbs & Cox he continually kept performance and maintenance data of the ship.

Once the decision had been made to go ahead with the construction of the *SS United States*, then it was Dad's task to convince a lethargic Congress to okay the subsidies required for construction and ultimate operation. This required many trips to Washington, D.C. over a period of about three years after he was honorably discharged from the U.S. Army. The success of his efforts resulted in the Company receiving the necessary subsidies; thereby permitting Mr. Gibbs and his firm, working with the Newport News Shipbuilding and Dry Dock Company, VA., to begin construction.

Those in the shipping business at the time referred to the ship as Ray's Ship because of the effort he put in. In this connection, Dad had to overcome the efforts of the English lobbyists to prevent such construction which would result in competition for the Atlantic passenger. Fortunately, their efforts failed.

As an aside, the United States Government during the war paid the English Government the equivalent of three times the costs of the *Queen Mary* and *Queen Elizabeth* for transporting our troops to & from Europe. This fact alone encouraged the Congress to affirm their decision relative to the Big "U."

We were fortunate to see the launching and to have been on the delivery trip bringing her up to New York to begin her cruising the Atlantic. The English continued their unsuccessful efforts to stop the launching, and Dad had a hoarse throat when we picked him up in Union Station, Washington, D.C., after having spent that morning arguing for the ship.

I will never forget the delivery trip and the churned water from the propellers as far as you could see to the horizon. We were told at the time that we were going the equivalent of 50 miles an hour.

As a final word on this story, my brother Ray and I have the greatest respect for Dad and his effort to give the American people the greatest ship of her kind in the world. And we appreciate the collective efforts of so many people who want the *SS United States* to sail again.

Maiden Voyage

by Laura Franklin Dunn

I was on the maiden voyage of the *SS United States* - an unforgettable experience. We sailed on July 3rd, 1952.

My mother and father (who was President of the U.S. Lines, the company that owned the ship), and I, accompanied by a friend from Baltimore, Sally Chapman, were in the Duck Suite, on the starboard side

The Maiden Voyage of the United States. *(Courtesy of John McFarlane)*

of the ship, and Margaret Truman, and her friend, Drucie Snyder, were in the Shell Suite, on the port side.

I was asked by my father to go over to Miss Truman's suite, to make sure she had everything she needed. I did, and met Margaret Truman, Drucie Snyder, and Mrs. Truman, who was saying good-bye to her daughter. I didn't see any sign of a secret service person. Everything was much more relaxed in those days.

Life aboard was a constant celebration. We were leading a conga line about 2 a.m., having danced the night away. Everyone seemed to sense the ship was going to break the record. We went up to the bridge, and Commodore Harry Manning, who was at the helm, let me put my finger on the helm as we broke the record. Three days, ten hours, and forty minutes, after passing Ambrose Light, the Big U steamed past Bishop Rock, the official finish line. On her victorious crossing from New York, a distance of 2,942 miles, she had averaged a speed of 35.59 knots, 5 1/2 knots faster than the *Queen Mary*. She had won the Blue Riband trophy, which had not been won by an American ship for nearly one hundred years.

The first port of call was Le Havre, France. There were at least ten newspaper reporters on board who had all ready phoned their respective papers to tell them we had broken the record. We were surrounded by boats in the harbor all decorated with American flags, and signs saying: "Congratulations to the Big U." She responded with several blasts of her very unladylike ship's horn.

It was one of the most exciting times of my life.

"Sea Baby Born on the Maiden Voyage of the Blue Ribbon Liner"

by Emma Elisabeth Arbenz

"Pink Ribbon for a Blue Ribbon Liner" read the ship's bulletin headlines announcing the birth of its youngest passenger. The year was 1952 and my entrance into the world was quite extraordinary and very special in so many ways.

You see, I (formerly Barbara Jo Allen) was born on the maiden voyage of the *SS United States* on July 8, 1952, while the ship was docked in the port city of Le Havre, France (latitude 48° 28.5 and longitude 075 E). Being a premature baby and measuring only 15 inches long and weighing 3 lbs. 11 oz., I was definitely the ship's tiniest and brightest little star. This, of course, made me a celebrity and instantly gave me my 15 minutes of fame at birth.

My parents, Dr. and Mrs. M.J. Allen were traveling on a business trip to England when I was born quite unexpectedly en route to Southampton. Dr. Frank Ciparelli of Kings County Hospital in Brooklyn (New York) was the ship's doctor and was at my mother's side when I was born. Dr. Ciparelli also attended my christening and kept in close contact with my parents for many years after the "blessed event."

The *SS United States* or "Queen of the Seas" as she was also known, made history as being the fastest and most famous merchant ship ever built at Newport News. The record-breaking crossing only took 3 days, 10 hours, and 40 minutes with Commodore Harry Manning (Captain, U.S.N.R.) at the helm of the eastbound voyage.

My star shone especially bright upon the *SS United States*' return to New York City and was hailed as the "Blue Ribbon Baby" by all who knew of my birth. On coming home to Madison, New Jersey, it was noted in

Emma Elisabeth Arbenz at her christening, at one year old with a birthday cake with the ship on it, and boarding the ship with her mother on a later voyage.

the local papers that I was the "Small Talk of the Town." Of course, I was too young to appreciate the attention for being one of such international personage.

As I grew up, my parents and I moved many times from the East Coast (New Jersey) to the West Coast (California) and back again to the East Coast (Maryland). In the summer of 1970, we move to England, where I entered into my first year as a student of Textile Design and Art History at Canterbury College of Art.

The years passed and I found myself back on American shores where I did much traveling and grew to the person that I am today. My adventures have taken me on locations as far as Australia, Mexico, Canada, and Western Europe to ones much closer a field such as New York (Hudson River Valley) and New England, which includes my favorite city, Boston.

I am now settled in Doylestown, Bucks County, Pennsylvania where my love of the environment, animals, and photography takes me on many long walks in the countryside searching for that "perfect picture." My passions in life are still very much connected to the sea, enjoying the ocean and its surroundings whenever possible.

Everyone Cheered! 1953
by Robert P. Bracken

As a merchant seaman in the early 1950s, I had seen the *United States* many times in Bremerhaven and New York, but the greatest thrill I got was when we saluted her going into the English Channel. I believe this was in 1953 and she was leaving the channel on her way to New York and broke the speed record on that trip. I was aboard a US Army transport at the time and when she acknowledged our salute, every soldier on that transport cheered. I still get chills when I see her laying up in Philadelphia, she deserves better than that.

Fortunate To Sail
by M. Boyd

In 1954 my two children and I were fortunate enough to sail on the *United States* to join my husband who was stationed in France. In 1957 luck was with us again when the entire family returned stateside on that wonderful ship. Nearly two years ago my husband passed away and in sorting out footlockers and chests and papers we relived our sailings by going over menus, napkins, pictures, daily news bulletin, etc. that we had saved.

I Set Sail In 1956
by Guenter Ziegler

It was 1955, and I was living in East Germany. I decided that I no longer wanted to live under the repressive communists who were in power. I got a visa and took the train to West Germany. There, I stayed with relatives, and then made arrangements with my brother who was already over here to come to the United States. I set sail on the *SS United States* in April of 1956. I was in tourist class in a room with three other young men.

We decided to go to the swimming pool, not paying much attention to the fact that it was reserved for first class passengers. We were able to sneak in. The lifeguard asked to have our wallets for safe keeping. When he discovered that we were tourist class, he gave us a look, but allowed us to stay.

During the voyage I had a good time swimming, dancing, and eating in the dining hall. It was a thrill to see the Statue of Liberty when we arrived in New York Harbor. I became a U.S. citizen, and will never forget my trip across the ocean on this wonderful ship. Now, I live near Philadelphia, and every time I see it as I drive across the Walt Whitman Bridge where it is docked nearby, I hope and pray to see it restored to its former glory.

Europe to New York City on the *United States* July 6, 1957

by Cynthia A. Sandor

My parents, Gertrude Kerschner and Robert Sandor met during World War II. My mother worked as a waitress in a coffee shop, while my father fought against Hitler's Third Reich, on the banks of the Blue Danube River, in Linz, Austria. The German Army occupied the Postingburg side of the river, while the Austrian and American Armies occupied the Linz side of the Danube River.

As my father was patrolling the streets, he came across the St. Moritz coffee shop. He decided to stop in for a cup of coffee. Looking for a place to sit down, he noticed an empty chair in the back corner of the room. People stared at him as he walked by — his dark green uniform depicts a sense of security for the people of Austria. His riffle strapped to his back, the ammunition wrapped around his waist, the heavy boots he wore all symbolized to the Austria people how American was standing beside their country. My father sat and waited to be served.

A little blonde haired, brown eyed waitress standing five-foot two, wearing a black and white uniform walked up to him. "Was mochte Sie?" She asked in her Austria dialect. "I cannot speak German" my father replied. "Was would you like trink?" my mother said. "Coffee." She turned and walked away.

My father's eyes gazed at her full body as it walked away from him. A few moments she returned with his coffee. This was the first time my parents met.

They spent their time fishing and boating in the lakes of Gmunden, hiking the mountains; my father in his army uniform and my mother in her suite and hiking boots. My father transformed my mother from a waitress, into a queen. My mother starting wearing panty hose for the first time, beautiful suits and make-up.

Since my mother spoke Austrian, and my father spoke a broken German, it was difficult for them to communicate. My mother's brother and sister, Franzel and Anita, would accompany my mother on all her excursions with my father. They were never alone. The four of them traveled the country side together.

Then one day, my father proposed to my mother. He asked my mother to marry her. Funny how my mother did not understand him and Uncle Franz and Tante Anita translated his marriage proposal.

My parents were married on May 8th and embarked on their first trip to the United States on the *SS United States* in July 6, 1957. She was 19 and my father was 21. My mother was dressed as a lady traveling first class — wearing a black suit and a full length red fox fur coat. My father walked in front of her wearing his black and white tweed coat, Dick Tracy hat, suit, tie and dark glasses. He looked like Elvis Presley in disguise. In the background, a sign reads "This Way For the *United States*." My mother had no ideas of the opportunities which laid before her.

As my parents boarded the ship and made their way up to their stateroom, Captain L.H. Alexanderson, Captain, U.S.N.R. prepared the ship for sail. As my parents stood next to the railing overlooking the thousands of people waiving below, the large brass whistle blew. Streamers were flying. Confetti was falling in her hair. People were happy. This great American ship was setting sail to the Promised Land — the Home of the Free — away from a World War and a country whose cities lie in ruins. My parents took each other's hand and kissed. The great ship gently moved from the dock. The lines were cast. This great ship, full of American soldiers and civilian passengers were making their passage to New York City.

The Gala Dinner that evening was formal. Even though the ship ran into a horrific storm, my parents decided to attend the formal dinner that evening. Dressed in their best, they dined on Smoked Salmon, Mushrooms

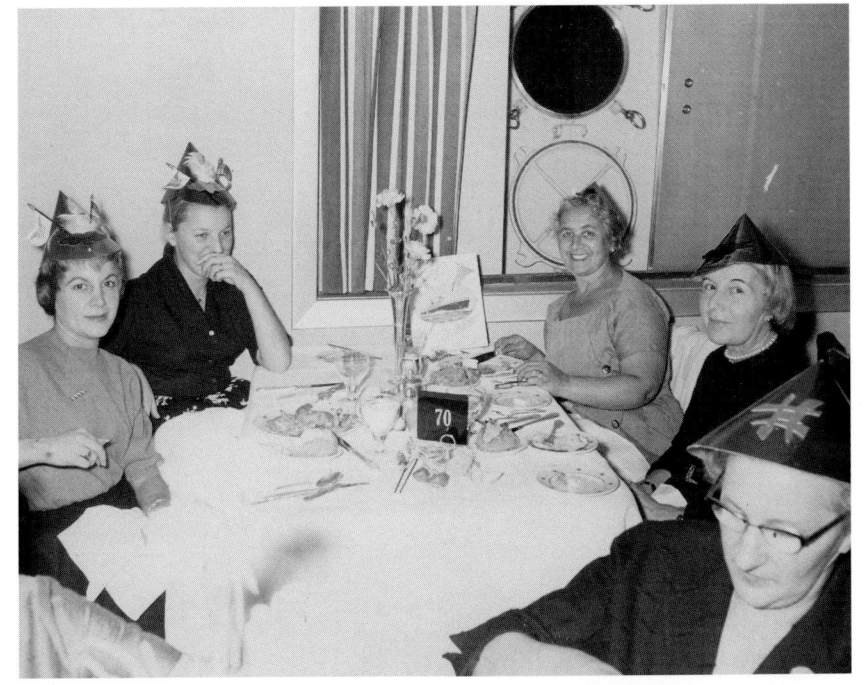

Passengers in the First Class Dining Saloon on A Deck in the 1950s. (Courtesy of Bill DiBenedetto)

a la Francaise and Chilled Fresh Fruit Cup, Maraschino. Their entree consisted of Fried Baby Lobster Rails, Sause Remoulade, And Cole Slaw, Roast Leg of Southdown Lamb au Jus with English Mint Sauce with Corn on the cob, Haricots Verts, Petitis Pois a la Francaise, Brussel Sprouts and the Cheif's Salad with Special Dressing. They finished their evening with Vienna Mocha Layer Cake, French Ice Cream, Stilton, Roquefort and Brie Cheese and Toasted Crackers. Most of the people on board had fallen ill that evening. My mother remembers telling me how, as the waves crashed over the bow of the ship, my parents were only one of two couples dancing in the formal ball room.

Over the next 35 years, my parents worked hard to build their own home and raise a family in Greenwich, Connecticut. My parents instilled work ethics, morals, family values and principles in me which live onto this very day. Work hard and take pride in the services you perform. You only have one brother and sister so take care of them. And be fair in all your business dealings.

My parents have since passed away. The pictures of them boarding the *United States*, overlooking the railing and their menu from July 6, 1957 hangs on my dining room wall. I missed my parents dearly, but their legacy will continue as long as their story is told.

A Brief Moment
by Joseph Rota

We were Westbound about two days out of New York, at about 8:00 a.m. on a summer morning in 1957. My duties as Radio Bell Boy required me to be at the ships radio room, which is next to the ships bridge. It seemed there were an extra number of ships officers on the bridge that morning. I then heard Commodore Anderson say, "there she is" as he pointed to starboard. I moved a few steps so I could see out and there was a submarine surfacing about 300 yards off our starboard bow. The first exciting thing, of many, was how could a submarine surface and keep up with us; we were doing better than 32 knots. The next thing that happened was a message by flashing light from the submarine's bridge tower. In less than one minute the sub was back under the ocean, like she had never been there.

I asked the chief radio operator, "What was that all about?" He smiled and said, "You didn't see that." Later I found out that the submarine commander was Admiral H. Rickover, and his wife was a passenger on board our ship. The flashing message was, HAPPY BIRTHDAY! The submarine was, of course, the first atomic submarine *Nautilus*.

Many exciting and wonderful things happened on that great ship in the four years that I served as a crew member ... this was just one story of many.

A Trip of a Lifetime 1958
by William Wood

My trip on the *United States* truly was one of a lifetime, for it brought me to America. I was born in Orleans, France in 1956, and adopted by an American couple stationed there. I cruised in First Class in January 1958 with from Le Havre to New York City on the same trip with the Duke and Duchess of Windsor. My folks later recalled that I had my days and nights mixed up, and would wake up in the middle of the night telling my father I wanted to walk saying "Promenade Daddy, Promenade!" Each time I hear about the *United States*, I feel a lump in my throat, for it was my one way ticket to America.

Encounter With Royalty
by Madelaine Fratello

It was a transatlantic cruise. The ocean waves were higher than our main floor port window. At dinner time, I could not understand why the waiter would casually pour half a pitcher of water on the table as he held a napkin precisely folded on his bent arm, standing at full attention. My parents would laugh at my expression every night during this event but I would sit quietly and mysteriously watch every time. I knew the water helped the dishes from sliding across the table during the violent storm but I could not understand why the lip on the rim of the table was not enough. Being strapped to the table with a belt around the chair made sense, but the water being poured over the table cloth did not fit the elegance of the dinning room. Sometime after dinner my parents gave me money to go purchase some cigars for my grandfather in the gift shop. It was tough walking the hallways. So! The steps were really a struggle and at times you could recognize the pattern of the waves and prepare for the big wave that would really make that one step extra hard. Some people that you passed in the halls were in wheel chairs or were wearing a cast or bandage. Apparently, they did not walk the halls in the rough waters as well as I did. But, there was one particular wave, which was too much for me to handle and knocked me down on the way back from the gift shop. The cigar box hit the wall and the box and I landed on the floor. All the cigars were displaced and suddenly a cabin door opened revealing a very tall, distinguished man, who said nothing, but simply gave one deliberate, warm smile at me and immediately help me stand-up and gathered all the cigars. He led me into his room where there was a lady sitting at the desk putting on perfume. She walked over to me, greeted me and invited me to neaten up the box of cigars. Together and with her guidance we reassembled all the cigars with their labels all facing in the same direction. She had a gentle voice and a patient way about her, as so did the man. We chatted and after some time I was slowly escorted, holding the gentleman's hand, back to my room where my parents were waiting for me. He smiled all the way and I remember him looking into my eyes even as we walked. I felt there was something special about him but I was too young to consider anything any further, after all, what would it have mattered for anything beyond a smile at that age. For the remainder of the trip I heard the names of those lovely people many time, but I, a ten year old, could not understand why there was so much talk about the Duke and Duchess of Windsor.

A telegram received by Catherine Brady on board January 28, 1960.

Catherine Brady (right rear with flower on shoulder) at the gala dinner on Saturday January 30, 1960 aboard the SS United States.

Recollections New York to Southampton on the *SS United States*

January 27, 1960 – February 1, 1960

By Catherine Brady

The following are a few recollections of my trip aboard the ship:

• High floral arrangement being delivered to my cabin, a parting gift from mother and daughter which were close friends at the time. I believe the flowers were Irises. It was very special as I had never received anything like that before.

• As the *SS United States* pulled out of New York harbor, we saw the very new and beautiful *France* berthed alongside at the pier.

• I was taking a parakeet back to London with me. The cage hung on a string between the closet and bureau, I think, so that the cage could swing to and fro as the ship rode the waves. The stewardess visited my cabin often to see and chat with my parakeet named "Fidal" after Castro who had paid a visit to New York at the time I got him. I liked the name!

• I remember going to the movies. I think the movie was "Home is the Hunter." In the theater the heavy drapes on either side of the screen swayed to and fro as the liner sped along. It behooved one not to look at them or you could be seasick!

• I was traveling alone but met a few nice people at meal times. One, a gentleman tulip grower from Holland returning home after a business trip. Another, a lady from Detroit going to Wales to see her mother for the last time.

• I recall that I was one of the few who ventured to the dining room for dinner on a rather rough day at sea. I recall also, not being able to go out on deck because of the extreme cold and rough weather – after all it was the end of January in the North Atlantic! The strength of the winds was too great. I tried once to open the door to go out and look around but it was impossible to do so. I would have been blown overboard.

• I regret not taking advantage of roaming around the beautiful ship and seeing as much as I could and also for not keeping a diary.

My heart is full of joy and full of sorrow as I have put my long ago memories on paper. Joy for the fact that I had the privilege of traveling on the one and only magnificent *SS United States*. And great sorrow that such a treasure was allowed to be torn apart, desecrated until nothing was left but a shell.

However, I look forward and long for the day when "The *SS United States*" is saved for posterity and returned to her former glory. And I thank all who are doing their very best for this great miracle to happen.

Working On The SS United States

by Dan McSweeney

My parents met in the New York subway the day before my dad sailed for Europe on the *SS United States*.

It was 1963 and by that time my father, a native of Glasgow, Scotland, had been working on the *SS United States* for all of the eleven years that she'd been sailing.

My mother, who had recently moved to New York from San Juan, Puerto Rico, was with her girlfriend that evening. They were on their way to a dance on the East Side, but got a little lost in the Times Square station. Seeing my dad walk by, they decided to ask him for directions. (He must have looked trustworthy enough and this was before crime started to get bad in the City.)

After showing them where to catch the shuttle train, my dad made some small talk and told them he was sailing for Europe the next day. They asked about his job

Dan McSweeney and sisters in London.

Dan McSweeney

McSweeney's SS United States Crew Pass

and he described the *United States* to them. I'm sure he was not at a loss for words, as he was always very proud of the ship and of the variety of jobs, from silver service steward to librarian's assistant, that he'd held aboard her.

I think my mom and dad were intrigued by the each other's voices. Perhaps the sound of their accents hinted at the idea that each had different, complementary perspectives on New York and on America in general. My father had visited Puerto Rico on a previous voyage and had spent a lot of time in Spain, so it was easy for him to relate to my mom. My mother didn't know a lot about Scotland, but she was no doubt curious about Europe. I'm sure she was also impressed by all the different kinds of people who had moved to New York to make new lives for themselves.

During the course of that first conversation, my dad invited my mother and her friend to see him off when the ship sailed the following afternoon. They agreed and exchanged telephone numbers. The next day, however, the ladies didn't show. My dad made the voyage and when he got back a couple of weeks later, he called my mom at home. So began their friendship, which after about a year evolved into a courtship and then marriage.

My sister was born in 1965 and I was born in 1970, just after the *United States* stopped sailing. My dad continued working aboard her until that time, completing 18 years of service aboard the ship, from her maiden voyage to her final, 400th trip. (Obviously, he didn't make every single voyage.)

During the early part of my parents' marriage, my father took my mom aboard the ship on the short leg from Southampton, England to Bremerhaven. He had planned to trick her by saying that they were going to take a small ferry to Germany. Needless to say, it worked. She still recalls how impressed she was by the size and comfort of the ship, and by all of my dad's crew mates, who went out of their way to take extra care of the newlyweds.

My dad had a seemingly endless supply of stories about the ship and her passengers. One that sticks out in my mind is the time when Sean Connery was aboard and some crew members told him that another Scotsman — my dad — worked on the ship. My dad and Mr. Connery spoke briefly on the ship's telephone, the actor saying that he couldn't meet my dad in person because a bunch of teenagers on board had him by a part of his anatomy!

My father also told stories about meeting W. Somerset Maugham, Judy Garland, John Wayne, and many other passengers throughout the 1950s and 1960s aboard the *United States*.

The ship has always loomed large in my consciousness. In some ways, I feel I owe my existence to her, as my father moved to the United States expressly to work aboard the ship. She is a symbol to me, of the opportunity that America has always represented and that, as a first-generation American, I feel compelled to explore to the fullest.

If, somehow, we can take action to save her, we will be fulfilling and preserving her tremendous promise, both for ourselves and for future generations. On a personal level, if I can help in the effort to save her, I'll no doubt have the sense that my father is looking down and smiling on me and the *United States* — both his beloved ship and his adopted country.

The Biggest Moving Giant
by Chris Parker

In 1967, my father had accepted a job teaching English in Turkey. We were to cross the Atlantic on the *SS United States* during that summer. Being only 9 years old, my expectations were unclear. Being raised in the desert southwest I had never seen a ship at all. Was this a row boat to take me across a lake? When I first encountered the *SS United States* in New York, I was amazed after seeing the biggest moving giant I had ever seen in my life.

Our family friends were allowed to board this ship with us to bid us farewell. While my parents entertained them in our stateroom, my brother and I decided to sneak off and explore the huge ship. We got hopelessly lost. Meanwhile it was time for our friends to leave the ship, as it was about to depart. My mother was desperately worried, thinking that we had gotten off the ship with their friends. But she found us looking out the window of one of the public rooms, as the ship backed away from the dock.

Later as we entered he Atlantic Ocean we experienced some very dense fog. The fog horns blasted every minute. I was very much frightened, thinking the ship was doomed. But my mother, who had been on other transatlantic passenger ships, assured me that it was fine. Later, were the lifeboat drills which worried me too.

After a while I really enjoyed our journey across the ocean on this great ship. There was a children's party, where we sang songs, and received balloons and sailor hats. I was so proud of that hat, with the name of the ship on it, that I went out on deck and pretended to be part of the crew. The strong wind blew my hat off my head, and down into the ocean it went. But they were nice, and gave me a new one. We enjoyed the movies, the swimming pool and meals every day of our journey. When we arrived in England, my father went to pick up our new car, then off to Turkey we drove.

Ten Crossings
By Paul Geiger

As a young man I was fortunate to have had the opportunity to make ten crossings and a couple of cruises as a stewards department crew member aboard the "Big U." It is so very sad to see her now languishing at a dock in Philadelphia because she was the finest ship that I ever had the pleasure to board. I couldn't tell you how many hours I spent at the very tip of the bow in much the same fashion as was shown in the movie "Titanic." The speed that we traveled was really remarkable and just watching the flying fish jump out of the way as we plunged from wave to trough and back up again could keep me mesmerized for hours.

On a particular trip in August 1968 we were held up in NY by a labor dispute. The *United States* was given special dispensation to sail, because of its importance to the National Maritime Union due to the 1,200 crew members and the fact that the voyage would have to be cancelled if the dispute lasted more than 15 hours.

We managed to leave port about 14 hours late and we were able to make up about 9 hours of that time and made the second fastest crossing from ambrose light to bishops rock on record. We did the crossing in 3 days,

17 hours and 11 minutes. Her maiden voyage time was 3 days, 10 hours and 40 minutes. The ship was almost 20 years old by then and if the sea had been calmer we would have been able to challenge her Blue Riband time. I was able to "sneak" down to the engine spaces and the steam valves had lots left. I wouldn't be surprised if we were doing 35 or 36 knots. It was still in such pristine condition though that if I hadn't known better I would have thought it was brand new. The entire rear third of the ship was shaking like a paint mixer when they cranked it up at night and the wake we churned up was awesome. I went scuba diving around the ship on a cruise to Panama and I got to sit on those propellers! They were four massive props with a steep pitch and I could sit on the hub and wrap my legs around it. The inboard screws were connected to the propeller shafts that extended almost to amidships and I could lay my finger on them when we were under way and it was smooth as glass.

Another story that I remember is that the ship was believed to be haunted. As the story was related to me (by a man who broke his leg running away from the ghost) went like this. In the early fifties there was a wedding in NY and the bride and groom had booked passage to Europe for their honeymoon on the *United States*. The husband was killed in a traffic accident on his way to the ship. His bride was traveling in another car and was unaware of what happened until after the ship had sailed. When she found out about the tragedy she apparently went to the stern the first night out of NY and threw herself overboard. They found her shoes on the deck and she was never seen alive again. I spoke with many fire watch and stewards department crew members who claimed to have seen her.

She only would be seen on trans-Atlantic crossings on the first night out of NY or the last night before arrival when returning. They related getting into elevators and asking what deck the young lady would like to go to, only to find that she had vanished. Others related following her into blind passageways and she would just go right through the bulkhead. I never saw her myself, but despite the fact that I was very skeptical at first, I talked to too many first hand witnesses to disregard it all together.

I live about an hour from Philadelphia now and it seems so strange that there are two battleships sitting in the river as tourist attractions while the *United States*, which could be used for so many possible functions, riverboat casino, hotel, shopping and restaurant center etc., sits there. I hope the right person in our government wakes up and realizes that it's too important a part of America in the twentieth century to let it go to the breakers.

Except for the *Queen Mary* and the *France* she is the only one left from a long line of Ocean Liners that helped to make this country what it is.

As A Night Porter 1969

by Alan Stark

I was an 18 1/2 year old teenager just graduated from John Bowne High School in Flushing Queens New York and a night Porter on the *SS United States* in August of 1969. My first experience on a ship and what a ship it was. I think it took me two days to find my bunk. To travel across the ocean and look out on the deck and see nothing but stars and water, working at night did have its advantages. I met many crew members from different countries and they took me under their wing and made this a most memorable two weeks. I mopped the deck, cleaned the passenger theatre and snuck into the pantry to eat some of the good passenger food. I gambled a little down below but made sure to come home with some money, that seemed like so much back then. I loved my journey on The Big U and hope it's restored someday.

Fifty Years of Admiration

by Ronald P. Jensh, Ph.D.

It is as exciting to see the majestic ship today as it was for me 50 years ago. Although presently a peeling, rusty lady of the seas, she still has an overpowering impact. Driving north on the Delaware Avenue in Philadelphia, suddenly the huge smoke stacks loom above the neighboring warehouses, stunning in their magnitude. Walking on the pier where she is berthed, one feels small and insignificant, but at the same time, proud of this American icon – a symbol of man's creative abilities.

I first saw this magnificent lady almost 50 years ago. I was in ninth grade (1953-1954) from a small New Jersey town outside of New York City. We regularly took class trips into NYC to visit museums and other "sites." That year, our teacher was able to obtain tourist passes for our class to board the *SS United States* for a tour preceding (I believe) its maiden voyage. This was the biggest event happening at the time, and we all were excited at the prospect of seeing something so stunning. We had seen her on television, but in those days TV screens were small and black and white. Little did we know what was in store for us.

I have been an amateur photographer since grade school. This was a wonderful opportunity to bring my Brownie Hawkeye camera (with a handful of flash bulbs) along for the adventure. I took about a dozen interior and exterior photographs from all angles. The negatives were filed and forgotten.

In 1962 I moved to Philadelphia, little knowing the famous ship would eventually arrive in the same city. When I became aware of her plight several years ago, I wrote two letters to the *Philadelphia Inquirer*. The response from readers was overwhelming. So many had remembered the ship with great fondness.

I retrieved my negatives, digitized them, and brought them to modern day quality. What a joy to see this unique vessel once again in her glory through those photographs.

I would like to see her stay here in Philadelphia/Camden as part of the revitalization of the waterfront together with the *USS New Jersey*, the Aquarium, and Penn's Landing. However, I realize the most important issue is to preserve this beauty no matter where she rests.

The *SS United States* was, is, and will always be a testament to our creative abilities and a symbol of our country, much like the Eiffel tower for France, the Pyramids for Egypt, the London Bridge and Big Ben for England. Once you have seen her you know she must be saved at all costs.

Last Call
July 4th, 2000,
Pier 84, NYC

by Joseph G. Mizii,

It was humid, very humid, but the cloud cover kept the temperature tame, at least until midday. Some people at work had wondered why I would get involved in an effort to save a ship that I had never sailed on and had not even seen, other than in pictures, until March of 1998. At that point, she was a shell of her former self, but seeing her for the first time had left me speechless even then, notwithstanding the shape she was in. She still gets to me even now.

So here I was, standing on Pier 84 in New York, right next to the *USS Intrepid*, which ironically, now occupies the Big U's old home berth. I was there because I was supporting the SS United States Foundation's efforts to spread the word about our grand old lady, and hopefully garner a number of new members in the process. You would think that such an idea couldn't fail. The crowds were huge, but I wish I could say the same for the interest. Most people were only there to watch the tall ships sail by. Our little display didn't attract much attention, and the attention it did attract that day was more along the lines of people having disoriented and quizzical looks on their faces, wondering what it is the *SS United States* was, and why they should care. But that didn't stop me. In fact, there was no place I would have rather been on that day than standing there on Pier 84, in support of our nation's flagship, ready to answer questions and hear some stories. Usually, the question was similar to the question I had gotten from people at work - "Why is this important?" This just really underscores the idea of how people are completely ignorant of what this ship stands for and has accomplished.

I did actually get a few people drop by and ask me some questions. One gentleman (he was in his mid 40s) said, "I remember that ship. I used to come watch her sail every time she was in. She was a beauty – clean, sleek, big and magnificent. There wasn't anything like her in port then, and there hasn't been anything like her since." And of course, you know, he was absolutely right.

Well, that's what I have to say about July 4th, 2000, a day I chose to help out, in a very personal way, with the Foundation's efforts to spread awareness. I felt so much pride being there, far more so than in writing letters, because there's no real interface with a letter. I think people start to understand better when they can detect someone else's enthusiasm. It's contagious.

The Majestic SS United States. (Courtesy of Bill DiBenedetto)

16

Supplemental History
Written by Bill DiBenedetto

Much has been written about the events concerning the service life of the *SS United States*, her abrupt removal from service on November 11, 1969. The following pages will attempt to describe the events that have transpired since that time. The Big U was laid up at Newport News Ship Building and Drydock Co. During June of 1970 she was moved across the James River to Norfolk International Terminals. She remained berthed there when title was passed from United States Lines to MarAd during 1973, for the remaining amount due on the mortgage approximately $25 million.

Moon Engineering was engaged to lay up the *SS United States* for future employment. The engineering plant was secured with condensers opened up., intakes sealed, boilers cleaned and opened. Giant dehumidifiers were installed, and all exterior openings sealed except two. A remote fire detection system was installed with the warning indicator board installed at the B deck entrance instead of the Damage Control Room, on the Bridge. This would allow the watchmen to keep watch of both the gangway and the fire control board in the remote chance of a fire.

She was being preserved correctly for future use. Still on board were all the articles that were used during her service life: furniture, silver, china, linens, beds, lamps, artwork and thousands of other items required for a great sea going hotel. Pictures taken during the 1970s early 1980s reveal an interior that looked like the last crewmen left and locked the door. Everything remained, just like it was in November 1969.

During the next few years MarAd courted many purchasers. At one point there were plans developed to turn the Big U into a hospital ship. However, the Navy felt the ship was too large and expensive to operate, and showed no real interest. They had already laid up all of their *Iowa* Class Battleships because they were so expensive to operate. Another potential purchaser was the Norwegian flag Kloster Group. They were looking for a large second hand liner to be placed in the booming Caribbean trade. After looking at several ships including the *United States* they chose the *France*. There were many other ideas and schemes but nothing became of any, until United States Cruises, owned by Richard Hadley purchased the Big U during 1980.

Mr. Hadley's initial plans were to do a simple refit and put the *United States* into service around the Hawaiian Islands. The former American Export Liners the *Independence* and the *Constitution* were currently cruising the islands and were successfully financially, while being operated under the American flag. Much of this success was due to the Jones White Act which restricted any port to port transportation in the United States to American flagged vessels. Because the *United States* would be restricted, due to her size, from many ports, Mr. Hadley plans called for two large tenders to be placed on the forward deck, much like the *Norway* (the former *France*).

Another plan that Mr. Hadley team developed was to use the *United States* as a floating condominium. This called for the staterooms to be sold and each owner would be a timeshare participant. Several staterooms were remolded and brochures were printed. New deck plans were created and plans for remodeling were drawn up. However, this idea did not attract many purchasers and was finally abandoned.

Many more plans were made and by 1984 the *SS United States* was to be sent to Germany for her new refit. The infamous auction was held during October of 1984. Virtually everything was offered for sale: silverware, china, furniture, crystal, even the bridge equipment, helms, telegraphs etc., gauges from the engine room. Thousands and thousands of items. Those items that were not sold at auction continued to be sold for many years afterwards to those seeking keepsakes of this great ship. With the ship to be totally refitted, most of these items were redundant and would no longer be used.

Many attempts were made by Richard Hadley to gain the financing required for the planned refit. Plans at the beginning were quite simple; cleaning, painting and automation of the boiler and engine rooms, to save staffing. Only one engine room was to be used, the forward boiler room and engine room would be used for other purposes. The propellers were to changed to allow for more economical fuel consumption. The estimated cost approximately $25 million. As time went on the plans called for much more than a normal refit. Cabins were to be ripped out and replaced, portholes moved, public rooms replaced and decks added. The estimates for the improvements soared, MarAd was approached

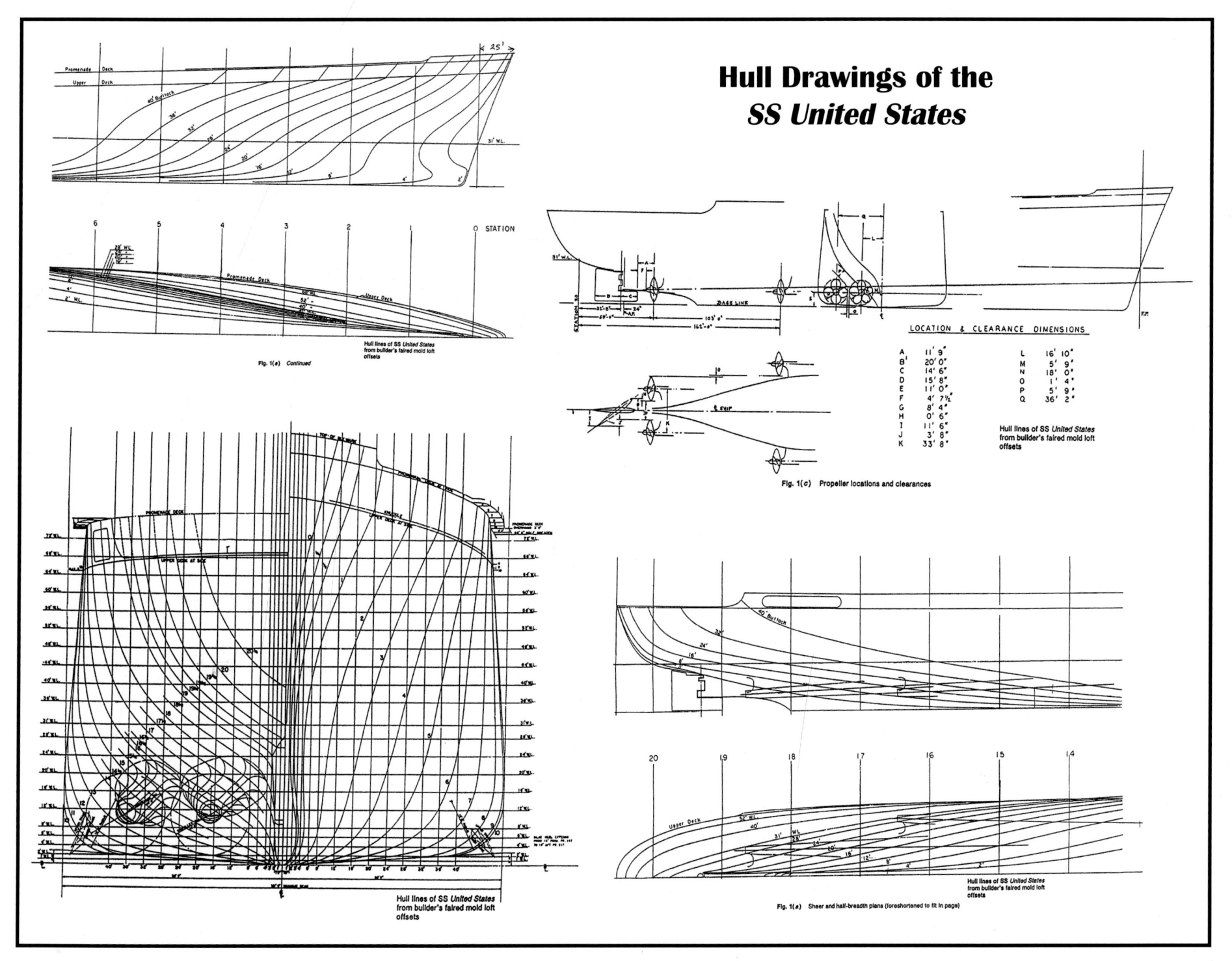

Hull Drawings of the *SS United States*

Fig. 1(a) Continued

Fig. 1(c) Propeller locations and clearances

LOCATION & CLEARANCE DIMENSIONS

A	11' 9"	L	16' 10"
B	20' 0"	M	5' 9"
C	14' 6"	N	18' 0"
D	15' 8"	O	1' 4"
E	11' 0"	P	5' 9"
F	4' 7½"	Q	36' 2"
G	8' 4"		
H	0' 6"		
I	11' 6"		
J	3' 8"		
K	33' 8"		

Hull lines of SS *United States* from builder's faired mold loft offsets

Fig. 1(a) Sheer and half-breadth plans (foreshortened to fit in page)

164

for a guaranteed loan of $80 million. Plans and estimates continued to rise with no financing in sight. Bills continued to accumulate until one creditor, Norfolk International Terminals, threaten to seize the ship for unpaid docking fees. Negotiations followed, the debt was to be forgiven provided that the SS United States was moved.

A contract was agreed to with CSX, for rental of a old coal pier in Newport News less than 2 miles from her birth place. On March 4, 1989 she was moved across Hampton Roads from Norfolk to Newport News. Promises were made, the Big U would be in service soon, but in reality nothing was occurring except the scraping of many valuable metals from the interior and exterior. Bills continued to mount until finally even the security guards quit since they were not being paid, the end was in sight. During October 1991 CSX Transportation filed suit and had the United States arrested for non payment of docking fees in the amount of $280,000. In addition the mortgagor Skopbank of Finland, (held the 1st trust of $5 Million) joined the lawsuit for non-payment of the mortgage.

News of the arrest spread among enthusiasts, the SS United States Preservation Society was formed in Northern Virginia to try and gain support to protect the ship from scrapping or foreign sale. Congressman Don Young (R) of Alaska, introduced HR 4163, SS United States Preservation Act of 1992 a bill to provide storage and prevent foreign sale until a plan could be put together to find proper usage for the Big U. Letters were written to the editor of every major seaport city newspaper in the United States. The Deptartment of Navy was approached on the basis the power plant was classified and she could still be used as a high speed transport. They declined and responded that the information was no longer classified and that the Navy had no use for the United States. Several cities were approached on the possibility obtaining the Big U and creating a east coast Queen Mary. Representatives from Quincy, Mass actually came to Newport News to inspect the ship with the possibility of using the ship as a floating hotel in Quincy. However, the refitting costs were prohibitive causing the city to lose their interest.

In a surprise move Richard Hadley declared bankruptcy for United States Cruises. This diversion lasted only about a week after which Judge Dumar stated the auction would continue on the original scheduled date. The Chairman of CSX, John Snow was approached by Congresswoman Helen Bentley for a 90 day Postponement. He agreed, but Judge Dumar rejected the plea on Monday morning and the auction began at noon April 27, 1992.

There were six bidders: Three scrap dealers, from Taiwan, India, and Canada. The bank representatives (Skopbank), a representative wanting to turn the ship into a museum, and Fred Mayer, chairman of Marmara Marine. It was clearly obvious from the beginning that Mr Mayer was going to get the ship. All the bidders, except the scrappers from India and Mr Mayer had dropped out at approximately $1.5 million. During the bidding there was a little humor, when the Scrappers from India raised the bid in $1 increments. Mr. Mayer would counter with $25,000 increases.

Mr Mayer succeeded in placing the winning bid of $2.6 million under the company name of Mamara Marine, a corporation registered in Delaware. Mr. Mayer was the owner of a Travel Agency

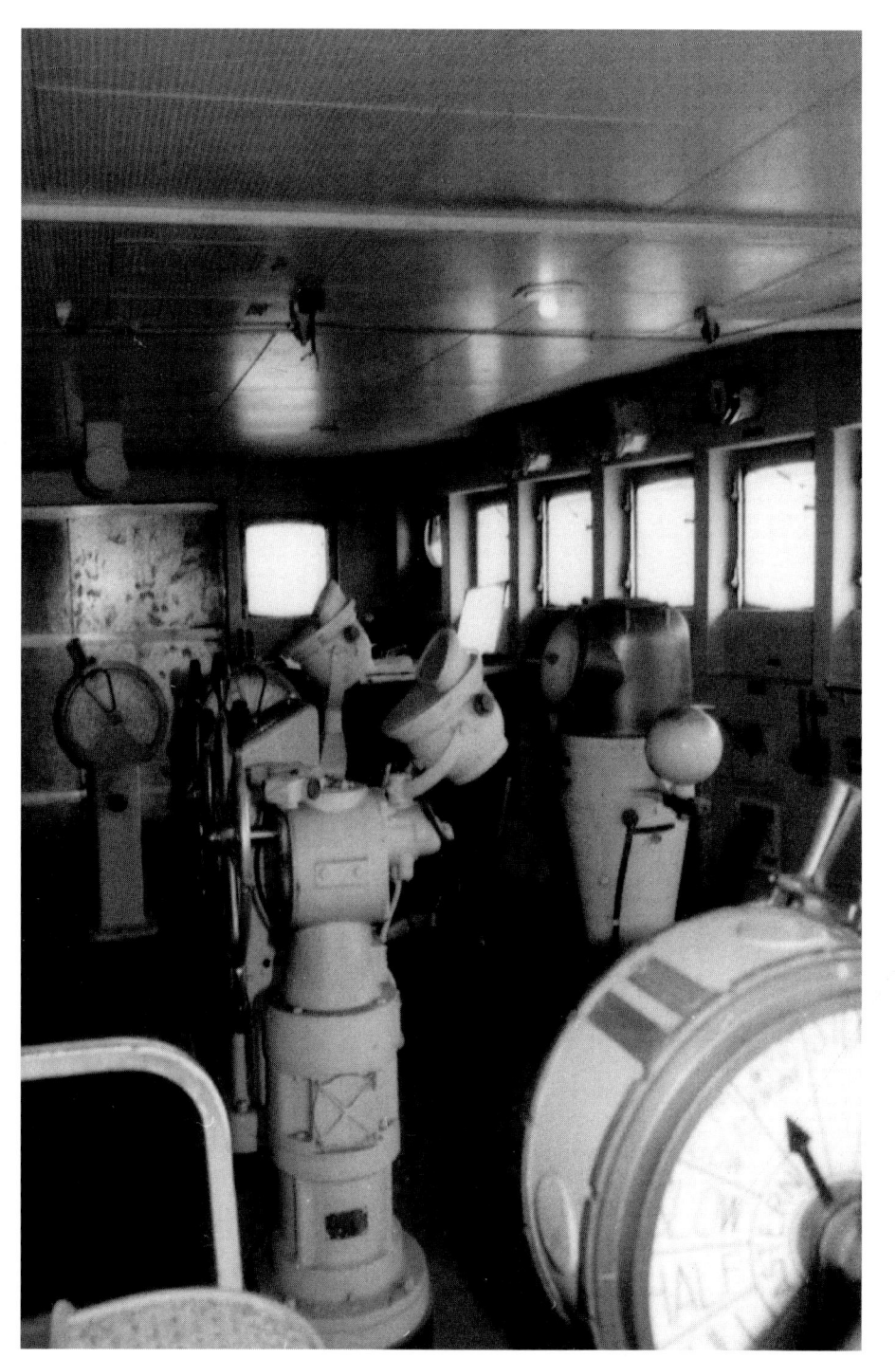

The Bridge on the SS United States in July 1981. (Courtesy of Bill DiBenedetto)

Fred Mayer (in center with glasses and beard) with partner, Kahraman Sadikoglu, (behind paper in Mayer's hand) at the auction at the Federal Courthouse Norfolk, Virginia April 27, 1992 (Courtesy of Bill DiBenedetto)

in New York City. He was also a member of the Board of Directors of Regency Cruise Lines. It was also learned that he had a partner, a Turkish ship yard owner, Kahraman Sakikoglu. Kahraman had restored another of Mr Gibbs other ships, the yacht *Savarona* of 1931. Plans were made to move the ship to Turkey within the next 3 to 6 weeks pending MarAd's approval for foreign sale.

The SS United States Preservation Society went into high gear. Congressmen were contacted to support the bill in Congress HR 4163. MarAd was contacted to prevent foreign sale, Public Law 92-296 of 1972 had directed the purchase of the *SS United States* from United States Lines and amendment 865a sponsored by Congresswomen Helen Bentley of Maryland specifically forbade foreign sale of the *SS United States* and the *SS Independence*. Apparently these laws meant little since both were approved for foreign sale by MarAd. The good news was the new owner never reflagged the Big U! She has always remained U.S. flagged.

The Bill HR 4163 was stalled in committee, by the Chairman of the Subcommittee on Merchant Marine, Congressman Walter Jones of North Carolina. Further discussions resulted in a impasse and the decision to move the bill along could not be reached. Efforts continued but time had run out. Mr. Mayer contracted with Clyde Marine Services of Long Beach CA to prepare the *SS United States* for the tow to Turkey.

Charles Deeney of Clyde Marine lead the team in preparing the ship for sea for the first time in 23 years. Portholes were covered on the inside with 1 inch steel plates, water ballast was loaded, water tight doors were closed and many other details were attended to. The home port of "New York" was repainted on her stern replacing "Seattle." From her mast flew a replica of the Blue Ribbon placed by Jim Rindfleisch and at her stern flew the American flag.

At approximately 12:30 p.m. on June 4, 1992 the last cable holding the *SS United States* parted and she started her way to Turkey towed by the sea going tug *Smit Rotterdam*. As she started to move, all of the tugs hailed the mighty ship by sounding their horns, in a sustained chorus of sound. It was all quite moving, a large crowd and the tugs singing a salute. Faded and rusted she was still the Queen of the American Merchant Marine. A comment made at Cape Henry, Virginia: "Its unbelievable, the queen of the American Merchant Marine being towed to sea as a derelict!"

The journey to Turkey was her slowest ever across the Atlantic Ocean. Her average speed approximately 7 knots, quite a bit slower than her record breaking 36.6 knots! After 36 days at sea she arrived in the Sea of Mamara, just outside Istanbul, Turkey, on July 9th. No piers were available and on July 11th, several miles from shore, a great effort to anchor without power was begun. After considerable effort, using matches and a single Bic lighter for light, the anchor was dropped for the first time in 23 years by John DeVenny. The new owners had big plans for their new ship, new decks, discos and a complete refit. The Turkish government had also agreed to guarantee a loan of $96 million towards the renovation. Still short of the required $150-200 million but a very significant amount toward the proposed renovation.

By November the Big U was still at anchor approximately 2 miles from shore. During a storm that month the anchor chain parted and she drifted ashore against a breakwater in the Bay of Tuzla. Fortunately no damage occurred due to the sandy bottom. She was towed back out to her anchorage and a new anchor was added to the end of the anchor Chain.

The ship departing for Turkey towed by Smit Rotterdam at the CSX Coal Pier, Newport News, Virginia June 4, 1992. (Courtesy of Bill DiBenedetto)

Once in Turkey the *SS United States* attracted the attention of Greenpeace. The plans for the refit called for the removal of all the interior walls constructed of marinite which was a fireproof material composed of asbestos. The engineering areas were also to be cleared of all asbestos materials. The SS United States Preservation Society researched and obtained instructions of the methods, used by the US Navy to remove asbestos from older U.S. Navy ships. These instructions were forwarded to the new owners in Istanbul. The Turkish press along with Greenpeace called the *United States* the ship of death (asbestos). The reality was the work, could with the proper removal methods, be completed with complete safety to the workers.

Rumors abounded that Cunard/Crown would lease and operate the *United States* in partnership with the QE 2. Greenpeace continued their campaign against the Big U for many months. Debates and controversy appeared in the local newspapers and television. During April 1993 Kahraman Sadikoglu, the majority owner, eventually announced that the ship would not be refurbished in Turkey due to a skilled labor shortage. Greenpeace won the battle! Bids were solicited from European yards and even a few from the U.S. Up to this time the *United States* has remained a U.S. flagged ship. Federal laws stipulated that only minor repair work could be performed in foreign yards otherwise the ship could not remain a U.S. Flagged vessel.

The *United States* remained at anchor until mid-October 1993 when she was once again attached to a tow line and was moved past Istanbul thru the Bosporus and into the Black Sea. After a trip of almost 340 miles

Kahraman Sadikoglu confronting Greenpeace June 1993 while the United States *was anchored just outside Istanbul, Turkey. (Courtesy of Captain Osman Ondes)*

she arrived at her destination at the former Soviet Naval base located at the port of Sevastopol in the Ukraine.

Here work began at the Naval yard to remove all of her interior marinite walls (cabins, public rooms, hallways, etc) In addition all asbestos was removed from the engineering areas such as engine and boiler rooms. The workers were very careful, even to the extent of bringing up the fire control system, in case of fires. Later inspection revealed that meticulous care was taken, on all aspects, on the removal of asbestos laden materials.

While the Big U was in Sevastopol her owners obtained a mortgage in the amount $5,555,500 + int. & pomc. from Edward A. Cantor located in Camden NJ, USA. The mortgage was probably used to pay for the asbestos removal and other associated expenses. While she was in Sevastopol the *United States* was dry docked and the bottom painted. Inspections performed at that time revealed the hull to be in excellent condition. All four of the propellers were removed at that time and placed on the decks at the stern.

During February of 1994 a great majority of the plans for the *United States* were purchased from Seaworthy in Essex Conn. They numbered close to 7,000 drawings and filled 300 boxes. While these are a small amount compared to the original 1.4 million blueprints, they provided most of the required information needed for the renovations. Seaworthy had performed many of the design studies for Richard Hadley, the previous owner. On February 17, 1994 these were flown to Kahraman Sadikoglu in Istanbul. The fact these were purchased indicated that the owner were getting serious about starting the proposed renovations. The drawings would be required for any work to be performed on this great liner.

167

Back in Istanbul, Kahraman Sadikoglu purchased the adjoining shipyard and had a berth dredged to accommodate the *United States*. During April of 1994 the Big U was towed back across the Black Sea to her new berth near Istanbul. Her interiors we now cleaned of all asbestos and now ready for a new life.

Over the next year press conferences were held, inspections conducted of the engineering areas, estimates given, shipyards contacted and more estimates given. However, the age old problem of available money once again became a problem. At one point the author was contacted by one of the owners and offered the main propulsion turbines (for a price). During this time the application for reflagging expired and the owners did not renew the application, good news!

While the Big U was berthed at Kahraman Sadikoglu's new shipyard, opportunity provided by the missing marinite walls was taken advantage of. Scrapping began to take place on materials that were once behind walls. Over time the scrapping claimed the, aluminum lifeboat davits and even the lifeboats themselves. Refitting for service, utilizing U.S. Coast Guard regulations, would have required all new lifesaving equipment Apparently Kahraman Sadikoglu wanted to get his investment back whether or not the *United States* was refitted!

News of the scraping eventually got back to Edward A. Cantor and Fred Mayer and they made an immediate move to protect their investment. Clyde Marine was once again hired to prepare the ship for sea. When Charles Deeney first arrived in Istanbul he was refused access to the ship by Kahraman Sadikogulu. After several attempts by Clyde Marine to gain access, Kahraman had the *United States* towed out to the sea of Mamara and anchored. Once she was at anchor Mr Deeney was allowed to prepare the ship for the tow.

At this point in time the first choice of a new lay-up pier was to be Portugal. On June 15, 1996 the *United States* was once again connected at the end of a tow line. Pulled by the *Smit New York* she began her journey to a new lay-up berth. The interesting part of the whole operation was there was no confirmed destination. Phone conversations with the Captain of the *Smit New York* revealed that he was told to head to the east coast of the United States and that further instructions would follow later.

Partially thru the trip the *Smit New York* paused briefly at Gibraltar for a progress payment on the tow charge. After a short break the journey began once again. By this point Mr. Mayer was still frantically looking for a berth. Mr. Cantor tried to persuade the city of Philadelphia to allow the Big U to berth at the former Philadelphia Navy Yard. The idea was to use the *United States* as the first civilian project at the Navy yard. Negotiations broke down and the owners still needed to find a pier capable of docking a 990 foot ship. They soon learned that piers this size are extremely rare, especially one's allowing long term berthing!

After the negotiations for the Philadelphia Navy Yard broke down the owners found a new berth at the Black Falcon Cruise Terminal near Logan Airport, Boston Mass. Alas, this too soon fell apart, the FAA would not allow a structure the height of a 13 story building near the airport. The owners frantically looked for another pier near Boston. A pier was finally located at the former Bethlehem Steel Shipbuilding plant in Quincy, Mass. Again problems, a crane which towered 165 feet prevented the *United States* from using the pier.

The owners had hired Clide Marine Services once again to dock the Big U. Charles Denney was in charge once again and hired a crew to get docking supplies. They were sent to Baltimore to purchase mooring supplies. The first item purchased was 5,700 feet of 10 inch line. Various other diameters were also purchased. The magnitude of the materials to moor a ship as large as the *United States* cannot be comprehended unless seen by the observer.

The Captain of the *Smit New York* was now instructed to head for the original destination of Philadelphia! On Friday the 19th of July 1996 the Captain was instructed to head toward the mouth of the Delaware Bay and wait for further instructions. On Monday July 22nd the *Smit New York* was instructed to bring the Big

SS United States *moored at the Tulza Shipyard September 1994. (Courtesy of Captain Osman Ondes)*

U up the Delaware River to Philadelphia. Last ditch efforts resulted in permission to dock the *United States* temporarily at The Packer Marine Terminal immediately south of the Walt Whitman Bridge, on the Pennsylvania side of the river. The main pier was parallel to the river and 2,000 feet long, the Big U was going to be about half the length of the pier. Much larger than the container ships which normally docked there.

The *Smit New York* started the run up the Delaware Bay and River at approximately 6:30 a.m. on Tuesday July 23rd. The plan was to arrive during slack tide at 7:00 a.m. on morning of July 24th. True to pattern, while the pilot boat and tugs waited, the *United States* arrived like a lady, fashionably late. At approximately 9:30 a.m. the *Smit New York* and the mighty *SS United States* suddenly appeared around the bend in the river near the Philadelphia Navy Yard. With the mothballed Navy carriers in the background the Big U still looked magnificent with her faded, pealing paint and lack of lifeboats.

The tug and ship finally arrived at the pier at around 10:30 a.m. and the remainder of the day was spent maneuvering and tying the ship up. The first business of the day started with trying to get the docking crew on board. The rope ladder hanging from the Promenade Deck had come apart on one end and was unusable. The docking crew had to be placed on board using a personnel carrier attached to the container crane. The ride was exciting and the clearance to the deck less than 15 feet to the deck. The *United States* was so large she had to be moved from dock so the huge container cranes could be moved around her. Her superstructure would interfere with the crane arms when she was alongside the pier.

She was finally moved to the north end of the Terminal. Her bow was placed under the Walt Whitman Bridge. Her bow lines were attached to mooring dolphins on the north side of the bridge. Her stacks were so tall they were higher than the bottom of the bridge deck, which is at least 150 from the level of the river. The bridge was the furthest most point the Big U could travel up the river. From Delaware Ave. The *SS United States* totally dominated the bridge, with her huge bow nestled under the bridge.

The remainder of the day was spent securing the ship to the dock, a long arduous process, since there was no power on board to use the windlass equipment. All the mooring lines, 10 inches, in diameter were moved manually by the deck crew, no small task! Time was spent trying to untangle the line. By 7:30 p.m. the Big U was secured to the dock. However, 2 tugs were retained to keep pushing the ship against the pier, the lines would stretch upwards of 12 feet when the tugs moved away from the ship. The following day more lines were added and the ship was finally secured adequately.

Investigation revealed that while all the interior marinite walls were removed, there was no hint of moisture or odors. She appeared like she did while under construction, yellow primer everywhere waiting for walls and interior to be installed. In the engineering areas, engine room, boiler rooms etc. all asbestos had been removed. During her first day after being berthed the EPA arrived and conducted tests to determine if there was any asbestos contamination! These tests revealed the workers in the Ukraine had done an excellent job and the ship received a clean bill of health. She was now ready for the long awaited rebuilding.

Negotiations continued with the City of Philadelphia. Since her stay at Packer Terminal was to be temporary, a new berth needed to be located as soon as possible. The city was very nervous with so large a vessel moored up against one of the major commuter routes into the city. A berth further upriver was being considered, However, survey's would be required to determine if the Big U would fit under the bridge.

Several weeks later, after several surveys were undertaken the City of Philadelphia approved the movement of the ship upriver. In order for the *United States* to fit under the Walt Whitman Bridge the 15 foot mast on the forward funnel, had to be unbolted and removed. When the Big U was finally maneuvered at dead low tide there was less than 5 foot of clearance from the top of the forward funnel to the bottom of the bridge deck! There were numerous city officials observing the move, to ensure that the ship did not collide into the bridge. Although sightings and calculations were done several times, the atmosphere was still tense. The *United States* then made the short trip to Pier 96 without mishap. It would have been quite a sight watching from the top of the funnel!

SS United States *towed by the* Smit New York, *Philadelphia, Pennsylvania July 24, 1996. (Courtesy of Bill DiBenedetto)*

At this point in time many suggestions on what to do with the ship abounded. The cheapest was to remodel the ship into a floating hotel. The second was to turn her into a gambling ship based in Philadelphia. The last and most expensive was to turn her back into a sea going cruise ship. One rumor was that the owners were considering outfitting the interior with casinos, and attach two sea going tugs and push her around like a barge. This option overcame the problem of renovating the engineering plant. What a humiliating existence this would have been, the fastest ocean liner ever built, doomed to pushed around by tugs.

After several months of inactivity the *United States* was moved to Pier 82 a short distance further north on the same side of the Delaware River. Visitors were not allowed and the ship once again was silent. A lonely guard stood vigil at the gangway.

During January 1997 the *United States* was arrested again by the U.S. Marshall Service in Philadelphia. The Plaintiff in the Case was Everette A. Cantor and the defendant was Mamara Marine. The reason stated in the arrest record was nonpayment of the mortgage since November 1994. Edward A. Cantor Inc. was now the legal custodian of the ship until the case was heard in court. The total lien stated in the legal documents was over 6 million dollars.

The arrest was advertised in the *Philadelphia Daily News* over the next several weeks. Claims were allowed to be registered up to April 21, 1997. After the final filing the judge had to make the decision on the final course of action. During the filing period there was no interest or action taken by the other partners.

At this point there were several possible outcomes. Mr Cantor could purchase the ship for amount of the lien. The Big U could be sold at auction once again with the possibility of being scrapped. Or the partners could pay Mr. Cantor the amount he is owed.

By August 1997, very little had taken place. The final figures for the lien amount were in excess of $11 million. The judge had finalized all the documents and authorized the auction. During this period Mr. Cantor contacted the Virginia Port Authority, in Norfolk, looking for a pier large enough to moor the *United States*. Piers 1,000 feet long were in short supply and the Big U remained at her pier in Philadelphia.

After a long spring and hot summer some action finally took place. A decision was finally reached by the court and the auction, for nonpayment of the mortgage. The auction would finally take place on Thursday, November 6, at 11:00 a.m. The site of the auction would be the Federal Courthouse at 601 Market Street, Philadelphia, just outside the Marshall's office.

The SS United States *in Philadelphia, Pennsylvania November 1996. (Courtesy of Sam Galbreath)*

On a side note the City of Philadelphia was currently conducting negotiations with a Norwegian shipbuilding company, Kvaerner Asa. The deal included public money, up to $470 million from Federal, State and City Governments and the now closed Philadelphia Navy Yard. Future plans include the building of 3 new cargo Ships. There was some speculation that Mr. Cantor had some discussions with Kvaerner Asa. However, people in the know stated nothing had taken place. In any event, any renovations concerning the *United States* would need to be privately funded.

The auction of the *SS United States* took place at the Federal Courthouse in Philadelphia, on November 6, at 11:00 a.m. Unlike the April 1992, auction in Norfolk, which attracted hundreds of spectators, the press, and many bidders, very few people showed. The press was absent and with the exception of one or two spectators all the remaining people involved were Mr. Cantor, his attorneys and the sheriff. Mr. Cantor was very disappointed that there no other bidders. Not a single other interested party showed up to bid, including the scrappers. When the sheriff started the bidding Mr. Cantor stepped forward and exercised a portion of his credit bid in the amount of $6 million, and became the new legal owner of the *SS United States*. The auction was over in less than a minute. This was great news at the time, the Big U avoided the scrappers once again. The new owner is a well respected and wealthy businessman in the Philadelphia area.

Mr. Cantor worked hard in trying to do something with the ship before he became the owner. This demonstrated that he cared for the ship and did have plans local Manhattan Community Board No. 4 wanted to see the pier used as a waterfront park.

Mr. Plattner was present at the Philadelphia auction in November, and had been in negotiation with Mr. Cantor for sometime. The rumor at the time was that Mr. Plattner had been waiting for the November Mayoral elections to be completed, to help ensure that the project had enough political support to be approved by the city. Time showed that getting approval was very difficult caused by the many concerned special interest groups. As of this printing approval had not been secured.

Pier 76 is approximately 800 feet long, which would mean that the *SS United States* would extend 200 feet into the Hudson River. The Coast Guard would certainly not allow this obstruction and part of the cost would be extending the pier an additional 200 feet, after all the appropriate approvals. The cost of converting the ship into a floating hotel is probably the most feasible of all the proposed uses. The one great advantage for this proposal was Location, Location, Location – the great definition of great real estate. The cost of total refurbishment would be less than the purchase of land and construction costs for a land based hotel. The project would almost certainly pay for itself quickly once approved.

During July a rumor started that the Big U was in a dry-dock at the Philadelphia Naval Yard, creating an atmosphere of anticipation. Phone calls and research revealed that the rumor was false and the ship still resided at Pier 82. At the same time it was learned the *SS United States* was being offered for sale for $30 million. The good news was no scrappers would be interested at that price.

for the vessel. As for the future Mr. Cantor did not have much to say. Rumors once again began to circulate, gambling ship, cruise ship and perhaps a great floating hotel. One thing Mr. Cantor did was to hire a crew that performed maintenance on the ship. Leaks were stopped and the interior was cleaned of accumulated debris.

On March 10, 1998 a startling announcement was made by a New York City developer, David Plattner. He had approached the City of New York for a long term lease for Pier 76. The plan was to make a floating hotel out of the *SS United States* to service the Javits Convention Center on 34th Street in Manhattan. The current plans for Pier 76, at the time, called for a Heliport. The

Bibliography

Elijah Baker III. *Introduction To Steel Shipbuilding*. McGraw-Hill Book Company New York, NY, 1953

Frank Braynard. *The Big Ship*. The Mariners Museum, Newport News, VA, 1981

Frank Braynard. *By Their Works Ye Shall Know Them* Gibbs & Cox, Inc, 1968

William H. Miller. *S.S. United States*. W.W. Norton & Company, Inc. 500 Fifth Ave, New York, NY 10110 , 1991

Denis Griffiths. *Power Of The Great Liners*. Patrick Stephens Limited, Sparkford, New York, Somerset, BA22 7JJ 1990

Robert Gardiner editor. *The Golden Age Of Shipping*. Naval Institute Press, 118 Maryland Ave, Annapolis, MD 21402-5035 1994

Frederick E. Emmons. *American Passenger Ships*. Associated University Presses, 440 Forsgate Drive, Cranbury, NJ 08512 1985

Robert Wall. *Ocean Liners*. Quarto Limited, Chartwell Books Inc, 110 Enterprise Ave, Secaucus, New Jersey 07094 1977

W.A. Baker and Tre Tryckare, *The Engine Powered Vessel*. Grosset & Dunlap Inc. New York, NY 1965

John Townsend Gibbons. *Palaces That Went To Sea*. Nereus Publishing Company, 10501 Cedar Lake Road, Suite 205, Minnetonka, MI 55343 1990

Robert B. Hopkins, editor, *Shipyard Bullletin*. Volume 14, No 8, 9, 10, 11, 12, Newport News Shipbuilding and Dry Dock Company, Newport News, VA 1952

Frank O. Braynard. *Famous American Ships*. Hastings House, Publishers, New York, NY 1978, 1956

Thomas C. Gillmer, *Modern Ship Design*. Naval Institute Press, Annapolis, MD 21402 1975, 1970

Arnold Kludas, *Great Passenger Ships Of The World Vol 5*. Patrick Stephens Limited, Wellingborough, Northamptonshire, England 1977

Index

A

Ackroyd, Cuthbert L. 104
Adenauer, Konrad 90
Airviews, Thomas 59
Aldrich, Winthrop W. 94
Alexander, Mike 2, 148
Alexanderson 110, 132, 133, 135, 137, 138, 143
Alexanderson, L.H. 156
Alexanderson, Leroy 2, 110, 111, 130, 135, 143
Alfano, Mike 2
Allen, Barbara Jo 73, 154
Allen, Milton J. 73, 154
Allendorfer, Harry 10
Altenburg, Charles J. 10, 28, 32
Ambrose, M.L. 139
Anderson 80, 81, 90, 94, 96, 99, 104, 107, 108, 111, 112, 113, 122, 123, 130, 139, 157
Anderson, George 115
Anderson, John 10, 79, 92, 108
Arbenz, Emma Elisabeth 154, 155
Arntz, Heinz 135
Asa, Kvaerner 170
Astor, Vincent 89, 95
Atkins, G.T. 90
Atkinson, Brooks 66
Austin, Freddy 112

Aylward 59, 103, 104
Azarraga, Luis 101

B

Bachko, Nicholas 10, 33, 83, 140
Bachman, Walter 10, 27, 31, 71
Bak, Mrs. William 10
Baker, Elijah, III 171
Baker, Ernest 63
Baker, W.A. 171
Bamberger, Werner 125, 126, 138
Barber, Samuel 114
Barkley, Alben W. 56
Barnard, Constance 48
Bates, F.A. 72
Bates, James L. 30, 35
Bates, Lawrence J. 10
Battersby, Alan 107
Baylis, John S. 137
Beall, Lester 67, 68
Beattie, Denny B. 10, 134
Beauregard, Elie 81
Beaverbrook 110
Bemelmans, Ludwig 92
Benzaria, David 113
Berger, Meyer 104
Berry, Richard 10
Besse, Sumner 48

Bilder, A.K. 92
Billings, Henry 92
Bishop, Jim 111
Bismarck, Otto 56, 95, 96
Blewett, William E., Jr. 48, 55, 71, 83, 118
Blinn, Jeff 10, 66
Bonner, Herbert C. 110
Bontempo, William 21
Bori, Lucretia 82
Borum, Linwood 103
Boston, William T. 104
Bowen, Harold G. 27
Bowers, John 141, 143
Boyd, M. 155
Bracken, Robert P. 155
Brady, Catherine 158
Brando, Marlon 98, 99
Braynard, Frank 2, 3, 8, 10, 148, 171
Brennan 54, 87
Brennan, John 53, 69
Brennan, Patrick 57
Brougham, Helen 143
Brown, Alexander Crosby 10, 60, 127
Brown, David P. 53
Brown, John 29
Brunel, Isambard Kingdom 11, 12
Buermann, Thomas 10, 30

Burgess, Robert H. 10
Burns, Robert S. 121
Burrow, Edwin 73, 75

C

Calhoon, Jesse M. 132
Callahan, John P. 119
Callan, Michael 122
Cameron, James 148
Cantor, Edward A. 147, 167, 168
Cantor, Everette A. 170
Cantor, H.B. 114
Carlsen, Henrik Kurt 78
Carson, Rachel 54
Casey, Ralph E. 106, 114, 120
Caune, M. Jean 10
Cavanagh, Edward F. 62
Cerio, Thomas 66
Chapin, E.B. 111
Chapman, Paul Wadsworth 37
Chapman, Sally 153
Christiansen, Ralph 60
Christie, Malcolm 83
Christoffersen 54
Christoffersen, J.A. 44, 83
Christy, William G. 80
Chu, Pauline 2
Churchill 75
Ciparelli, Frank 73, 154

Clark, Dane 94
Cochrane, Edward L. 40, 43, 50, 56, 59, 60, 64, 78
Coddaire, David J. 38
Cole, G.D. 50
Collins, Floyd 86
Collister, Gaynor 48
Colton, Arthur 48
Congdon, Alfred L. 34, 49
Connally, Tom 48, 50, 82
Connelly 5
Connery, Sean 160
Considine, Robert 47, 78
Cook, Barton O. 32, 33, 34
Cook, E.R. 100
Cooke, Richard P. 59, 87
Cooper, Gary 91
Cooper, J. Lester 83
Corcoran, Kevin 122
Coune, J. 115
Cove, George E. 71
Crain, Jeanne 94
Cramp, William 27
Cravath, Vera 111
Crawford, Joan 98, 134
Cronican, Frank 61
Cronkite, Walter 90, 95
Cruz, Ramon 124
Culpepper, H.L. 10, 21
Curran, Joseph 20, 35, 40, 62, 82, 87, 130, 132, 144

D

Dali, Salvador 98, 99, 107
Dallas, Rebekah T. 10
Daniel, Clifton 71
Daniels, Josephus 17
Davies, Mrs. Joseph E. 92
Davis, Emery 86
Davis, Meyer 86
Day, William B. 125
de Beuregard, Alain Costa 92
de Carlo, Yvonne 82
de Chambrun, Rene 94
de Cler, Hendrikus P.G. 89
de Lamerie, Paul 66
De Limure, Ivan 81
De Marzo 70
Deckert, Mamie 99
Deeney, Charles 166, 168
Deitz, Carla 66
Delasio, Marcel 61
Dennis, Elizabeth A. 2
DeVenny, John 166
Devlin 53, 80, 87, 90, 103
Devlin, James 108
Devlin, Jones F. 44
DiBenedetto, Bill 3, 41, 42, 43, 45, 46, 52, 58, 88, 96, 97, 102, 118, 120, 121, 127, 138, 145, 146, 156, 162, 163, 165, 166
Dietz, Carla 48
Disney, Walt 122, 123
Doyle, Robert 10
DuBois, George 72, 89
Duffy, James Edmund 73, 74
Dugan, James 103
Dunn, Laura Franklin 153
Durling, E.V. 106

E

Earhart, Amelia 56
Eastwold, E.R. 134
Edwards, E.D. 59
Eisenhower, Dwight 70, 91, 107, 112, 114, 120, 135, 143
Eisle, Gerhard 72
Emmet, W.L.R. 16
Emmons, Frederick E. 171
Erwin, Ray 65
Euvrard 96
Ewen, Theodore 99
Ewen, William Hopkins 99

F

Fagan, Arthur 79, 80
Farley, James A. 95
Farnsworth, George S. 100
Farrell, Frank 66
Fender, Frederick 66, 92, 94, 96, 99, 110, 130
Ferguson 105
Ferguson, Homer L. 25
Fernanders, J.C. 10
Ferris, Theodore 17, 32
Finnegan, Joe 89
FitzGerald, David T. 137
Ford, Glenn 123, 124
Ford, J. Duncan 92
Forrest, Matthew 10, 28, 29, 30, 31, 32, 33, 34, 38, 46, 79
Forsyth, William 99
Franke, William B. 112, 121
Franklin 8, 31, 35, 44, 53, 60, 62, 64, 65, 67, 69, 72, 75, 76, 83, 89, 90, 92, 93, 106, 112, 119, 121, 125, 126
Franklin, John M. 24, 31, 36, 153
Franklin, Philip A.S. 17, 21, 24, 25
Fratello, Madelaine 157
Freeman, Ira Henry 89
Friedlander, Paul 65, 129
Fulton, Robert 133
Fulton, Tom 2
Furness, Viscountess 94

G

Gabor, Eva 91
Gabor, Magda 91
Gabor, Zsa Zsa 91
Galbreath, Sam 170
Gallagher, Hugh 94
Gardiner, Robert 171
Garland, Judy 98, 145, 160
Garmatz, Edward A. 122
Garson, Greer 113
Gautier, Kenneth 10, 87, 90, 114, 122, 132, 138
Gayton, Cynthia 2
Gehrig, Clarence P. 10, 94, 132
Geiger, Paul 160
Gibbons, C.D. 119
Gibbs 20, 24, 30, 36, 40, 46, 48, 50, 61, 62, 63, 69, 71, 77, 87, 111, 122, 139
Gibbs, Albert E. 90
Gibbs, Frederic 5, 10, 11, 14, 16, 17, 19, 24, 26, 28, 33, 35, 36, 43, 63, 83, 111
Gibbs, Susan 2, 3
Gibbs, Vera Cravath 4
Gibbs, William Francis 2, 4, 6, 8, 10, 11, 12, 13, 14, 15, 16, 17, 18, 19, 21, 24, 25, 26, 27, 28, 29, 30, 31, 32, 33, 34, 35, 36, 37, 38, 39, 40, 43, 44, 47, 48, 49, 50, 51, 53, 54, 60, 61, 64, 67, 69, 70, 71, 73, 74, 75, 77, 78, 79, 81, 82, 83, 92, 93, 94, 99, 103, 104, 106, 107, 110, 112, 115, 118, 121, 125, 130, 133, 134, 137, 138, 139, 144, 149, 153
Gibson, Andrew E. 142
Gilfford, Walter S. 75
Gill, Brendon 112
Gill, "Gus" 48
Gingold, Hermione 99, 137
Gleason, Jackie 91
Glenny, Charles F. 104
Gmelin, Stephan 83
Godby, Joseph P. 38, 39
Grady, Henry Francis 30
Grainger, Isaac B. 111
Grant, Cary 98, 99
Grant, Francis 130
Grattidge, Harry 70
Gray, Harold 95
Green, William J. 10
Griffin, Merv 139
Griffith, James M. 10
Griffiths, Denis 171
Griffiths, John Willis 111
Gruenberg, Cholly 110
Guerrier, Albert 72

H

Hadley, Richard 10, 144, 145, 163
Hague, Robert L. 112
Hailey, Howard 79
Hales 81, 82, 83, 86, 119
Hales, Harold Keates 53
Halsey, P.F. 50
Hamilton, Alexander 80
Hamshar, Walter 38, 40, 43, 44, 48, 49, 50, 59, 70, 73, 83, 123
Hannigan, Thomas 130
Hardy 56
Hardy, A.C. 77
Hardy, Porter, Jr. 38
Harris, Basil 31
Harris, Clyde 99
Harris, Dick 111
Hart, Eugene 97
Hayworth, Rita 80, 81, 127
Hearst, William Randolph 24, 57
Hepburn, Katherine 65
Herbert, Frederic 18
Hertenger, Albert 76
Hertzler, John R. 39
Hicks, D. Scott 153
Hicks, Raymond M. 56, 153
Hicks, Rex L. 61
Hitchcock, Alfred 80
Hoffman, Clare E. 63
Hogan, Ben 92
Hogan, Frank S. 110
Hogge 48
Holman, Nat 81
Holmes, Oliver Wendell 142
Hope, Bob 80
Hopkins, Robert 38, 47, 48, 50, 60
Horka, Archie 142
Horne, George 37, 38, 43, 48, 49, 56, 59, 60, 70, 71, 72, 95, 106, 133, 140
Hughes, Richard 125
Hughes-Hallett, C.C. 75
Huntington, Henry 25
Hurd, Charles 36
Hurley, Edward N. 18
Hurok, Sol 90, 119
Hutton, Barbara 94
Huxley, Julian 99
Hyde, Fillmore 60

I

Iddon, Don 72
Impellitteri, Vincent R. 62, 66, 76
Ireland, Mark 33
Ismay, Bruce 89

J

Jackson, Mahalia 123
Jensh, Ronald P. 161
Jessel, George 80
Johansen 127
Johnson 139
Jones 46
Jones, Gerald Norman 82
Jones, Robert J. 66

173

Jones, Walter 39, 45, 47, 48, 50, 62, 65, 71, 78, 83, 90, 93, 94, 95, 111, 166
Jordan, Allan E. 10

K

Kahler, Bruce E. 10
Kaiser 66, 76, 78, 87, 92, 106, 111, 138
Kaiser, Harold 123
Kaiser, William 44, 53, 57, 75, 106, 137, 139
Kane 61, 113
Kane, John 10, 18, 32, 33, 38, 40, 61, 112, 118, 140
Kaufman, George S. 90, 100
Keating 62
Keaton, Buster 81
Kefauver, Estes 80
Keller, Allan 130
Kelly 5
Kelly, Ardie L. 10
Kelly, John 21
Kennedy 120, 122, 135, 148
Kennedy, John F. 28
Kennedy, Joseph 28, 92, 95, 99
Kerschner, Gertrude 156
Kidde, Walter 139
Kiepura, Jan 86
King, Thomas A. 10
Kirk, Tommy 122
Klein, Anne 106
Krebs 19
Krudener, Bill 61
Kunze, Gustave 137

L

Lafayette 94
Laflen, Edward C. 137
Laise, Steve 10
Lancaster, Burt 98, 99
Land, Emory S. 29
Landiak, Nicholas 113
Lardner, John 86
Lasker, Albert 24, 26
Lawrence, Newbold T. 53, 81
Le Roux, Charles 135
le Toumelin, Jacques-Yves 73
Lea, Robert B. 103
LeBarge, Arthur 70
Lee 53
Lehman, Bill 150
Lehman, Bruce A. 2
Lehmann, Hilde M. 133
Leviero, Anthony 29
Lewis, John L. 108
Lindsay, John 144
Lipton, Seymour 60
Lloyd 48
Lloyd, Harold 113
Lloyd, Wilson 48
Lock, John 66, 70, 94, 96
Logue, John M. 137, 144
Long, Stephen 112
Lux, Gwenn 56, 69, 71
Lydiard, Hugh 2

M

MacMurray, Fred 122
Majalca, Anna Maria 122
Malmsea, Andrew 9, 66, 80, 91, 98, 105, 107, 108, 123, 124, 131, 135
Malmstrom, Walter 10
Maloney, Walter E. 81
Manning 56, 59, 61, 63, 64, 66, 71, 72, 73, 75, 82, 89, 90
Manning, Harry 53, 56, 70, 77, 79, 138, 154
Manning, Stephen 48, 76
Marckwald, Dorothy 27, 34, 39, 43, 54, 57, 67, 69
Marie, Jean 115
Marine, Clyde 168
Marshall, George C. 43, 81
Marx, Hans 10
Masefield, John 47, 51
Maugham, W. Somerset 160
Maxwell, Elsa 110, 111
Mayer, Fred 166
Mayer, Louis B. 99
McAllister 66
McBride, Bill 85, 100, 101, 116, 117, 128, 136
McBride, Thomas F. 110
McCrann, William 143
McDonald, Jim 48
McEntee, William 19
McFarlane, John 134, 154
McGranery, James P. 64, 86
McKay, Donald 12, 61, 132
McMullen, John J. 140, 142
McNeill, James 29
McQuillan 21
McSweeney, Daniel 2, 159
Mead, Margaret 152
Meany, George 99, 113
Mellon, Grenville 36
Menjou, Adolph 81
Menotti, Gian-Carlo 114
Menuhin, Yehudi 108
Mercer, Emanuel 99
Meseck, John A. 66
Mesta, Perle 80
Meyer, Henry 10, 21, 30
Milland, Ray 82
Miller, James Nathan 124
Miller, William 148, 150, 171
Mizii, Joseph G. 162
Molony, Charles 43
Monroe, Bob 62, 66
Monroe, T.A. 90
Montgomery, Robert 95
Moore, Albert V. 79
Moore, L. Porter 140
Moorer, T.H. 140
Morgan, Clifford S. 10, 132
Morgan, J.P. 12, 16, 17, 18, 24, 29, 31, 90, 111
Morgan, Junius S. 90
Morse, Clarence C. 105, 113
Morse, Huntington 35
Moynihan, Vincent A. 10, 32
Muchulsky, Joseph 133
Mueller, Henry 96
Mueller, Hermann 66, 135
Mumma, Albert G. 106
Mundy, Archie 79, 80
Murray, John E. 10
Murrow, Edward R. 92

N

Nash, Frank C. 35
Nash, Harry 49
Nevard, Jacques 50, 112
Newell, William S. 79
Niarchos, Stavros 105
Nixon, B.J. 10
North, John Ringling 99
Novak, Kim 123

O

Oates, Walter E. 10
Oberon, Merle 107, 113
O'Byrne, Patrick 103
Olefeldt, Sven 9, 80, 91, 98, 105, 107, 108, 123, 124, 131
Ondes, Osman 167, 168
O'Neill, J.R.P. 10
Ostuni, Peter 55
Outerbridge, William W. 106

P

Pahlavi, T. 89
Palmedo, Betsey 89
Parker, Chris 160
Parkhurst, Cliff E. 133
Patrick, G.S. 121
Patz, Frank 10
Pearce, Laer 2
Peavy, Nat 111
Peet, Creighton 119
Perkins, David E. 10
Perkins, Walter B. 10
Perry, William 141
Philips, Allan 47, 48
Phillips, McCandish 132
Pickford, Mary 104
Pidduck, Eric 75
Pineau, Suzanne L. 133
Pizer, Vernon 96
Plattner, David 171
Popkin, Harry 82
Presley, Elvis 156
Primrose, Durward 26
Purdon, Alexander 124, 139
Purves, Austin, Jr. 94

R

Radcliffe, William T. 59, 67
Ralston, Vera 80
Rand, William 53, 119, 122, 132, 135, 139
Ravenel, G.F. 48
Ray, Gilbert 105
Reavis, Logan U. 92, 93
Reed, Sherman W. 61
Reid, Charles 124
Reid, Whitelaw 90
Reil, Frank 47, 48, 50, 65
Reiner, Fritz 69
Rhodes, Margaret 94
Richter, Arthur 66
Rickover, Hyman G. 118, 157
Ridington, Richard W. 130, 137
Rigg, Ernest H. 28
Rindfleisch, Jim 166
Ripley, Bob 47
Robinson, Paul 2, 151
Rockefeller, Lawrence 80
Rodriguez, J. Fred, Jr. 147
Rogers, Charles "Buddy" 104
Rogers, Ginger 145
Rogers, Moses 11
Rollini, Adrian 65
Rolph 93

Roosevelt, Franklin 6, 28, 37
Rosenfeld, Stanley 44
Rota, Joseph 157
Rothschild, Louis S. 103
Ruggles, Anne 57
Runciman, Viscount 75
Ryan, Cornelius 111
Ryan, Joseph J. 108

S

Sadikoglu, Kahraman 166
Salisbury, Harrison 94
Saltonstall, Leverett 103
Sanchez, Jorge 125
Sanders 21
Sandor, Cynthia A. 156
Sandor, Robert 156
Sands, John O. 10
Sarnoff, David 69
Sawyer 57, 60, 63, 64, 65, 74, 80
Schlecht, Walter F., Jr. 122
Scotto, Anthony 141
Seixas, Victor 99
Selassie, Haile 95, 135
Seldin, Joel 108
Semler, Robert C. 2
Serig, Howard W., Jr. 142
Sheedy, John 66, 99, 112, 137, 143
Shelly, J.F. 64
Shepard, Richard F. 51, 124
Shere, Sam 48
Sherwood, William 123

Shindler, Michael 10, 92, 135
Short, V.C. 46
Skillman, Russell 103
Smith 82
Smith, Britton O. 10, 28, 60, 79, 99
Smith, Dick 111
Smith, Matt 150
Smith, Reginald 107
Smith, Richard Austin 110
Smith, William W. 33, 34
Smyth, Miriam 34
Snyder 97
Snyder, Drucie 154
Snyder, Frederick W. 89, 96
Soderberg, C.R. 27
Sorrell, Donald W. 69
Spector, Barbara 143
Sperie, Fred 123
Sperry, Elmer A. 103
Stanwyck, Barbara 91
Stark, Alan 161
Stedman, Giles 90
Stein, Barney 90
Steinway, Theodore 49
Stephens, Patrick J. 10
Stephenson, Phyllis 10
Stevens, Edwin 28
Stevens, John 28
Stoke, May 93
Strauss, Lewis 112
Sutton, Horace 78
Swanson, Gloria 7
Sweet 48

T

Taft 65, 70
Tait, Jack 66
Tastrom, Edward 59, 83, 86
Taylor 134
Taylor, Carol 110
Taylor, David W. 17, 26
Taylor, Elisabeth 145
Taylor, Robert 91
Theander, Robert L. 137
Thomas, Clifford 72
Thompson, Edna 111
Thompson, J. Walter 48
Thompson, Mark A. 2
Toledo, Ralph 61
Tollefson, Thor C. 110
Toomey, Elizabeth 72
Toomey, Jeanne 66, 69, 72, 76
Torrey, Owen C. 63, 66
Tracy, Spencer 65
Tromp, Martin Harpertzoon 70
Tross, Mildred 69
Truman, Harry S. 30, 37, 40, 44, 64, 72, 73, 75, 86, 104, 145, 154
Truman, Margaret 48, 69, 71, 72, 81, 110, 135, 154
Tucker, John S. 130, 144

U

Urquhart, Anne 10, 27, 34, 39, 43, 44, 54, 57, 67, 69

V

Valentino, Rudolph 7
Van Horne, Harriet 100
Van Tromp 82
van Zanten, Cornelius Veldhuyzen 89
Vanderbilt, Reginald C. 94
VanDyk, Arnulf R. 137
Vickery, Harold L. 30

W

Wagner, Robert 130
Waley-Cohen, Bernard N. 104
Wall, Robert 171
Wallace, De Witt 81
Wally, Deborah 122
Walsh, John P. 10
Walsh, William 122
Walters, Lou 125
Warren, Lindsay 37, 38, 40, 57, 60, 62, 63, 64
Warwick, Andrew 132
Watts 48
Wayne, John 160
Webb, William 61
Weigele, Raymond 132
Westover, Lawrence Robert 2
Westover, Robert Hudson 2, 3, 8, 144, 145, 148, 150, 151
Whalen, Grover 75, 90
Wheelock, C.D. 35
Whipple, Ward D. 101
White, Jones 163

Whitman, Walt 147, 156, 169
Wilhelm, Kaiser 99
Wilkie, Mrs. Wendell L. 139
Wilkinson, John J. 66
Wilkinson, William D. 10
Will, John M. 141
Williams, Tennessee 90, 100
Willis, Douglas 70
Willis, William 104
Wilson 19
Winchester, J.H. 26
Wise 48
Wood, William 157
Woodrum, Agnes 123
Woodward 40, 51, 59, 60, 61
Woodward, J.B., Jr. 36, 51
Wyman, Jane 122, 123

Y

Young, Don 165
Young, Theodore J. 49

Z

Zelin, Joseph 112
Ziegler, Guenter 155
Zippler, Norman 10, 21, 24, 28, 60, 78, 79
Zola, Francois J. Emile 94

175

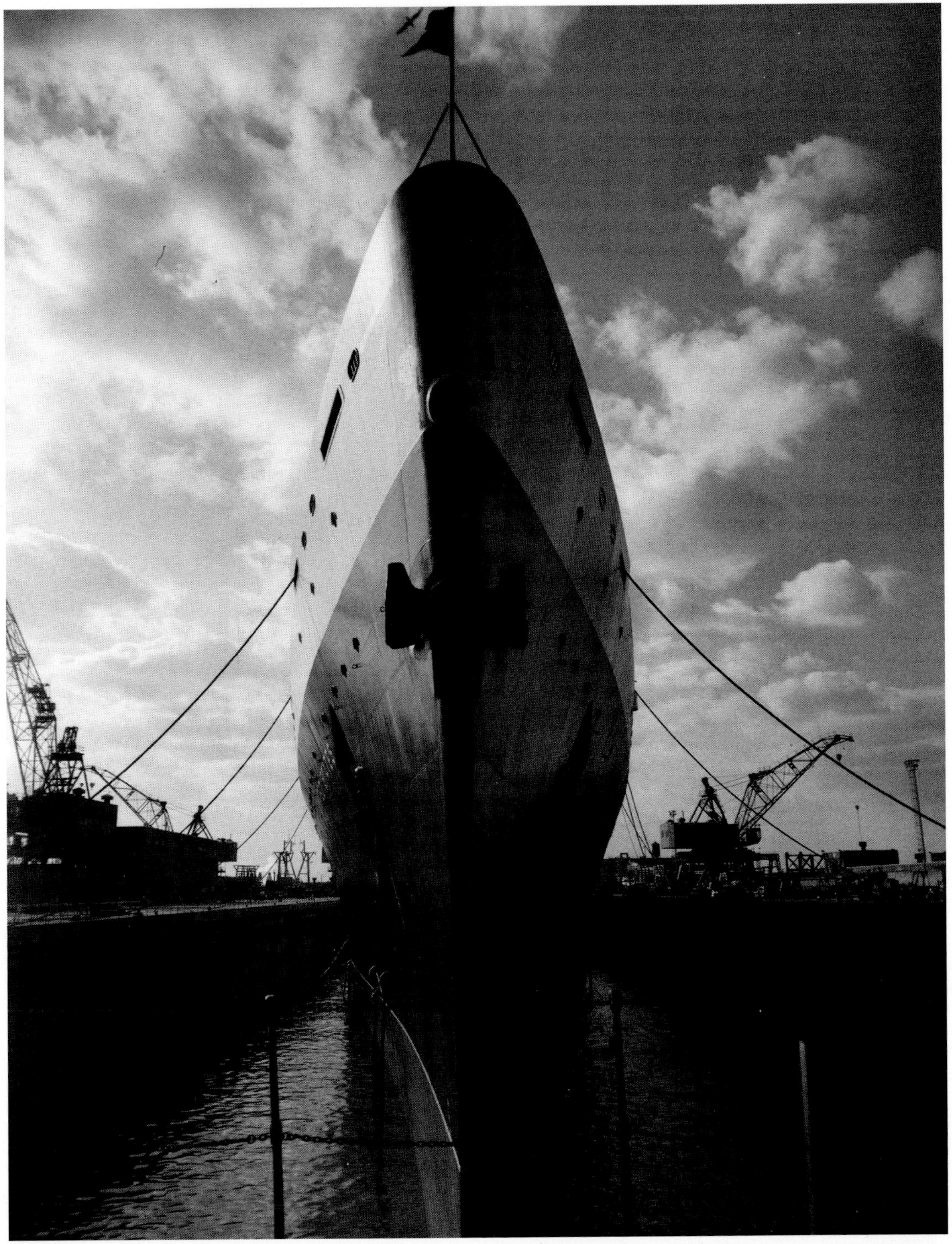